SOLUTIONS MANUAL

DYNAMIC MODELING AND CONTROL OF ENGINEERING SYSTEMS

SECOND EDITION

J. LOWEN SHEARER
BOHDAN T. KULAKOWSKI
JOHN F. GARDNER

PRENTICE HALL Upper Saddle River, NJ 07458

Acquisition Editor: ***Bill Stenquist***
Production Editor: ***Veronica Schwartz***
Production Coordinator: ***Julia Meehan***
Special Projects Manager: ***Barbara A. Murray***
Cover Designer: ***PM Workshop, Inc.***
Supplement Cover Manager: ***Paul Gourhan***

A Pearson Education Company
Upper Saddle River, NJ 07458

Printed in the United States of America

10 9 8 7 6 5 4 3 2

ISBN 0-13-719378-5

Prentice-Hall International (UK) Limited,London
Prentice-Hall of Australia Pty. Limited, Sydney
Prentice-Hall Canada Inc., Toronto
Prentice-Hall Hispanoamericana, S.A., Mexico
Prentice-Hall of India Private Limited, New Delhi
Prentice-Hall of Japan, Inc., Tokyo
Pearson Education Asia Pte. Ltd., Singapore
Editora Prentice-Hall do Brasil, Ltda., Rio de Janeiro

FOREWORD

This manual has been prepared primarily for instructors. It consists of two parts. Part I contains solutions to the problems appearing at the ends of the chapters of the book. Part II is a collection of special in-depth problems, which integrate the material covered in more than one chapter of the book. These special problems are suggested for possible use as case studies, computer projects or other major homework assignments.

The manual, accompanying the second edition of the book, differs only slightly from the manual developed for the first edition. The original manual was put into its final form by Dr. Kevin B. Todd, who was at that time a doctoral student in the Department of Mechanical Engineering at Penn State. We are very grateful to Kevin, who also checked most of the solutions of the end-of-chapter problems.

B.T.K. and J.F.G.

CHAPTER 1

PROBLEM 1.1

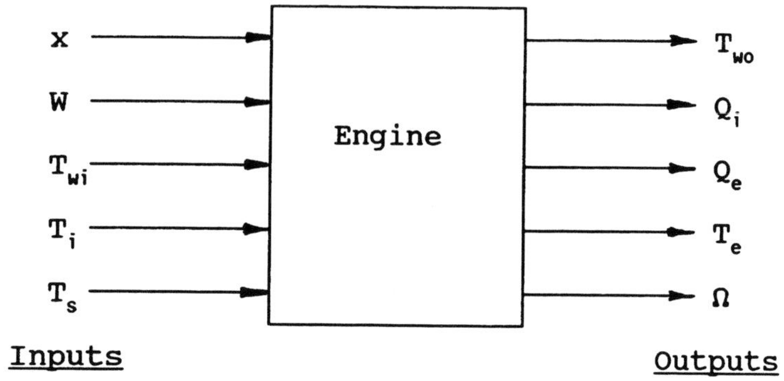

(T_s can also be considered an output)

PROBLEM 1.2

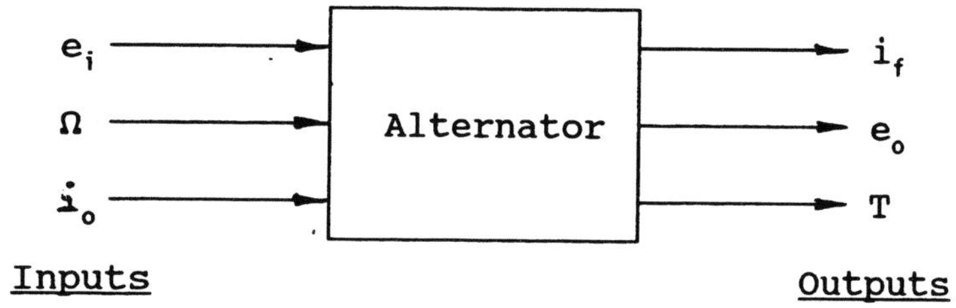

(i_o represents load and can be considered either an input or output)

PROBLEM 1.3

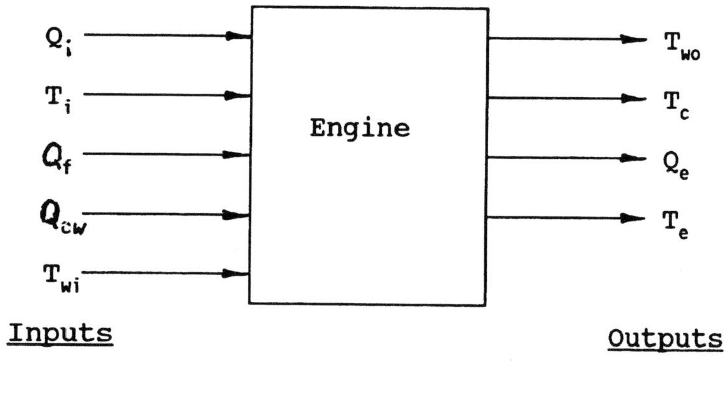

PROBLEM 1.4

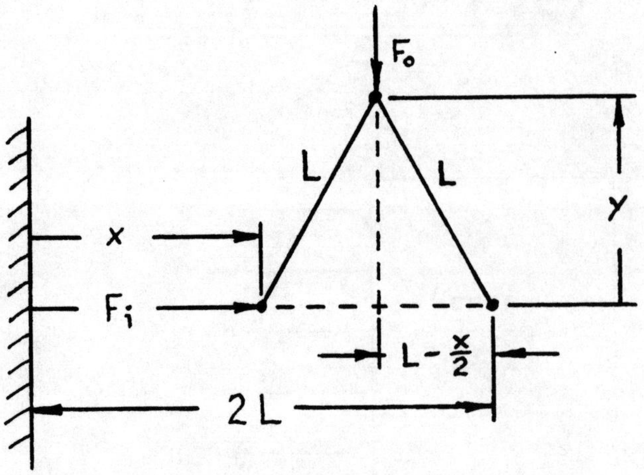

a) $y = (L^2 - (L - x/2)^2)^{.5} = (Lx - (x/2)^2)^{.5}$

$$\hat{y} = \left.\frac{dy}{dx}\right|_{x=\bar{x}} \cdot \hat{x} = \frac{(L - (\bar{x}/2))\hat{x}}{2(L\bar{x} - (\bar{x}/2)^2)^{.5}}$$

b) When $\bar{x} = L/2$,

$$\hat{y} = \frac{(3L/4)\ \hat{x}}{2(L^2/2 - L^2/16)^{.5}} = \frac{3\hat{x}}{2(7)^{.5}}$$

c) $\hat{F}_o\hat{y} = \hat{F}_i\hat{x}$

$$\hat{F}_o = \frac{2(7)^{.5}}{3}\hat{F}_i$$

PROBLEM 1.5

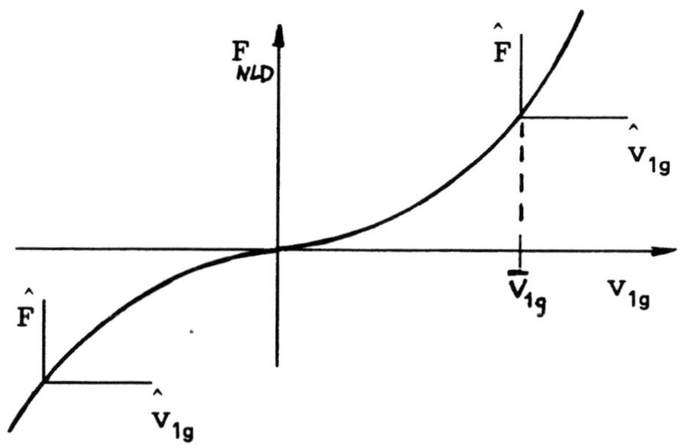

(The sign of $\hat{F}$ must always be the same as the sign of $\hat{v}_{1g}$)

a) $\bar{F}_{NLD} = C\,|\bar{v}_{1g}|\,\bar{v}_{1g}$

b) $$\hat{F} = \left.\frac{dF}{dv_{1g}}\right|_{\bar{v}_{1g}} \hat{v}_{1g}$$

$$= 2C\,|\bar{v}_{1g}|\,\hat{v}_{1g}$$

$$b_{inc} = 2C\,|\bar{v}_{1g}|$$

c)

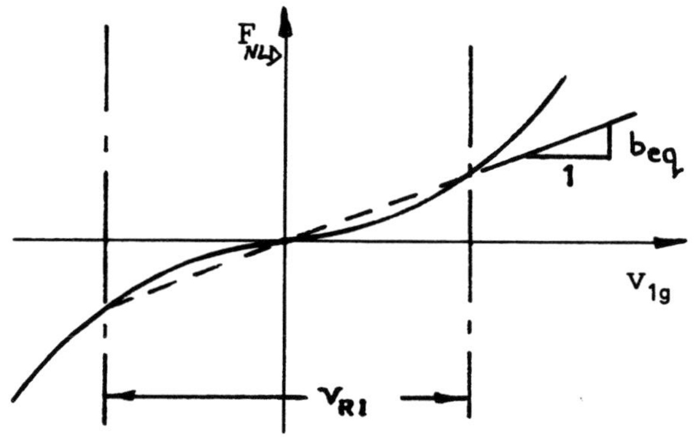

d)

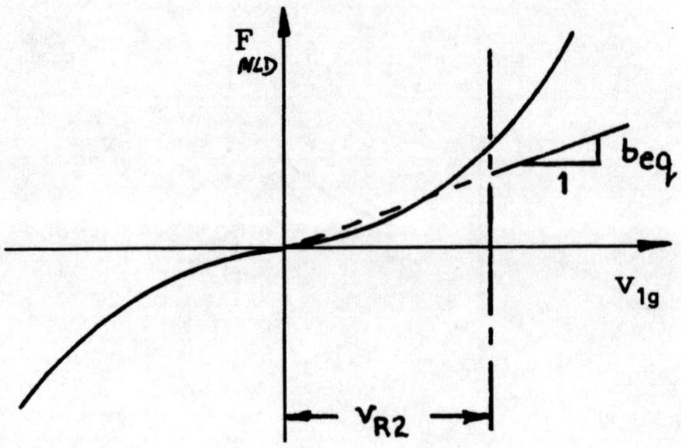

PROBLEM 1.6

a) At the normal operating point the liquid height is constant, so the mathematical model equation becomes

$$0 = -\frac{b\bar{y}}{A_0 + a\bar{y}} + \frac{\bar{Q}_i}{A_0 + a\bar{y}}$$

and hence the normal operating point value of liquid height is

$$\bar{y} = \frac{\bar{Q}_i}{b}$$

b) The model equation can be rewritten in the following form

$$\frac{dy}{dt} = -f_{NL1}(y) + f_{NL2}(y, Q_i)$$

where

$$f_{NL1}(y) = \frac{by}{A_0 + ay}$$

and

$$f_{NL2}(y, Q_i) = \frac{Q_i}{A_0 + ay}$$

The Taylor series expansion of f_{NL1} and f_{NL2} yields

$$f_{NL1}(y) \approx \frac{b\bar{y}}{A_0 + a\bar{y}} + \hat{y}\,\frac{b(A_0 + a\bar{y}) - ab\bar{y}}{(A_0 + a\bar{y})^2} = \frac{b\bar{y}}{A_0 + a\bar{y}} + \hat{y}\frac{bA_0}{(A_0 + a\bar{y})^2}$$

$$f_{NL2}(y, Q_i) \approx \frac{\bar{Q}_i}{A_0 + a\bar{y}} + \frac{\hat{Q}_i}{A_0 + a\bar{y}} - \hat{y}\frac{a\bar{Q}_i}{(A_0 + a\bar{y})^2}$$

Substituting the Taylor series expressions for f_{NL1} and f_{NL2} gives the linearized model equation

$$\frac{d\hat{y}}{dt} = -\frac{bA_0 + a\bar{Q}_i}{(A_0 + a\bar{y})^2}\hat{y} + \frac{1}{A_0 + a\bar{y}}\hat{Q}_i$$

Notice that constant terms from Taylor series expansions of f_{NL1} and f_{NL2} cancel out in the linearized equation.

CHAPTER 2

PROBLEM 2.1

a) Since the attached mass **m** is only five times the self-mass of the spring and the frequency of excitation may result in self-vibration of the spring, a massless spring model for the heavy spring is not suitable. Since the excitation frequency is less than the lowest natural frequency of the distributed-parameter model of the spring, the three-ideal-element model shown below should approximate its behavior in the 'clamped-clamped' mode (i.e. the mode in which it is constrained displacement-wise at both of its ends).

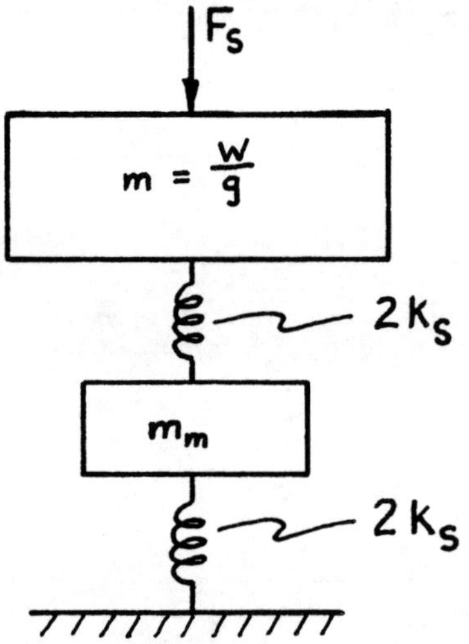

Here m_m is the mass which results in a natural frequency within the lumped-parameter model of the heavy spring which is equal to the lowest natural frequency of self-vibration of the distributed-parameter model of the spring.

This model will behave at very low frequencies like a pure spring have net stiffness k_s (since $1/k_s = 1/(2k_s) + 1/(2k_s)$), and at increasing frequencies of excitation it will begin to vibrate within itself in a manner very similar to that of the distributed-parameter model until the excitation frequency approaches the lowest natural frequency in the 'clamped-clamped' mode.

From Marks' Handbook, p. 5-75, the natural frequencies of the distributed-parameter model in the 'clamped-clamped' mode are given by:

$$f_n = c_n \left[\frac{gAE}{wl^2} \right]^{.5}, \qquad c_n = \frac{1}{2n}, \qquad n = 1, 2, 3, \ldots$$

For the lowest frequency mode, n = 1, so that

$$(f_n)_{distrib} = .5(k_s m_s)^{.5}$$

where k_s = AE/l = self-stiffness of spring

m_s = wl/g = self-mass of spring

A = spring rod area
E = modulus of elasticity
l = spring rod length
w = weight per unit length of rod
g = acceleration of gravity

From vibration theory the natural frequency of the three-lumped-element model:

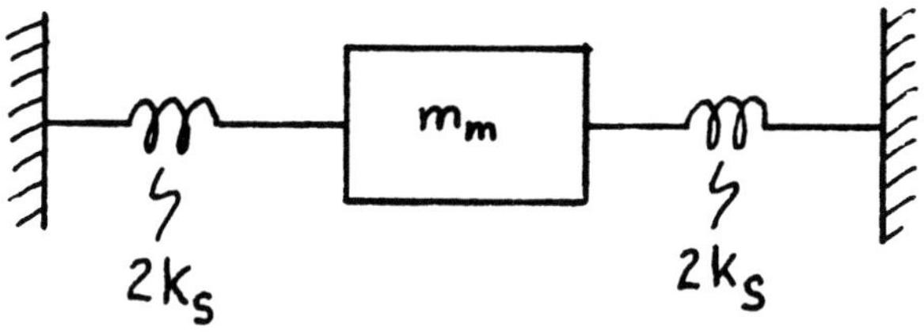

is given by:

$$(f_n)_{lumped} = \omega_n/2\pi = (1/2\pi)(4k_s/m_m)^{.5}$$

Equating $(f_n)_{distrib}$ and $(f_n)_{lumped}$ yields:

$$(1/2)(k_s/m_s)^{.5} = (1/\pi)(k_s/m_m)^{.5}$$

or

$$m_m = (4/\pi^2)m_s \approx 0.4\ m_s$$

b) Here the 'free-clamped' mode (left end constrained force-wise and right end constrained displacement-wise) of self-vibration for the distributed model is indicated, approximated by the following lumped parameter model:

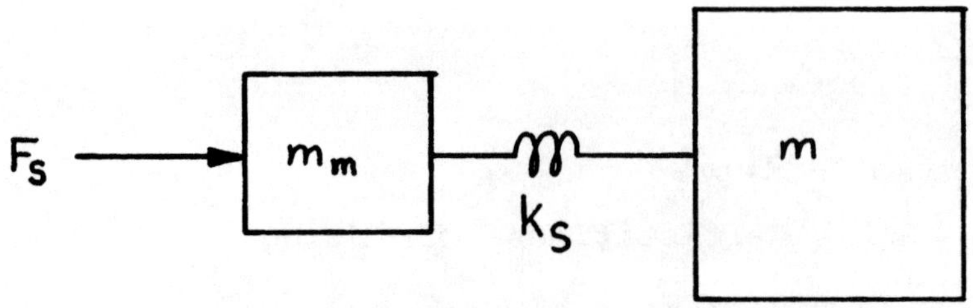

This model will behave as a pure spring having stiffness k_s at very low excitation frequencies because the portion of the transmitted force F_s required to accelerate the mass m_m will be negligible, and at increasing excitation frequencies, it will exhibit a self-vibration very similar to that of the distributed-parameter model until the excitation frequency approaches the lowest natural frequency in the 'free-clamped' mode of vibration for the distributed parameter model.

From <u>Marks' Handbook</u> again,

$$f_n = C_n \left[\frac{gAE}{wl^2} \right]^{.5} , \qquad C_n = \frac{2n - 1}{4}$$

so that the lowest frequency mode, $n = 1$, and

$$(f_n)_{distrib} = (1/4)(k_s/m_s)^{.5}$$

where k_s = self-stiffness of the spring
m_s = self-mass of the spring

From vibration theory the natural frequency for the two-lumped-element model:

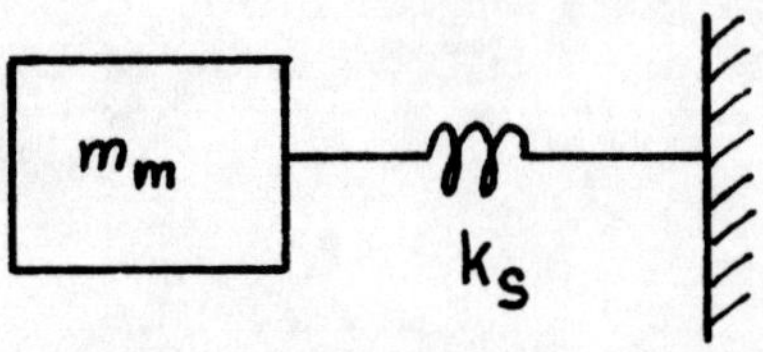

is given by:

$$(f_n)_{lumped} = \omega_n/2\pi = (1/2\pi)(k_s/m_m)^{.5}$$

Equating $(f_n)_{distrib}$ with $(f_n)_{lumped}$

$$(1/4)(k_s/m_s)^{.5} = (1/2\pi)(k_s/m_m)^{.5}$$

which is then solved for m_m giving,

$$m_m = (2/\pi)^2 m_s = 0.4 m_s$$

PROBLEM 2.2

a) The velocity vs. time graph and system diagrams requested in part a) are as follows:

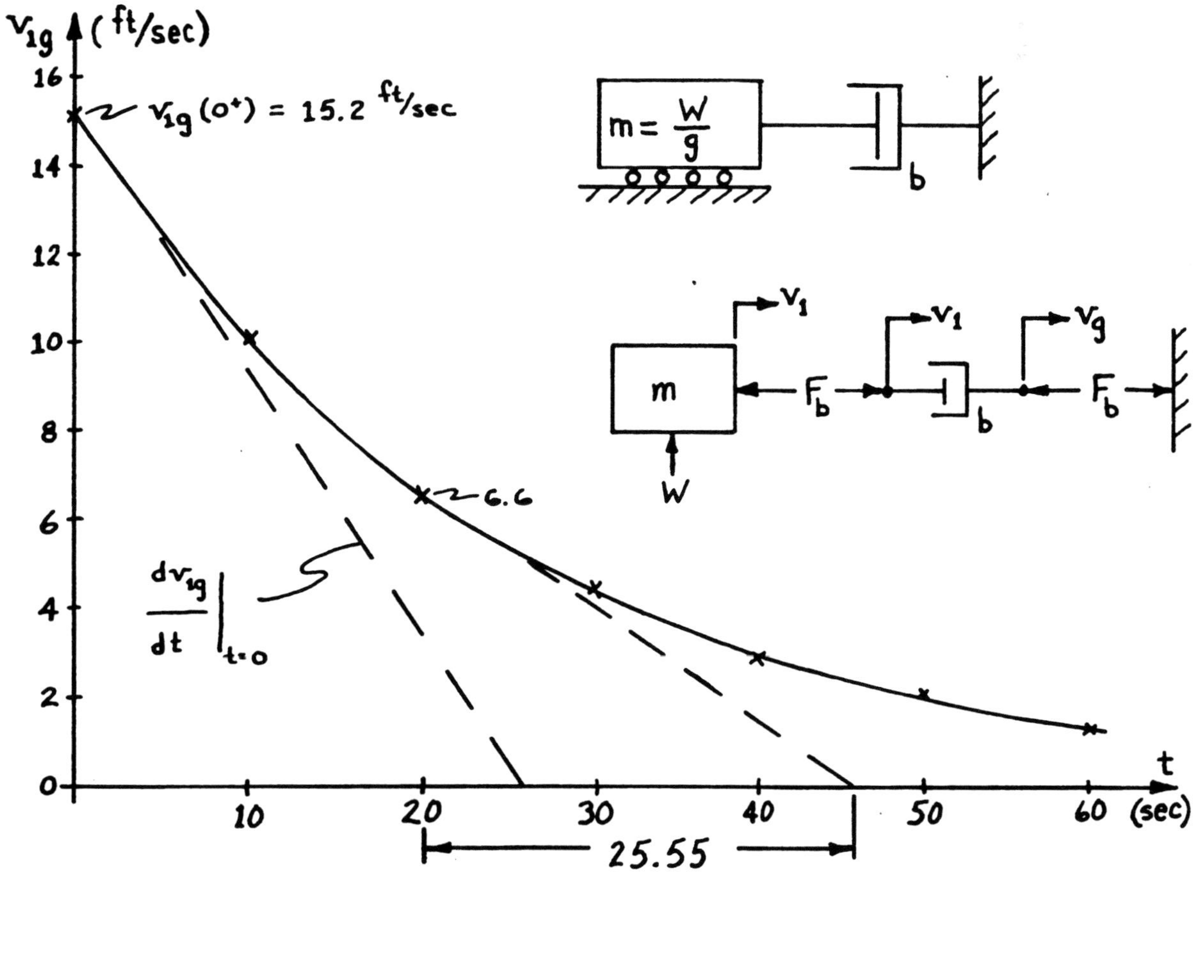

And the describing equations yield the system differential equation as follows:

$$m \frac{dv_{1g}}{dt} = -F_b = -bv_{1g}$$

so that

$$m \frac{dv_{1g}}{dt} + bv_{1g} = 0$$

b) The values of m and b are determined as follows:

$$m = W/g = (3000 \text{ lb})/(32.2 \text{ ft/sec})$$

$$= 93.7 \text{ lb-sec}^2/\text{ft} \quad \text{(or slugs)}$$

Using the system differential equation to solve for b at any time t after t = 0,

$$bv_{1g}(t) = -m \frac{dv_{1g}}{dt} \quad ; \quad b = (-m/v_{1g}(t)) \frac{dv_{1g}}{dt}$$

So that at time t = 0+,

$$b = (-m/v_{1g}(0+)) \left. \frac{dv_{1g}}{dt} \right|_{t=0+}$$

Yielding,

$$b = \frac{(93.17)(15.2)}{(15.2)(25.7)} = 3.62 \text{ lb-sec/ft}$$

Making another try at t = 20 sec,

$$b = \frac{(93.17)(6.6)}{(6.6)(25.55)} = 3.64 \text{ lb-sec/ft}$$

which is in pretty good agreement considering the rather crude gaphing techniques employed.

PROBLEM 2.3 (Hint: Check for Coulomb Friction)

The graph of the data and the system diagrams are shown below.

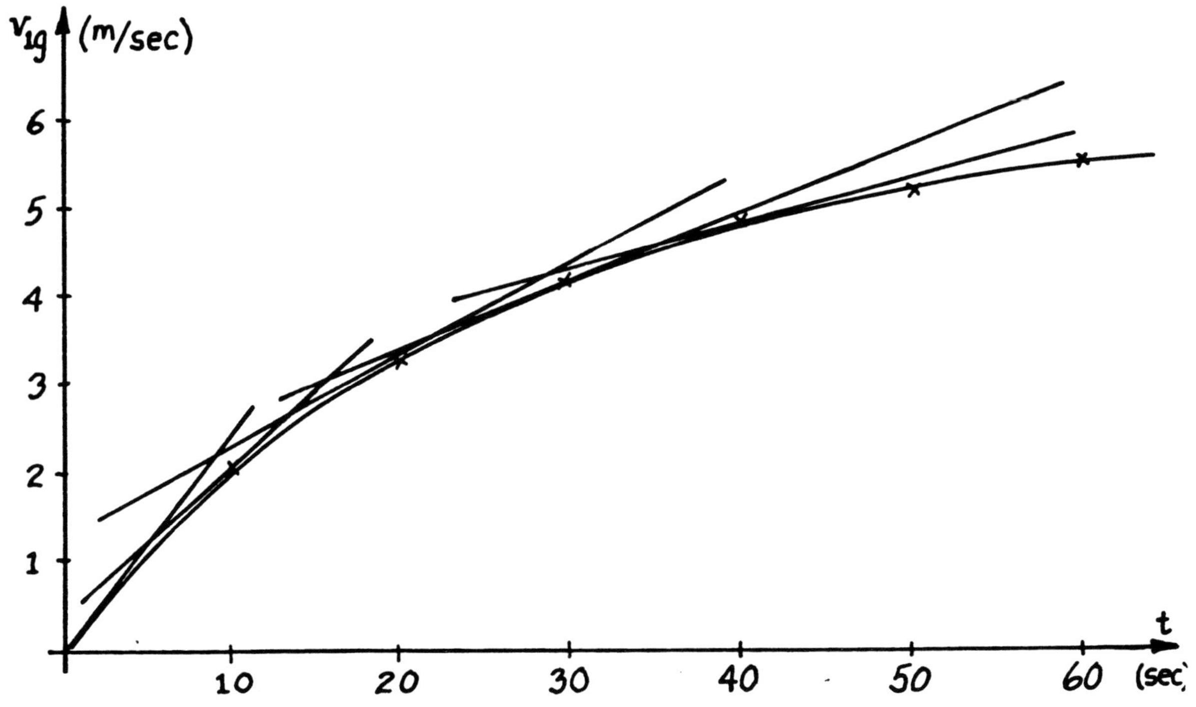

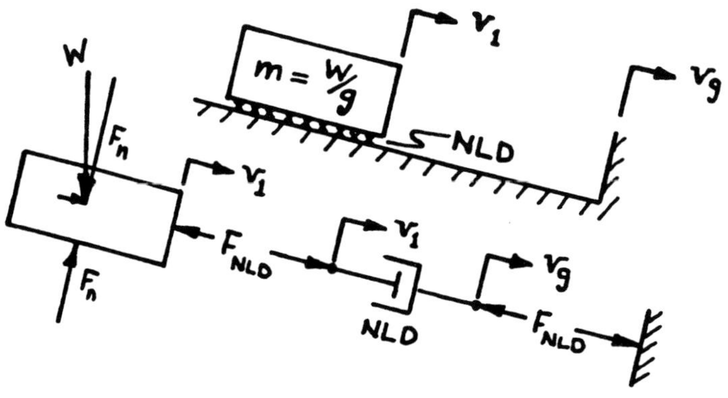

The describing equations and system differential equation are

$$m \frac{dv_{1g}}{dt} = W/10 - F_{NLD} \quad ; \qquad F_{NLD} = f_{NL}(v_{1g})$$

$$m \frac{dv_{1g}}{dt} + f_{NL}(v_{1g}) = W/10$$

Solving for F_{NLD} at any given time t after $t = 0$,

$$F_{NLD} = W/10 - m \frac{dv_{1g}}{dt}$$

where

$$m = 2200/2.2 = 1000 \text{ Kg} \quad (\text{or N-sec}^2/\text{m})$$

$$W = mg = (1000)(9.8) = 9800. \text{ N}$$

At $t = 0+$, $dv_{1g}/dt = 2.45/10 = .245 \text{ m/sec}^2$, and

$$F_{NLD}(0+) = 980 - (1000)(.245) = 735 \text{ N}$$

Since $v_{1g}(0+) = 0$, the possible linear damping term bv_{1g} is zero, and <u>all of</u> $F_{NLD}(0+)$ is a Coulomb Friction component $F_c = 735$ N.

At $t = 10$ sec, $dv_{1g}/dt = (3.75 - .4)/20 = .1675 \text{ m/sec}^2$, and

$$F_{NLD}(10) = F_c + bv_{1g}(10) = W/10 - m \left.\frac{dv_{1g}}{dt}\right|_{t=10}$$

We may now solve for b:

$$b = \left(W/10 - F_c - m \left.\frac{dv_{1g}}{dt}\right|_{t=10} \right)/v_{1g}(10)$$

$$b = [980 - 735 - (1000)(.1675)]/2.05 = 37.6 \text{ N-sec/m}$$

Given more time and persistance, a chart of computations for t = 10, 20, 30, and 40 shown below makes it possible to prepare the plot of $F_{NLD} = f_{NL}(v_{1g})$ vs. v_{1g} which then follows.

t	$v_{1g}(t)$	Slope data	dv_{1g}/dt	mdv_{1g}/dt	F_{NLD}
0	0	2.45/10	.245	245	735
10	2.05	(3.75-.4)/20	.1675	167.5	812.5
20	3.3	(5.4-1.3)/40	.102	102	878
30	4.15	(6.5-1.8)/60	.078	78	902
40	4.85	(5.9-3.75)/40	.054	54	926

Plotting F_{NLD} vs. v_{1g}:

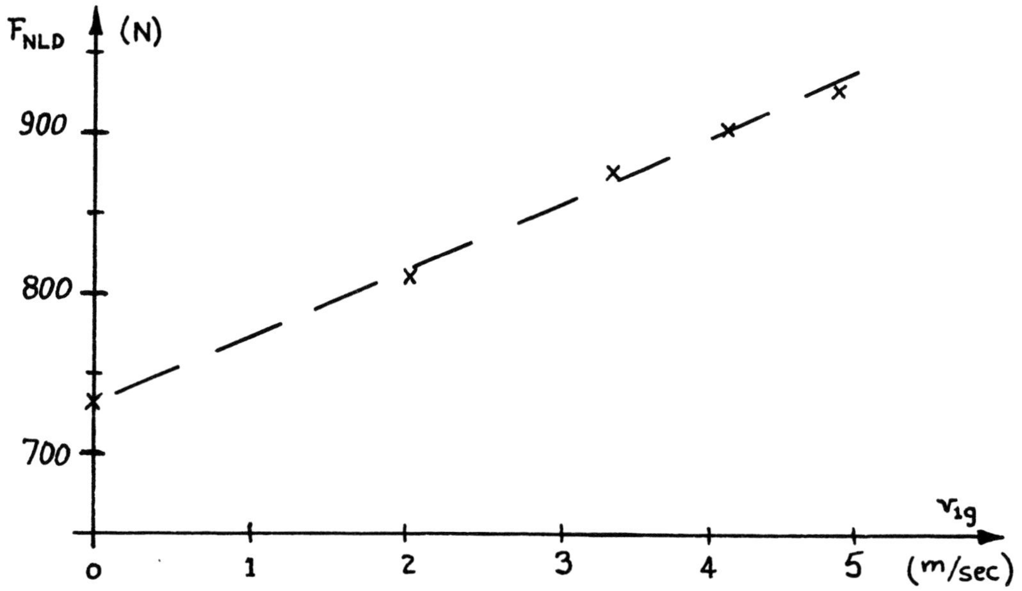

From this graph the damping coefficient b is the slope of the F_{NLD} vs. v_{1g} 'curve' which is nearly constant, allowing for experimental error and the crude graphing technique employed:

$$b = (926 - 735)/4.85 = 39.4 \text{ N-sec/m}$$

which compares fairly well with the value computed earlier at t = 10 sec.

PROBLEM 2.4

a) Preparing a graph of steady-state torque vs. shaft speed Ω_{1g}, noting that 600 RPM is equivalent to 62.8 rad/sec, from the 'Driven' data reveals negligible Coulomb friction torque T_c, and a very nearly linear damping torque characteristic having slope

$$B = 3.7/52.32 = .071 \text{ N-m-sec/rad}$$

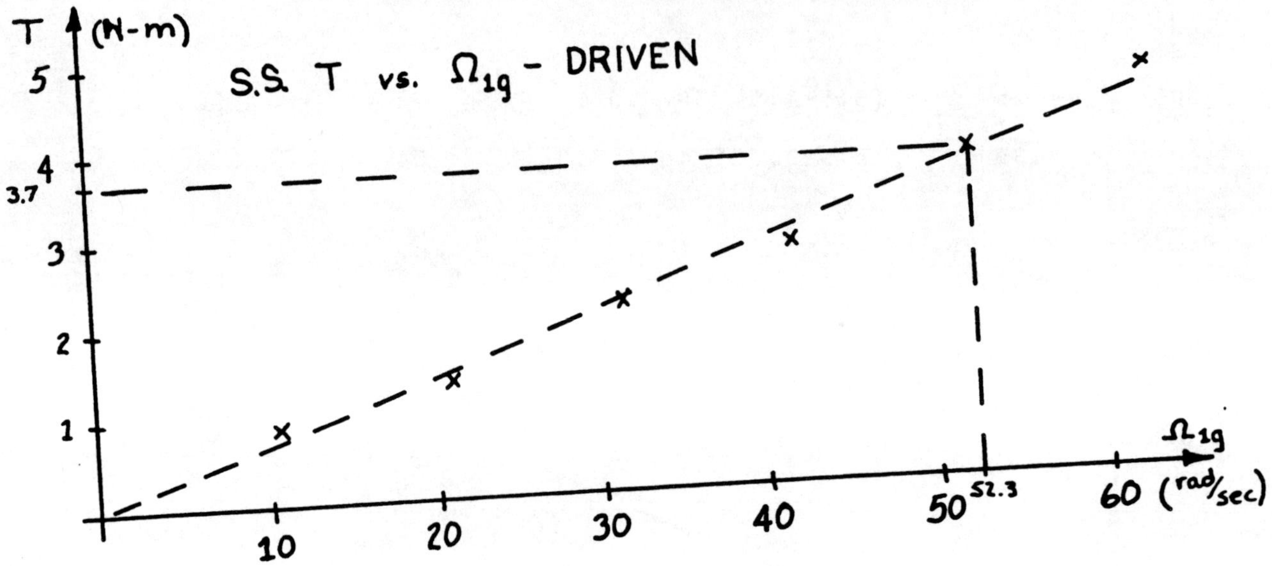

b) The system model is :

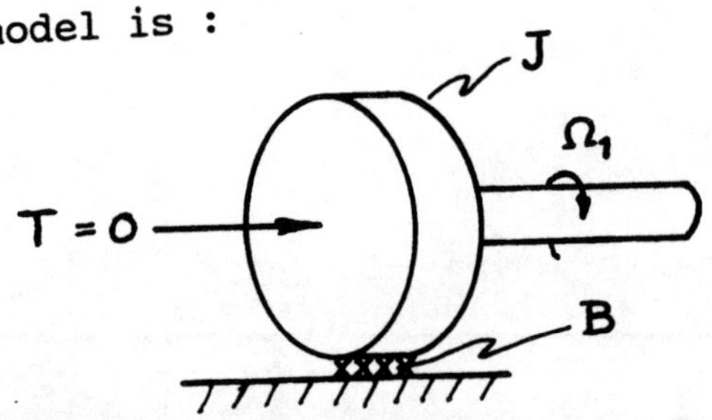

So that when coasting, the driving torque T is zero and

$$J \frac{d\Omega_{1g}}{dt} + B\Omega_{1g} = 0$$

c) Solving for J at any time t greater than zero

$$J = \frac{-B\Omega_{1g}}{\frac{d\Omega_{1g}}{dt}}$$

Preparing a graph of Ω_{1g} vs. t from the second set of data for the 'Coasting' case, makes it possible to determine $d\Omega_{1g}/dt$ at any time t by measuring the slope of this curve as shown below.

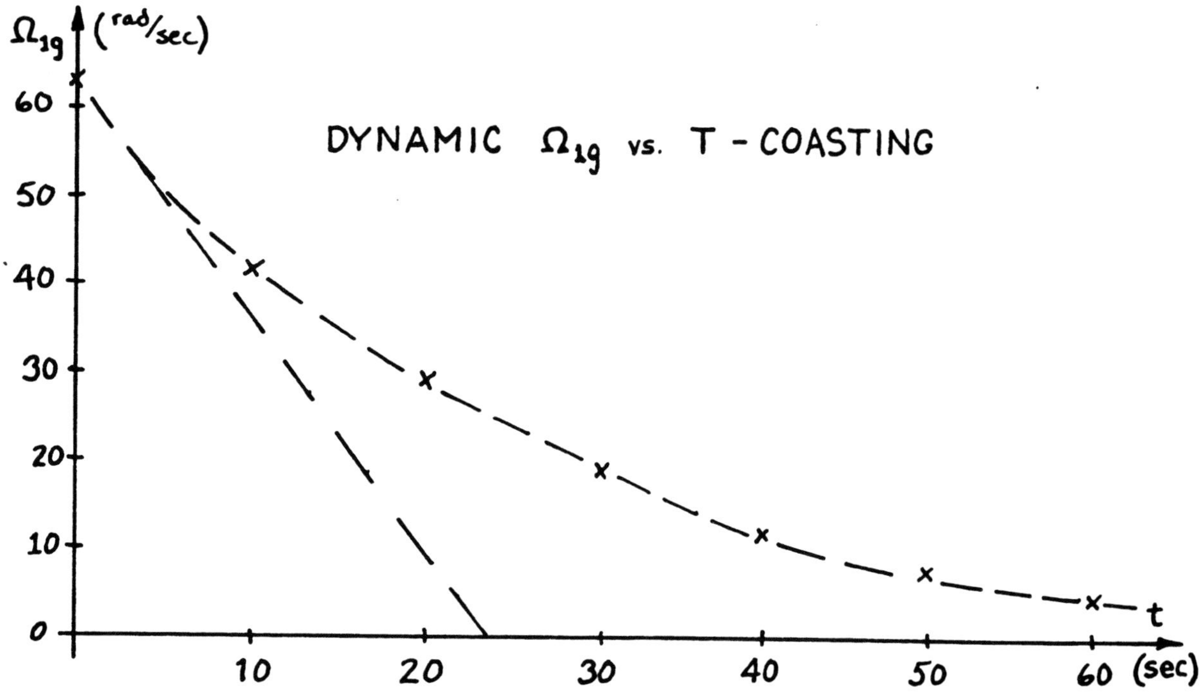

For example, at t = 0+,

$$\left.\frac{d\Omega_{1g}}{dt}\right|_{t=0+} = -62.8/23.5 = -2.67 \text{ N-m-sec}^2/\text{rad}$$

and $\Omega_{1g}(0+) = 62.8$ rad/sec, so that we have

$$J = \frac{B\Omega_{1g}(0+)}{\left.\frac{d\Omega_{1g}}{dt}\right|_{t=0+}} = (.071)(62.8)/2.67 = 1.669 \text{ N-m-sec}^2/\text{rad}$$

PROBLEM 2.5

a) The complete free-body diagram is

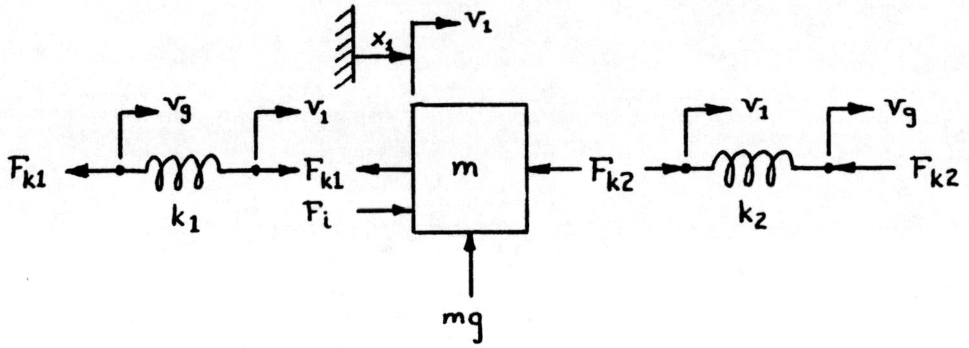

b) At rest with $(F_i)_o = 5.0$ lb

$$(F_i)_o - (F_{kl})_o - (F_{k2})_o = m\frac{dv_{1g}}{dt} = 0$$

$$(k_1 + k_2)(x_1)_{o2} = (F_i)_o$$

$$(x_1)_o = (F_i)_o/(k_1 + k_2) = 5.0/(k_1 + k_2)$$

c) From the describing equations

$$m\frac{dv_{1g}}{dt} = m\frac{d^2x_1}{dt^2} = F_i - F_{kl} - F_{k2} = F_i - (k_1 + k_2)x_1$$

Or when $F_i = 0$

$$m\frac{d^2x_1}{dt^2} + (k_1 + k_2)x_1 = 0$$

d) Since reducing the force suddenly to zero does not result in an infinite force on the mass, its velocity at $t = 0+$ is still zero. Since the mass is still not moving at $t = 0+$

$$x_1(0+) = x_1(0-) = (x_1)_o$$

PROBLEM 2.6

a) The describing equations and free-body diagram are

$$T_s - T_i = \frac{d\Omega_{2g}}{dt}$$

$$T_s = K_s(\theta_1 - \theta_2)$$

$$\Omega_{2g} = \frac{d\theta_2}{dt}$$

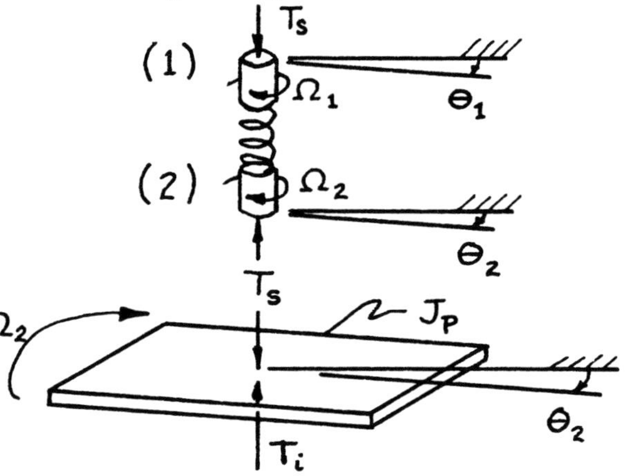

Combining to eliminate T_s and noting that $\theta_1 = 0$

$$J \frac{d^2\theta_2}{dt^2} + K_s\theta_2 = -T_i$$

b)

$$\omega_n = (K_s/J_p)^{.5}$$

From Marks' Handbook, p. 3-10

$$J_p = M_p(a^2 + b^2)/12 = 5(100 + 900)/12$$

$$J_p = 417 \text{ kg-cm}^2\text{/rad} = 4.17 \text{ N-cm-sec}^2\text{/rad}$$

From Marks' Handbook, p. 5-41

$$K_s = T_s/\theta_{12} = GI_p/L = G\pi d^4/32L$$

$$= (8.27\text{x}10^6)(3.14)(.5)^4/(30)(32)$$

$$= 1690 \text{ N-cm/rad}$$

$$\omega_n = (1690/4.17)^{.5} = 20.1 \text{ rad/sec} \quad \text{or} \quad 3.2 \text{ Hertz}$$

c) The inertia of the rod is very, very small

$$J_r = M_r r^2/2 = \rho L\pi d^4/32 = (.0078)(30)(3.14)(.5)^4/32$$

$$J_r = .0016 \text{ N-cm-sec}^2/\text{rad}$$

Therefore it is negligible compared to the plate inertia of 4.17 N-cm-sec²/rad, and should be of no concern in this problem.

PROBLEM 2.7

The complete free-body diagram (neglecting gravity) for this system is

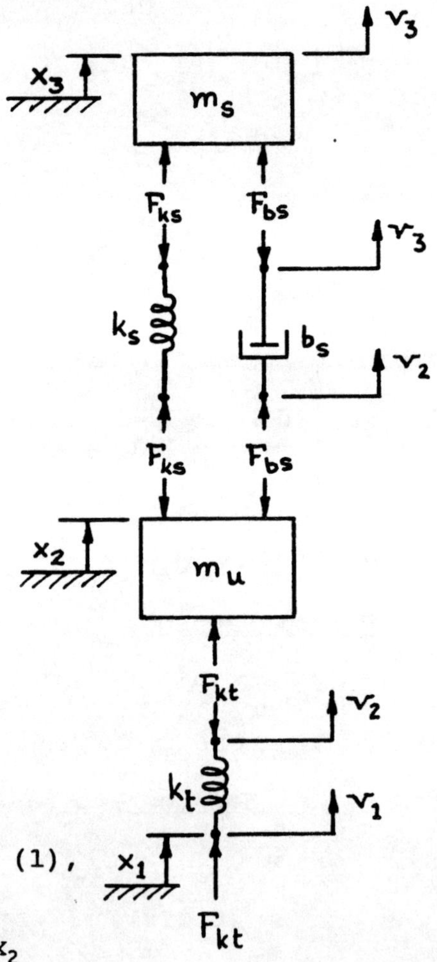

The complete set of describing equations is

(1) $$m_s \frac{d^2x_3}{dt^2} = F_{ks} + F_{bs}$$

(2) $$F_{ks} = k_s(x_2 - x_3)$$

(3) $$F_{bs} = b_s\left(\frac{dx_2}{dt} - \frac{dx_3}{dt}\right)$$

(4) $$m_u \frac{d^2x_2}{dt^2} = F_{kt} - F_{ks} - F_{bs}$$

(5) $$F_{kt} = k_t(x_1 - x_2)$$

They contain the five unknowns x_3, F_{ks}, F_{bs}, x_2, and F_{kt}.

a) To find $x_3 = f(x_1,t)$, equations (1), (2), and (3) are combined to produce

(6) $$m_s \frac{d^2x_3}{dt^2} + b_s \frac{dx_3}{dt} + k_s x_3 = b_s \frac{dx_2}{dt} + k_s x_2$$

Similarly equations (3), (4), and (5) are combined

$$(7) \qquad m_u \frac{d^2x_3}{dt} + b_s \frac{dx_2}{dt} + (k_s + k_t)x_2 = k_t x_1 + k_s x_3 + b_s \frac{dx_3}{dt}$$

Operating on equation (6) with $(m_s D^2 + b_s D + k_s)$, operating on equation (7) with $(b_s D + k_s)$, and rearranging

$$(6m) \qquad (m_u D^2+b_s D+k_s+k_t)(b_s D+k_s)x_2 = (m_u D^2+b_s D+k_s+k_t)(m_s D^2+b_s D+k_s)x_3$$

$$(7m) \qquad (m_u D^2+b_s D+k_s+k_t)(b_s D+k_s)x_2 = (b_s D+k_s)^2 x_3+k_t(b_s D+k_s)x_1$$

Subtracting (6m) from (7m) to eliminate x_2

$$[(m_u D^2+b_s D+k_s+k_t)(m_s D^2+b_s D+k_s)-(b_s D+k_s)^2]x_3 = k_t(b_s D+k_s)x_1$$

or

$$(8) \qquad m_u m_s \frac{d^4x_3}{dt^4} +(m_u+m_s)b_s \frac{d^3x_3}{dt^3} +[m_s k_s+m_s(k_s+k_t)\frac{d^2x_3}{dt^2} +b_s k_t \frac{dx_3}{dt} +k_t k_s x_3$$

$$= k_t b_s \frac{dx_1}{dt} +k_t k_s x_1$$

b) To find $F_{ks} = f(x_1,t)$, we need to eliminate x_2, x_3, F_{bs}, and F_{kt}. To do this, combine equations (1) and (3) to eliminate F_{bs} from equation (1)

$$(9) \qquad m_s \frac{d^2x_2}{dt^2} + b_s \frac{dx_3}{dt} = b_s \frac{dx_2}{dt} + F_{ks}$$

and then combine (3), (4), and (5) to eliminate F_{bs} and F_{kt} from equation (4)

$$(10) \qquad m_u \frac{d^2x_2}{dt^2} + b_s \frac{dx_2}{dt} + k_t x_2 = b_s \frac{dx_3}{dt} + k_t x_1 - F_{ks}$$

Now we need to use equation (2) to get an expression for x_2 in terms of F_{ks} and x_3

$$(11) \qquad x_2 = x_3 + (1/k_s)F_{ks}$$

which is then substituted in equations (9) and (10), leaving two equations, (12), and (13) with the two unknowns x_3 and F_{ks}

$$(12) \qquad m_s D^2 x_3 = [(b_s/k_s)D + 1]F_{ks}$$

$$(13) \qquad (m_u D^2 + k_t)x_3 = -(1/k_s)(m_u D_2 + b_s D + k_t + k_s)F_{ks}$$

Now operating on equation (12) with $(m_u D^2 + k_t)$ and on equation (13) with $m_s D^2$

(14) $$(m_u D^2+k_t)(m_s D^2)x_3 = [(b_s/k_s)D+1](m_u D^2+k_t)F_{ks}$$

(15) $$(m_u D^2+k_t)(m_s D^2)x_3 = -m_s D^2(1/k_s)(m_u D_2+b_s D+k_t+k_s)F_{ks}+k_t m_s D^2 x_1$$

makes it possible to eliminate x_3 by subtracting equation (15) from equation (14)

$$\{[(b_s/k_s)D+1](m_u D^2+k_t)+m_s D^2(1/k_s)(m_u D_2+b_s D+k_t+k_s)\}F_{ks} = k_t m_s D^2 x_1$$

or

(16) $$(m_s m_u/k_s)\frac{d^4F_{ks}}{dt^4} + (b_s/k_s)(m_s+m_u)\frac{d^3F_{ks}}{dt^3} + [m_u+(k_t+k_s)m_s/k_s]\frac{d^2F_{ks}}{dt^2}$$
$$+ (b_s k_t/k_s)\frac{dF_{ks}}{dt} + k_t F_{ks} = k_t m_s\frac{d^2x_1}{dt^2}$$

PROBLEM 2.8

a) The complete free-body diagram is

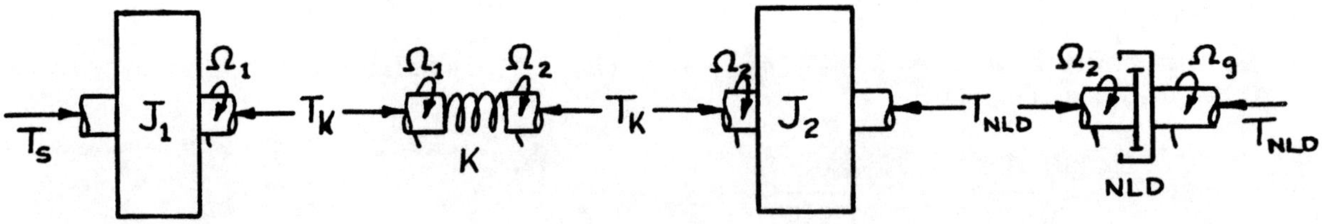

b) The necessary and sufficient set of describing equation,

(1) $$J_1 \frac{d^2\theta_1}{dt^2} = T_s - T_K$$

(2) $$T_K = K(\theta_1 - \theta_2)$$

(3) $$J_2 \frac{d^2\theta_2}{dt^2} = T_K - T_{NLD}$$

(4) $$T_{NLD} = T_o + C|\Omega_{2g}|\Omega_{2g}$$

contains the four unknowns θ_1, T_K, θ_2, and T_{NLD}. ($\Omega_{2g} = d\theta_2/dt$)

c) The corresponding set of small-perturbation equations consists of the following

(1sp) $$J_1 \frac{d^2\hat{\theta}_1}{dt^2} = \hat{T}_s - \hat{T}_K$$

(2sp) $$\hat{T}_K = K(\hat{\theta}_1 - \hat{\theta}_2)$$

(3sp) $$J_2 \frac{d^2\hat{\theta}_2}{dt^2} = \hat{T}_K - \hat{T}_{NLD}$$

(4sp) $$\hat{T}_{NLD} = 2C|\bar{\Omega}_{2g}|\hat{\Omega}_{2g}$$

and the normal operating point values are given by

$$\bar{T}_s = \bar{T}_K = \bar{T}_{NLD} = T_o + C\bar{\Omega}_{2g}^{\ 2}$$

and

$$\bar{\Omega}_{1g} = \bar{\Omega}_{2g}$$

because $d\bar{T}_K/dt \equiv 0$

d) Combining equations (1sp) and (2sp) to eliminate $\hat{T}_K$ from equation (1sp)

(5sp) $$J_1 \frac{d^2\hat{\theta}_1}{dt^2} = \hat{T}_s - K(\hat{\theta}_1 - \hat{\theta}_2)$$

and combining equations (2sp), (3sp), and (4sp) to eliminate $\hat{T}_K$ and $\hat{T}_{NLD}$ from equation (3sp) (noting that $\hat{\Omega}_{2g} \equiv d\hat{\theta}_2/dt$)

$$\text{(6sp)} \quad J_2 \frac{d^2\hat{\theta}_2}{dt^2} = K(\hat{\theta}_1 - \hat{\theta}_2) - 2C|\overline{\Omega}_{2g}| \frac{d\hat{\theta}_2}{dt}$$

so that equation (6sp) may be solved for $\hat{\theta}_1$.

$$\text{(7sp)} \quad \hat{\theta}_1 = (J_2/K)\frac{d^2\hat{\theta}_2}{dt^2} + \hat{\theta}_2 + (2C/K)|\overline{\Omega}_{2g}| \frac{d\hat{\theta}_2}{dt}$$

Substituting this expression for $\hat{\theta}_1$ into equation (5sp) yields

$$(J_1\frac{d^2\hat{\theta}_2}{dt^2} + K)[(J_2/K)\frac{d^2\hat{\theta}_2}{dt^2} + \theta_2 + (2C/K)|\overline{\Omega}_{2g}|\frac{d\hat{\theta}_2}{dt}] = \hat{T}_s + K\hat{\theta}_2$$

or

$$(J_1J_2/K)\frac{d^4\hat{\theta}_2}{dt^4} + (2J_1|\overline{\Omega}_{2g}|/K)\frac{d^3\hat{\theta}_2}{dt^3} + (J_1+J_2)\frac{d^2\hat{\theta}_2}{dt^2} + 2C|\overline{\Omega}_{2g}|\frac{d\hat{\theta}_2}{dt} + K\hat{\theta}_2 = \hat{T}_s + K\hat{\theta}_2$$

And since $d\hat{\theta}_2/dt = \hat{\Omega}_{2g}$

$$\text{(8sp)} \quad (J_1J_2/K)\frac{d^4\hat{\Omega}_{2g}}{dt^4} + (2J_1|\overline{\Omega}_{2g}|/K)\frac{d^3\hat{\Omega}_{2g}}{dt^3} + (J_1+J_2)\frac{d^2\hat{\Omega}_{2g}}{dt^2} + 2C|\overline{\Omega}_{2g}|\hat{\Omega}_{2g} = \hat{T}_s$$

PROBLEM 2.9

a) The complete free-body diagram is

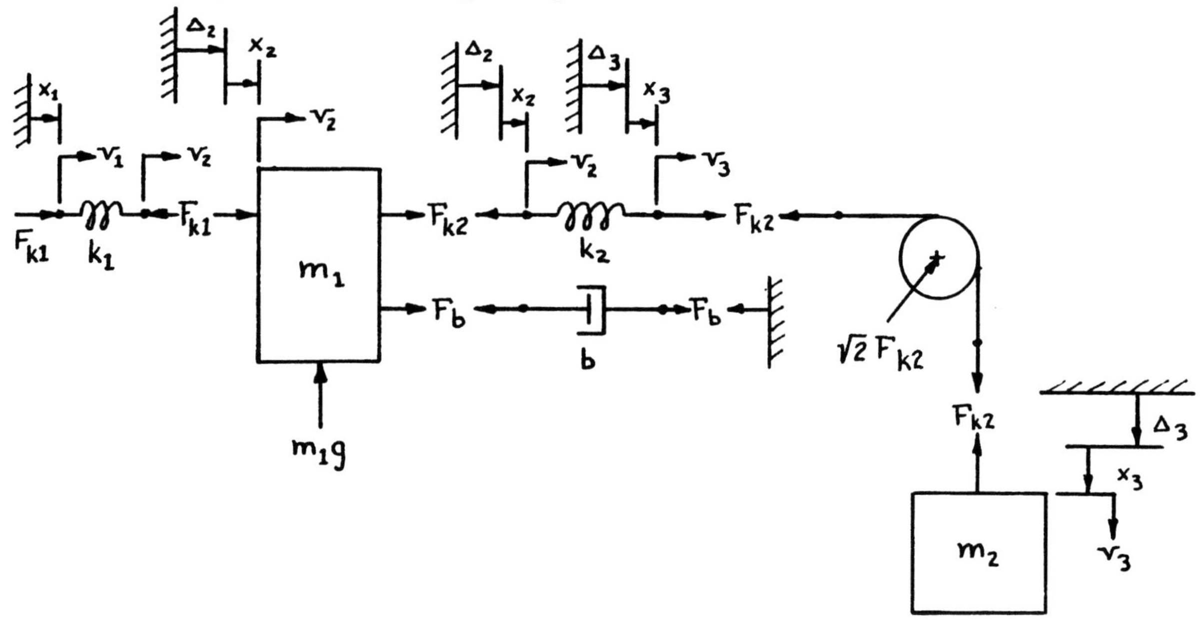

b) The displacement references are

$$\Delta_2 = m_2g/k_1$$

$$(\Delta_3 - \Delta_2) = m_2g/k_2$$

$$\Delta_3 = m_2g/k_1 + m_2g/k_2$$

$$= m_2g(k_1 + k_2)/k_1k_2$$

c) The necessary and sufficient set of describing equations

(1) $$m_1 \frac{d^2x_2}{dt^2} = F_{k1} + F_{k2} + F_b$$

(2) $$F_{k1} = k_1[x_1 - (\Delta_2 + x_2)]$$

(3) $$F_{k2} = k_2[(\Delta_3 + x_3) - (\Delta_2 + x_2)]$$

$$= k_2(x_3 - x_2) + k_2(\Delta_3 - \Delta_2)$$

(4) $$F_b = bv_{g2} = -b \frac{dx_2}{dt}$$

$$(5) \qquad m_2 \frac{d^2x_3}{dt^2} = m_2 g - F_{k2}$$

contain the five unknowns x_2, x_3, F_{k1}, F_{k2}, and F_b.

d) Combining equations (1), (2), (3), and (4), and noting that $k_1\Delta 2 = k_2(\Delta_3 - \Delta_2) = m_2 g$

$$(6) \qquad m_1 \frac{d^2x_2}{dt^2} = k_1(x_1 = x_2) + k_2(x_3 - x_2) - b\frac{dx_2}{dt}$$

and combining equations (3) and (5), and noting that $k_2(\Delta_3 - \Delta_2) = m_2 g$

$$(7) \qquad m_2 \frac{d^2x_3}{dt^2} = -k_2(x_3 - x_2)$$

Collecting terms in equations (6) and (7)

$$(6c) \qquad m_1 \frac{d^2x_2}{dt^2} + b\frac{dx_2}{dt} + (k_1 + k_2)x_2 = k_1x_1 + k_2x_3$$

$$(7c) \qquad m_2 \frac{d^2x_3}{dt^2} + k_2x_3 = k_2x_2$$

Solving (7c) for x_2 and substituting for x_2 in (6c)

$$[m_1\frac{d^2}{dt^2} + b\frac{d}{dt} + (k_1+k_2)][(m_2/k_2)\frac{d^2x_3}{dt^2} + x_3] = k_1x_1 + k_2x_3$$

or

$$(8) \quad (m_1m_2/k_2)\frac{d^4x_3}{dt^4}+(bm_2/k_2)\frac{d^3x_3}{dt^3}+[m_1+m_2(k_1+k_2)/k_2]\frac{d^2x_3}{dt^2}+b\frac{dx_3}{dt}+k_1x_3=k_1x_1$$

PROBLEM 2.10

a) The complete free-body diagram is

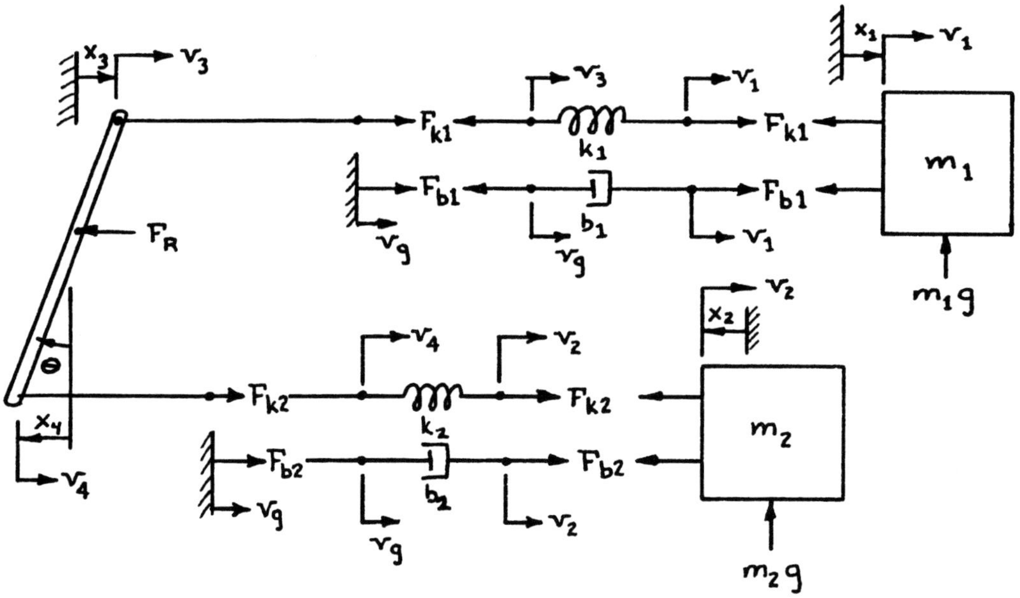

b) The necessary and sufficient set of describing equations

(1) $$m_1 \frac{d^2x_1}{dt^2} = F_s - F_{k1} - F_{b1}$$

(2) $$F_{k1} = k_1(x_1 - x_3)$$

(3) $$F_{b1} = b_1 \frac{dx_1}{dt}$$

(4) $$m_2 \frac{d^2x_2}{dt^2} = -F_{k2} - F_{b2}$$

(5) $$F_{k2} = k_2(x_2 - x_4)$$

(6) $$F_{b2} = b_2 \frac{dx_2}{dt}$$

(7) $$x_4 = -(b/a)x_3$$

(8) $$F_{k2} = (a/b)F_{k1}$$

contain the eight unknown variables $x_1, x_2, x_3, x_4, F_{k1}, F_{b1}, F_{k2}, F_{b2}$. In order to find $x_2 = f(F_s,t)$, it will be necessary to eliminate x_1, x_3, x_4, and all the forces. Combining equations (1), (2), and (3) to eliminate F_{k1} and F_{k2} from (1)

$$(9) \qquad m_2 \frac{d^2x_1}{dt^2} + b_1 \frac{dx_1}{dt} + k_1x_1 = F_s + k_1x_3$$

and combining equations (4), (5), (6), and (7) to eliminate F_{k2}, F_{b2}, and x_4

$$(10) \qquad m_2 \frac{d^2x_2}{dt^2} + b_2 \frac{dx_2}{dt} + k_2x_2 = k_2(-b/a)x_3$$

Combining equations (2), (5), (7), and (8) results in an expression for x_1 in terms of x_2 and x_3

$$(11) \qquad x_1 = (bk_2/ak_1)x_2 + [1 + (b^2k_2/a^2k_1)]x_3$$

which is then substituted in equation (9) to yield

$$(12) \qquad (k_2b/k_1a)(m_1 \frac{d^2x_2}{dt^2} + b_1 \frac{dx_2}{dt} + k_1x_2) =$$

$$-[1 + (k_2b^2/k_1a^2)](m_1 \frac{d^2x_3}{dt^2} + b_1 \frac{dx_3}{dt} + k_1x_3) + k_1x_3 + F_s$$

Equations (10) and (12) contain only the two unknowns x_2 and x_3. Solving (10) for x_3

$$(13) \qquad x_3 = (-a/k_2b)(m_2 \frac{d^2x_2}{dt^2} + b_2 \frac{dx_2}{dt} + k_2x_2)$$

which is then substitutedd into equation (12) to yield

$$(k_2b/k_1a)(m_1 \frac{d^2x_2}{dt^2} + b_1 \frac{dx_2}{dt} + k_1x_2) = F_s +$$

$$\{k_1-[1+(k_2b^2/k_1a^2)](m_1 \frac{d^2}{dt^2}+b_1\frac{d}{dt}+k_1)\}(-a/k_2b)(m_2\frac{d^2x_2}{dt^2}+b_2\frac{dx_2}{dt}+k_2x_2)$$

Rearranging and collecting terms

(14) $$\left(1 + \frac{k_2b^2}{k_1a^2}\right)m_1m_2 \frac{d^4x_2}{dt^4} + \left(1 + \frac{k_2b^2}{k_1a^2}\right)(m_1b_2 + m_2b_1)\frac{d^3x_2}{dt^3} + \left[\frac{k_2b^2}{k_1a^2}k_1m_2 + \left(1 + \frac{k_2b^2}{k_1a^2}\right)b_1b_2 + m_1k_2\right]\frac{d^2x_2}{dt^2} + \left(\frac{k_2b^2}{k_1a^2}k_1b_2 + b_1k_2\right)\frac{dx_2}{dt} = (-k_2b/a)F_s$$

Problem 2.11

Figure 2.9:

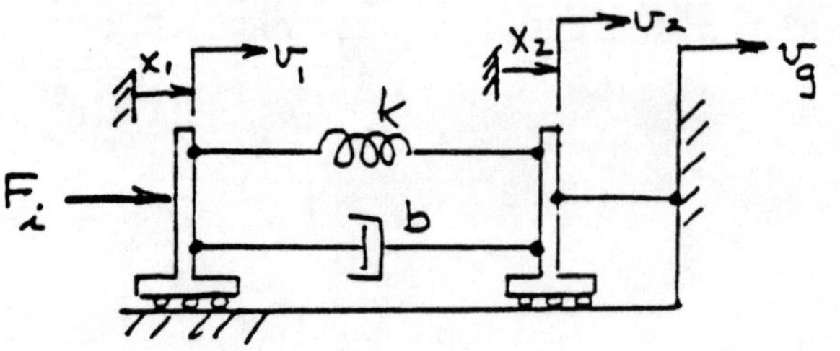

a) Rearranging Equation (2.23):

$d(x_1-x_2)/dt = (1/b)[F_i - k(x_1-x_2)]$

Starting with Summer having inputs F_i and $F_K=k(x_1-x_2)$ followed by a coefficient (1/b), an Integrator, and another Summer the simulation block diagram is formed:

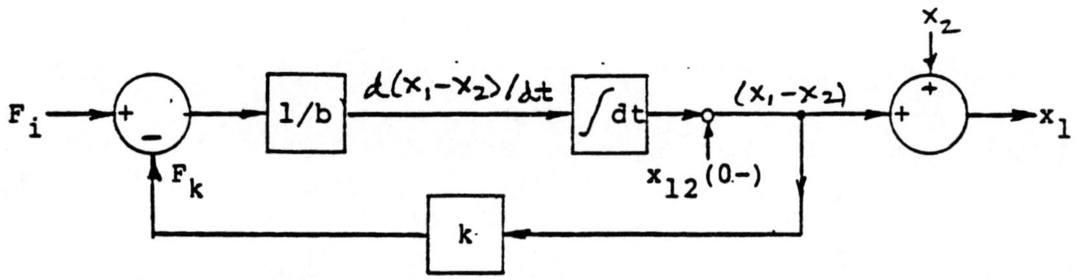

Discussion. Assuming that the system has been initially at rest with $F_i = 0$, the first effect of a change in the input force F_i starting at t = 0 is an initial rate of change of spring deflection:

$$d(x_1-x_2)/dt = F_i(0+)/b$$

As time goes by this simulated velocity is integrated to produce the simulated spring deflection (x_1-x_2), which, when multiplied by the spring stiffness coefficient, k, simulates the spring force F_k. The action of the increasing spring force opposing the input force F_i is simulated by summing it with a negative sign in the left-hand Summer. This effectively closes the loop with negative feedback, so that all the variables interact continuously in closed loop fashion to simulate the dynamic behaviour of the system. Such simulations are commonly carried out through the use of analog, digital, or hybrid (analog-digital) computers. For the case when x_2 is also an input to this system, the motion x_1 is simulated by adding x_2 to the spring deflection (x_1-x_2) with the right-hand Summer.

b) Adding a coefficient block (1/b) between the input force F_i and the left-hand Summer, removing the (1/b) block from between the Summer and Integrator, and changing the feedback block to (k/b) yields the same system in normalized form:

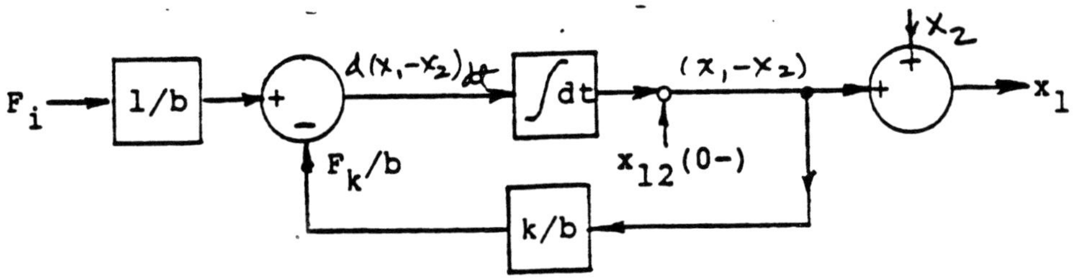

Problem 2.12

Figure 2.10:

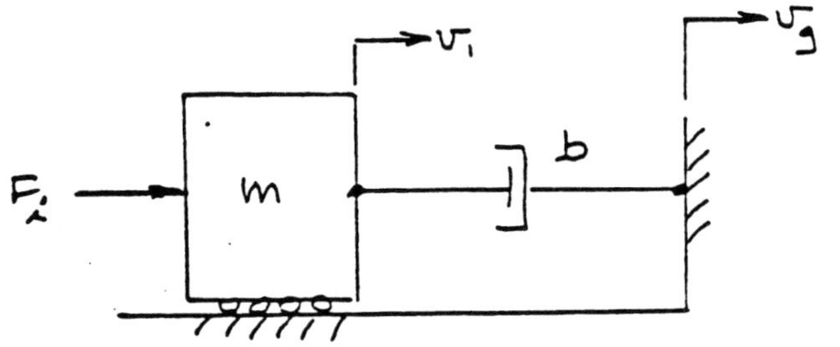

Rearranging Equation (2.27):

$$dv_{1g}/dt = (1/m)[F_i - b(v_{1g} - v_{2g})]$$

Beginning with the input force F_i acting into a Summer together with the damper force $F_b=b(v_{1g}-v_{2g})$ followed by a Coefficient (1/m) and an Integrator the simulation block diagram takes the form:

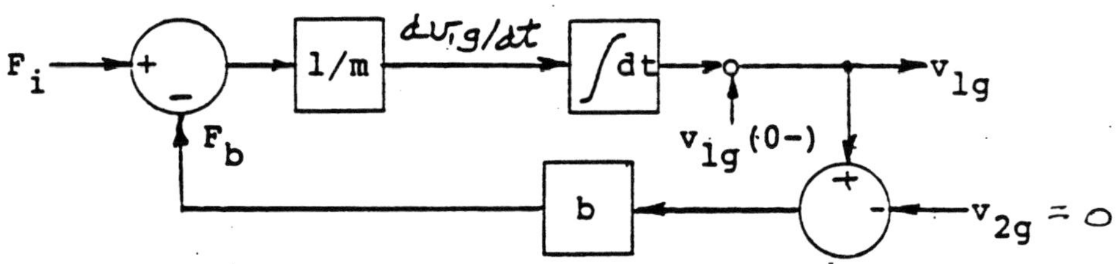

Assuming that the system has been initially at rest with F_i = 0, the first effect of a change in the input force F_i at t = 0 is to produce an initial change in the acceleration of the mass:

$$dv_{1g}/dt = F_i(0+)/m$$

As time goes by this simulated acceleration is integrated to produce the simulated velocity v_{1g} which is continuously compared in the right-hand Summer with the possible input velocity v_{2g} to simulate damper velocity difference $v_{1g}-v_{2g}$. Using the coefficient block (b) produces the simulated damper force $F_b=(v_{1g}-v_{2g})$, which is then summed with a negative sign to simulate its opposition to the input force F_i. This effectively closes the loop with negative feedback and all the variables then interact continuously to simulate the dynamic behaviour of this system.

Here the role of (m) and (b) are analogous to the roles of (b) and (k) respectively in Problem 3.11, while the behaviour of v_{1g} is analogous to the behaviour of x_1 in Problem 3.1.

Problem 2.13

Figure 2.11:

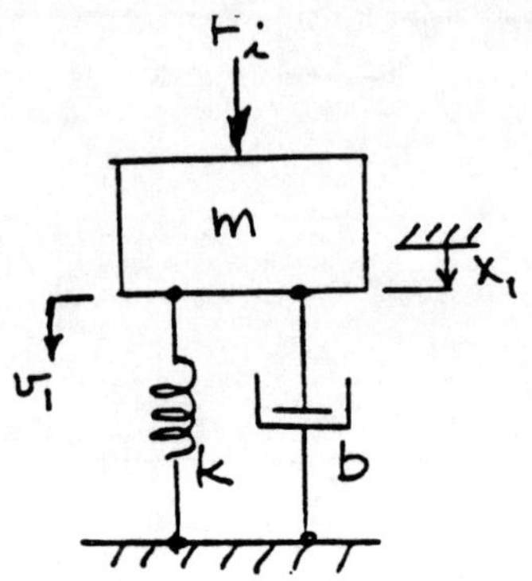

Rearranging Equation (2.33):

$d^2x_1/dt^2 = (1/m)(F_i - bdx_1/dt - kx_1)$

a) Starting with F_i, the simulation block diagram is assembled as follows:

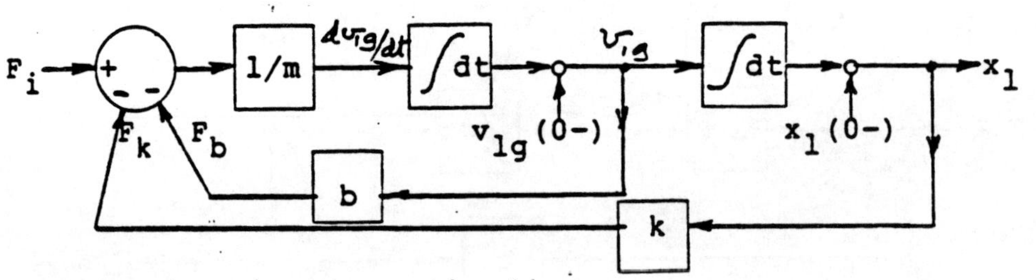

b) The coefficient block (k) is removed from the outer feedback path as follows:

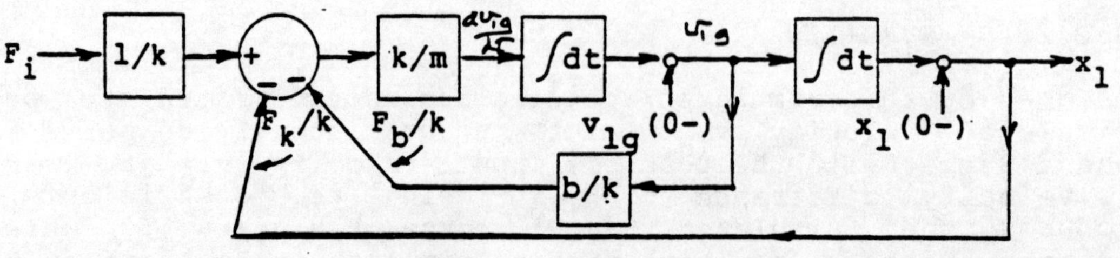

c) Compared with Problem 2.12, this system has two integrators and two closed loops, each with negative feedback. The inner loop, acting around only the first Integrator, produces a more immediate effect on the simulated motion of the mass than the outer loop which acts around both Integrators. This system needs two Integrators in its simulation block diagram because it contains two energy storage elements, (m) and (k), instead of the single energy storage element (k) in Problem 2.12, corresponding to the second-order input-output differential equation as compared to the first-order differential equation describing the system of Problem 2.12.

Problem 2.14

Figure 2.12:

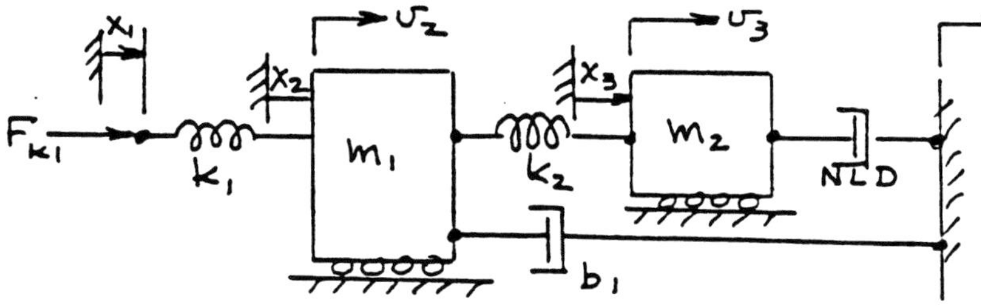

Rearranging Equation (2.41):

(1) $d^2x_2/dt^2 = (1/m_1)[k_1x_1 + k_2x_3 - b_1dx_2/dt - (k_1+k_2)x_2]$

Rearranging Equation (2.42):

(2) $d^2x_3/dt^2 = (1/m_2)[k_2x_2 - f_{NL}(dx_3/dt) - k_2x_3]$

a) Starting with x_1 and Equation (1) and then proceeding with Equation (2) the simulation block diagram takes the following form:

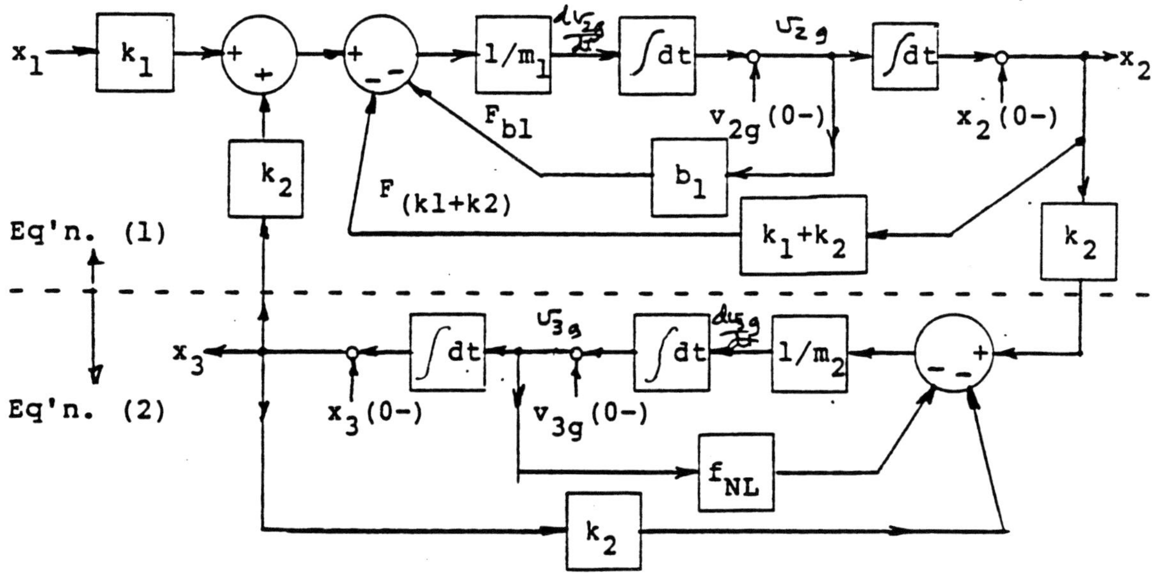

b) The block diagram for the linearized system is the same as above except for the use of a "b_{inc}" block instead of the "f_{NL}" block, where

$$b_{inc} = dF_{NLD}/dv_{3g}\Big|_{\bar{v}_{3g}}$$

and all variables become 'hat' values.

Problem 2.15

Figure 2.17:

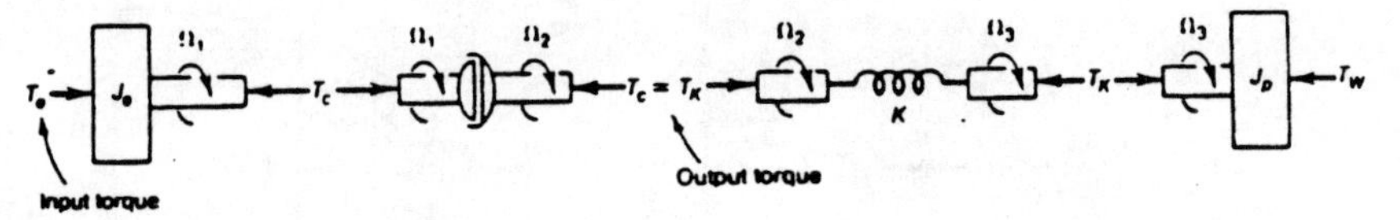

The three state-variable equations are:

(2.54) $d\Omega_{3g}/dt = (1/J_p)(T_K - T_w)$

(2.55) $d\Omega_{1g}/dt = (1/J_e)(T_e - T_K)$

(2.56) $dT_K/dt = K(\Omega_{2g} - \Omega_{3g}) = K[f_{NL}(\Omega_{1g}, T_K) - \Omega_{3g}]$

$= K[SSR(\Omega_{1g}^2 - T_K/C_c) - \Omega_{3g}]$

where $\Omega_{2g} = f_{NL}(\Omega_{1g}, T_K) = SSR(\Omega_{1g}^2 - T_K/C_c)$

or using Equation (2.57a) from Chapter 2,

(2.57a) $\Omega_{2g}^2 = \Omega_{1g}^2 - T_K/C_c$

a) Starting with the simulation of Equation (2.55), using $\Omega_{2g} = f_{NL}(\Omega_{1g}, T_K)$ in simulating Equation (2.56), and then simulating Equation (2.54) leads to the following simulation block diagram:

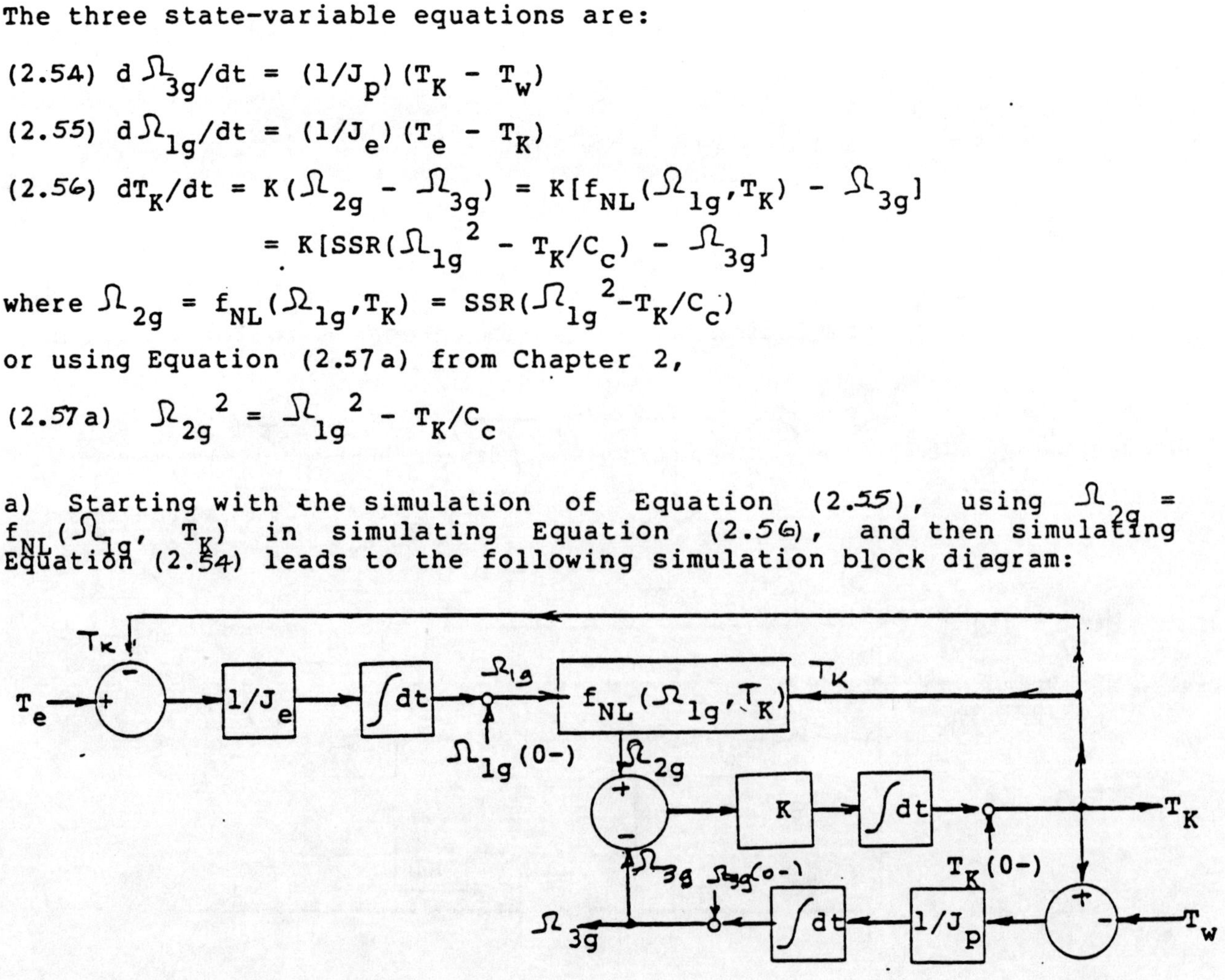

b) Using (2.51a) to linearize the relationship of Ω_{2g} to Ω_{1g} and T_K,

$$2\bar{\Omega}_{2g}\hat{\Omega}_{2g} = 2\bar{\Omega}_{1g}\hat{\Omega}_{1g} - (1/C_c)\hat{T}_K$$

or

(2.51sp) $$\hat{\Omega}_{2g} = (\bar{\Omega}_{1g}/\bar{\Omega}_{2g})\hat{\Omega}_{1g} - (1/2C_c\bar{\Omega}_{2g})\hat{T}_K$$

for which the simulation diagram is:

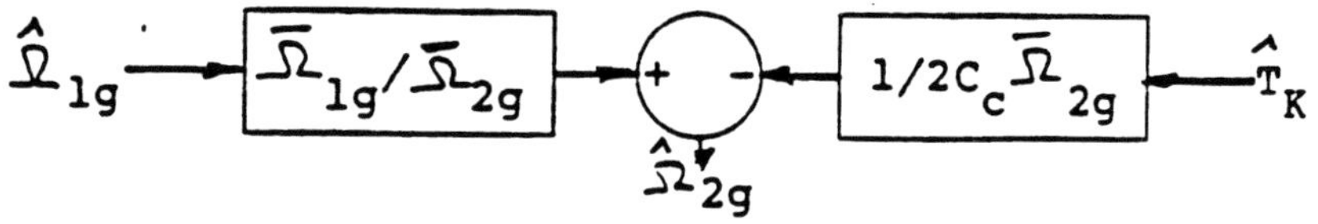

This block diagram segment then replaces the "f_{NL}" block in the diagram above, and of course all variables are then 'hat' values.

c) The simulation of the nonlinear function may be carried out as follows:

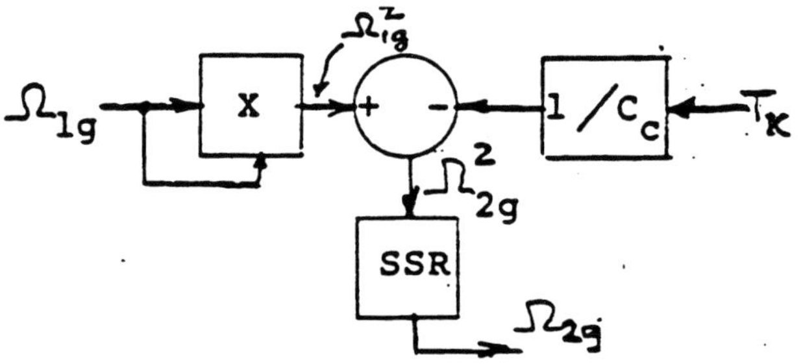

CHAPTER 3

Problem 3.1

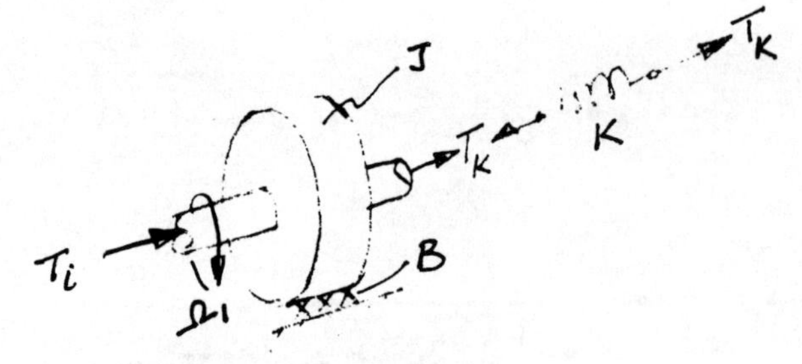

$$T_B = B\Omega_{1g} = B\dot{\theta}_1$$

$$T_K = K\theta_1$$

Newton's Second Law

$$J\dot{\Omega}_{1g} + T_B + T_K = T_i(t)$$

$$J\dot{\Omega}_{1g} + B\Omega_{1g} + K\theta_1 = T_i(t)$$

a)

T-type variable	$q_1 = T_K$	Two energy storing elements in the system - two state variables
A-type variable	$q_2 = \Omega_{1g}$	

Differentiating both sides of expression for T_K gives

$$T_K = K\theta_1 \quad \text{or} \quad \dot{T}_K = K\Omega_{1g}$$

which is the first state variable equation. The second state state variable equation is obtained from Newton's second law.

$$\dot{\Omega}_{1g} = -(K/J)\,\theta_1 - (B/J)\,\Omega_{1g} + (1/J)\,T_i(t)$$

or

$$\dot{\Omega}_{1g} = -(1/J)\,T_K - (B/J)\,\Omega_{1g} + (1/J)\,T_i(t)$$

The output equation is

$$y = \theta_1 = (1/K)\, T_K$$

b) Select the state variables: θ_1 and Ω_{1g}

State variable equations are

$$\dot{\theta}_1 = \Omega_{1g}$$

$$\dot{\Omega}_{1g} = -(K/J)\,\theta_1 - (B/J)\,\Omega_{1g} + (1/J)\,T_i(t)$$

The output equation is

$$y = \theta_1$$

Problem 3.2

Combining the state variable equations derived in problem ~~4.1b~~ 3.1b gives the following input/output equation

$$J\ddot{\theta}_1 + B\dot{\theta}_1 + K\theta_1 = T_a(t)$$

Problem 3.3

The free body diagram:

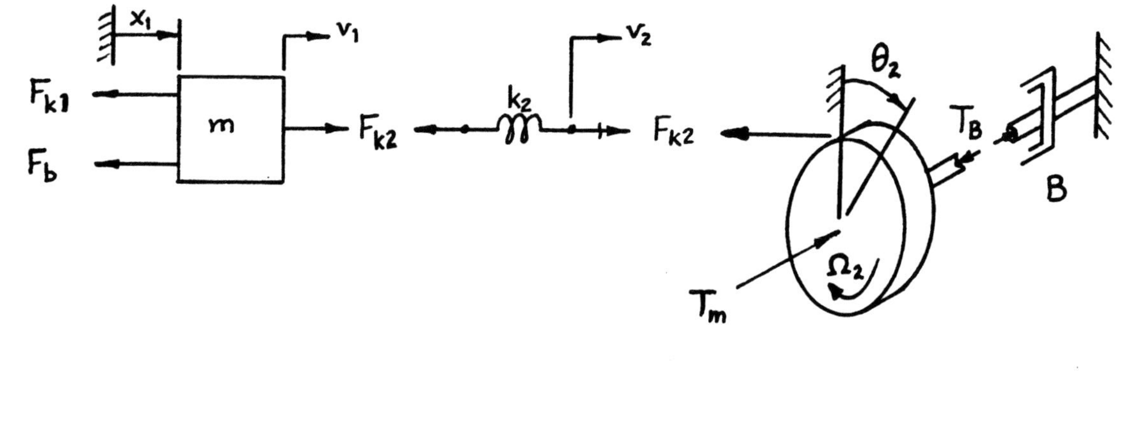

Elemental equations:

$$F_{k1} = k_1x \qquad T_B = B\Omega_{1g}$$

$$F_b = bv_{1g}$$

$$F_{k2} = k_2(x_2 - x_1) = k_2(R\theta_2 - x_1)$$

The complete set of describing differential equations (from Newton's second law)

(1) $$m\dot{v}_{1g} + bv_{1g} + k_1x_1 = k_2(R\theta_2 - x_1)$$

(2) $$J\dot{\Omega}_{2g} + B\Omega_{2g} + k_2R(R\theta_2 - x_1) = T_m$$

Three choices of state variables.

<u>First set of state variables</u>: T and A-type variables:

$$q_1 = F_{k1} \qquad q_2 = v_{1g} \qquad q_3 = T_{k2} \qquad q_4 = \Omega_{2g}$$

The state equations are

(3) $$\dot{F}_{k1} = k_1v_{1g}$$

(4) $$\dot{v}_{1g} = -(1/m)F_{k1} - (b/m)v_{1g} + (1/mR)T_{k2}$$

(5) $$\dot{T}_{k2} = -k_2Rv_{1g} + k_2R^2\Omega_{2g}$$

(6) $$\dot{\Omega}_{2g} = -(1/J)T_{k2} - (B/J)\Omega_{2g} + (1/J)T_m(t)$$

The output equations are

$$x_1 = (1/k_1)F_{k1}$$

$$x_2 = (1/k_2R)T_{k2} + (1/k_1)F_{k1}$$

State model in matrix form:

$$\begin{bmatrix} \dot{q}_1 \\ \dot{q}_2 \\ \dot{q}_3 \\ \dot{q}_4 \end{bmatrix} = \begin{bmatrix} 0 & k_1 & 0 & 0 \\ -1/m & -b/m & 1/Rm & 0 \\ 0 & -k_2R & 0 & k_2R^2 \\ 0 & 0 & -1/J & -B/J \end{bmatrix} \begin{bmatrix} q_1 \\ q_2 \\ q_3 \\ q_4 \end{bmatrix} + \begin{bmatrix} 0 \\ 0 \\ 0 \\ 1/J \end{bmatrix} u(t)$$

$$\begin{bmatrix} y_1 \\ y_2 \end{bmatrix} = \begin{bmatrix} 1/k_1 & 0 & 0 & 0 \\ 1/k_1 & 0 & 1/k_2R & 0 \end{bmatrix} \begin{bmatrix} q_1 \\ q_2 \\ q_3 \\ q_4 \end{bmatrix}$$

<u>Second choice of state variables</u>: Two variables and their derivatives:

$$q_1 = x_1 \qquad q_2 = \dot{x}_1 \qquad q_3 = \theta_2 \qquad q_4 = \dot{\theta}_2$$

The state variable equations are

(7) $\dot{x}_1 = v_{1g}$

(8) $\dot{v}_{1g} = -[(k_1 + k_2)/m]x_1 - (b/m)v_{1g} + (k_2R/m)\theta_2$

(9) $\dot{\theta}_2 = \Omega_{2g}$

(10) $\dot{\Omega}_{2g} = (k_2R/J)x_1 - (k_2R^2/J)\theta_2 - (B/J)\Omega_{2g} + (1/J)T_m(t)$

The output equations are

$$y_1 = x_1$$

$$y_2 = x_2 = R\theta_2$$

The state model in matrix form:

$$\begin{bmatrix} \dot{q}_1 \\ \dot{q}_2 \\ \dot{q}_3 \\ \dot{q}_4 \end{bmatrix} = \begin{bmatrix} 0 & 1 & 0 & 0 \\ -(k_1+k_2)/m & -b/m & k_2R/m & 0 \\ 0 & 0 & 0 & 1 \\ k_2R/J & 0 & -k_2R^2/J & -B/J \end{bmatrix} \begin{bmatrix} q_1 \\ q_2 \\ q_3 \\ q_4 \end{bmatrix} + \begin{bmatrix} 0 \\ 0 \\ 0 \\ 1/J \end{bmatrix} u(t)$$

$$\begin{bmatrix} y_1 \\ y_2 \end{bmatrix} = \begin{bmatrix} 1 & 0 & 0 & 0 \\ 0 & 0 & R & 0 \end{bmatrix} \begin{bmatrix} q_1 \\ q_2 \\ q_3 \\ q_4 \end{bmatrix}$$

Third choice of state variables: One variable and its successive derivatives

$$q_1 = x_1 \qquad q_2 = \dot{x}_1 \qquad q_3 = \ddot{x}_1 \qquad q_4 = \dddot{x}_1$$

The state variable equations are

(11) $\dot{q}_1 = q_2$

(12) $\dot{q}_2 = q_3$

(13) $\dot{q}_3 = q_4$

To obtain fourth state variable equation rewrite equations (1) and (2) as follows

(14) $m\ddot{x}_1 + b\dot{x}_1 + (k_1+k_2)x_1 - k_2R\theta_2 = 0$

(15) $J\ddot{\theta}_2 + B\dot{\theta}_2 + k_2R^2\theta_2 - k_2Rx_1 = T_m$

From eq. (14)

(16) $\theta_2 = (m/k_2R)\ddot{x}_1 + (b/k_2R)\dot{x}_1 + [(k_1+k_2)/k_2R]\,x_1$

Substituting (16) into (15) yields the fourth state equation

$$\frac{Jm}{k_2R}\ddddot{x}_1 + \frac{Jb+Bm}{k_2R}\dddot{x}_1 + \left[\frac{J(k_1+k_2)+Bb}{k_2R} + Rm\right]\ddot{x}_1$$

$$+ \left[\frac{B(k_1+k_2)}{k_2R} + Rb\right]\dot{x}_1 + Rk_1x_1 = T_m(t)$$

The output equations are

$$y_1 = x_1$$

$$y_2 = x_2 = [(k_1+k_2)/k_2]\,q_1 + (b/k_2)\,q_2 + (m/k_2)\,q_3$$

The state variable model in matrix form:

$$\begin{bmatrix} \dot{q}_1 \\ \dot{q}_2 \\ \dot{q}_3 \\ \dot{q}_4 \end{bmatrix} = \begin{bmatrix} 0 & 1 & 0 & 0 \\ 0 & 0 & 1 & 0 \\ 0 & 0 & 0 & 1 \\ a_{41} & a_{42} & a_{43} & a_{44} \end{bmatrix} \begin{bmatrix} q_1 \\ q_2 \\ q_3 \\ q_4 \end{bmatrix} + \begin{bmatrix} 0 \\ 0 \\ 0 \\ k_2R/Jm \end{bmatrix} u(t)$$

where

$$a_{41} = -\frac{R^2k_1k_2}{Jm}$$

$$a_{42} = -\frac{B(k_1+k_2)+R_2bk_2}{Jm}$$

$$a_{43} = -\frac{J(k_1+k_2)+Bb+k_2R^2m}{Jm}$$

$$a_{44} = -\frac{Jb+Bm}{Jm}$$

and

$$\begin{bmatrix} y_1 \\ y_2 \end{bmatrix} = \begin{bmatrix} 1 & 0 & 0 & 0 \\ (k_1+k_2)/k_2 & b/k_2 & m/k_2 & 0 \end{bmatrix} \begin{bmatrix} q_1 \\ q_2 \\ q_3 \end{bmatrix}$$

Problem 3.4

Substitute $q_1 = \bar{q}_1 + \hat{q}_1$, $q_2 = \bar{q}_2 + \hat{q}_2$ and $u = \bar{u} + \hat{u}$ into the nonlinear state variable equations

(1) $$\dot{\bar{q}}_1+\dot{\hat{q}}_1 = -4(\bar{q}_1+\hat{q}_1) + 10(\bar{q}_2+\hat{q}_2) + 4(\bar{u} + \hat{u})$$

(2) $$\dot{\bar{q}}_2+\dot{\hat{q}}_2 = 0.5(\bar{q}_1+\hat{q}_1) - f_{NL}\{\bar{q}_2+\hat{q}_2\}$$

where $f_{NL}\{q_2\} = 2|q_2|q_2$.

At the normal operating point $\hat{q}_1 = 0$, $\hat{q}_2 = 0$, $\hat{u} = 0$, and hence

(3) $$-4\bar{q}_1 + 10\bar{q}_2 + 4\bar{u} = 0$$

(4) $$0.5\bar{q}_1 - f_{NL}\{\bar{q}_2\} = 0$$

Using (3) and noticing that $\dot{\bar{q}}_1 = 0$, eq. (1) becomes

(5) $$\dot{\hat{q}}_1 = -4\hat{q}_1 + 10\hat{q}_2 + 4\hat{u}$$

which is the first linearized state variable equation.

Now linearize $f_{NL}\{q_2\}$ in the vicinity of the normal operating point using Taylor's theorem

(6) $$f_{NL} \approx f_{NL}\{\bar{q}_2\} + \hat{q}_2 \left.\frac{df_{NL}\{q_2\}}{dq_2}\right|_{\bar{q}_2} = 2|\bar{q}_2|\bar{q}_2 + 4|\bar{q}_2|\hat{q}_2$$

Substituting (6) and (4) into (2) yields the second linearized state variable equation

(7) $$\dot{\hat{q}}_2 = 0.5\hat{q}_1 - 4|\bar{q}_2|\hat{q}_2$$

Combining eqs (5) and (7), the input/output equation is obtained

$$2\ddot{\hat{q}}_2 + 8(|\bar{q}_2| + 1)\dot{\hat{q}}_2 + (32|\bar{q}_2| - 10)\hat{q}_2 = 4\hat{u}$$

Problem 3.5

The state variable equations are

(1) $$\dot{q}_1 = - 3q_1 - 19q_2$$

(2) $$\dot{q}_2 = q_1 - 2q_2 - u$$

The output equation is

(3) $$y = 2q_2$$

From equation (2)

$$q_1 = \dot{q}_2 + 2q_2 + u$$

Substituting into equation (1)

$$\ddot{q}_2 + 5\dot{q}_2 + 25q_2 = -3u - \dot{u}$$

From eq. (3), $q_2 = 0.5y$, hence the input/output equation

$$0.5\ddot{y} + 2.5\dot{y} + 12.5y = -3u - \dot{u}$$

Problem 3.6

a) Applying D operator to the system differential equations gives

(1) $$(D^2 + 4D + 4)y = (2D + 2)x$$

(2) $$(2D + 1)x - y = u(t)$$

From equation (1)

(3) $$x = \frac{D^2 + 4D + 4}{2D + 2}y$$

Substituting (3) into (2)

$$\frac{(2D + 1)(D^2 + 4D + D)}{2D + 2}y - y = u(t)$$

Hence

(4) $$(2D^3 + 9D^2 + 10D + 2)y = (2D + 2)u(t)$$

Replacing D operator by corresponding time derivatives yields

(5) $$\dddot{y} + 4.5\ddot{y} + 5\dot{y} + y = \dot{u} + u$$

Equation (5) is the system input/output model.

b) Select the following state variables

$$q_1 = z \qquad q_2 = \dot{z} \qquad q_3 = \ddot{z}$$

where z is an auxiliary variable satisfying the equation

(6) $$\dddot{z} + 4.5\ddot{z} + 5\dot{z} + z = u$$

The state variable equations for the system described by (6) are

$$\dot{q}_1 = q_2$$

$$\dot{q}_2 = q_3 \tag{7}$$

$$\dot{q}_3 = -q_1 - 5q_2 - 4.5q_3 + u$$

The output equation is as equation (4.23) in the text

$$y = b_o q_1 + b_1 q_2$$

where (from eq. (5)) $b_o = 1$ and $b_1 = 1$, and thus

$$y = q_1 + q_2 \tag{8}$$

Rewriting equations (7) and (8) in matrix form

$$\begin{bmatrix} \dot{q}_1 \\ \dot{q}_2 \\ \dot{q}_3 \end{bmatrix} = \begin{bmatrix} 0 & 1 & 0 \\ 0 & 0 & 1 \\ -1 & -5 & -4.5 \end{bmatrix} \begin{bmatrix} q_1 \\ q_2 \\ q_3 \end{bmatrix} + \begin{bmatrix} 0 \\ 0 \\ 1 \end{bmatrix} u(t)$$

$$y = \begin{bmatrix} 1 & 1 & 0 \end{bmatrix} \begin{bmatrix} q_1 \\ q_2 \\ q_3 \end{bmatrix}$$

Problem 3.7

A complete free body diagram is shown below

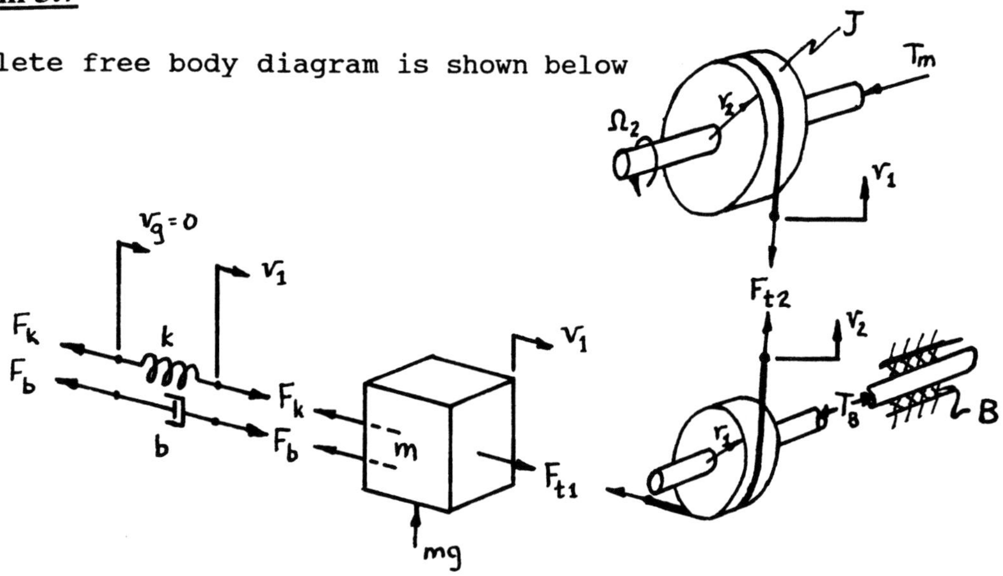

The describing equations are

(1) $$F_{t1} - F_b - F_k = m \frac{dv_{1g}}{dt}$$

(2) $$F_k = k\ x_1$$

(3) $$F_b = b\ v_{1g}$$

Combining (1), (2), and (3)

(4) $$m \frac{dv_{1g}}{dt} + b\ v_{1g} + k\ x_1 = F_{t1}$$

The describing equations for the pulley

(5) $$T_B = r_1(F_{t2} - F_{t1})$$

(6) $$T_B = B\ \Omega_{1g}$$

(7) $$\Omega_{1g} = v_{1g}/r$$

Combining (5), (6), and (7)

(8) $$\frac{B}{r_1^{\,2}} v_{1g} = F_{t2} - F_{t1}$$

The describing equation for the rotational inertia

(9) $$T_m - r_2 F_{t2} = J \frac{d\Omega_{2g}}{dt}$$

The angular velocities Ω_{1g} and Ω_{2g} are related as

(10) $$\Omega_{1g} r_1 = \Omega_{2g} r_2$$

Substituting Ω_{2g} from equation (10) into (9) and solving for F_{t2} gives

(11) $$F_{t2} = -J \frac{r_1}{r_2^2} \frac{d\Omega_{1g}}{dt} + \frac{1}{r_2} T_m$$

Combining equation (7), (8), and (11) yields an epression for F_{t1}

(12) $$F_{t1} = - \frac{B}{r_1^2} v_{1g} - \frac{J}{r_2^2} \frac{dv_{1g}}{dt} + \frac{1}{r_2} T_m$$

Substituting (12) into (4)

(13) $$(m + \frac{J}{r_2^2}) \frac{dv_{1g}}{dt} + (b + \frac{B}{r_1^2}) v_{1g} + k\, x_1 = (1/r_2)\, T_m$$

Selecting x_1 and v_{1g} as the state variables, the state variable equations are

(14) $$\dot{x}_1 = v_{1g}$$

(15) $$\dot{v}_{1g} = - \frac{k}{m+J/r_2^2} x_1 - \frac{b+B/r_1^2}{m+J/r_2^2} v_{1g} + \frac{1}{mr_2+J/r_2} T_m$$

Problem 3.8

Differentiating both sides of equation (15) from the solution to Problem 4.7, we obtain

(1) $$(m + \frac{J}{r_2^2}) \ddot{v}_{1g} + (b + \frac{B}{r_1^2}) \dot{v}_{1g} + k\, v_{1g} = (1/r_2)\, \dot{T}_m$$

Now substitute

(2) $$v_{1g} = r_2 \Omega_{2g}$$

to obtain the desired input-output equation

$$(3) \qquad (mr_2 + \frac{J}{r_2})\,\ddot{\Omega}_{2g} + (br_2 + \frac{Br_2}{r_1^{\,2}})\,\dot{\Omega}_{2g} + kr_2\,\Omega_{2g} = (1/r_2)\,\dot{T}_m$$

Problem 3.9

The free body diagram for the rack and pinion part of the system is shown in Figure ~~10.9~~ P3.9.

The differential equation of motion for the inertia J_m is

$$(1) \qquad J_m\dot{\Omega}_{1g} + B\Omega_{1g} + T_{NL}\{\theta_1,\theta_2\} = T_i(t)$$

The equation describing the translational part of the system is

$$(2) \qquad m\dot{v}_{1g} + F_{NLD}\{v_{1g}\} + kx_1 = 1/R\ T_{NLS}\{\theta_1,\theta_2\}$$

Substituting $x_1 = \theta_2 R$ into eq. (2) gives

$$(3) \qquad mR\ddot{\theta}_2 + F_{NLD}\{v_{1g}\} + kR\theta_2 = 1/R\ T_{NLS}\{\theta_1,\theta_2\}$$

a) Select the following state variables

$$q_1 = \theta_1 \qquad q_2 = \Omega_{1g} \qquad q_3 = \theta_2 \qquad q_4 = \Omega_{2g}$$

Using equations (1) and (2), the state variable equations are derived as follows:

$$(4) \qquad \dot{\theta}_1 = \Omega_{1g}$$

$$(5) \qquad \dot{\Omega}_{1g} = -\ 2/J_m\ |\theta_1-\theta_2|\,(\theta_1-\theta_2) - B/J_m\ \Omega_{1g} + 1/J_m\ T_i(t)$$

$$(6) \qquad \dot{\theta}_2 = \Omega_{2g}$$

$$(7) \qquad \dot{\Omega}_{2g} = 2/mR^2\ (\theta_1-\theta_2)\,|\theta_1-\theta_2| - k/m\ \theta_2 - 2R^2/m\ \Omega_{2g}^3 - 4/m\ \Omega_{2g}$$

where the nonlinear friction force was expresses as

$$(8) \qquad F_{NLD}\{v_{1g}\} = 2v_{1g}^3 + 4v_{1g} = 2R^3\Omega_{2g}^3 + 4R\Omega_{2g}$$

Substituting numerical values for the model parameters and using general symbols, the nonlinear state variable equations take the following form:

$$(9) \qquad \dot{q}_1 = q_2$$

(10) $\dot{q}_2 = -10(q_1-q_3)|q_1-q_3| - 150q_2 + 5T_i(t)$

(11) $\dot{q}_3 = q_4$

(12) $\dot{q}_4 = 0.5(q_1-q_3)|q_1-q_3| - 1.25q_3 - 0.25q_4 - 0.03125q_4^3$

b) The system is at rest at the normal operating point and thus the velocities will be zero.

$$\bar{\Omega}_{1g} = \bar{q}_2 = 0 \quad \text{and} \quad \bar{\Omega}_{2g} = \bar{q}_4 = 0$$

To find $\bar{\theta}_1$ and $\bar{\theta}_2$ substitute $q_1 = \bar{q}_1$, $q_2 = \bar{q}_2$, $q_3 = \bar{q}_3$, $q_4 = \bar{q}_4$, and $T_i = \bar{T}_i = 0.8$ into the state variable equations to obtain

$$0 = -10(\bar{q}_1-\bar{q}_3)|\bar{q}_1-\bar{q}_3| - \cancelto{0}{150\bar{q}_2} + 5\bar{T}_i$$

$$0 = 0.5(\bar{q}_1-\bar{q}_3)|\bar{q}_1-\bar{q}_3| - 1.25\bar{q}_3 - \cancelto{0}{0.25\bar{q}_4} - \cancelto{0}{0.03125\bar{q}_4^3}$$

Solving the above two equations for $\bar{q}_1$ and $\bar{q}_3$, gives

$$\bar{q}_1 = \bar{\theta}_1 = 0.792 \text{ rad;}$$

$$\bar{q}_3 = \bar{\theta}_2 = 0.16 \text{ rad;} \qquad (\bar{x}_1 = 0.08 \text{ m})$$

c) There are two nonlinear functions in the model equations that need to be linearized. Denote those functions by f_1 and f_2 and linearize using Taylor's theorem.

(13) $f_1 = (q_1-q_3)|q_1-q_3|$

$$\approx (\bar{q}_1-\bar{q}_3)|\bar{q}_1-\bar{q}_3| + (\hat{q}_1-\hat{q}_3)2|\bar{q}_1-\bar{q}_3|$$

$$= 0.4 + 1.264\hat{q}_1 - 1.264\hat{q}_3$$

(14) $f_2 = q_4^3 \approx \bar{q}_4^3 + \hat{q}_4 3\bar{q}_4^2 = 0 \qquad \text{for } \bar{q}_4 = 0$

The linearized state variable equations become

(15) $$\dot{\hat{q}}_1 = \hat{q}_2$$

Substituting (13) into (10) and cancelling constant terms yields

(16) $$\dot{\hat{q}}_2 = -\ 12.64\hat{q}_1 - 150\hat{q}_2 + 12.64\hat{q}_3 + 5\hat{T}_i(t)$$

(17) $$\dot{\hat{q}}_3 = \hat{q}_4$$

Using (13) and (14), the last linearized state equation is

(18) $$\dot{\hat{q}}_4 = 0.632\hat{q}_1 - 1.882\hat{q}_3 - 0.24\hat{q}_4$$

d) Combining equations (17) and (18) gives

$$\ddot{\hat{q}}_3 = 0.632\hat{q}_1 - 1.882\hat{q}_2 - 0.25\dot{\hat{q}}_3$$

Hence

(19) $$\hat{q}_1 = 1.58\ddot{\hat{q}}_3 + 3.0\hat{q}_3 + 0.4\dot{\hat{q}}_3$$

Combining equations (15) and (16)

(20) $$\ddot{\hat{q}}_1 = -\ 12.64\hat{q}_1 - 150\dot{\hat{q}}_1 + 12.64\hat{q}_3 + 5\hat{T}_i$$

Substituting $\hat{q}_1$ and its derivatives from (19) and (20) and grouping like terms, yields

(21) $$1.58\ddddot{\hat{q}}_3 + 237.4\dddot{\hat{q}}_3 + 83\ddot{\hat{q}}_3 + 455\dot{\hat{q}}_3 + 25.36\hat{q}_3 = 5\hat{T}_i$$

Substituting $\hat{q}_3 = \hat{\theta}_2 = \hat{x}_1/R$ into (21) gives the input/ouput equation

(22) $$\ddddot{\hat{x}}_1 + 150.25\dddot{\hat{x}}_1 + 52.5\ddot{\hat{x}}_1 + 288\dot{\hat{x}}_1 + 16.05\hat{x}_1 = 1.58\hat{T}_i(t)$$

Problem 3.10

As mentioned in the Errata sheet (available via the INTERNET at Mathwork's FTP server: `ftp://ftp.mathworks.com/pub/books`), the problem statement should refer to Figure P2.10 (not 2.15 as stated in the text book.) Figure P2.10 is a two-mass system with a massless lever coupling them through springs.

Begin with the three Free Body Diagrams:

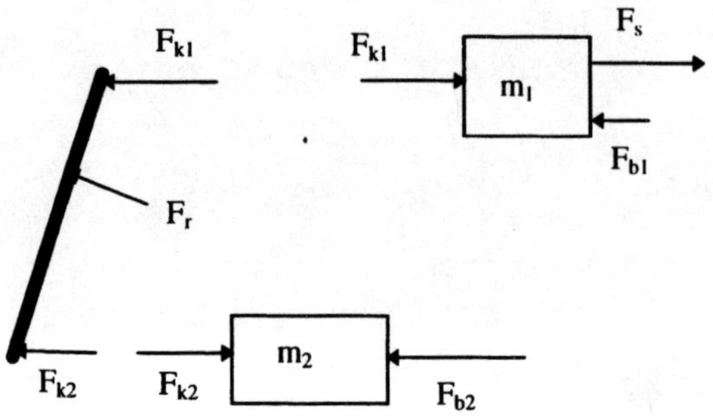

From which we can find these three equations:

$$m_1\dot{v}_1 = F_{k1} + F_s - F_{b1} \qquad (1)$$

$$m_2\dot{v}_2 = F_{k2} - F_{b2} \qquad (2)$$

$$F_{k1}a\cos\theta - F_{k2}b\cos\theta = 0 \qquad (3)$$

where

$$F_{k1} = k_1(a\sin\theta - x_1) \qquad (4)$$

$$F_{k2} = k_2(-b\sin\theta - x_2) \qquad (5)$$

$$F_{b1} = b_1 v_1 \qquad (6)$$

$$F_{b2} = b_2 v_2 \qquad (7)$$

Using the 'small angle assumption' and substituting, we get:

$$m_1\dot{v}_1 = F_{k1} + F_s - b_1 v_1 \qquad (8)$$

$$m_2\dot{v}_2 = F_{k2} - b_2 v_2 \qquad (9)$$

$$F_{k1} = k_1(a\theta - x_1) \qquad (10)$$

$$F_{k2} = k_2(-b\theta - x_2) \qquad (11)$$

$$aF_{k1} - bF_{k2} = 0 \qquad (12)$$

We need to find state equations for this system using a state vector of [v_1 v_2 F_{k1}]. Therefore, we take the time derivative of equation (10) and use equations (11) and (12) to eliminate F_{k2} and θ from the system. The complete state equations are:

$$\dot{v}_1 = -\frac{b_1}{m_1}v_1 + \frac{1}{m_1}F_{k1} + \frac{1}{m_1}F_s \qquad (13)$$

$$\dot{v}_2 = -\frac{b_2}{m_2}v_2 + \frac{a}{bm_2}F_{k1} \qquad (14)$$

$$\dot{F}_{k1} = -\frac{k_1 k_2 b^2}{k_2 b^2 + k_1 a^2}\left[\frac{a}{b}v_2 + v_1\right] \qquad (15)$$

The second part of the problem asks the student to derive an input/output representation of the system using $F_s(t)$ as the input and v_2 as the output.

We can make our task slightly easier by re-writing the state equations in the D-operator form:

$$m_1 Dv_1 = -b_1 v_1 + F_{k1} + F_s \qquad (13a)$$

$$m_2 Dv_2 = -b_2 v_2 + \frac{a}{b}F_{k1} \qquad (14a)$$

$$rDF_{k1} = -k_1\left[\frac{a}{b}v_2 + v_1\right] \qquad (15a)$$

where $r = \left(1 + \frac{k_1 a^2}{k_2 b^2}\right)$

Solve (13a) for F_{k1}:

$$F_{k1} = (m_1 D + b_1)v_1 - F_s \quad (16)$$

Substitute (16) into (14a) and (15a):

$$(m_2 D + b_2)v_2 = \frac{a}{b}\left[(m_1 D + b_1)v_1 - F_s\right] \quad (17)$$

$$rD\left[(m_1 D + b_1)v_1 - F_s\right] = -k_1\left[\frac{a}{b}v_2 + v_1\right] \quad (18)$$

Solve (18) for v_1:

$$v_1 = \frac{rDF_s - \frac{k_1 a}{b}v_2}{rm_1 D^2 + rb_1 D + k_1} \quad (19)$$

Finally, substitute (19) into (17) and group like terms:

$$rm_1 m_2 \frac{d^3}{dt^3}v_2 + r(m_1 b_2 + m_2 b_1)\frac{d^2}{dt^2}v_2 + \left[rb_1 b_2 + m_2 k_1 + \frac{a^2}{b^2}m_1 k_2\right]\frac{d}{dt}v_2$$
$$+\left[k_1 b_2 + \frac{a^2}{b^2}k_1 b_1\right]v_2 = -\frac{a}{b}k_1 F_s \quad (20)$$

Where: $r = \left(1 + \frac{k_1 a^2}{k_2 b^2}\right)$

While the answer is in somewhat different form, it is equivalent to the solution of problem 2.10

<u>Problem 3.11</u>

This problem demonstrates a subtle variation in the rule of "one state variable per energy storing element". As noted in the footnote on page 61 in the text (2nd edition), we use one state variable for each independent energy storing process. In this problem, since the disk is free to slip as well as roll on the cart, it stores kinetic energy in both rotational and linear modes, which are independent.

There are five independent energy storing processes, which can be represented by the following state variables:

Kinetic energy of m_c:	v_c
Potential energy of spring, k_c	F_{kc} or x_c
Potential energy of spring, k_r	F_{kr}
Kinetic energy of m_r, linear	v_r
Kinetic energy of J_r, rotational	Ω_r

Free-body diagrams of the components:

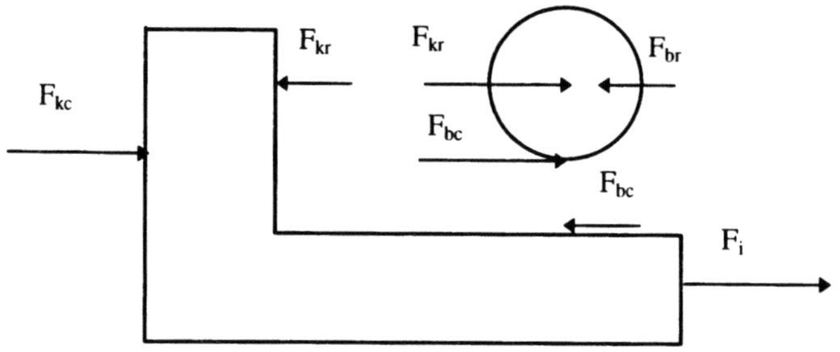

Through basic mechanics, we write the following equations:
Summation of forces for the cart:

$$m_c \dot{v}_c = F_{kc} + F_i - F_{kr} - F_{bc} \qquad (1)$$

The springs:

$$F_{kc} = -k_c x_c \qquad (2)$$

$$F_{kr} = k_r(x_c - x_r) \qquad (3)$$

Summation of forces for the disk:

$$m_r \dot{v}_r = F_{kr} - F_{br} + F_{bc} \qquad (4)$$

And summation of torques:

$$J_r \dot{\Omega}_r = T_i + rF_{bc} \qquad (5)$$

where: $F_{br} = b_r v_r$

Equations (1)-(5) will become our state equations. We need to take the derivative of (3) with respect to time, and we need to resolve the force due to the damping between the disk and the cart, F_{bc}.

Let's take a closer look at the interface between the two, and define two points, P_c and P_r which lie at the closest approach between the two objects.

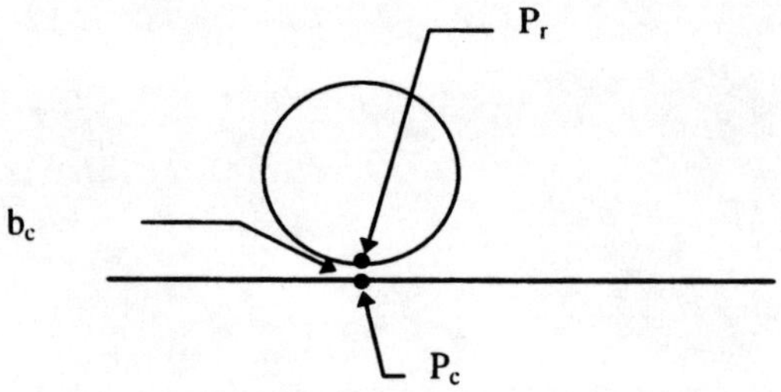

The force F_{bc}, as shown on the free body diagrams, can be defined as:

$$F_{bc} = b_c v_{rel} = b_c\left(v_{P_c} - v_{P_r}\right) \tag{6}$$

Since the cart is not rotating, all points on the cart move at v_c. The point P_r, has motion due to the linear motion of the disk, v_r and rotational motion, Ω_r. Therefore, the force between the disk and the cart is:

$$F_{bc} = b_c\left(v_c - v_r - r\Omega_r\right) \tag{7}$$

Re-arranging, we can show the five state equations in matrix form:

$$\begin{bmatrix} \dot{v}_c \\ \dot{x}_c \\ \dot{v}_r \\ \dot{\Omega}_r \\ \dot{F}_{kr} \end{bmatrix} = \begin{bmatrix} \frac{-b_c}{m_c} & \frac{-k_c}{m_c} & \frac{b_c}{m_c} & \frac{rb_c}{m_c} & \frac{-1}{m_c} \\ 1 & 0 & 0 & 0 & 0 \\ \frac{b_c}{m_r} & 0 & \frac{-(b_c+b_r)}{m_r} & \frac{-rb_c}{m_r} & \frac{1}{m_r} \\ \frac{rb_c}{J_r} & 0 & \frac{-rb_c}{J_r} & \frac{-r^2b_c}{J_r} & 0 \\ k_r & 0 & -k_r & 0 & 0 \end{bmatrix} \begin{bmatrix} v_c \\ x_c \\ v_r \\ \Omega_r \\ F_{kr} \end{bmatrix} + \begin{bmatrix} \frac{1}{m_c} & 0 \\ 0 & 0 \\ 0 & 0 \\ 0 & \frac{1}{J_r} \\ 0 & 0 \end{bmatrix} \begin{bmatrix} F_i \\ T_i \end{bmatrix} \tag{8}$$

CHAPTER 4

Problem 4.1

Rewrite the system input/output equation

(1) $$\dot{y} + 2.5y = 2.5u(t)$$

a) The system time constant is (eq. ~~5.28~~ 4.21)

$$\tau = 1/2.5 = 0.4 \text{ s}$$

The steady-state value of the step response for $u(t) = U_s(t)$ is

$$y_{ss} = 2.5/2.5 = 1.0$$

Using eq 5.40, the complete expression for the system unit step response is

(2) $$y(t) = 1 - (1 - 2)e^{-t/0.4} = 1 + e^{-2.5t}$$

b) For y(0) = 0, equation (2) becomes

(3) $$y(t) = 1 - e^{-2.5t}$$

c) For a unit impulse input, the response can be obtained by differentiating the part of the step response given by equation (2) due to the step input and then using equation 5.50.

(4) $$\hat{y}_i(t) = \frac{d}{dt}\left\{\left(1 - e^{-t/\tau}\right)\right\} + (2 - 0)e^{-t/\tau}$$

$$= (1/\tau)e^{-t/\tau} + 2e^{-t/\tau} = 4.5e^{-2.5t}$$

d) Differentiating equation (3) gives

$$\hat{y}_i(t) = 2.5e^{-2.5t}$$

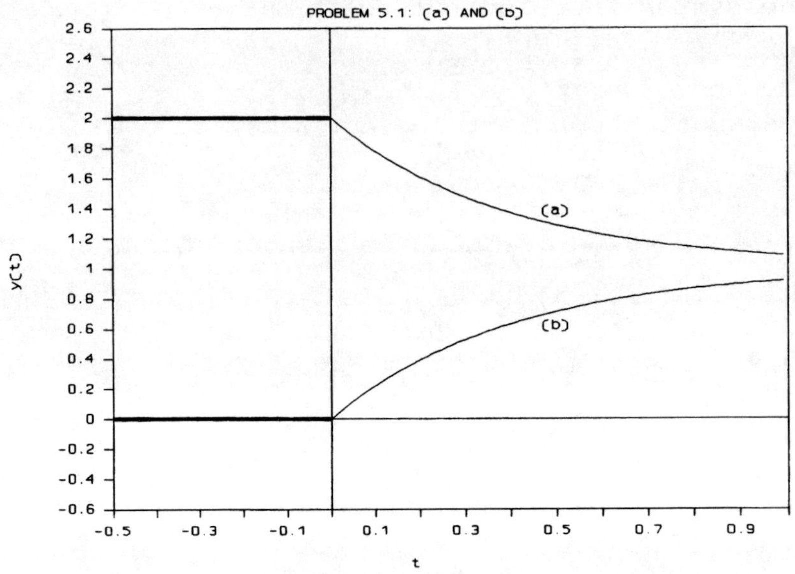
PROBLEM 5.1: (a) AND (b)
y(t)
t
(a)
(b)
2.6
2.4
2.2
2
1.8
1.6
1.4
1.2
1
0.8
0.6
0.4
0.2
0
-0.2
-0.4
-0.6
-0.5
-0.3
-0.1
0.1
0.3
0.5
0.7
0.9

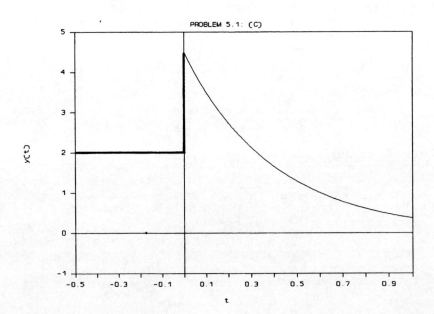

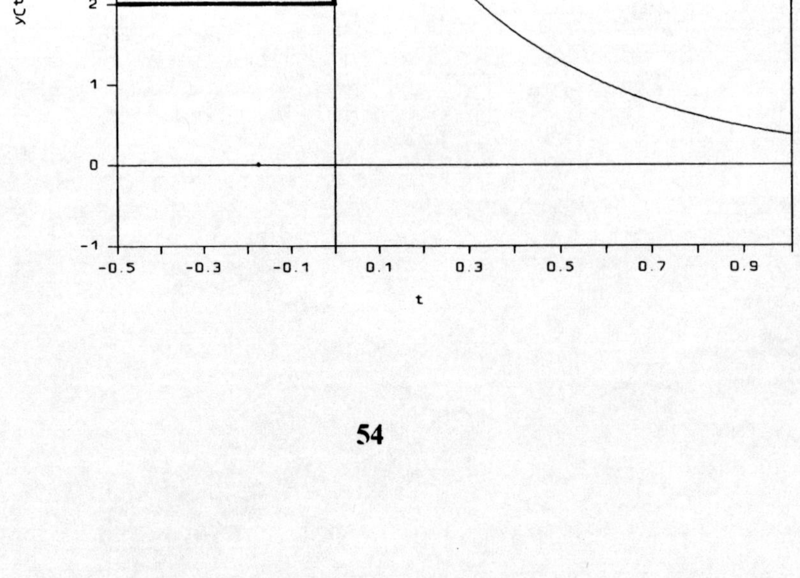
PROBLEM 5.1: (C)
y(t)
t
5
4
3
2
1
0
-1
-0.5
-0.3
-0.1
0.1
0.3
0.5
0.7
0.9

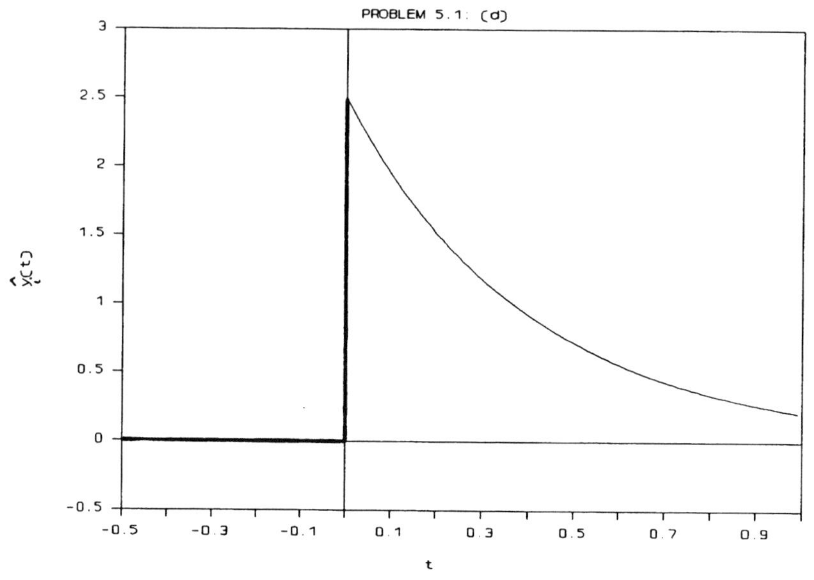

Problem 4.2

a) First, find the characteristic equation

$$(p - p_1)(p - p_2) = 0$$

$$(p + 1 - j)(p + 1 + j) = 0$$

(1) $$p^2 + 2p + 2 = 0$$

Hence, the differential input/output equation is

(2) $$\ddot{y} + 2\dot{y} + 2y = U_s(t)$$

The natural frequency, damping ratio, and damped natural frequency are

$$\omega_n = (2)^{.5} = 1.41 \text{ rad/s}$$

$$\zeta = 2/2(2)^{.5} = 0.707$$

$$\omega_d = 1.41(1 - .707^2)^{.5} = 1 \text{ rad}$$

The peak time and overshoot are

$$t_p = \pi/\omega_d = 3.14 \text{ sec}$$

$$M_p = 4.3\%$$

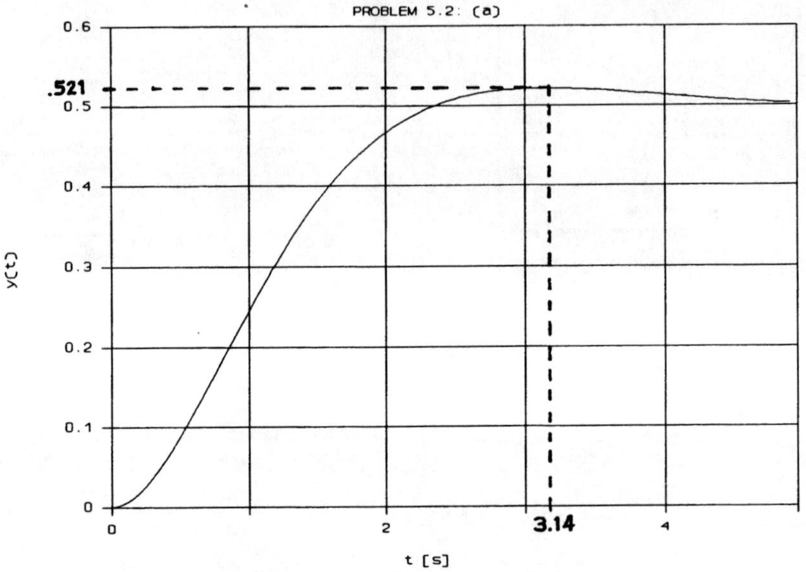

b) The characteristic equation is

$$(p - 1 - j)(p - 1 + j) = 0$$

(3) $$p^2 - 2p + 2 = 0$$

The input/output equation:

(4) $$\ddot{y} - 2\dot{y} + 2y = U_s(t)$$

Homogeneous solution:

$$y_h(t) = e^t(K_3\cos(t) + K_4\sin(t))$$

Particular solution:

$$y_p(t) = y_{ss} = 0.5$$

Hence, the complete solution:

(5) $$y(t) = 0.5 + e^t(K_3\cos(t) + K_4\sin(t))$$

K_3 and K_4 can be found from the initial conditions.

$$y(0) = 0.5 + K_3 = 0 \rightarrow K_3 = -0.5$$

and

$$\dot{y}(t) = e^t(K_3\cos(t)+K_4\sin(t))+e^t(-K_3\sin(t)+K_4\cos(t))$$

$$\dot{y}(0) = K_3 + K_4 = 0 \rightarrow K_4 = 0.5$$

The system step response is

$$y(t) = 0.5 + e^t(-0.5\cos(t) + 0.5\sin(t))$$

$$= 0.5 + 0.5e^t(\sin(t) - \cos(t))$$

The response in this case grows without bound because the roots of the characteristic equation are located in the right hand side of the complex plane.

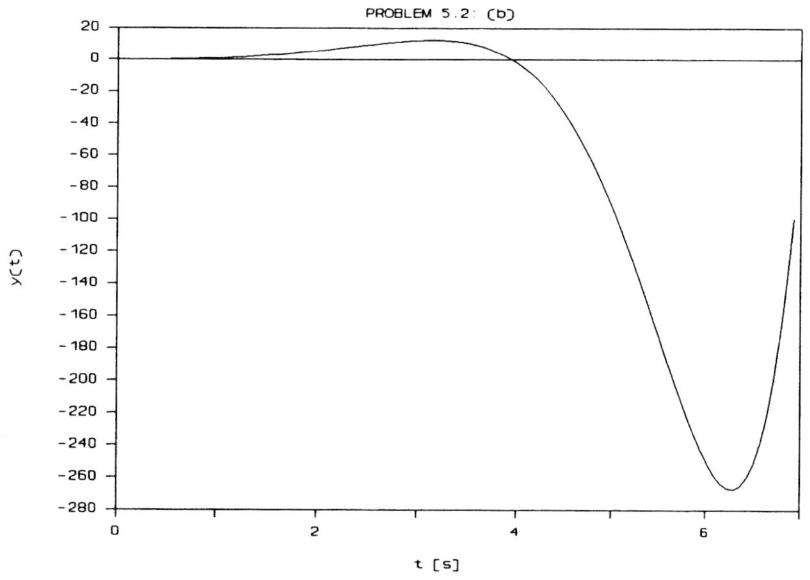

Problem 4.3

To meet the condition for steady-state velocity, take limit for time approaching infinity of both sides of the system model equation

(1) $$B\Omega_{ss} = \overline{T} \rightarrow B = \overline{T}/\Omega_{ss}$$

where $\overline{T}$ = 10 Nm and Ω_{ss} = 50 rpm. Adjusting units of Ω_{ss} to rad/s gives

(2) $$B = 60\overline{T}/2\pi\Omega_{ss} = 1.9 \text{ Nms/rad}$$

To meet the other condition, notice that the step response drops below 5% of its steady-state value after approximately three time constants. This condition can, therefore, be written as

(3) $$3\tau = 160 \times 10^{-3}\text{s}$$

The system time constant is

(4) $$\tau = J/B$$

The value of J meeting the requirement for the speed of response is, from equations 3 and 4,

(5) $$J = B(160 \times 10^{-3})/3 = 0.1 \text{ Nms}^2\text{/rad}$$

Problem 4.4

Use equation 5.37

a) $y(0) = 4$ $\quad y_{ss} = 1$ $\quad \tau = 0.5$

$$y(t) = 1 - (1 - 4)e^{-t/0.5} = 1 + 3e^{-2t}$$

b) $y(0) = -4$ $\quad y_{ss} = 3$ $\quad \tau = 0.4$

$$y(t) = 3 - (3 + 4)e^{-t/0.4} = 3 - 7e^{-2.5t}$$

Problem 4.5

The system equation of motion is

(1) $$m\dot{v} + bv = F(t)$$

Hence, the time constant

(2) $$\tau = m/b = 1.5/300 = 5 \cdot 10^{-3}\text{s}$$

The steady-state velocity for $F(t) = 100$ lb and t approaching infinity, from equation (1)

(3) $$v_{ss} = F_{ss}/b = 0.33 \text{ ft/s}$$

Using equations (2) and (3) and the initial condition, $v(0) = 0$

(4) $$v(t) = v_{ss} - [v_{ss} - v(0)]e^{-t/\tau} = 0.33(1 - e^{-200t})$$

Problem 4.6

a) Free body diagram for the turbine before the shaft breaks

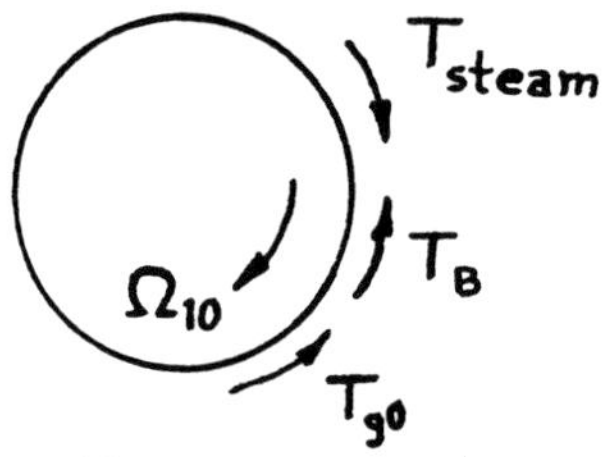

(1) $$T_{g0} = T_{steam} - B\Omega_{10}$$

b) After the shaft breaks, $t > t_0$, the system is described by the equation

(2) $$J\dot{\Omega}_{1g} + B\Omega_{1g} = T_{steam}$$

Hence, the time constant is

(3) $$\tau = J/B$$

c) In accordance with considerations in chapter 1.2, lacking an infinite torque, the speed of the turbine cannot change suddenly, and thus

(4) $$\Omega_{1g}(0^+) = \Omega_{1g}(0^-) = \Omega_{10}$$

d) Given $\Omega_{1g}(0) = \Omega_{10}$, $\Omega_{1gss} = T_{steam}/B$, and $\tau = J/B$, the system step response is

(5) $$\Omega_{1g}(t) = T_{steam}/B - \left[(T_{steam}/B) - \Omega_{10}\right]e^{-B/J\ t}$$

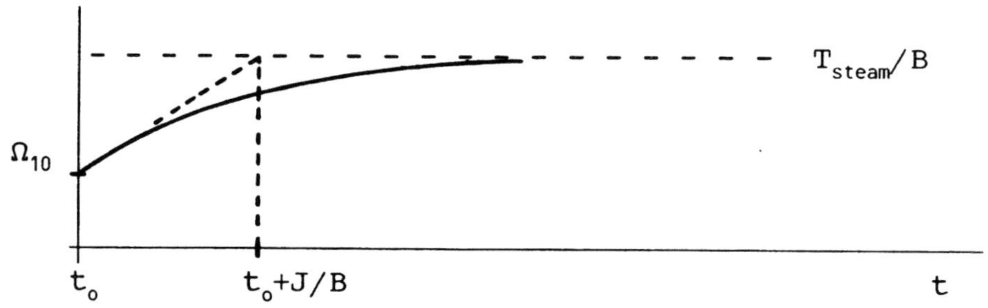

e) This condition can be expressed mathematically as

(6) $\Omega_{1g}(t_x) \le 0.01\Omega_{10}$

Using equation (5) and solving for t_x yields

$$t_x = -\frac{1}{\tau} \ln\left(\frac{\Omega_{ss} - 1.05\Omega_{10}}{\Omega_{ss} - \Omega_{10}}\right)$$

where $\tau = J/B$ and $\Omega_{ss} = T_{steam}/B$

Problem 4.7

Rewriting the model equation

(1) $\dot{y} - ay = bU_s(t)$

The steady-state value of y, and the time constant can be found

(2) $y_{ss} = -b/a \qquad \tau = -1/a$

Using (2) and the initial condition, the unit step response

(3) $y(t) = -b/a - (-b/a - 0)e^{at} = -b/a(1 - e^{at})$

From the two initial conditions

(4) $y(0.5) = -b/a(1 - e^{0.5a}) = 1.2$

and

(5) $\lim_{t\to\infty} y(t) = (-b/a) = 2$

Solving (4) and (5) for a and b gives

$a = -1.8326 \qquad b = 3.6652$

The system model is thus

(6) $\dot{y} + 1.8326y = 3.6652u(t)$

Problem 4.8

The system state variable equations are

(1) $$\dot{q}_1 = -6q_1 + 2q_2$$

(2) $$\dot{q}_2 = -6q_2 + 5u$$

From equation 1

(3) $$q_2 = 0.5\dot{q}_1 + 3q_1$$

and

(4) $$\dot{q}_2 = 0.5\ddot{q}_1 + 3\dot{q}_1$$

Substituting (3) and (4) into (2)

(5) $$\ddot{q}_1 + 12\dot{q}_1 + 36q_1 = 10u$$

Hence, the damping ratio $\zeta = 12/2(36)^{.5} = 1$ → the system is critically damped.

The steady-state solution:

$$q_{1ss} = 10/36 = 0.2778$$

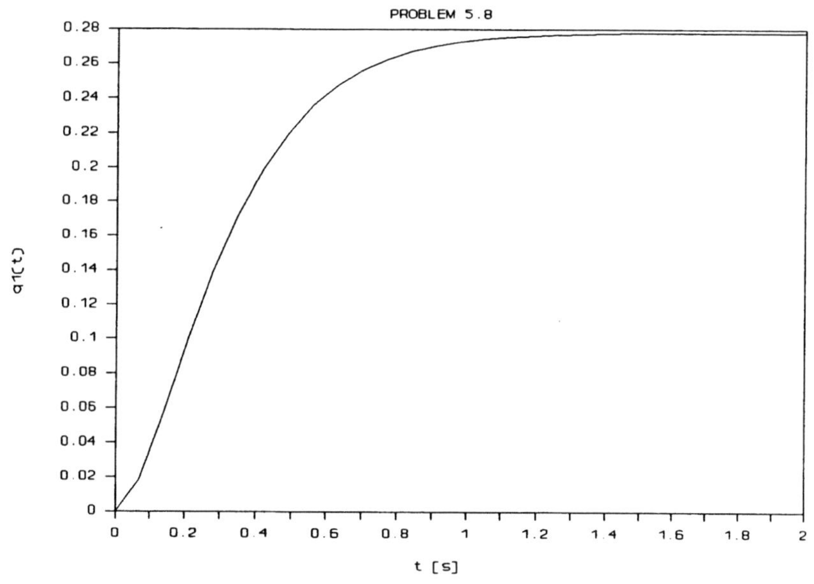

Problem 4.9

Free body diagram of the system:

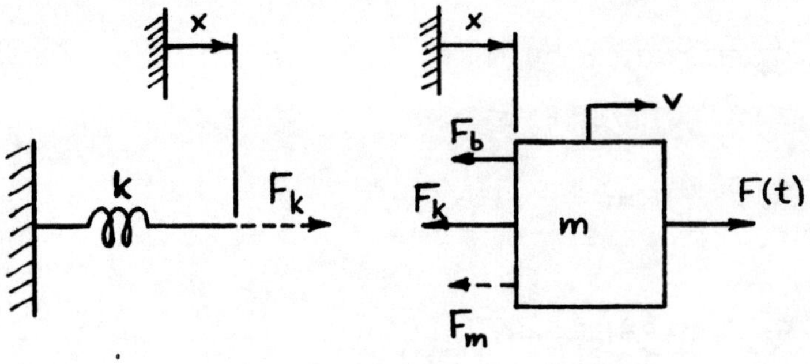

(1) $$F_m + F_b + F_k = F(t)$$

(2) $$4\ddot{x} + b\dot{x} + kx = F(t)$$

At steady state, both derivatives in eq. (2) become zero, and hence

(3) $$kx_{ss} = F_{ss}$$

From Figure ~~P5.3~~ P4.9, x_{ss} = 0.1 m. Also F_{ss} is given, which determines the value of k.

(4) $$k = F_{ss}/x_{ss} = 10/.01 = 100 \text{ N/m}$$

From the step response in Figure ~~P5.3~~ P4.9, M_p = 0.163.

Using equation ~~5.111~~ 4.106, the corresponding value of the damping ratio is found to be

(5) $$\zeta = 0.5$$

From equation (2)

(6) $$\zeta = b/2(4k)^{.5}$$

and hence

(7) $$b = \zeta 2\{4k\}^{.5} = (0.5)2\{4(100)\}^{.5} = 20 \text{ Ns/m}$$

Problem 4.10

From the defintion of the logarithmic decay ratio

(1) $$LDR = \ln(16.5/55) = -1.2$$

Using equation 4.109 expressing LDR in terms of ζ, we have

(2) $$-2\pi\zeta/(1 - \zeta^2)^{.5} = -1.2$$

Solving for ζ, gives

(3) $$\zeta = 0.195$$

Now, the system damped natural frequency is

(4) $$\omega_d = \{\ k(1 - \zeta^2)/m\ \}^{.5}$$

But

(5) $$\omega_d = 2\pi/T_d$$

Equating right hand sides of equations (4) and (5) yields

(6) $$2\pi/T_d = \{\ k(1 - \zeta^2)/m\ \}^{.5}$$

which gives

(7) $$k = 205.2 \text{ N/m}$$

Using the expression for the damping ratio

(8) $$\zeta = b/2(km)^{.5}$$

and solving for b,

(9) $$b = 12.5 \text{ Ns/m}$$

Problem 4.11

a) The input/output equation is

(1) $$m\dot{v} = F \qquad \text{where} \quad F = U_s(t)$$

To obtain the unit step response, divide both sides of equation (1) by m and integrate from 0 to t

$$\dot{v} = (1/m)U_s(t)$$

(2) $$v = (1/m)\int_0^t U_s(t) = (1/m)t$$

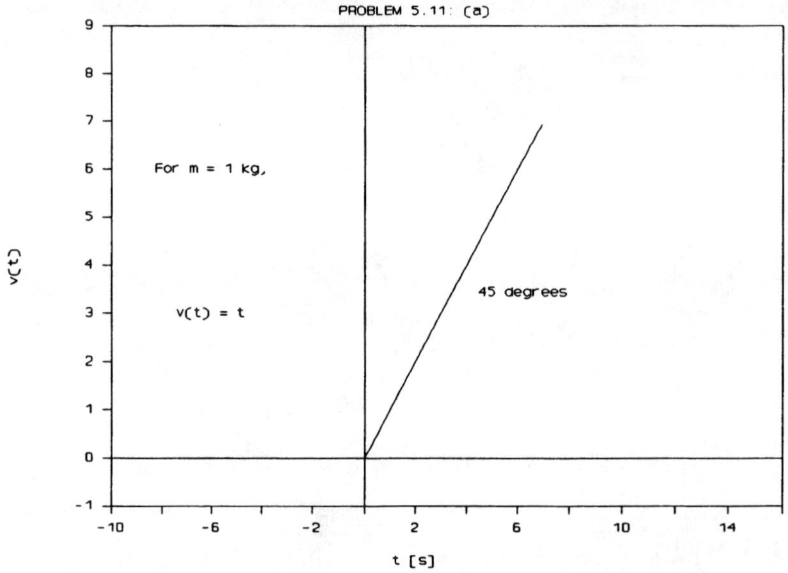

b) The input/output equation for system (b) is

(3) $$m\dot{v} + bv = F \qquad \text{where} \quad F = U_s(t)$$

From equation (3) the time constant and the steady-state velocity, v_{ss}, can be found

(4) $$v_{ss} = (1/b)\lim_{t\to\infty}\{\ F(t)\ \} = 1/b = 1 \text{ m/s}$$

$$\tau = m/b = 1 \text{ s}$$

The unit step response is thus

(5) $$v(t) = v_{ss} - (v_{ss} - v_0)e^{-t/\tau} = 1 - e^{-t}$$

Assuming zero initial condition, $v_0 = 0$

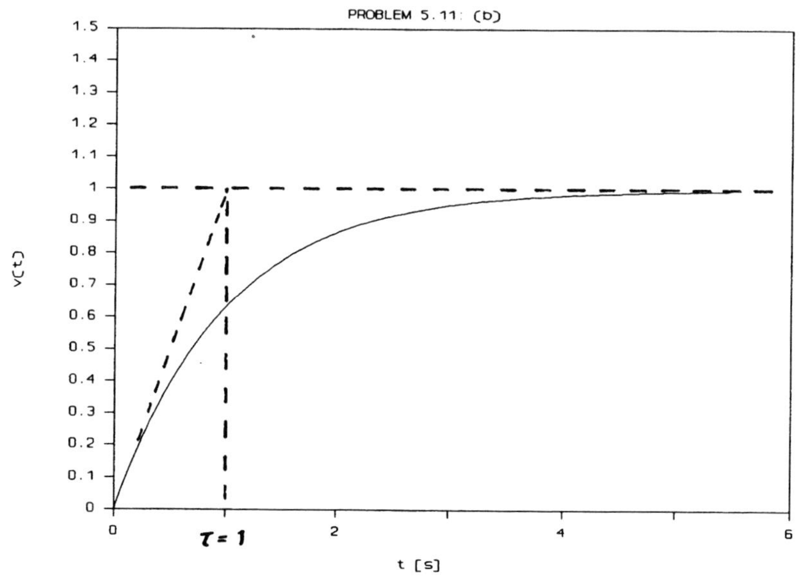

c) The input/output equation in this case is

(6) $$m\ddot{x} + b\dot{x} + kx = F \qquad \text{where} \quad F = U_s(t)$$

Substituting numerical values for m, b, and k, gives

(7) $$\ddot{x} + 6.28\dot{x} + 45.6x = U_s(t)$$

The following specifications of the system step response can be determined from equation (7).

$$x_{ss} = 1/45.6 = 0.022 \text{ m}$$

$$\zeta = 6.28/2(45.6)^{.5} = 0.465$$

$$\omega_n = (45.6)^{.5} = 6.75 \text{ rad/s}$$

$$\omega_d = \omega_n(1 - \zeta^2)^{.5} = 5.976 \text{ rad/s}$$

$$T_d = 2\pi/\omega_d = 1.05 \text{ s}$$

$$t_p = T_d/2 = 0.525 \text{ s}$$

$$M_p\% = 100e^{-\{\pi\zeta/(1-\zeta^2)^{.5}\}} = 19.2\%$$

$$x_{max} = 1.192x_{ss} = .026 \text{ m}$$

These specifications will aid in sketching the system unit step response.

The exact solution of equation (7) is (from equation ~~5.91~~ 4.86)

$$x(t) = 0.022[1 - e^{-3.14t}\{\cos(5.976t)+0.593\sin(5.976t)\}]$$

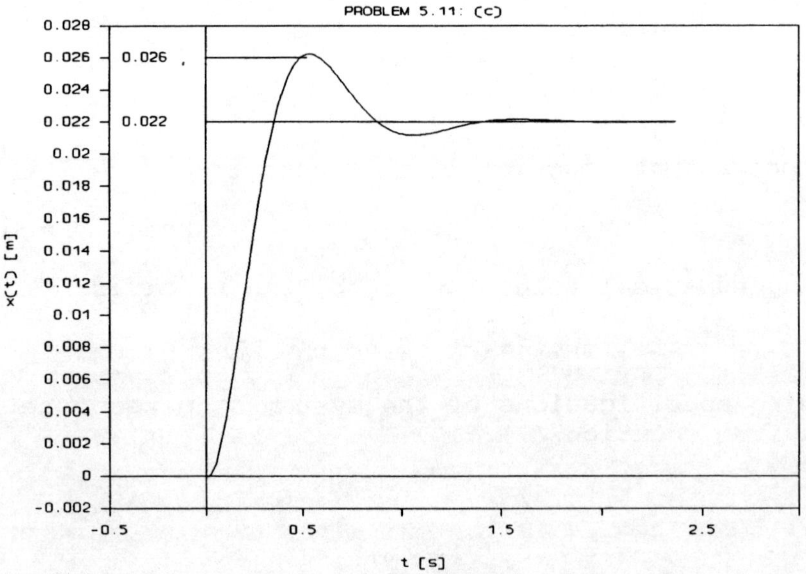

Problem 4.12

The characteristic equation of the third order model is

(1) $$p^3 + 12p^2 + 25p + 50 = 0$$

The roots of this equation are:

$$p_1 = -10 \qquad p_2 = -1+2j \qquad p_3 = -1-2j$$

The complex roots are located much closer to the imaginary axis and, therefore, are considered the dominant roots. Neglecting the distant real root, $p_1 = -10$, the second order characteristic equation is obtained.

(2) $$(p - p_2)(p - p_3) = 0$$

Substituting the values of p_2 and p_3 gives

(3) $$p^2 + 2p + 5 = 0$$

The homogeneous differential equation having a characteristic equation in this form is

(4) $$\ddot{y} + 2\dot{y} + 5y = 0$$

The peak overshhot and the period of oscillation of this model are

$$\omega_n = (5)^{.5} = 2.23 \text{ rad/s}$$

$$\zeta = 2/2(5)^{.5} = 0.447$$

$$\omega_d = 2.23(1 - 0.447^2)^{.5} = 2.0 \text{ rad/s}$$

$$T_d = 3.14 \text{ sec}$$

$$M_p\% = 20.8\%$$

Comparison of the two models:

Model Order	Mp%	Td, sec
3	18.8	3.34
2	20.8	3.14

Problem 4.13

The system free body diagram:

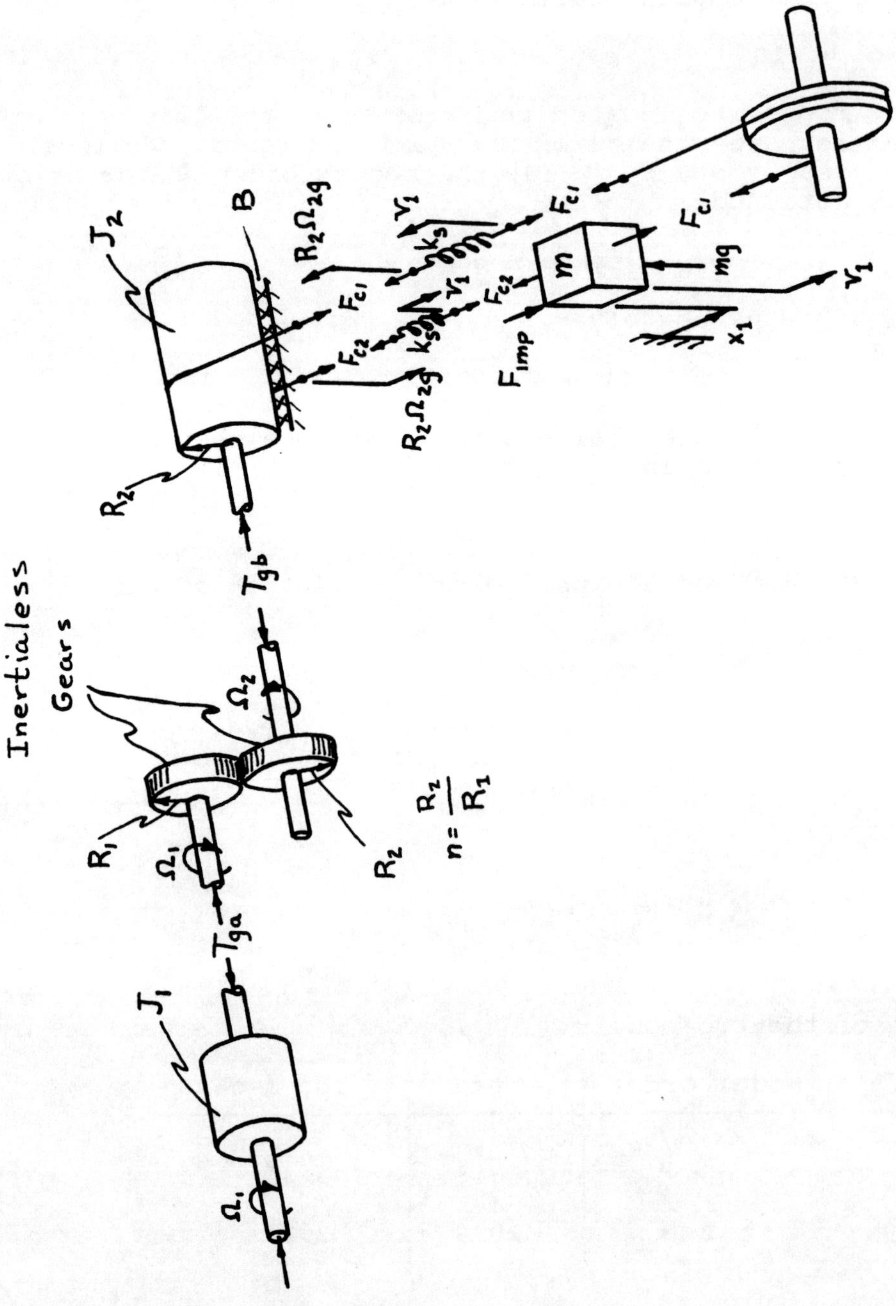

The describing equations for the system are:

For inertia J_1 -

(1) $$T_m - T_{ga} = J_1 \frac{d\Omega_{1g}}{dt}$$

For the gears -

(2) $$T_{ga} = -(1/n)\ T_{gb} \qquad n=R_2/R_1$$

(3) $$\Omega_{2g} = -(1/n)\ \Omega_{1g}$$

For inertia J_2 -

(4) $$T_{gb} - F_{C1}R_2 + F_{C2}R_2 - T_B = J_2 \frac{d\Omega_{2g}}{dt}$$

(5) $$T_B = B_{eq}\Omega_{2g}$$

(6) $$F_{C1} = k_s(R_2\theta_2 - x_1)$$

(7) $$F_{C2} = -k_s(R_2\theta_2 - x_1)$$

For mass m_s -

(8) $$F_{imp} + F_{C1} - F_{C2} = m_s \frac{dv_{1g}}{dt}$$

There are three independent energy storing elements: 1) combined inertias J_1 and J_2; 2) cable; 3) spindle mass m_s. The system will therefore be described by three state-variable equations. Select

$$q_1 = \Omega_{2g} \qquad q_2 = v_{1g} \qquad q_3 = R_2\theta_2 - x_1$$

as the state-variables. The state-variable equation for q_3 is simply

$$R_2\dot{\theta}_2 - \dot{x}_1 = R_2\Omega_{2g} - v_{1g}$$

or

(9) $$\dot{q}_3 = R_2 q_1 - q_2$$

To derive the two other state equations, first combine equations (1), (2), and (3) to obtain

(10) $$T_{gb} = -J_1 n^2 \dot{\Omega}_{2g} + nT_m$$

Substitute (10) into (4)

(11) $$(J_2 + n^2J_1)\dot{\Omega}_{2g} + T_B + R_2(F_{C1} - F_{C2}) = nT_m$$

Substitute (6) and (7) for F_{C1} and F_{C2} and (5) for T_B

(12) $$(J_2 + n^2J_1)\dot{\Omega}_{2g} + B_{eq} + 2R_2k_s(R_2\theta_2 - x_1) = nT_m$$

Hence the state-variable equation for $\dot{\Omega}_{2g}$ is

(13) $$\dot{\Omega}_{2g} = -\frac{B_{eq}}{J_{eq}}\Omega_{2g} - \frac{2R_2k_s}{J_{eq}}(R_2\theta_2 - x_1) + \frac{n}{J_{eq}}T_m$$

or

(13') $$\dot{q}_1 = -\frac{B_{eq}}{J_{eq}}q_1 - \frac{2R_2k_s}{J_{eq}}q_3 + \frac{n}{J_{eq}}T_m$$

where

(14) $$J_{eq} = J_2 + n^2J_1$$

To obtain the third state variable equation, combine (6), (7), and (8).

(15) $$m_s\frac{dv_{1g}}{dt} - 2k_s(R_2\theta_2 - x_1) = F_{imp}$$

Hence

(16) $$\dot{v}_{1g} = \frac{2k_s}{m_s}(R_2\theta_2 - x_1) + \frac{1}{m_s}F_{imp}$$

or

(16') $$\dot{q}_2 = \frac{2k_s}{m_s}q_3 + \frac{1}{m_s}F_{imp}$$

Equations (9), (13), and (16) constitute the set of state-variable equations for this system. Now find an input-output equation relating Ω_{2g} to F_{imp} for $T_m = 0$. Combining the state-variable equations to eliminate q_2 and q_3 yields

$$\frac{J_{eq}}{2R_2k_s}\dddot{q}_1 + \frac{B_{eq}}{2R_2k_s}\ddot{q}_1 + \frac{m_sR_2^2+J_{eq}}{m_sR_2}\dot{q}_1 + \frac{B_{eq}}{m_sR_2}q_1 = \frac{1}{m_s}F_{imp} \tag{17}$$

Hence, the system characteristic equation is

$$\frac{J_{eq}}{2R_2k_s}p^3 + \frac{B_{eq}}{2R_2k_s}p^2 + \frac{m_sR_2^2+J_{eq}}{m_sR_2}p + \frac{B_{eq}}{m_sR_2} = 0 \tag{18}$$

Since the order of the characteristic equation is odd, one of the roots must be real. Also, because the system behavior was very oscillatory, the other two roots must be complex. To find the roots of equation (18) first use the approximation of the real root gevin in the problem statement.

$$p_1 \approx -\frac{a_0}{a_1} = -\frac{B_{eq}}{m_sR_2^2+J_{eq}} \tag{19}$$

If the two complex roots are $p_2 = \alpha + j\beta$ and $p_3 = \alpha - j\beta$, then the following is true

$$p^3+(a_2/a_3)p^2+(a_1/a_3)p+(a_0/a_3) = (p-p_1)(p-\alpha-j\beta)(p-\alpha+j\beta) \tag{20}$$

and hence

$$p^3+(a_2/a_3)p^2+(a_1/a_3)p+(a_0/a_3) = p^3-(2\alpha+p_1)p^2 + (\alpha^2+\beta^2+2\alpha p_1)p - (\alpha^2+\beta^2)p_1 \tag{21}$$

Equating constant terms in (21) gives

$$(a_0/a_3) = -(\alpha^2+\beta^2)p_1 \tag{22}$$

But the natural frequency associated with a pair of complex roots is

$$\omega_n = [\ \alpha^2 + \beta^2\ ]^{.5} \tag{23}$$

Now, from (22) and (23)

$$\omega_n = [\ a_0/(a_3p_1)\ ]^{.5} \tag{24}$$

Substituting for a_0 and a_3 from equation (18) and for p_1 from (19) yields

$$\omega_n = [\ \{\ 2k_s(m_sR_2^2+J_{eq})\ \}/(m_sJ_{eq})\ ]^{.5} \tag{25}$$

Now, equating second order terms in equation (21)

$$a_2/a_3 = -\ (2\alpha + p_1)$$

Substituting for a_2, a_3 from (18) and for p_1 from (19) and solving for α, we find

$$(26) \qquad \alpha = -\frac{1}{2}\left(p_1 + \frac{a_2}{a_3} \right) = -\frac{1}{2}\left(\frac{B_{eq}}{J_{eq}} - \frac{B_{eq}}{m_s R_2^2 + J_{eq}} \right)$$

Using equation (5.75) to find ζ

$$(27) \qquad \zeta = -\frac{\alpha}{\omega_n} = \frac{1}{2\omega_n}\left(\frac{B_{eq}}{J_{eq}} - \frac{B_{eq}}{m_s R_2^2 + J_{eq}} \right)$$

From equations (25) and (27) the effect of system parameters on the damping ratio can be determined. To reduce oscillations in the system response, the parameters must be changed to increase ζ. Some of the changes that would provide more damping in the system are: increasing B_{eq}, decreasing k_s, decreasing R_2, decreasing n.

CHAPTER 5

Problem 5.1

Solve problem 4.1(a) using the MATLAB script from Table 5.1 using time steps of 0.1 and 0.02 seconds.

Recall Problem 4.1(a):

$$2\dot{y} + 5y = 5u(t)$$

where u(t) is the unit step function and y(0) = 2.0.

First, modify the file EULMETH.M (Table 5.1 but also available from the MATLAB FTP server) to accommodate the new equation, the new initial conditions and the time step. This problem also has a smaller time constant than the one shown in the example, therefore, it is advisable that we change the final time as well (4 seconds is a good choice).

The new script is listed below:

```
%
%       Set up the sample time, initial time and final times
%
dt   =  0.1;
t(1) =  0.0;
tf   =  4.0;
%
%       Set the initial condition
%
x(1)=2.0;
%
%       Loop through the times, numerically evaluating the integral
%
for i=2:tf/dt+1,

        xd=5/2*(1-x(i-1));
        x(i)=x(i-1)+xd*dt;
        t(i)=t(i-1)+dt;

end;
%
%       Plot the results using MATLAB's plot command
%
plot(t,x);
```

You can get a clearer plot by manipulating the scales using MATLAB's AXIS command.

The two computed responses are shown below with the circles indicating the response computed at the 0.1 time step, while the '+''s show the response at the finer time step (0.02).

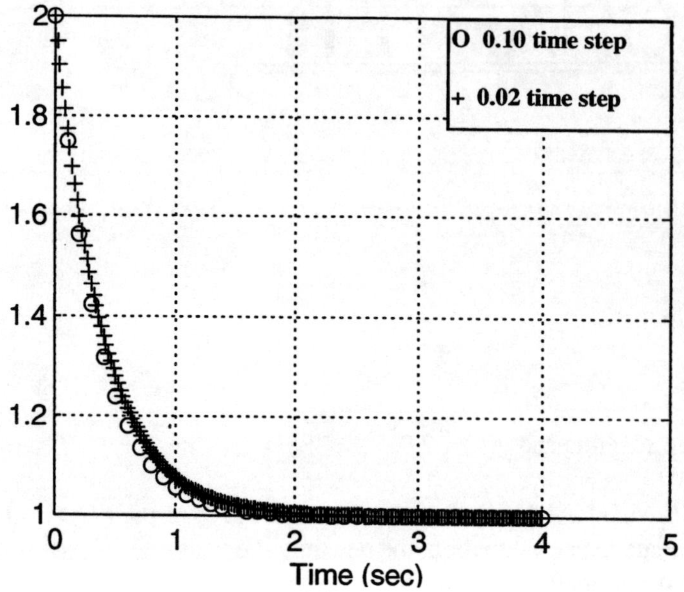

<u>**Problem 5.2**</u>

Again, we will solve the equation of 4.1(a). The script file has already been modified for the previous problem. This problem is solved by re-running the script many times and comparing it to the exact solution, which is:

$$y(t) = 1 + e^{-2.5t}$$

The time constant for this problem is 0.4 seconds. Therefore, the candidate time steps are: 0.04, 0.08, 0.2, 0.4, 0.8 and 2.0 seconds. We will construct a table similar to the ones shown in the text to compare the various time steps. Note that the smallest time step will yield 100 points in the time interval from 0 to 4 seconds. For the sake of compactness, we will only show 10 time steps in the table.

Time(s)	**Exact**	**Δt=0.04**	**Δt=0.08**	**Δt=0.2**	**Δt=0.4**	**Δt=0.8**	**Δt=2.0**
0	2.0	2.0	2.0	2.0	2.0	2.0	2.0
0.4	1.3679	1.3487	1.3277	1.25	1.0		
0.8	1.1353	1.1216	1.1074	1.0625	1.0	0.0	
1.2	1.0498	1.0424	1.0352	1.0156	1.0		
1.6	1.0183	1.0148	1.0115	1.0039	1.0	2.0	
2.0	1.0067	1.0052	1.0038	1.0010	1.0		-3.0
2.4	1.0025	1.0018	1.0012	1.0002	1.0	0.0	
2.8	1.0009	1.0006	1.0004	1.0001	1.0		
3.2	1.0003	1.0002	1.0001	1.0000	1.0	2.0	
3.6	1.0001	1.0001	1.0000	1.0000	1.0		
4.0	1.0000	1.0000	1.0000	1.0000	1.0	0.0	17.0

Problem 5.3

Modify the script from Table 5.1 to implement the improved Euler method and solve the equation from Problem 4.1a.

The modification is made within the loop which computes the estimates. A partial listing of the script file showing the modifications can be seen below:

```
x(1)=2.0;
%
%       Loop through the times, numerically evaluating the integral
%
for i=2:tf/dt+1,

        xd1=2.5*(1-x(i-1));       %compute the derivative at beginning
        xhat=x(i-1)+xd1*dt;       %compute estimate of state at end
        xd2=2.5*(1-xhat);         %compute estimate of derivative at end
        xd=1/2*(xd1+xd2);         %compute average of derivatives
        x(i)=x(i-1)+xd*dt;        %compute estimate of state
        t(i)=t(i-1)+dt;
end;
%
```

It should be noted that, for this simple script, the derivative function is actually encoded twice (both `xd1` and `xd2`). A more sophisticated approach would have the derivative as an external function that would be called from a more generic integration script file.

For a time step of 0.2 seconds, we can compare the Improved Euler method and the Euler method in the table below:

Time (s)	Exact Solution	Euler $\Delta t=0.2$	Improved Euler $\Delta t=0.2$
0.0	2.0000	2.0000	2.0000
0.4	1.3679	1.2500	1.3906
0.8	1.1353	1.0625	1.1526
1.2	1.0498	1.0156	1.0596
1.6	1.0183	1.0039	1.0233
2.0	1.0067	1.0010	1.0091
2.4	1.0025	1.0002	1.0036
2.8	1.0009	1.0001	1.0014
3.2	1.0003	1.0000	1.0005
3.6	1.0001	1.0000	1.0002
4.0	1.0000	1.0000	1.0001

Problem 5.4

Once again, we solve problem 4.1(a), but this time we use the 4th order RK method, using Table 5.4 in the text. We modify the loop in which the derivatives are computed, the result will look something like this:

```
%
%       Loop through the times, numerically evaluating the integral
%
for i=2:tf/dt+1,

        k1=2.5*(1-x(i-1));
        xhat1=x(i-1)+k1*dt/2;
        k2=2.5*(1-xhat1);
        xhat2=x(i-1)+k2*dt/2;
        k3=2.5*(1-xhat2);
        xhat3=x(i-1)+k3*dt;
        k4=2.5*(1-xhat3);

        x(i)=x(i-1)+dt/6*(k1+2*k2+2*k3+k4);
        t(i)=t(i-1)+dt;

end;
%
```

And the results are compared with the previous methods:

Time (s)	Exact Solution	Euler Δt=0.2	Improved Euler Δt=0.2	RK–4 Δt=0.2
0.0	2.0000	2.0000	2.0000	2.0000
0.4	1.3679	1.2500	1.3906	1.3682
0.8	1.1353	1.0625	1.1526	1.1355
1.2	1.0498	1.0156	1.0596	1.0499
1.6	1.0183	1.0039	1.0233	1.0184
2.0	1.0067	1.0010	1.0091	1.0068
2.4	1.0025	1.0002	1.0036	1.0025
2.8	1.0009	1.0001	1.0014	1.0009
3.2	1.0003	1.0000	1.0005	1.0003
3.6	1.0001	1.0000	1.0002	1.0001
4.0	1.0000	1.0000	1.0001	1.0000

Problem 5.5

Use RK-4 and check against the analytical solution of Problem 4.3. Recall the equation of Problem 4.3:

$$J\dot{\Omega} + B\Omega = T(t)$$

Problem 4.3 asks us to find values of J and B for which the system will meet the following two conditions:

(a) the steady-state speed is 50 rpm for a steady state torque of 10 N-m input.

(b) the speed drops to 5% of it's steady state value 160 ms after the torque is removed.

This is solved iteratively using the numerical simulation. First, modify the RK script file for this problem. A portion of the modified file is shown below:

```
%       Set the parameter values
%
J = 1.0;
B = 1.0;
%
%       Define the input
%
Tin = 10.0;
%
%       Loop through the times, numerically evaluating the integral
%
for i=2:tf/dt+1,

        k1=1/J*(Tin-B*x(i-1));
        xhat1=x(i-1)+k1*dt/2;
        k2=1/J*(Tin-B*xhat1);
        xhat2=x(i-1)+k2*dt/2;
        k3=1/J*(Tin-B*xhat2);
        xhat3=x(i-1)+k3*dt;
        k4=1/J*(Tin-B*xhat3);

        x(i)=x(i-1)+dt/6*(k1+2*k2+2*k3+k4);
        t(i)=t(i-1)+dt;

end;
%
```

We set both J and B equal to 1.0 as a starting place. Our previous experience with differential equations tells us that the steady state speed is a function of only the input and B (since steady-state implies that the derivatives equal zero). Therefore, we iteratively run the script file, changing B and noting the steady state value of the speed. Some trial runs are summarized in the table below. Note that the target steady-state speed, 50 rpm, should be converted to its equivalent speed in rad/s (5.236 rad/s).

B	Ω_{ss}
1.0	10.0
2.0	5.0
1.9	5.263
1.92	5.2083
1.91	5.235

B= 1.91 is deemed close enough.

The second part sets the value of J. We modify the script file so that it the final time is 0.160 seconds, and set the integration step time to 0.01 seconds. We then run the file, modifying J to find the value for which the speed is 5% of the steady state value at a time of 0.160 seconds. The target speed is 0.2618 rad/s.

J	Ω_{ss}
1	2.8573
2	4.4941
0.1	0.2465
0.15	0.6827
0.11	0.3254

At which point, we deem J=0.1 to be close enough for our purposes.

The final answer is:

J=0.1 Nms^2/rad
B=1.91Nms/rad

which match the results from Problem 4.3.

Problem 5.6

Solve the problem of 4.5 numerically using both Improved Euler and RK-4.

The equation of motion for this problem is :

$$m\dot{v} = -bv + F(t)$$

where m=1.5 lb-sec^2/ft, b=300 lb sec/ft and the force input is a step of 100 lb and t=0 seconds. The initial value of the velocity is zero. We manipulate the equation and solve for the derivative:

$$\dot{v} = \frac{1}{1.5}[100 - 300v]$$

The improved Euler script is modified to look like this:

```
%
%       Set the initial condition
%
x(1)=0.0;
%
%       Loop through the times, numerically evaluating the integral
%
for i=2:tf/dt+1,

        xd1=1/1.5*(100-300*x(i-1));    %compute the derivative at beginning
        xhat=x(i-1)+xd1*dt;            %compute estimate of state at end
        xd2=1/1.5*(100-300*xhat);      %compute estimate of derivative at end
        xd=1/2*(xd1+xd2);              %compute average of derivatives
        x(i)=x(i-1)+xd*dt;             %compute estimate of state
        t(i)=t(i-1)+dt;
end;
%
```

The RK-4 script is also modified:

```
%       Set the initial condition
%
x(1)=0.0;
%
%
%       Define the input
%
Fin = 100.0;
%
%       Loop through the times, numerically evaluating the integral
%
for i=2:tf/dt+1,

        k1=1/1.5*(100-300*x(i-1));
        xhat1=x(i-1)+k1*dt/2;
        k2=1/1.5*(100-300*xhat1);
        xhat2=x(i-1)+k2*dt/2;
        k3=1/1.5*(100-300*xhat2);
        xhat3=x(i-1)+k3*dt;
        k4=1/1.5*(100-300*xhat3);

        x(i)=x(i-1)+dt/6*(k1+2*k2+2*k3+k4);
        t(i)=t(i-1)+dt;

end;
%
```

The two methods can be compared using a rather coarse time step. The time constant of this equation is 5 ms, so we'll use that as the time step. The figure below compares the two methods, with the circle representing the RK method while the '+' s show the improved Euler computation.

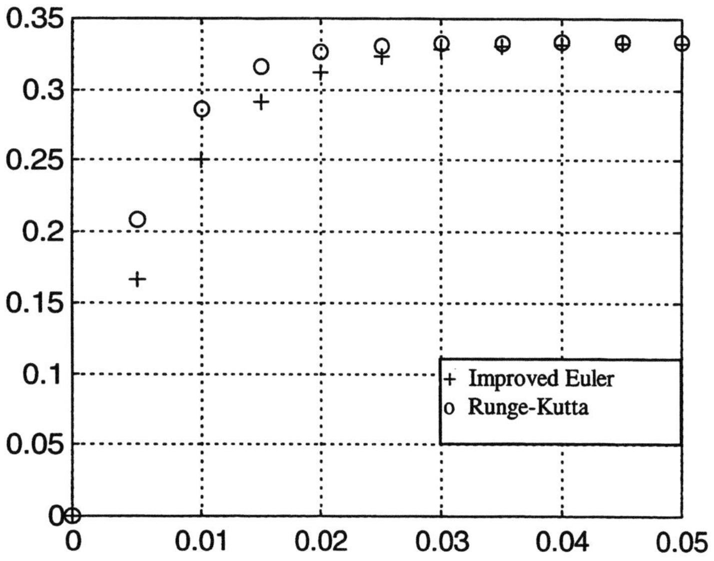

Problem 5.7

First, the script from Table 5.1 is modified to allow for the integration of 2 differential equations. We will introduce two state variables, x_1 and x_2. The equation to be integrated is:

$$\ddot{x} = \tfrac{1}{9}[0.1 - 4\dot{x} - 4x]$$

Which can be transformed into state space form with x_1 as the velocity and x_2 as the displacement.

$$\dot{x}_1 = \tfrac{1}{9}[0.1 - 4x_1 - 4x_2]$$
$$\dot{x}_2 = x_1$$

The script file looks like this:

```
%       Set up the sample time, initial time and final times
%
dt=    0.2;
t(1)= 0.0;
tf=    20.0;
%
%       Set the initial condition
%
x1(1)= 0.0;
x2(1)= 0.0
%
%       Loop through the times, numerically evaluating the integral
%
for i=2:tf/dt+1,
        xd1=1/9*(0.1-4*x1(i-1)-4*x2(i-1));
        xd2=x1(i-1);
        x1(i)=x1(i-1)+xd1*dt;
        x2(i)=x2(i-1)+xd2*dt;
        t(i)=t(i-1)+dt;
end;
%
%       Plot the results using MATLAB's plot command
%
plot(t,x2);
```

And the step response:

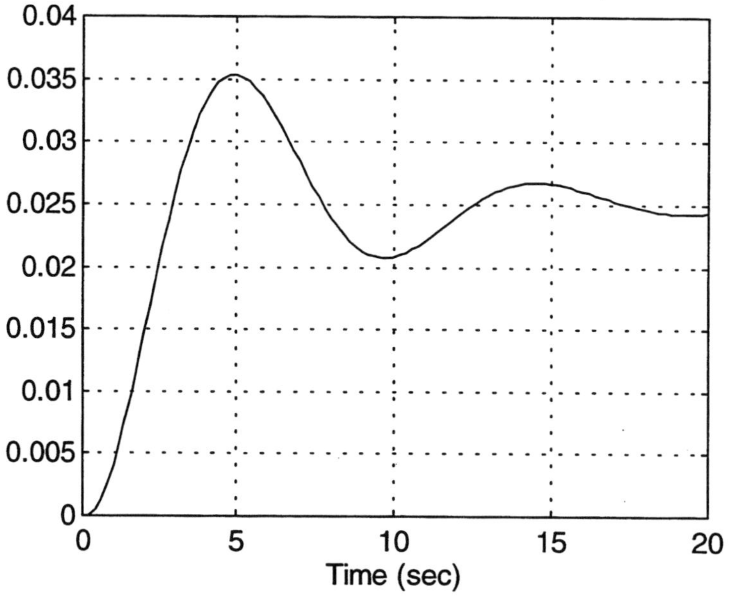

From the plot we can pull off the performance parameters:

Percent overshoot = [(0.35-0.25)/0.25]*100% = 40%
t_p (time at first peak) = 5.0 seconds (or just under)
DR (decrement Ratio) = [(0.268-0.25)/(0.35-0.25)] = 0.18

You can use the DR to predict ζ, the damping ratio, using equation (4.108):

ζ=0.2633

Note that the analytical solution in Chapter 4 predicts a ζ of 0.33 and M_p of 32.94%.

In this example, I used a time step of 0.2 seconds. If you refine the time step, the approximation improves.

Problem 5.8

Building on the previous solution, we can expand the script to handle a third order equation from Problem 4.12:

$$\dddot{y} + 12\ddot{y} + 25\dot{y} + 50y = u(t)$$

and u(t) is a step function of magnitude 50.

Assigning the following state variables:

$$x_1 = \ddot{y}$$
$$x_2 = \dot{y}$$
$$x_3 = y$$

The script file looks like this:

```
%
%       Set up the sample time, initial time and final times
%
dt=   0.05;
t(1)= 0.0;
tf=   10.0;
%
%       Set the initial condition
%
x1(1)= 0.0;
x2(1)= 0.0;
x3(1)= 0.0;
%
%       Loop through the times, numerically evaluating the integral
%
for i=2:tf/dt+1,

        xd1=50.0-12*x1(i-1)-25*x2(i-1)-50*x3(i-1);
        xd2=x1(i-1);
        xd3=x2(i-1);

        x1(i)=x1(i-1)+xd1*dt;
        x2(i)=x2(i-1)+xd2*dt;
        x3(i)=x3(i-1)+xd3*dt;

        t(i)=t(i-1)+dt;

end;
%
%       Plot the results using MATLAB's plot command
%
plot(t,x3);
```

And the step response:

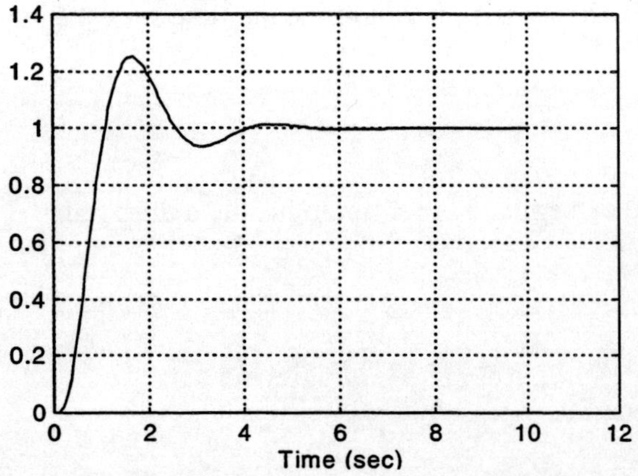

Which resembles the plot in the textbook (Figure P4.12) but has some significant differences, again, if the step size is refined or a higher-order method used, the approximation improves.

Problem 5.9

(a) Determine the N.O.P. by setting the derivatives to zero and substituting the nominal input force (F_a=15 N)

The state equations give us:

$$0 = \bar{v}$$

$$0 = -\frac{1}{m}\left[-k\bar{x} - F_{NLD}(\bar{v}) + \bar{F}_a\right]$$

The first equation tells us that the nominal velocity is zero, which allows us to solve for nominal displacement:

$$\bar{v} = 0$$

$$\bar{x} = 2.8$$

(b) Linearize about the NOP. This is easily done as the only nonlinear portion is the nonlinear damping force.

$$\dot{\hat{x}} = \hat{v}$$

$$\dot{\hat{v}} = \tfrac{1}{m}\left[-k\hat{x} - \hat{v} + \hat{F}_a\right]$$

These linearized equations yield the following characteristic equation:

$$p^2 + 0.1p + 0.5 = 0$$

From which we conclude:

ω_n = 0.7071 rad/s
ζ = 0.071

And the period of damped oscillation is:

T_d=8.9 seconds

c) Modify the RK script file (Table 5.4) to handle second order equations. This is done more easily if we make a separate file to handle the evaluation of the derivatives. The file `fdervs.m` is created for this purpose. It is a MATLAB function file (as opposed to script file) and has this form:

```
function       [x1d,x2d]=fdervs(x,f,t);
%
%
%       x(1) = x,  displacement
%       x(2) = v,  velocity
%       f    = Fa, input force
%       t    = time
%
x1d=x(2);
FNLD=x(2)^2+x(2)+1;
x2d=1/10*(-5*x(1)-FNLD+f);
```

Then the RK script file can be modified to handle two state variables. One possible solution would look like this:

```
%
%       Set up the sample time, initial time and final times
%
dt=     0.4;
t(1)=   0.0;
tf=     50.0;
%
%       Set the initial condition to match N.O.P.
%
x1(1)= 2.8;     % initial displacement
x2(1)= 0.0;     % initial velocity
%
Fa=15;
%
%       Loop through the times, numerically evaluating the integral
%
for i=2:tf/dt+1,
%
%       Apply step at 10 seconds
%
        if(t(i-1))>10
                Fa=15+1.5;
        end;


        [k11,k12] = fdervs([x1(i-1) x2(i-1)],Fa,t(i-1));
        xhat11=x1(i-1)+k11*dt/2;
        xhat21=x2(i-1)+k12*dt/2;
%
        [k21,k22]=fdervs([xhat11 xhat21],Fa,t(i-1)+dt/2);
        xhat21=x1(i-1)+k21*dt/2;
        xhat22=x2(i-1)+k22*dt/2;
%
        [k31,k32]=fdervs([xhat21 xhat22],Fa,t(i-1)+dt/2);
        xhat31 = x1(i-1)+k31*dt/2;
        xhat32 = x2(i-1)+k32*dt/2;
%
        [k41,k42]=fdervs([xhat31 xhat32],Fa,t(i-1)+dt);


        x1(i) = x1(i-1)+dt/6*(k11+2*k21+2*k31+k41);
        x2(i) = x2(i-1)+dt/6*(k12+2*k22+2*k32+k42);
        t(i)=t(i-1)+dt;

end;
%
%       Plot the results using MATLAB's plot command
%
plot(t,x1);
```

Note that the script starts with the nominal input (F_a=15) and with the initial displacement set at the NOP (2.8). The disturbance input is applied 10 seconds after the start of the simulation. This allows us to check the equilibrium at the NOP. An integration step size of 0.4 was used following the suggestion of making it 5% of the period of damped oscillation.

The step results of this simulation is shown below:

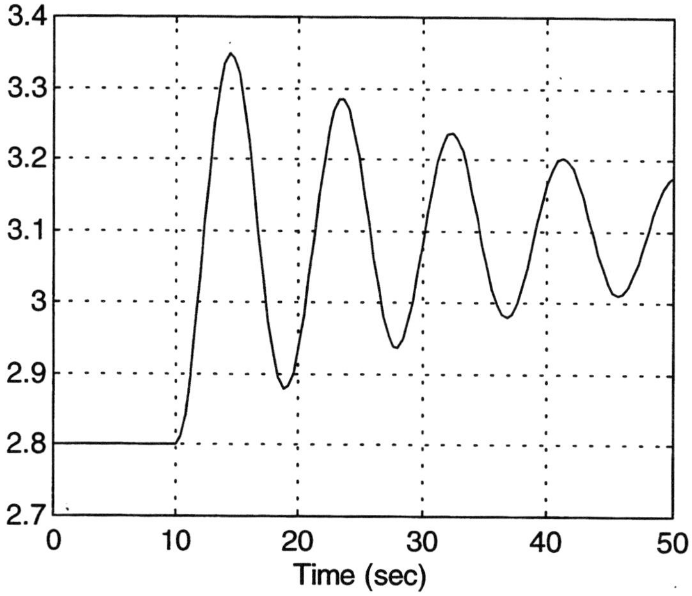

From this plot (or by examining the vector x_1) we can pull off some parameters:

Td (period of damped oscillation) = 8.8 seconds

DR (decrement ratio) = [(3.28-3.1)/(3.35-3.1)] = 0.72

Therefore: ζ= 0.052, ω_n = 0.714

The natural frequency matches well, but the damping ratio is a bit lower than that shown by the linear model.

(d) The numerically computed step response for a disturbance step of 15 N is shown below:

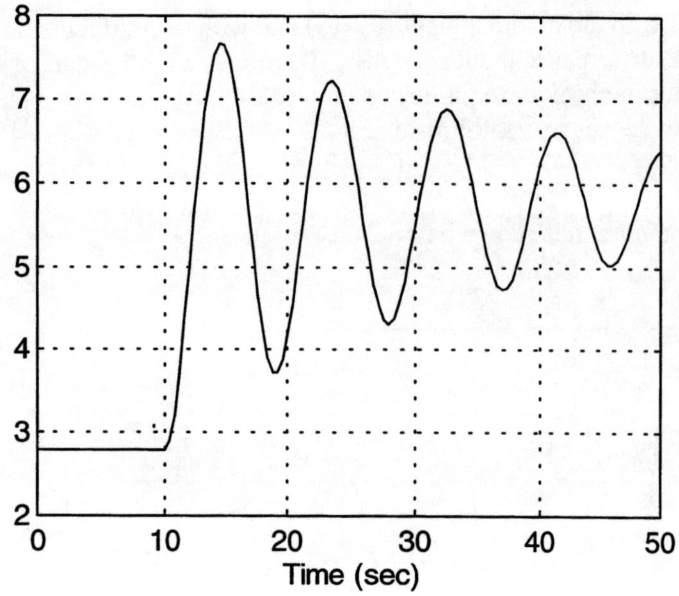

Which yields the following 2nd order parameters:

T_d = 8.8 sec
DR = 0.753
ω_n = 0.714
ζ = 0.04515

(e), (f) and (g)

The linearized model is used to compute the trajectory, then added to the NOP (2.8) and plotted with the computed nonlinear solution in the following two graphs:

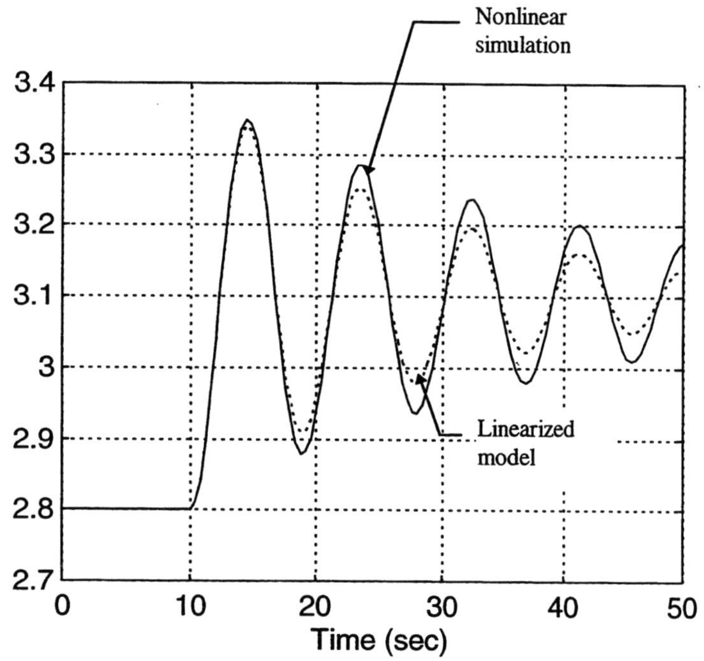
Nonlinear simulation
Linearized model
3.4
3.3
3.2
3.1
3
2.9
2.8
2.7
0
10
20
30
40
50
Time (sec)

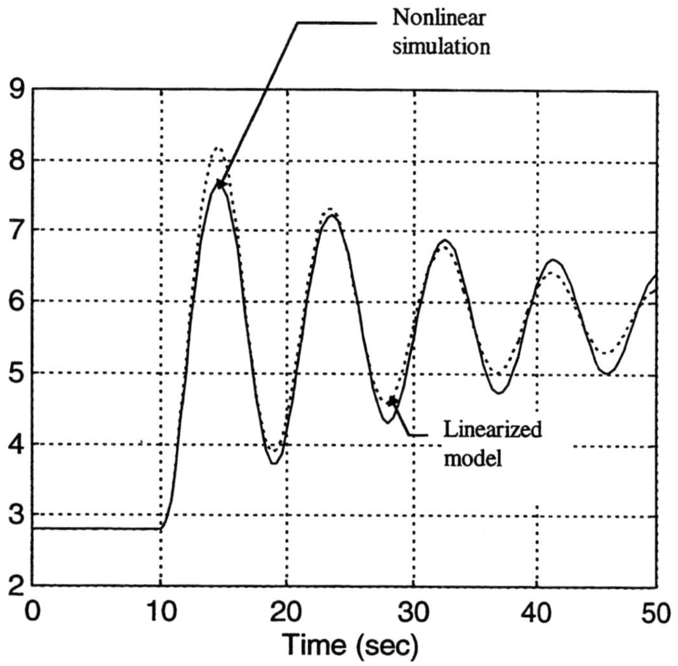
Nonlinear simulation
Linearized model
9
8
7
6
5
4
3
2
0
10
20
30
40
50
Time (sec)

Problem 5.10

(a) We'll use the same approach outlined in the solution of Problem 5.9. A separate function is created to evaluate the derivatives.

```
function       [x1d,x2d,x3d]=fd510(x,u,t);
%
%
%       x(1) = x,  displacement
%       x(2) = x-dot, first derivative
%       x(3) = x-2-dot, second derivative
%       u    = input
%       t    = time
%
x1d=x(2);
x2d=x(3);
x3d=20*u-40-10*x(3)-4*x(2);
```

Additionally, the RK routine must be modified to allow for three state variables as shown below:

```
%       Set up the sample time, initial time and final times
%
dt=     0.1;
t(1)=   0.0;
tf=     15.0;
%
%       Set the initial condition to match N.O.P.
%
x1(1)= 0.0;     % initial displacement
x2(1)= 0.0;     % initial velocity
x3(1)= 0.0;
%
%
u=1.0;
%
%       Loop through the times, numerically evaluating the integral
%
for i=2:tf/dt+1,
%


        [k11,k12,k13] = fd510([x1(i-1) x2(i-1) x3(i-1)],u,t(i-1));
        xhat11=x1(i-1)+k11*dt/2;
        xhat21=x2(i-1)+k12*dt/2;
        xhat31=x3(i-1)+k13*dt/2;


%
        [k21,k22,k23]=fd510([xhat11 xhat21 xhat31],u,t(i-1)+dt/2);
        xhat21=x1(i-1)+k21*dt/2;
        xhat22=x2(i-1)+k22*dt/2;
        xhat23=x3(i-1)+k23*dt/2;
%
        [k31,k32,k33]=fd510([xhat21 xhat22 xhat23],u,t(i-1)+dt/2);
        xhat31 = x1(i-1)+k31*dt/2;
        xhat32 = x2(i-1)+k32*dt/2;
        xhat33 = x3(i-1)+k33*dt/2;
%
        [k41,k42,k43]=fd510([xhat31 xhat32 xhat33],u,t(i-1)+dt);


        x1(i) = x1(i-1)+dt/6*(k11+2*k21+2*k31+k41);
        x2(i) = x2(i-1)+dt/6*(k12+2*k22+2*k32+k42);
        x3(i) = x3(i-1)+dt/6*(k13+2*k23+2*k33+k43);
        t(i)=t(i-1)+dt;

end;
%
```

For a unit step input and zero initial conditions, the three state variables behave as shown below:

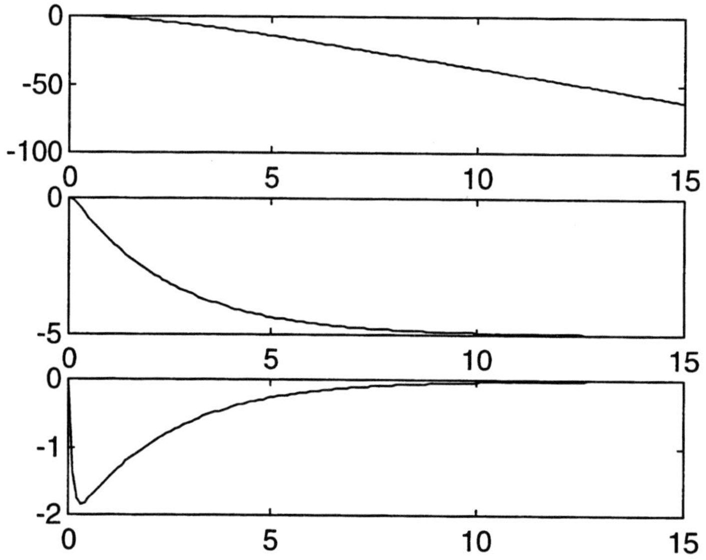

(b) We'll use the same function to evaluate the derivatives in our modification of the improved Euler method. The new script file for this one looks like:

```
%       Set up the sample time, initial time and final times
%
dt    = 0.1;
t(1)  = 0.0;
tf    = 15.0;
%
%       Set the initial condition
%
x1(1) =  0.0;
x2(1) =  0.0;
x3(1) =  0.0;
%
u=1.0;
%
%       Loop through the times, numerically evaluating the integral
%
for i=2:tf/dt+1,
        [xd11 xd12 xd13]=fd510([x1(i-1) x2(i-1) x3(i-1)],u,t(i-1));
%
        t(i)=t(i-1)+dt;
%
        x1hat=x1(i-1)+xd11*dt;
        x2hat=x2(i-1)+xd12*dt;
        x3hat=x3(i-1)+xd13*dt;
%
        [xd21 xd22 xd23]=fd510([x1hat x2hat x3hat],u,t(i));
%
        x1(i)=x1(i-1)+0.5*(xd11+xd21)*dt;
        x2(i)=x2(i-1)+0.5*(xd12+xd22)*dt;
        x3(i)=x3(i-1)+0.5*(xd13+xd23)*dt;

end;
%
%       Plot the results using MATLAB's plot command
%
subplot(3,1,1),plot(t,x1,'w-');
subplot(3,1,2),plot(t,x2,'w-');
subplot(3,1,3),plot(t,x3,'w-');
```

And the three responses look like:

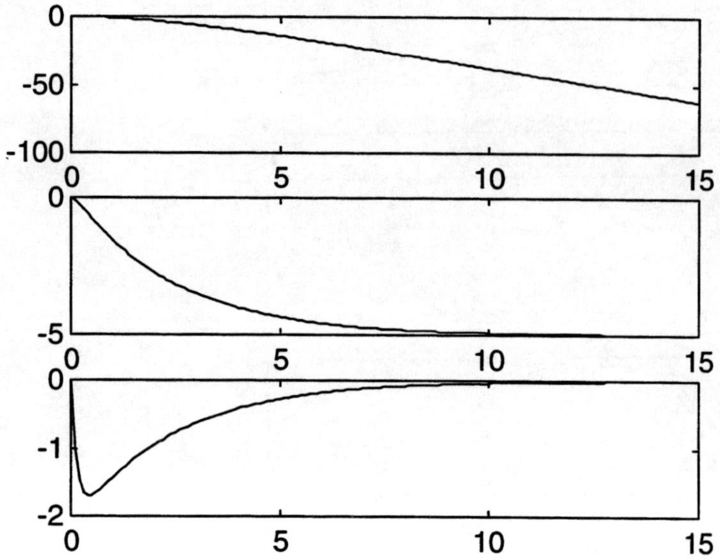

Part c)

The analytical solution for this problem is:

$$x(t) = 12.5 - 5t + 0.0238e^{-9.5826t} - 12.5238e^{-0.4174t}$$

and if we plot x(t) and it's first two derivatives on the same scales as the numerical solution above, we get:

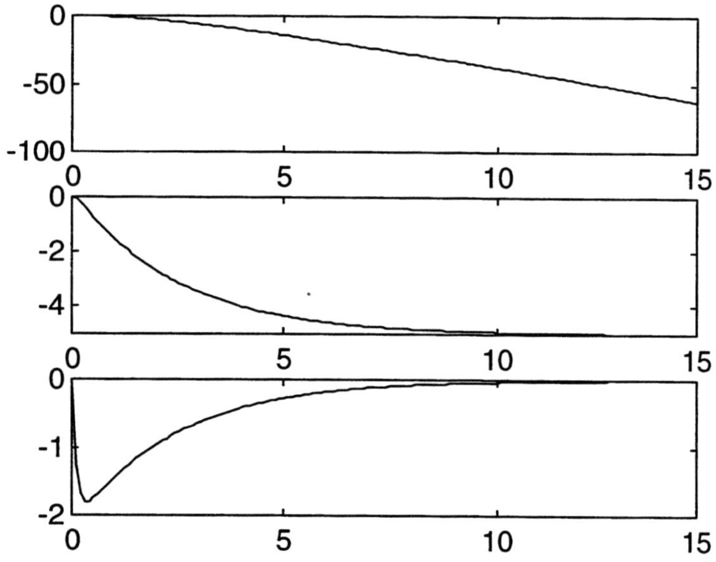

Which looks like a close match.

One final comparison, let's look at the second derivative of the variable, and compare the two numerical solutions with the analytical solution, shown below:

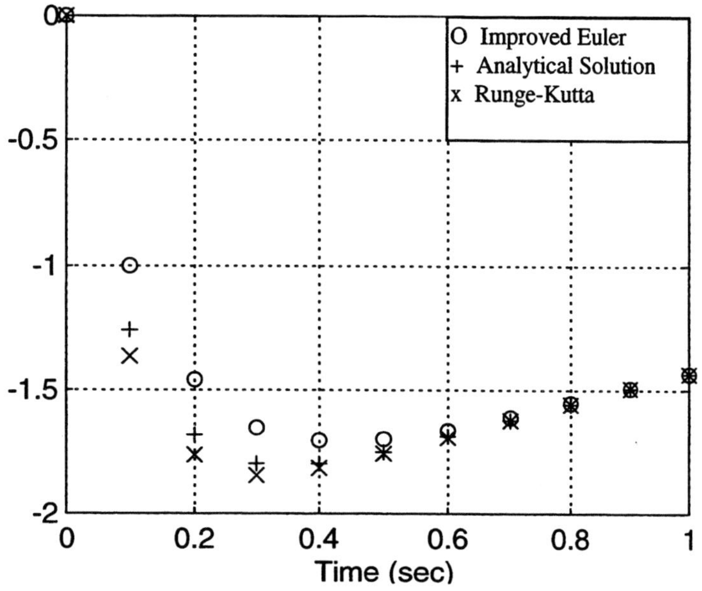

CHAPTER 6

Problem 6.1

The point of this problem is to make an impulse function by summing two step inputs, and then apply it to the 2nd order system which has been used as an example. The modified SIMULINK diagram might look something like this:

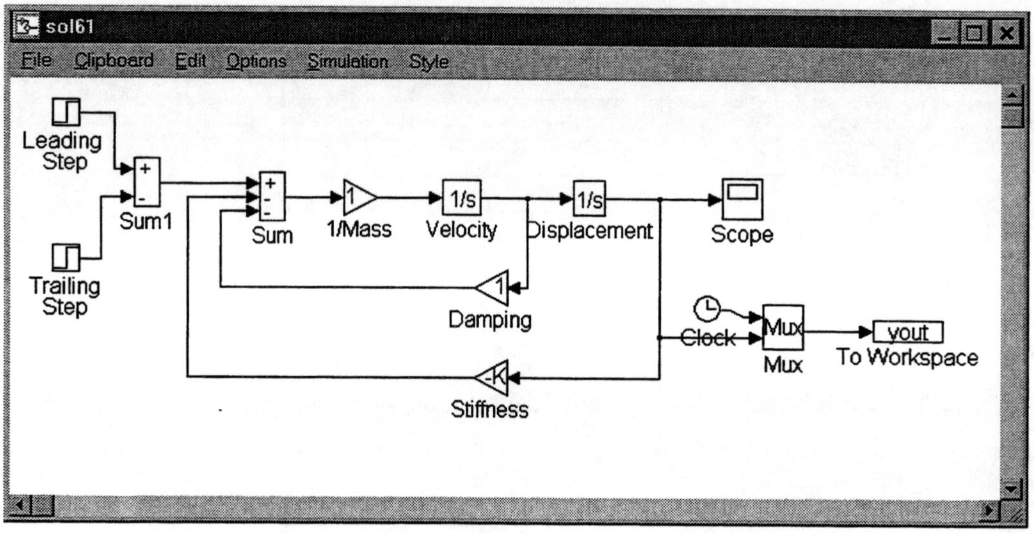

The Leading Step is set to go from 0 to 100/dt at 1.0 seconds. The trailing step goes from 0 to 100/dt at 1.0+dt seconds. The summing junction assures that the two will cancel out. The magnitude of the pulse remains constant at 100 and the variable dt can be set from the MATLAB prompt. Here is a series of responses taken from dt=1.0 to dt=0.1. The system was integrated using RK-4, minimum step=0.0001, maximum step =0.1.

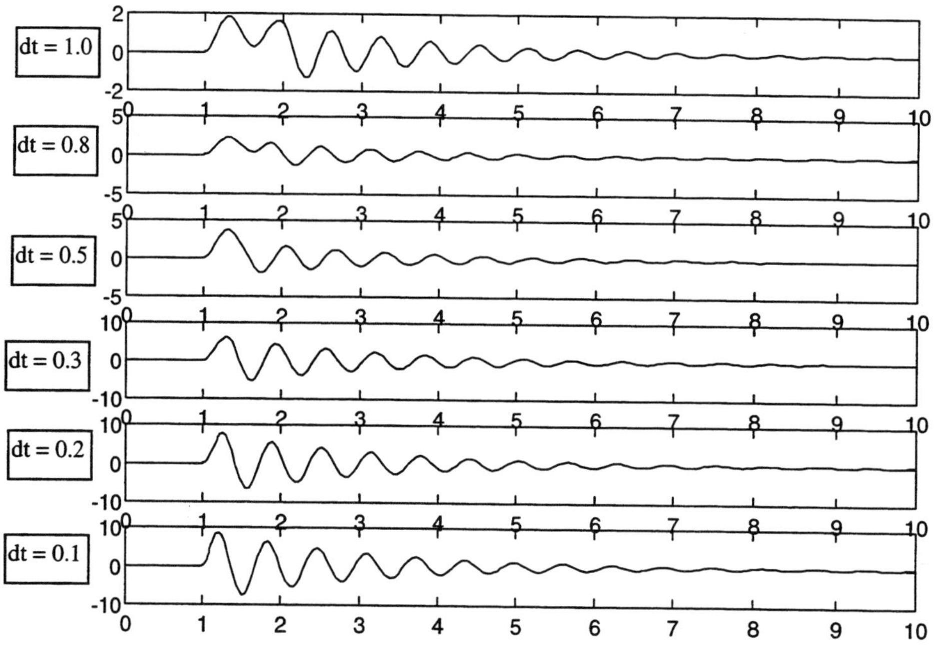

Problem 6.2

The modified SIMULINK diagram looks like this:

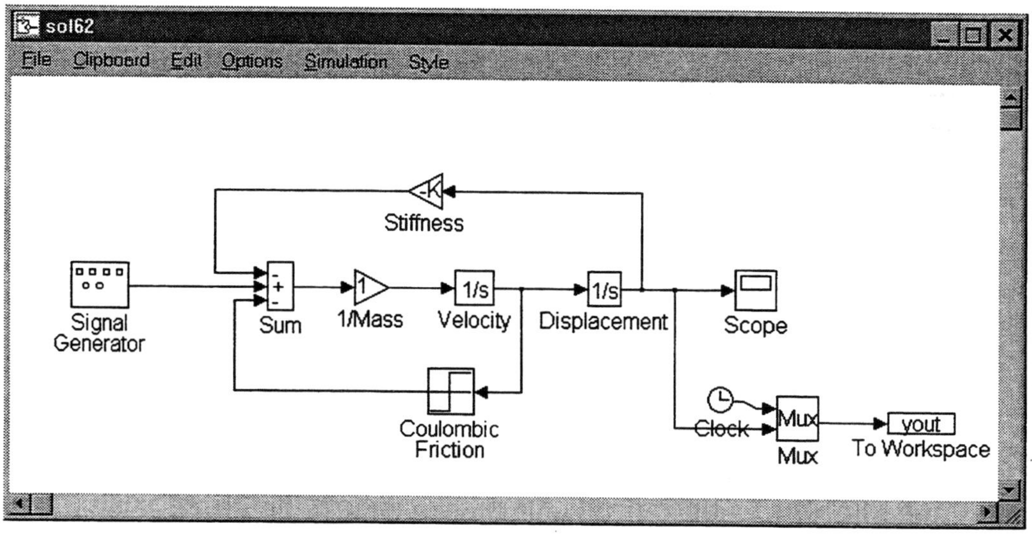

And it's response to a sine wave of magnitude 50, frequency of 1 rad/sec looks like this:

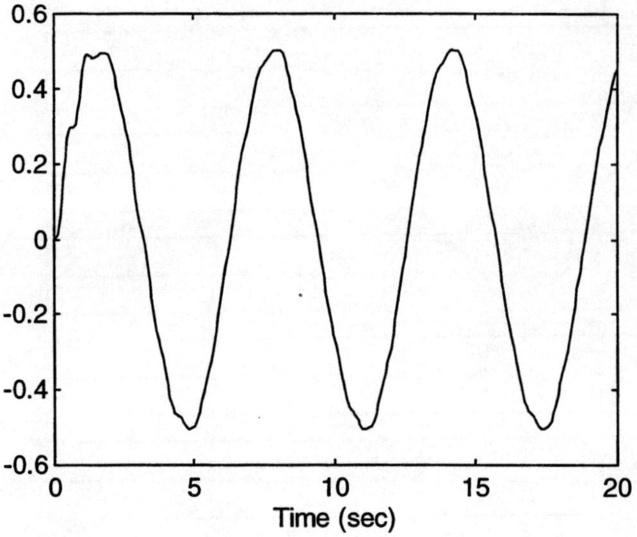

Problem 6.3

The more sophisticated friction law requires the use of the SIMULINK function block. The SIMULINK model is modified to look like this:

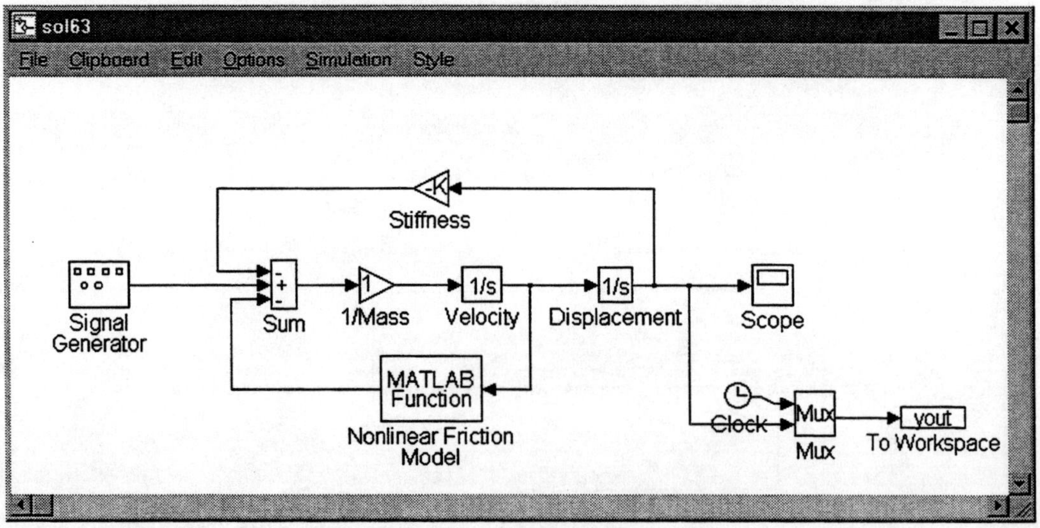

The MATLAB function block refers to an M-file called `p63.m`, which is shown below:

```
function  [f]=p63(v)
%
%
if v>0
        f=6.25*v^2-5*v+2;
else
        f=-6.25*v^2-5*v-2;
end
```

And the response to the 1 rad/sec sine wave is:

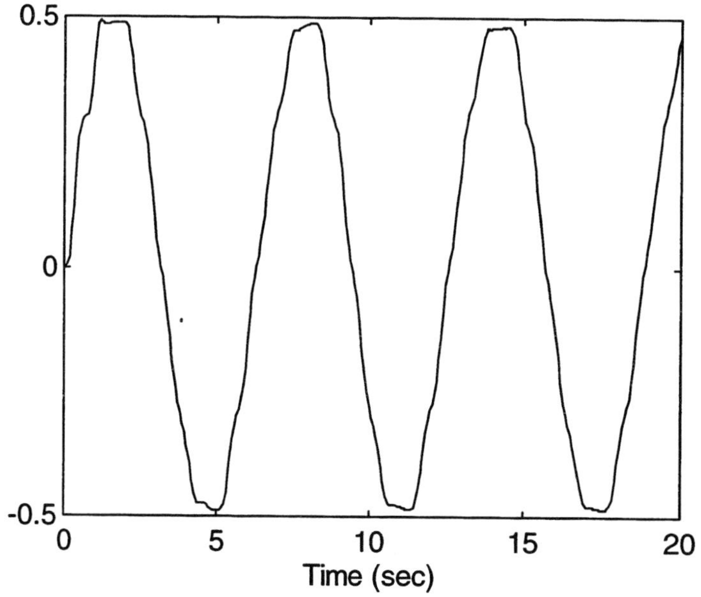

Problem 6.4

Now the nonlinear element is in the displacement feedback path. In this case, as simple f( ) block can be used since the relationship can be easily expressed in one line.

The modified block diagram:

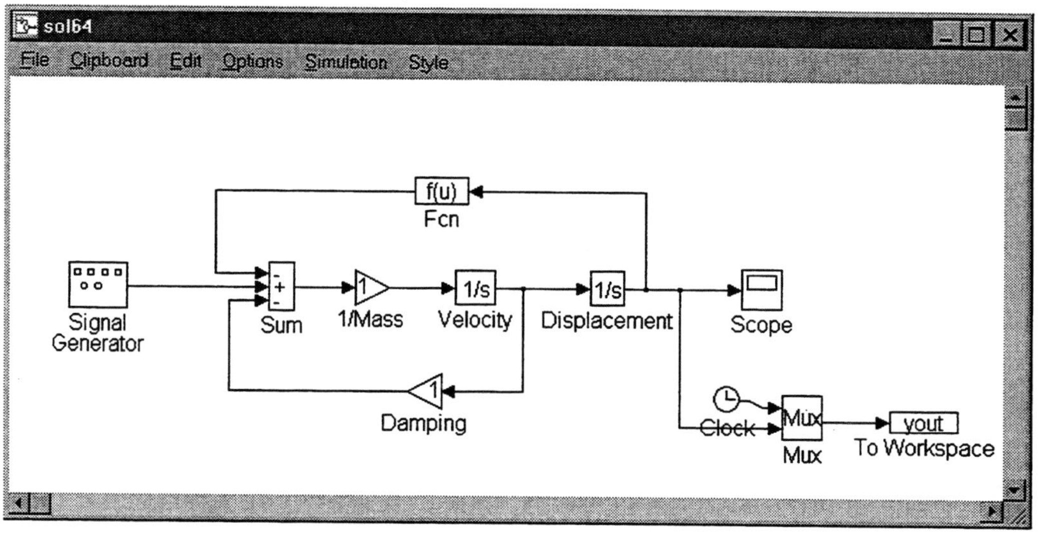

Set the cubic law by double-clicking on the f(u) block. Fill in the dialog box to look like this:

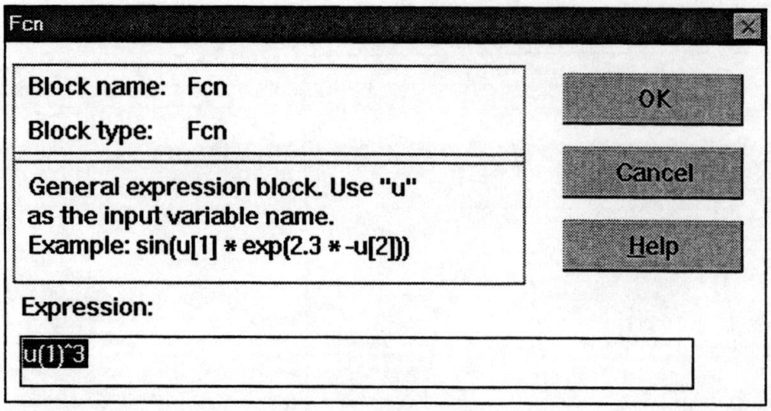

For fairly small inputs, the response looks rather linear. For example, if the input sine wave has a magnitude of 1.0, the response looks like this:

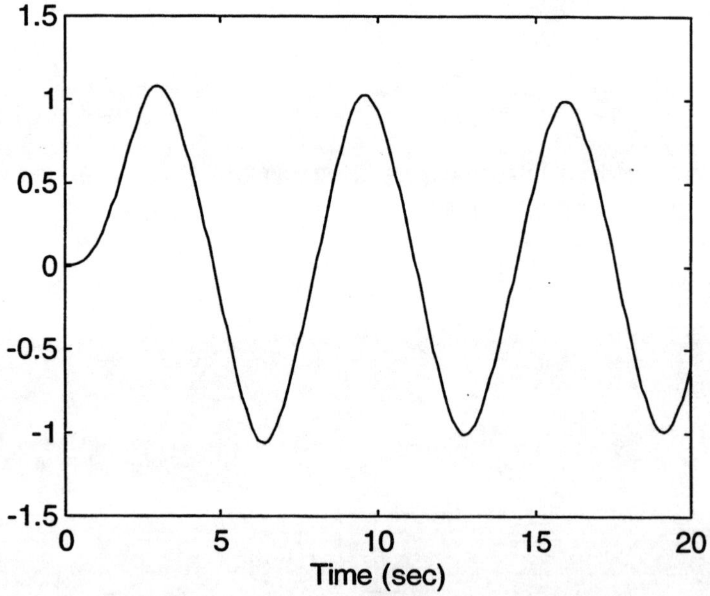

If, on the other hand, the magnitude is 10.0, then the response is:

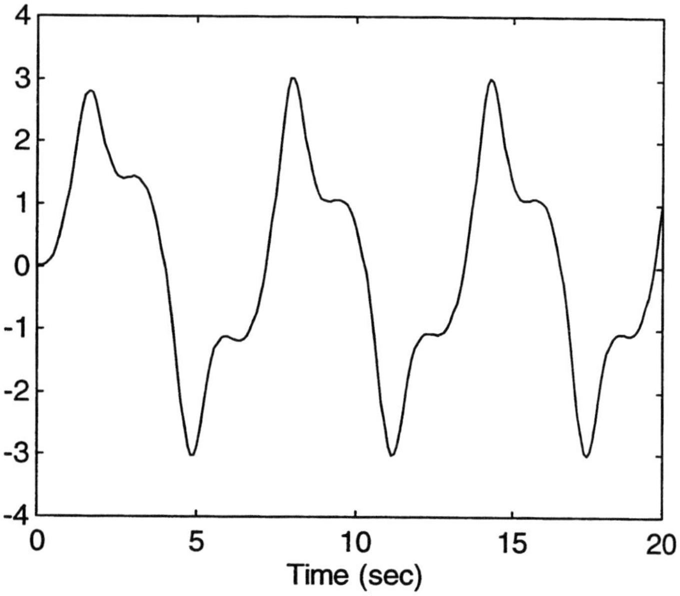

Which clearly shows the nonlinear nature of this system.

<u>Problem 6.5</u>

The quarter-car model shown in Problem 2.7 has two masses, therefore, the simulation requires 4 integrators. The figure below shows one possible solution for this problem. Note that the forces in the spring and tire are present in the block diagram. This, in my opinion, makes for a cleaner simulation and one that is easier to work with. It has been my experience that students will "over-manipulate" the equations before sitting down to do the block diagram and the forces will not explicitly appear in the simulation. One implication of this approach, aside from requiring many more blocks, is that the system parameters such as tire stiffness and damping constant, occur in more than one block. This makes parametric studies difficult.

The problem statement gave no parameter values, however students are encouraged to use their engineering judgment to find sets of parameters which are in the right ballpark for an automobile. One such set follows:

m_s = 500/386 (quarter-car model of a 1-ton automobile)
m_u = 80/386 (approximate mass of hub, wheel and tire)
k_s = 300 lb/in
k_t = 1200 lb/in (actually, the tire is highly nonlinear, this approximates its stiffness around the nominal load)

The damping factor (b_s) is a bit more problematic. You can encourage your students to recall their experience with automobiles. They should realize that automobile suspensions are underdamped, but not by much (one overshoot at most). Therefore, they can experiment with the simulation using step inputs, adjusting the damping factor to an appropriate value. (This technique is not far from the methods used by engineers is similar settings.) My experimentation leads to this value of b_s.

$b_s = 80$ lb sec/in.

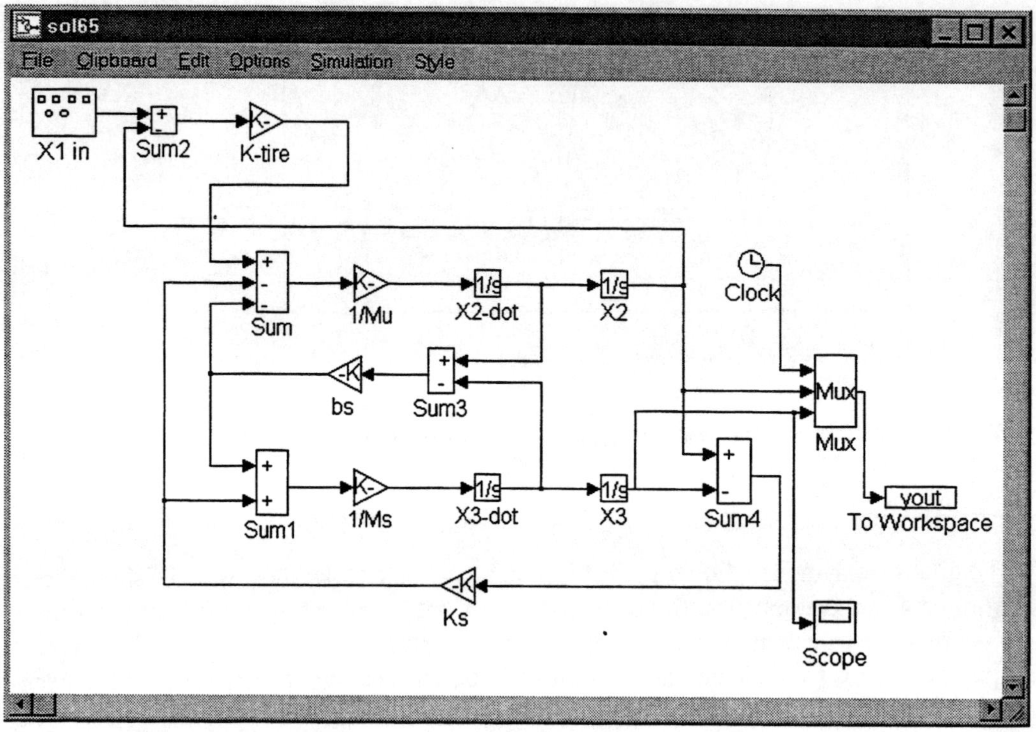

Adjusting the input to be a random noise function with nominal amplitude of 1 inch, the following response can be seen:

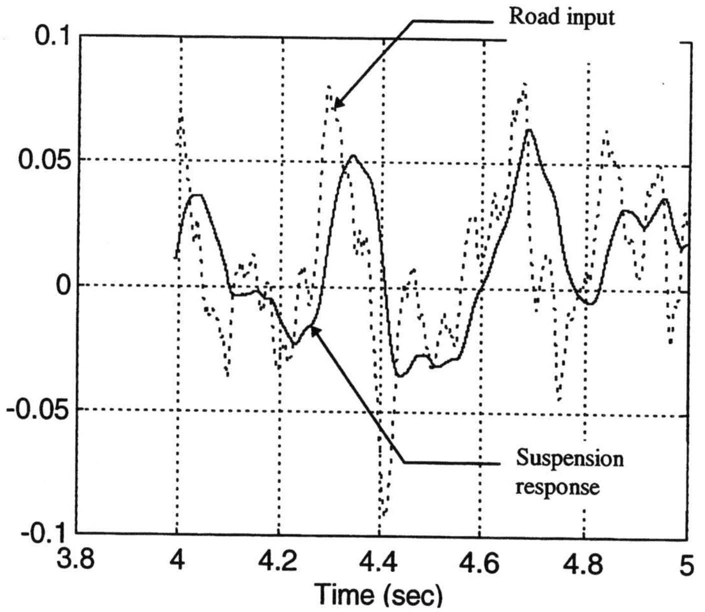

The simulation above assumes linear behavior of the springs and dampers. The last part of the problem asks the student to consider the case of suspension closing the spring to its solid height. It is possible to model this behavior as a piece-wise linear spring. SIMULINK has many ways of representing this kind of function. I will use a function m-file to carry it out. Replacing the Ks gain block with a function block, we can write an m-file to find fksnl.

```
function    [FNL]=fksnl(u)
%
%
%       u = relative displacement of spring where zero
%       relative displacement corresponds to the equilibrium
%       height of the spring
%
%       We assume that the spring has about 6 inches of useful
%       travel, after which it closes to solid height and then
%       exhibits a much higher stiffness.
%
if (u<=6),
        FNL=300.0*u;
elseif (u>6),
        FNL=300*6+10E6*(u-6);
end;
```

Problem 6.6

The system shown in Problem 2.8 is a third order system, although students are tempted to use four integrators because the shaft torque is a function of differential displacement. This can be avoided by making the torque itself a state of the system, as is the case below:

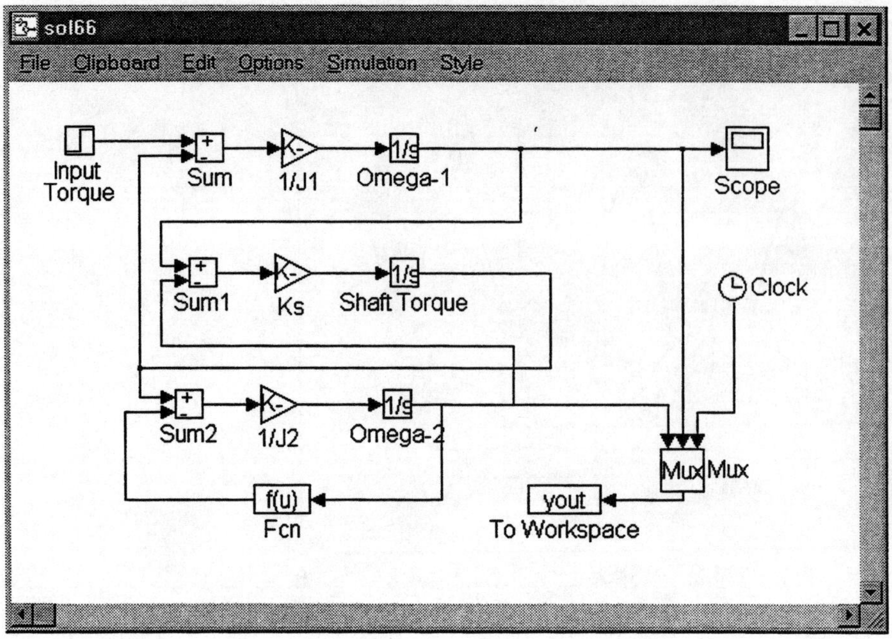

The nonlinear torque is computed in the Fcn block. The dialog box for that block is set up to look like this:

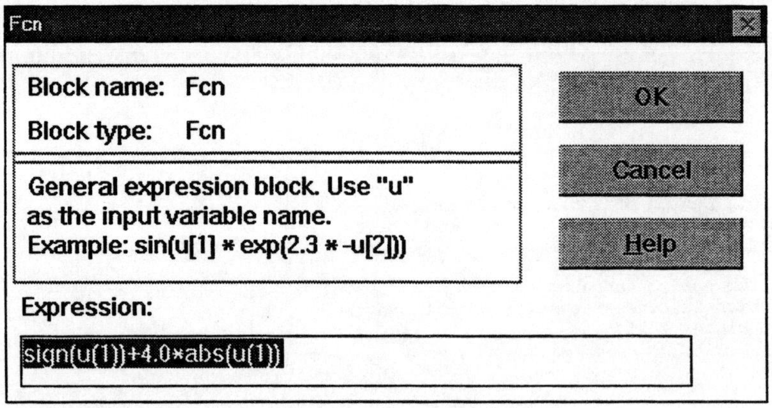

Note that no value was given for T_0 and it is assumed to be unity.

The family of step responses for C=0.5 to 5.0 is seen below:

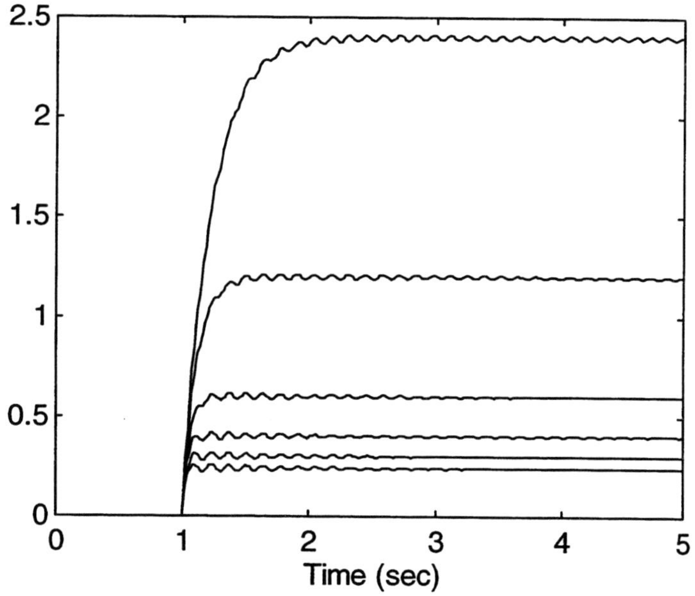
2.5
2
1.5
1
0.5
0
0
1
2
3
4
5
Time (sec)

CHAPTER 7

Problem 7.1

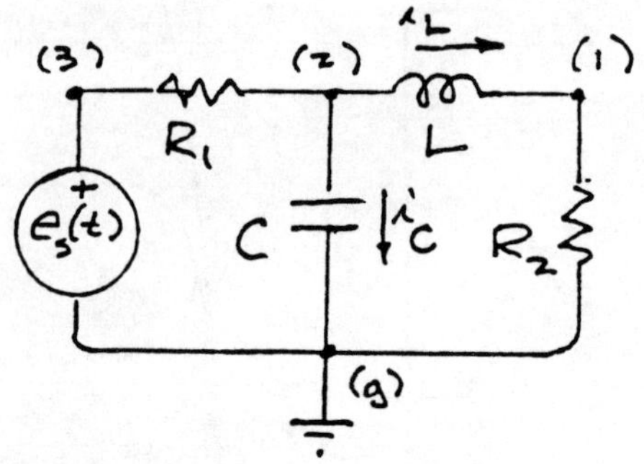

Because e_s has been zero for a long time, previous transients will have decayed and all variables at t=0- are zero. Thus there is no energy initially stored in either C or L. (An exceptional case would be that of an oscillatory system having zero damping, which obviously does not exist here.) Therefore $e_{32}(0-)=0$; $e_{1g}(0-)=0$

a) Since the step change in e_s only produces a sudden change in i_{R1}, which can only start to change e_{2g}, then $e_{2g}(0+)=e_{2g}(0-)=0$. Thus at t=0+, $e_{32}(0+) = e_s(0+) - e_{2g}(0+) =$ 10 volts.

b) To suddenly change the current i_L at t = 0 would require that e_{21} be infinite at t=0, an obvious impossibility, so $i_L(0+) = i_L(0-) = 0$, and $e_{1g}(0+) = R_2 i_L(0+) = 0$

Problem 7.2.

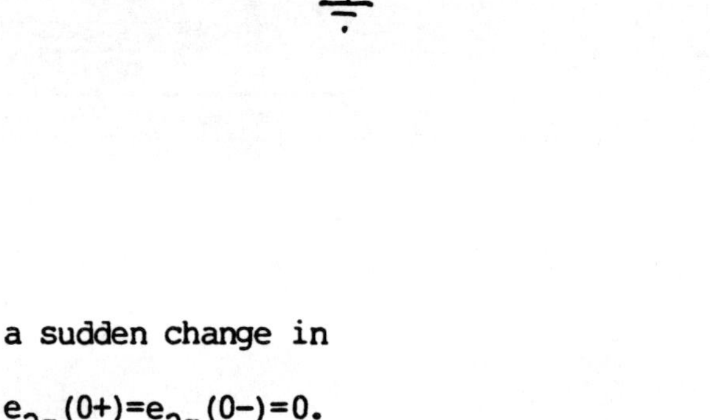

With e_s having been constant for a long time, all possible transients from previous inputs will have decayed, and all variables at t=0- will be constant.

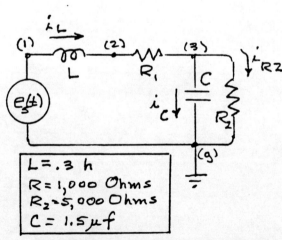

L=.3 h
R=1,000 Ohms
R_2=5,000 Ohms
C= 1.5μf

a) Since $i_L(0-)$ = constant, $e_{12}(0-) = 0$,

and since $e_{3g}(0-)$ = constant, $i_C(0-) = 0$.

Thus $i_L(0-) = i_{R1}(0-) = i_{R2}(0-) = e_s/(R_1+R_2) = 5.0/(6000)$ = .000833 amp.

1.0 h= 1.0 v-sec/a
1.0 Ohm= 1.0 v/a
1.0 f= 1.0 a-sec/v

Since there is no infinite source of voltage to change i_L at t=0,

$\underline{i_L(0+)} = i_L(0-) = \underline{.000833}$ $\underline{\text{amp.}}$

As t approaches infinity, all transients will have decayed so that

$e_{12}(\infty) = 0$ and $i_C(\infty) = 0$, and $\underline{i_L(\infty)} = e_s(\infty)/(R_1+R_2)$

$= 7.0/6000 = \underline{.001\ 67}$ $\underline{\text{amp.}}$

b) Furthermore $\underline{e_{3g}(0-)} = R_2 I_L(0-) = R_2 i_{R2}(0-) = 5000\text{x}(.000833)$

$= \underline{4.166}$ $\underline{\text{volts.}}$

Since there is no source of infinite current to change e_{3g} at t=0,

$\underline{e_{3g}(0+)} = e_{3g}(0-) = \underline{4.166}$ $\underline{\text{volts.}}$

As t approaches infinity, all transients will have decayed so that

$e_{12}(\infty) = 0$ and $i_C(\infty) = 0$, and $\underline{e_{3g}(\infty)} = e_s(\infty)R_2/(R_1+R_2) =$

$7.0\text{x}5000/6000 = \underline{5.833}$ $\underline{\text{volts.}}$

c) Since $e_{12}(0-) = 0$, $\underline{e_{2g}(0-)} = e_s(0-) = \underline{5.0}$ $\underline{\text{volts.}}$

Then $\underline{e_{2g}(0+)} = e_{3g}(0+) + e_{23}(0+) = 4.166 + R_1 i_{R1}(0+) =$

$4.166 + R_1 i_L(0+) = 4.166 + 1000\text{x}(.000833) = \underline{5}$ $\underline{\text{volts.}}$

Finally, since $e_{12}(\infty) = 0$, $\underline{e_{2g}(\infty)} = e_s(\infty) = \underline{7.0}$ $\underline{\text{volts.}}$

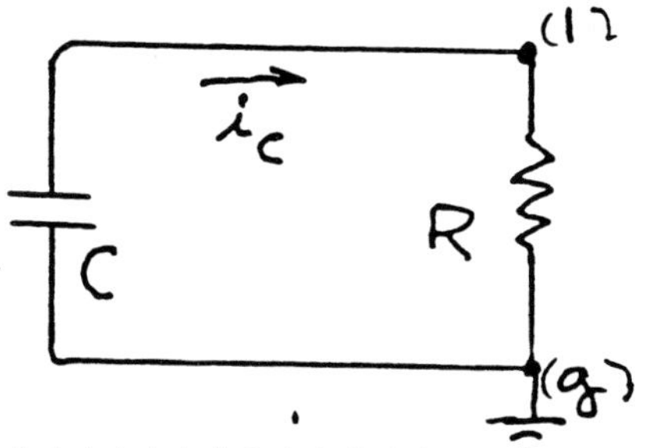

Problem 7.3.

Switch closes at t=0. Then the capacitor voltage at t=0+, $e_{1g}(0+) =$ 12.5 volts. The given data graphed vs. time reveals what appears to be a typical decaying exponential response having time constant tau = 35 sec.

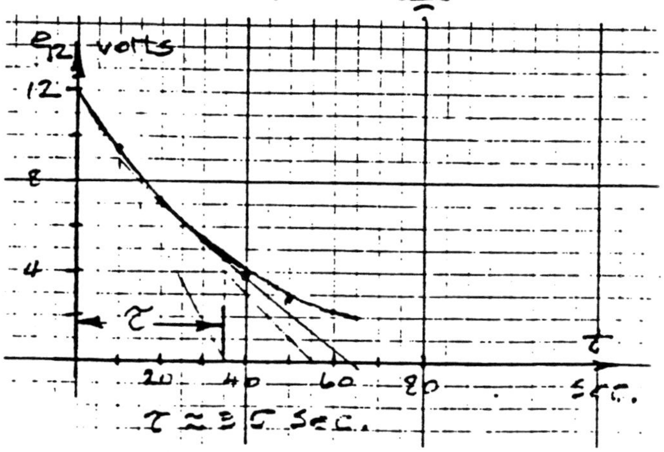

a) The system differential equation is derived from $i_C = Cde_{g1}/dt = e_{1g}/R$, and since $e_{g1} = -e_{1g}$, we obtain the homogeneous differential equation:

$$RCde_{1g}/dt + e_{1g} = 0$$

having time constant tau = RC . Equating RC with the experimentally determined value from the graph yields

$$C = tau/R = 35/10^5 = 3.5x10^{-6} \text{ f (or amp-sec/volt)}$$

Problem 7.4

The circuit diagram for t>0 and the graphed data are as follows:

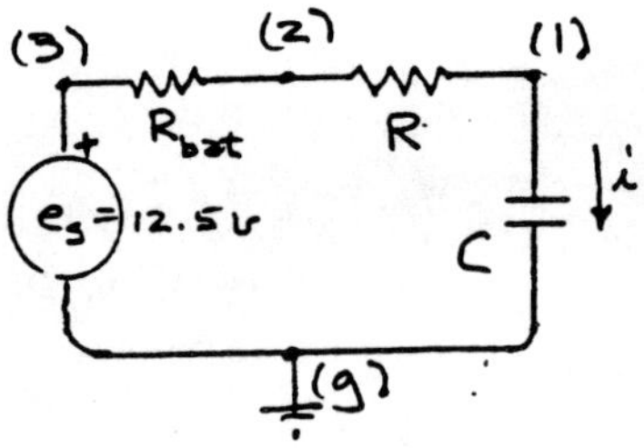

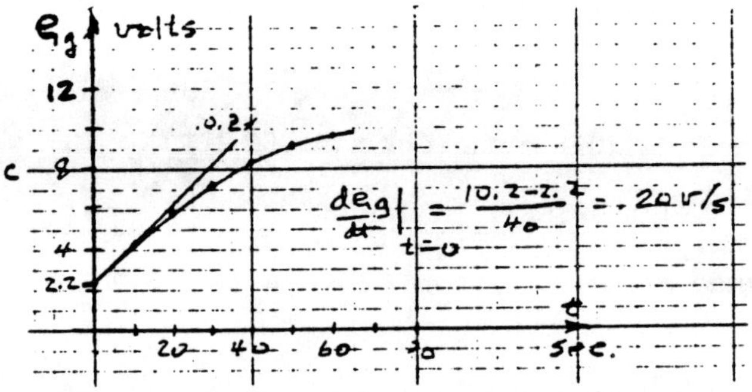

At t=0+, $e_{3g}(0+)$ = 12.5 v, and $e_{1g}(0+)$ = 2.2 v., (apparently from a left-over charge!)

For t>0, $e_s = (R_{bat}+R)i_C + e_{1g}$, where $i_C = Cde_{1g}/dt$, yielding the system differential equation:

$$(R_{bat}+R)Cde_{1g}/dt + e_{1g} = e_s$$

Solving for R_{bat},

$$\underline{R_{bat}} = -R + (1/C)(e_s - e_{1g}(0+))/de_{1g}/dt\Big|_{t=0+}$$

$$= -10^5 + (10^5/35)(10.3/.20)$$

$$= \underline{4.7x10^4 \text{ ohms}}$$

Problem 7.5

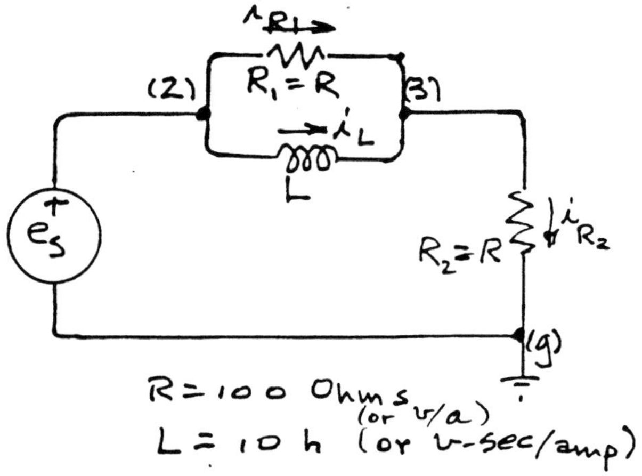

a) For L, $e_{23} = Ldi_L/dt$ . . (1)

For R_1, $e_{23} = R_1 i_{R1}$ . . (2)

For R_2, $e_{3g} = R_2 i_{R2}$ . . (3)

Kirchhoff's current law at node (3),

$i_{R2} = i_{R1} + i_L$ . . (4)

Kirchhoff's voltage law for outer loop,

$e_s = e_{23} + e_{3g}$ . . (5)

The above 5 equations contain the five unknowns e_{23}, e_{3g}, i_{R1}, i_L, and i_{R2}, from which we need to eliminate e_{23}, i_{R1}, i_L, and i_{R2}. First combine (1) and (4)

$e_{23} = Ld(i_{R2}-i_{R1})/dt$ . . (6)

Then combine (2), (3), and (6)

$e_{23} = (L/R_2)de_{3g}/dt - (L/R_1)de_{23}/dt$ . . (7)

Combine (7) and (5)

$e_s - e_{3g} = (L/R_2)de_{3g}/dt - (L/R_1)d(e_s-e_{3g})/dt$ . . (8)

Rearranging (8)

$L(1/R_1+1/R_2)de_{3g}/dt + e_{3g} = (L/R_1)de_s/dt + e_s$ . . (9)

b) Since e_s has been zero for a very long time, the system is initially relaxed at t=0−, so that all variables are zero and $di_L/dt\big|_{t=0-} = 0$. Thus $\underline{e_{3g}(0-)} = e_s(0-) = \underline{0}$.

At t=0+, $i_L(0+) = i_L(0-) = 0$ so that $i_{R2}(0+) = i_{R1}(0+)$.

From Kirchhoff's voltage law, for t=0+: $e_s(0+) = e_{23}(0+) + e_{3g}(0+)$

Substituting from (2) and (3) and solving for $i_{R2}(0+)$,

$i_{R2}(0+) = e_s(0+)/(R_1+R_2)$

Then solving the elemental equation (3) for $e_{3g}(0+)$,

$\underline{e_{3g}(0+)} = (R_2/(R_1+R_2))e_s(0+) = \underline{2.5\ v}$.

As $t \to \infty$, the system reaches a new equilibrium with all variables constant, so that $di_L/dt|_{t=\infty} = 0$, and $e_{23}(\infty) = 0$, leaving,

$\underline{e_{3g}(\infty)} = e_s(\infty) - e_{23}(\infty) = e_s(\infty) = \underline{5.0\ v.}$

c) The system time constant tau $= L(R_1+R_2)/(R_1R_2) =$

$4000/40000 = .1$ sec

The step response is then quickly sketched:

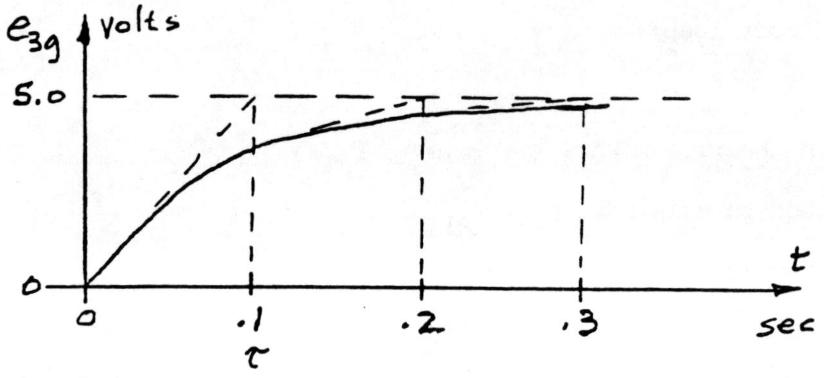

Problem 7.6

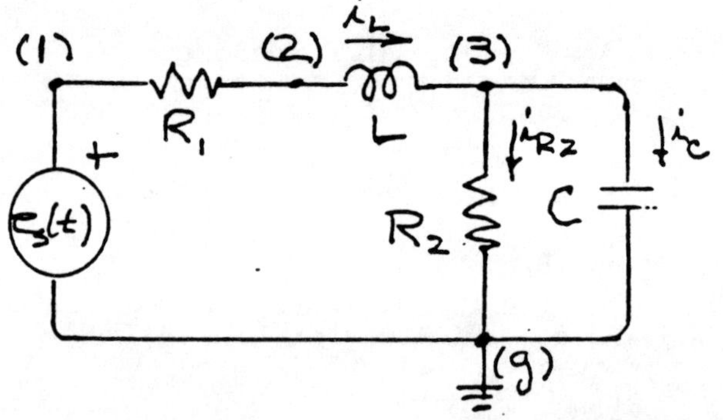

$R_1 = 2\ K = 2000$ Ohms

$R_2 = 8\ K$ (v/a)

$L = 27.6$ h (v-sec/a)

$C = 4.5\ \mu f$ μ(a-sec/v)

a) For R_1, $e_{12} = R_1 i_L$ . . (1)

For L, $e_{23} = L di_L/dt$ . . (2)

For R_2, $e_{3g} = R_2 i_{R2}$ . . (3)

For C, $i_C = C de_{3g}/dt$ . . (4)

Kirchhoff's current law,

$i_L = i_{R1} = i_{R2} + i_C$ . . (5)

Kirchhoff's voltage law,

$e_s = e_{12} + e_{23} + e_{3g}$ . . (6)

Combining (1), (2), and (6),

$L di_L/dt = e_s - R_1 i_L - e_{3g}$ . . (7)

Combining (3), (4), and (5),

$C de_{3g}/dt = i_L - (1/R_2) e_{3g}$ . . (8)

Combining (7) and (8) to eliminate i_L,

$L(Cd^2e_{3g}/dt^2+(1/R_2)de_{3g}/dt) = e_s - e_{3g} -$

$$R_1(Cde_{3g}/dt+(1/R_2)e_{3g}) \qquad . . (9)$$

Rearranging (9), and noting that $e_{3g} = e_o$,

$$\underbrace{LC}_{a_2}d^2e_o/dt^2 + \underbrace{[L/R_2 + R_1C]}_{a_1}de_o/dt + \underbrace{[(R_1+R_2)/R_2]}_{a_0}e_o = e_s$$

b) The undamped natural frequency is

$w_n = (a_0/a_2)^{.5} = [(R_1+R_2)/(R_2LC)]^{.5}$

$\underline{w_n} = [(10000)/(8000\text{x}27.6\text{x}4.5\text{x}10^{-6})]^{.5} = \underline{100.3}\ \underline{\text{rad/sec}}.$

The damping ratio is

zeta $= a_1/2(a_2a_0)^{.5} = (L+R_1R_2C)/2R_2[LC(R_1+R_2)/R_2]^{.5}$

$\underline{\text{zeta}} = (27.6+16\text{x}10^6\text{x}4.5\text{x}10^{-6})/(16000)[27.6\text{x}4.5\text{x}10^{-6}\text{x}10000/8000]^{.5}$

$= \underline{.5}$

c) No infinite sources, so

$\underline{i_1(0+)} = i_L(0-) = \underline{0}$

$\underline{e_o(0+)} = e_o(0-) = \underline{0}$

$\underline{de_o/dt}\Big|_{t=0+} = (1/C)[i_L(0+) - (1/R_2)e_o(0+)] = \underline{0}$

d) Then the sketched response of e_o vs. time t:

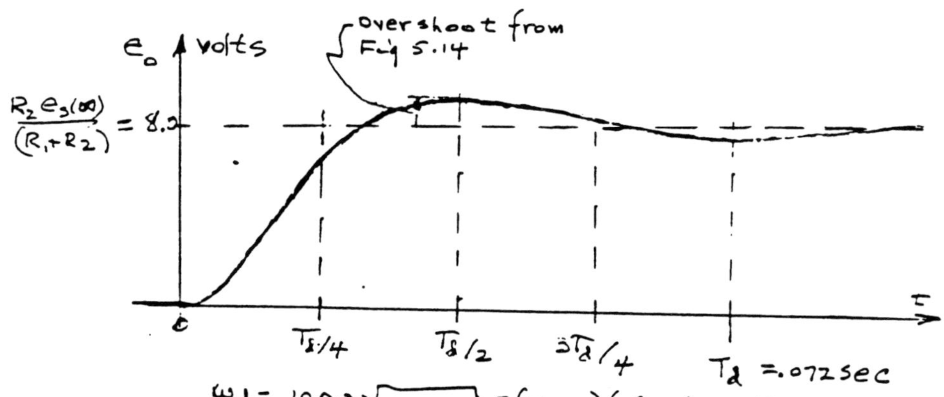

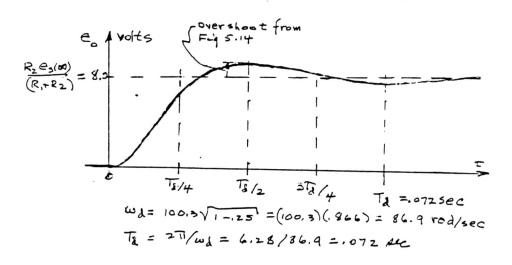

$\omega_d = 100.3\sqrt{1-.25} = (100.3)(.866) = 86.9$ rad/sec

$T_d = 2\pi/\omega_d = 6.28/86.9 = .072$ sec

Problem 7.7

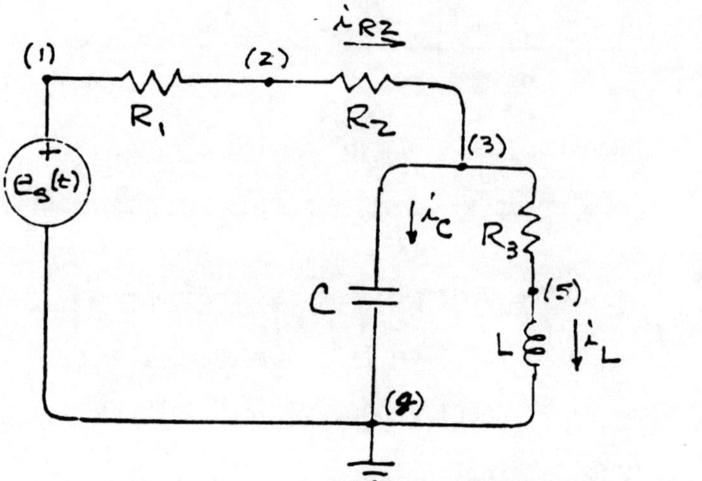

$R_1 = 80$ v/a
$R_2 = 320$ v/a
$L = 2.0$ v-sec/a
$C = 50 \times 10^{-6}$ a-sec/v

a) Starting with the elemental equation for C,

$Cde_{3g}/dt = i_C = i_{R2} - i_L =$

$(e_s - e_{3g})/(R_1+R_2) - i_L$ . . (1)

Then starting with the elemental equation for L,

$Ldi_L/dt = e_{5g} = e_{3g} - R_3 i_L$ . . (2)

Rearranging (1) and (2) yields the two state-variable equations:

$de_{3g}/dt = [-1/(R_1+R_2)C]e_{3g} + (-1/C)i_L + [1/(R_1+R_2)C]e_s$ . . (3)

$di_L/dt = (1/L)e_{3g} + (-R_3/L)i_L$ . . (4)

b) Since R_1 and R_2 are not completely independent, they may be lumped together into a single resistor $R_c = R_1+R_2$

Then the simulation blodk diagram is:

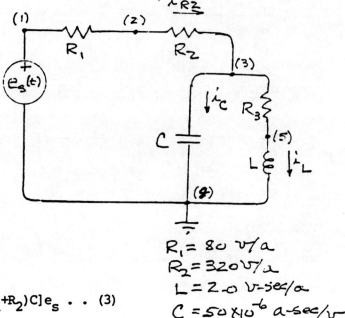

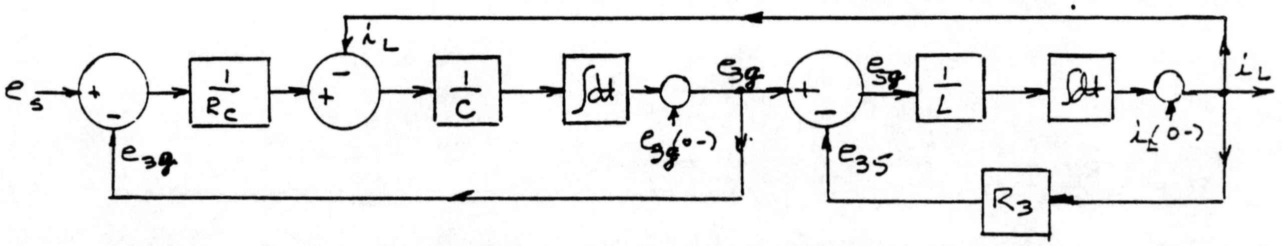

c) Combining (3) and (4) to eliminate i_L, yields the desired system differential equation:

$$Cd^2e_{3g}/dt^2 + [R_3C/L + (1/(R_1+R_2))]de_{3g}/dt + [1/L + (R_3/L(R_1+R_2))]e_{3g} =$$
$$[1/(R_1+R_2)]de_s/dt + [R_3/L(R_1+R_2)]e_s$$

d) At t=0- it is assumed that all previous transients have died away, hence $de_{34}/dt\big|_{t=0-} = 0$ and $di_L/dt\big|_{t=0-} = 0$.

It follows then that $i_C(0-) = 0$ and $e_{54}(0-) = 0$.

Then we may write,

$i_L(0-) = e_s(0-)/(R_1+R_2+R_3)$

and

$e_{34}(0-) = e_{35}(0-) = R_3 e_s(0-)/(R_1+R_2+R_3)$

Then, since e_{54} cannot be infinite at t = 0,

$\underline{i_L(0+)} = i_L(0-) = 5/(405) = \underline{.0123\ \text{amp}}$.

And since i_C cannot be infinite at t= 0,

$\underline{e_{34}(0+)} = e_{34}(0-) = 5x5/405 = \underline{.0617\ v}$.

At t=0+, the current $i_C(0+) = i_{R2}(0+) - i_L(0+)$, or

$i_C(0+) = [1/(R_1+R_2)](e_s(0+) - e_{34}(0+)) - e_s(0-)/(R_1+R_2+R_3)$

$\underline{i_C(0+)} = (1/400)(2 - .0617) - 5/405 = \underline{.00746\ \text{amp}}$.

$\underline{de_{34}/dt}\big|_{t=0+} = (1/C)i_C(0+) = -.00746/5x10^{-5} = \underline{-149.2\ \text{volts/sec}}$.

e) In order to sketch the response of e_{34} to the step decrease in e_s, we need the above-determined initial conditions plus the final value of e_{34} and the natural frequency and damping ratio of this second-order system.

As t approaches infinity, after the transient has died away, $i_C(\infty) = 0$, and $e_{54}(\infty) = 0$, so that the final value of e_{34} is:

$\underline{e_{34}(\infty)} = R_3 e_s/(R_1+R_2+R_3) = 5x2/405 = \underline{.0247\ v}$. [2/5 of.0617]

The undamped natural frequency is:

$\underline{w_n} = [(R_1+R_2+R_3)/LC(R_1+R_2)]^{.5} = [405/(2x5x10^{-5}x400)]^{.5}$

$= \underline{100.6\ \text{rad/sec}}$.

The damping ratio zeta is given by:

zeta = $[L+R_3C(R_1+R_2)]/\{2L(R_1+R_2)$

$[C(R_1+R_2+R_3)/(L(R_1+R_2)]^{.5}\}$

$= (2.+5x5x10^{-5}x400)/(2x2x400)\ (5x10^{-5}x405/2x400)^{.5}$

<u>zeta</u> = <u>.082</u>

The damped natural frequency is:

$\underline{w_d} = w_n(1-\text{zeta}^2)^{.5} = 100.6x(1-.0064)^{.5} = 100.6x(1-.0032) =$

$= 100.6x.9968 =$ <u>100.2</u> <u>rad/sec.</u>

The period of the underdamped oscillation is:

$\underline{T_d} = 2xPi/w_d = 6.28/100.2 =$ <u>.0627</u> <u>sec.</u>

Now the response is easily sketched from the parameters just calculated:

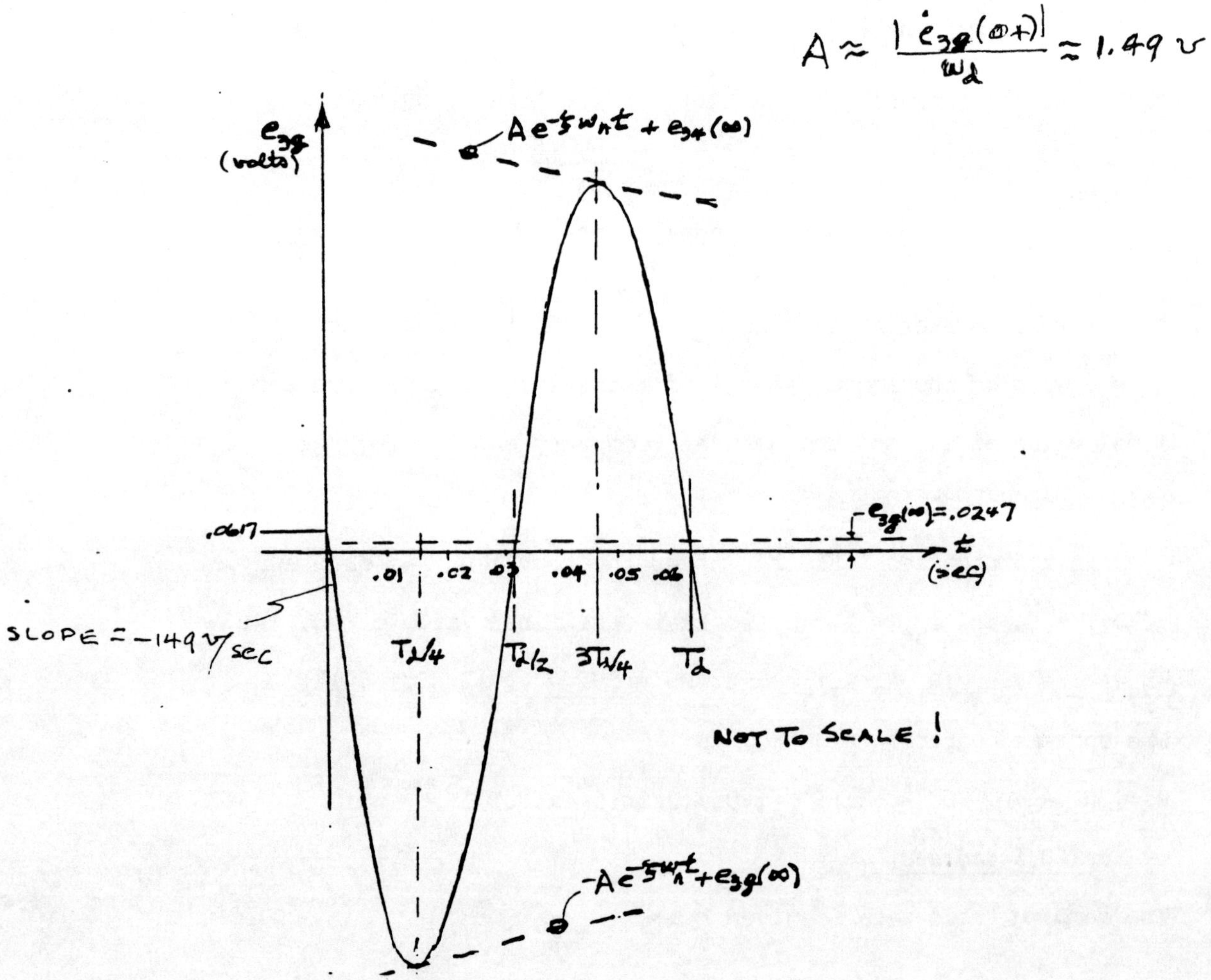

Problem 7.8.

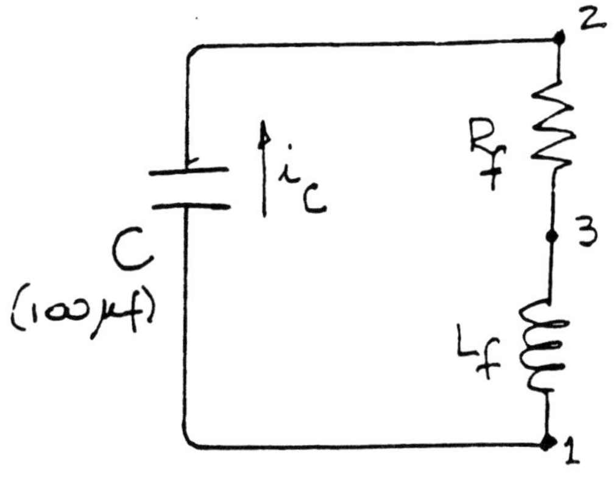

a) The circuit diagram shows the lumped resistance and lumped inductance in series because there is only a single current flowing through a single path (only one winding with a terminal at each end), in other words the resistance and inductance are occuring along the same single wire.

b) For C, $i_C = Cde_{12}/dt$ . . (1)

For R_f, $e_{23} = R_f i_{Rf} = R_f i_C$ . . (2)

For L_f, $e_{31} = Ldi_L/dt = Ldi_C/dt$ . . (3)

K's voltage law for loop,

$e_{12} + e_{23} + e_{31} = 0$ . . (4)

Starting with (4), (2), and (3),

$e_{12} = -e_{23} - e_{31} = - R_f i_C - Ldi_C/dt$ . . (5)

Now substituting for i_C from (1),

$e_{12} = -R_f Cde_{12}/dt - LCd^2e_{12}/dt^2$ . . . (6)

Rearranging (6),

$LCd^2e_{12}/dt^2 + R_f Cde_{12}/dt + e_{12} = 0$ . . (7)

c) The undamped natural frequency w_n is,

$w_n = (1/LC)^{.5}$ . . (8)

The damping ratio zeta is,

$zeta = R_f C/[2(LC)^{.5}]$ . . (9)

The per-cycle decay ratio is,

$DR = e^{-(zeta)w_n T_{per}}$

Substituting for DR = .8 and T_{per} = .18,
$-(\text{zeta})w_n(.18) = \ln(.8)$

or $(\text{zeta})w_n = -\ln(.8)/.18 = 1.24$ . . (10)

From (8) and (9) we also know that,

$(\text{zeta})w_n = R_f/2L$ . . (11)

So that,

$R_f/L = 2.48$ . . (12)

→ for later use

Now the damped natural frequency w_d is,

$w_d = w_n(1-\text{zeta}^2)^{.5} = 2x\text{Pi}/T_{per}$

$= 6.28/.18 = 34.9$ rad/sec . . (13)

or $w_n = w_d/(1-\text{zeta}^2)^{.5}$

Multiplying both sides by zeta yields the equation for zeta,

$(\text{zeta})w_d/(1-\text{zeta}^2)^{.5} = (\text{zeta})w_n$

Now since we have a numerical value for $(\text{zeta})w_n$ from (11) and w_d from (13), we have the equation needed to solve for zeta,

$34.9(\text{zeta}) = 1.24(1-\text{zeta}^2)^{.5}$

or $(34.9)^2(\text{zeta})^2 = (1.24)^2(1-\text{zeta}^2)$

or $\text{zeta} = 1.24/(34.9^2 + 1.24^2)^{.5} \doteq 1.24/34.92$

$= .036$

and $\text{zeta}^2 = .0013$

Finally we can now solve for L using

$L = (1/C)(1/w_n^2) = (1-\text{zeta}^2)/[C(w_d^2)]$

$= (1 - .0013)/(34.9^2 x 10^{-4}) = .9987/.1218$

<u>L = 8.2 h (or volt-sec/amp)</u>

and from (12) <u>R</u> = 2.48 L = <u>20.3 ohms (or volt/amp)</u>

Problem 7.9.

a) At the N. O. point, $\overline{i_C} = 0$,

and $\overline{e_{3g}} = 0$, so that

$\overline{e_{12}}+\overline{e_{23}} = R_1\overline{i_{NLR}}+3.0\text{x}10^6\overline{i_{NLR}}^3 = \overline{e_s} = 5.0$

Rearranging,

$3\text{x}10^6\overline{i_{NLR}}^3 + 400\overline{i_{NLR}} = 5$ . . (1)

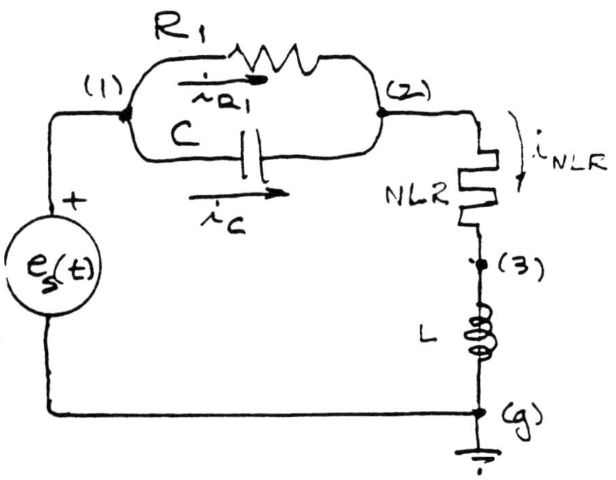

Solving (1) by a simple iteration,

$\overline{i_{NLR}} = 5/(400 + 3\text{x}10^6\overline{i_{NLR}}^2)$

which begins by using $\overline{i_{NLR}} = 5/400$ on the right-hand side to start with:

next $\overline{i_{NLR}} = 5/(400 + 3\text{x}10^6\text{x}(.0125)^2) = 5/(400 + 468.8)$

$= .0058$

next $\overline{i_{NLR}} = 5/(400 + 3\text{x}10^6\text{x}(.0058)^2) = .00998$

next $\overline{i_{NLR}} = 5/(400 + 3\text{x}10^6\text{x}(.01)^2) = .007$

etc. which converges in a few steps to ,

$\overline{i_{NLR}} = .008266$ . . (2)

$R_{inc} = 9\text{x}10^6\text{x}\overline{i_{NLR}}^2 = 9\text{x}10^6\text{x}(.008266)^2$

$\underline{R_{inc} = 614.7 \text{ ohms (or volt/amp)}}$ . . (3)

b) Starting with C, using the elemental and K's law eqns.,

$de_{12}/dt = (1/C)i_C = (1/C)(i_{NLR} - i_{R1})$

$= (-1/R_1C)e_{12} + (1/C)i_{NLR}$ . . (4) ← S-V Eqn. 1

Then going ahead with L, and appropriate elemental and K's law eqns.

$di_{NLR}/dt = (1/L)e_{3g} = (1/L)(e_s-e_{12}-e_{23})$

$= (-1/L)e_{12}+(-3\text{x}10^6/L)i_{NLR}^3+(1/L)e_s$ . . (5) ← S-V Eqn. 2

Linearizing (4) and (5),

$d\hat{e}_{12}/dt = (-1/R_1C)\hat{e}_{12} + (1/C)\hat{i}_{NLR}$ . . (6)

$d\hat{i}_{NLR}/dt = (-1/L)\hat{e}_{12} + (-R_{inc})\hat{i}_{NLR} + (1/L)\hat{e}_s$ . . (7)

Combining (6) and (7) to eliminate $\hat{i}_{NLR}$,

$$Cd^2\hat{e}_{12}/dt^2 + [1/R_1 + R_{inc}C/L]d\hat{e}_{12}/dt +$$
$$[1/L + R_{inc}/R_1L]\hat{e}_{12} = (1/L)\hat{e}_s \quad . . (8)$$

From here on it will help to use,

$a_2 = C = 5x10^{-6}$ amp-sec/volt

$a_1 = [1/R_1 + R_{inc}C/L] = 3.52x10^{-3}$ amp/volt

$a_0 = [1/L + R_{inc}/R_1L] = .845$ amp/volt-sec

c) The undamped natural frequency w_n is

$\underline{w_n} = (a_0/a_2)^{.5} = \underline{411\ rad/sec}$

The damping ratio zeta is

$\underline{zeta} = a_1/[2(a_2a_0)^{.5} = \underline{.853}$

The damped natural frequency is

$\underline{w_d} = w_n(1-zeta^2)^{.5} = .51w_n = \underline{214.2\ rad/sec}$

Since the output is $\hat{e}_{2g} = \hat{e}_s - \hat{e}_{12}$, the differential equation for $\hat{e}_{2g}$ is

$$a_2d^2\hat{e}_{2g}/dt^2 + a_1d\hat{e}_{2g}/dt + a_0\hat{e}_{2g} =$$
$$a_2d^2\hat{e}_s/dt^2 + a_1d\hat{e}_s/dt + [a_0-(1/L)]\hat{e}_s \quad . . (9)$$

To complete the analytical solution, we need to know the values of $e_{2g}(0+)$ and $de_{2g}/dt\big|_{t=0+}$.

Since e_{12} cannot change in zero time because i_C cannot become infinite at t=0,

$\underline{e_{2g}(0+)} = e_s(0+)-e_{12}(0-) = e_s(0+) = \underline{.5\ volt}$

Since $i_{NLR} = i_L$ cannot change in zero time because e_{3g} cannot become infinite at t=0,

$i_{NLR}(0+) = i_{NLR}(0-) = 0$

Then from K's current law at node (2),

$$i_C(0+) = i_{NLR}(0+) - i_{R1}(0+) = i_{NLR}(0+) - e_{12}(0+)/R_1$$

and because $e_{12}(0+) = 0$,

$$i_C(0+) = 0 - 0 = 0$$

and $de_{2g}/dt|_{t=0+} = de_s/dt|_{t=0+} - de_{12}/dt|_{t=0+}$

$$= 0 - (1/C)i_C(0+)$$

$$\underline{de_{2g}/dt|_{t=0+} = 0}$$

The solution for $\hat{e}_{2g}$ is of the form:

$$\hat{e}_{2g}(t) = A_0 + Ae^{-(zeta)w_n t}\cos(w_d t + \phi)$$

where the particular solution $A_0 = [(a_0-(1/L))/a_0]\hat{e}_s(0+)$

$$A_0 = (R_{inc}/R_1L)/[(R_1+R_{inc})/R_1L]\hat{e}_s(0+)$$

$$A_0 = [R_{inc}/(R_1+R_{inc})]\hat{e}_s(0+)$$

$$\underline{A_0} = [615/(400+615)]x.5 = \underline{.303\ volt}$$

At t=0+,

$$\hat{e}_{2g}(0+) = A_0 + A\cos\phi = .5 \text{ volt}$$

$$\underline{A\cos\phi} = .5 - .303 = \underline{.197\ volt}$$

$$de_{2g}/dt|_{t=0+} = 0 + Ae^0\sin\phi + A\cos\phi[-(zeta)w_n]e^0$$

$$0 = A\sin\phi + A\cos\phi[-(zeta)w_n]$$

$$\tan\phi = 1/[(zeta)w_n]$$

$$\underline{\phi} = \tan^{-1}[1/(zeta)w_n] = \underline{.0028\ rad}$$

And now for A:

$$\underline{A} = .197/\cos 0 = .197/.999996 = \underline{.197\ volt}$$

(CONTINUED ON NEXT PAGE)

The response is sketched as follows:

$$\bar{e}_{2g} = \bar{e}_s - R_i \bar{i}_{NLR}$$
$$= 1.69 \, v.$$
$$T_d = \frac{2\pi}{\omega_d} = \frac{6.28}{2.09}$$
$$= .03 \, sec$$

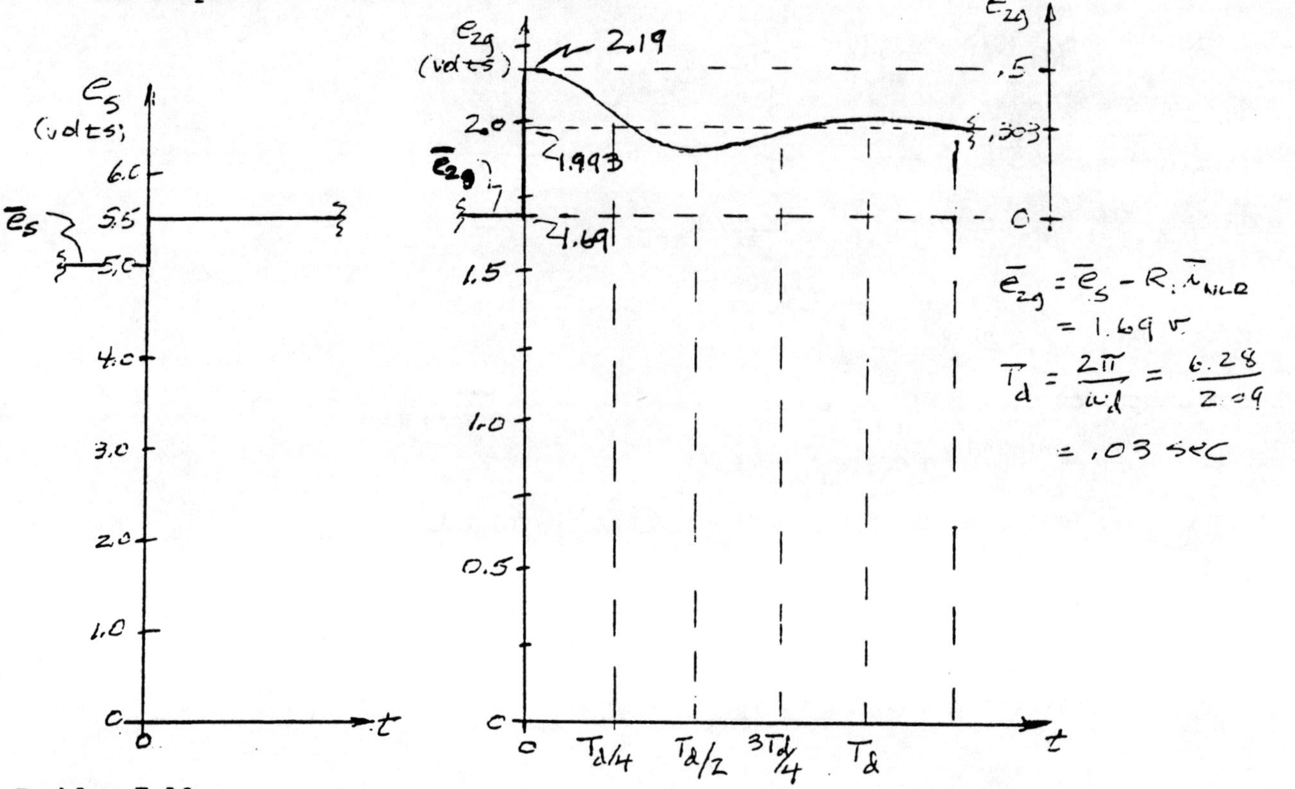

Problem 7.10.

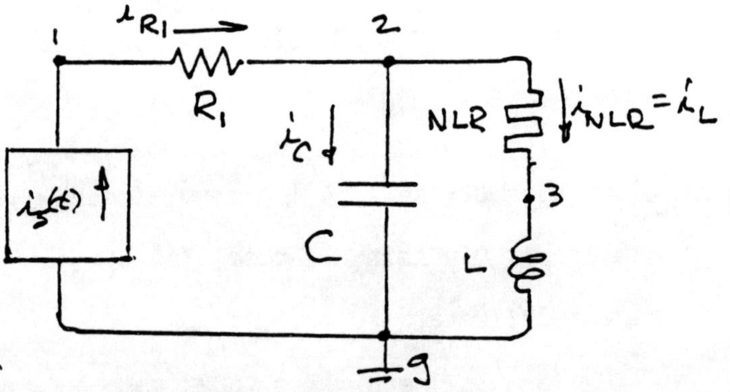

a) For C, $i_C = C \, de_{2g} \, dt$ . . (1)

For 1, $i_{R1} = e_{12}/R_1$ . . (2)

For NLR, $e_{23} = K_{NLR}(i_{NLR}{}^3)$ . . (3)

For L, $e_{3g} = L \, di_{NLR}/dt$ . . (4)

K's current law at node (2) is

$$i_{R1} = i_C + i_{NLR} \quad . . (5)$$

(Node (3) is taken care of by using i_{NLR} for i_L in (3), (4), and

(5).)

K's voltage law for the inner loop is,

$$e_{2g} = e_{23} + e_{3g} \quad . . (6)$$

(Outer loop is irrelevant here because there is no need to solve for

e_{1g} here.

Noting that $i_{R1} = i_s$ and starting with (1) and (2),

$de_{2g}/dt = (1/C)(i_s - i_{NLR})$

$de_{2g}/dt = 0 x e_{2g} + (-1/C) i_{NLR} + (1/C) i_s$ . . (7) ← S-V Eqn. 1

Then using (4), (6), and (3),

$di_{NLR}/dt = (1/L)(e_{2g} - e_{23}) = e_{2g}/L - (K_{NLR}/L)(i_{NLR}^3)$

or $di_{NLR}/dt = (1/L)e_{2g} + (-K_{NLR}/L)(i_{NLR}^3)$ . . (8) ← S-V Eqn. 2

b) At the N.O. point, given $\bar{e}_{12} = 1.2$v, $\bar{e}_{23} = 3.75$ v, find R_1 and $\bar{i}_{NLR}$.

The set of N.O.P. conditions must satisfy the following:

$\bar{i}_C = 0$; $\bar{e}_{3g} = 0$; $\bar{i}_{R1} = \bar{i}_s = \bar{i}_{NLR}$; $\bar{e}_{1g} = \bar{e}_{12} + \bar{e}_{23}$.

From (3) and given data,

$\bar{i}_{NLR}^3 = \bar{e}_{23}/10^7 = 3.75 x 10^{-7}$

$\bar{i}_{NLR} = (3.75 x 10^{-7})^{1/3}$ = <u>.00722 amp.</u>

From (2), and noting that $\bar{i}_{R1} = \bar{i}_s$,

$R_1 = \bar{e}_{12}/\bar{i}_s = 1.2/.00722$ = <u>166.2 ohms</u> (or volt/amp)

c) Linearizing (7) and (8),

$d\hat{e}_{2g}/dt = + (-1/C)\hat{i}_{NLR} + (1/C)\hat{i}_s$ . . (9)

$d\hat{i}_{NLR}/dt = (1/L)\hat{e}_{2g} + (-3K_{NLR}\bar{i}_{NLR}^2/L)\hat{i}_{NLR}$ . . (10)

d) The simulation block diagram for the linearized system is then drawn as follows:

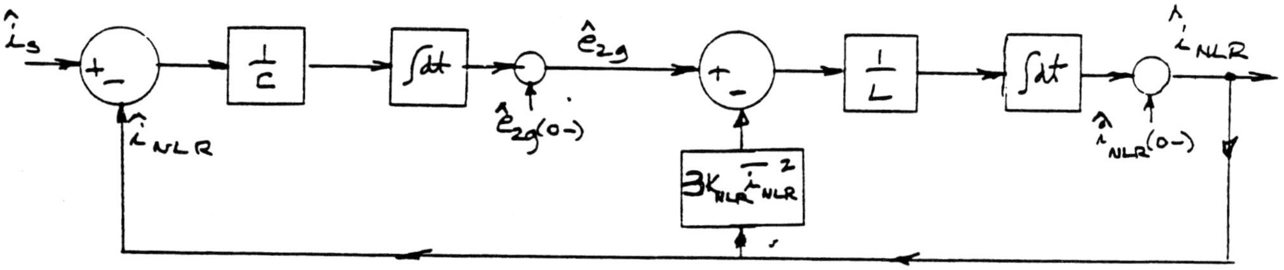

Problem 7.11.

a) For L, $e_{12} = L\, di_L/dt$ . . (1)

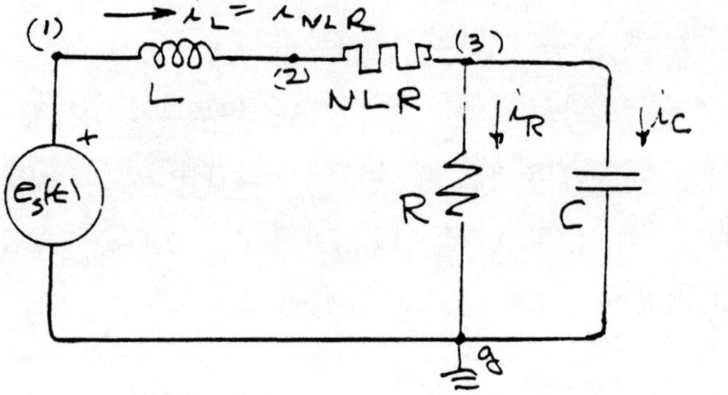

For NLR, using $i_L = i_{NLR}$,

$e_{23} = K|i_L|\, i_L$ . . (2)

For R, $i_R = e_{3g}/R$ . . (3)

For C, $i_C = C de_{3g}/dt$ . . (4)

K's current law for node (3),

$i_L = i_R + i_C$ . . (5)

K's voltage law for outer loop,

$e_s = e_{12} + e_{23} + e_{3g}$ . . (6)

Starting with (4), (5), and (3),

$de_{3g}/dt = (1/C)(i_L - i_R) = (1/C)(i_L - e_{3g}/R)$

or $de_{3g}/dt = (-1/CR)e_{3g} + (1/C)i_L$ . . (7) ← S-V Eqn. 1

Then proceeding with (1), (6), and (2),

$di_L/dt = (1/L)(e_s - e_{23} - e_{3g})$

or $di_L/dt = (-1/L)e_{3g} + (-K/L)|i_L|\, i_L + (1/L)e_s$ . . (8) ← S-V Eqn. 2

b) The incremental resistance R_{inc} is,

$R_{inc} = de_{23}/di_{NLR}\big|_{\bar{i}_{NLR}} = 2K|\bar{i}_{NLR}|$

c) Linearizing (7) and (8),

$d\hat{e}_{3g}/dt = (-1/CR)\hat{e}_{3g} + (1/C)\hat{i}_L$ . . (9)

$d\hat{i}_L/dt = (-1/L)\hat{e}_{3g} + (-R_{inc}/L)\hat{i}_L + (1/L)\hat{e}_s$ . . (10)

d) The simulation block diagram is as follows:

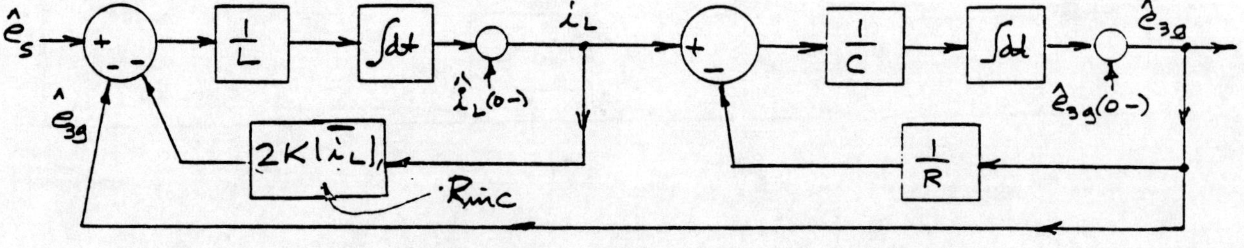

e) Combining (9) and (10) to eliminate i_L,

$$C d^2\hat{e}_{3g}/dt^2 + [(1/R) + (R_{inc}\, C/L)]d\hat{e}_{3g}/dt + [(1/L) + (R_{inc}/LR)]\hat{e}_{3g} = (1/L)\hat{e}_s$$

Problem 7.12.

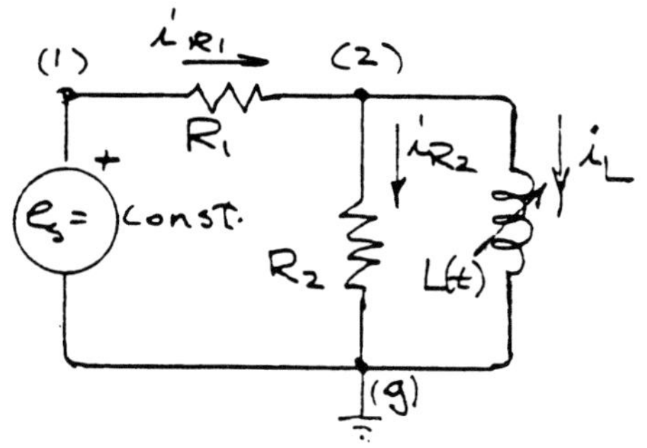

$L(t) = \bar{L} + \hat{L}(t) = 1.0 + 0.1 \sin 5t$

$e_{2g} \equiv d\lambda_{2g}/dt$

a) For L, $\lambda_{2g} = L(t)i_L$ . . (1)

For R_1, $i_{R1} = e_{12}/R_1$ . . (2)

For R_2, $i_{R2} = e_{2g}/R_2$ . . (3)

K's current law at node (2),

$i_{R1} = i_{R2} + i_L$ . . (4)

K's voltage law for either loop,

$e_s = e_{12} + e_{2g}$ . . (5)

Identity for λ_{2g},

$e_{2g} \equiv d\lambda_{2g}/dt$ . . (6)

Starting with (6), then (3), (4), (5), and (1),

$$\begin{aligned} d\lambda_{2g}/dt = e_{2g} &= R_2 i_{R2} = R_2(i_{R1} - i_L) \\ &= R_2[(e_s - e_{2g})/R_1 - \lambda_{2g}/L(t)] \\ &= (-R_2/R_1)e_{2g} + (-R_2/L(t))\lambda_{2g} + (R_2/R_1)e_s \end{aligned}$$

Noting that $e_{2g} \equiv d\lambda_{2g}/dt$, and rearranging,

$$d\lambda_{2g}/dt = [-R_2R_1/(R_1+R_2)]\lambda_{2g}/L(t) + [R_2/(R_1+R_2)]e_s \quad . . (7)$$

b) At the N.O. point, $d\lambda_{2g}/dt=0$; $\bar{e}_{2g}=0$; $L(t) = \bar{L}$, so that from (7),

$(R_2/\bar{L})\bar{\lambda}_{2g} = (R_2/R_1)e_s$

or $\underline{\bar{\lambda}_{2g}} = (\bar{L}/R_1)e_s = 1x6/12000 = \underline{.0005 \text{ volt-sec}}$

from (1), $\underline{\bar{i}_L} = \bar{\lambda}_{2g}/\bar{L} = e_s/R_1 = 6/12000 = \underline{.0005 \text{ amp}}$

$\underline{\bar{e}_{12}} = e_s = \underline{6\ v.}$

Linearizing (7) and noting that $e_s = 0$,

$$d\hat{\lambda}_{2g}/dt = [-R_1R_2/(R_1+R_2)\bar{L}]\hat{\lambda}_{2g}$$
$$+ [R_1R_2\bar{\lambda}_{2g}/(R_1+R_2)\bar{L}^2]\hat{L}(t) \quad . . (8)$$

c) Differentiating (8) with respect to time,

$$d\hat{e}_{2g}/dt + [R_1R_2/(R_1+R_2)\bar{L}]\hat{e}_{2g} =$$
$$[R_1R_2\bar{\lambda}_{2g}/(R_1+R_2)\bar{L}^2]d\hat{L}/dt \quad . . (9)$$

Problem 7.13.

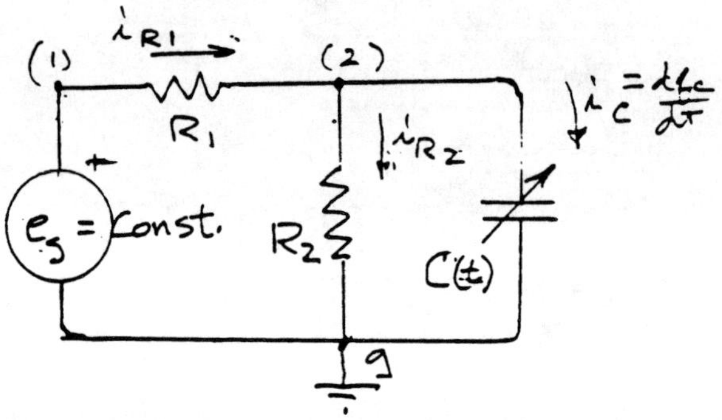

a) For C(t), $q_C = C(t)e_{2g}$ . . (1)

For R_1, $i_{R1} = e_{12}/R_1$ . . (2)

For R_2, $i_{R2} = e_{2g}/R_2$ . . (3)

K's current law,

$i_{R1} = i_{R2} + i_C$ . . (4)

K's voltage law,

$e_s = e_{12} + e_{2g}$ . . (5)

Identity for q_C,

$dq_C/dt \equiv i_C$ . . (6)

Starting with (6), then (4), (2), and (3),

$$dq_C/dt = i_C = i_{R1} - i_{R2} = e_{12}/R_1 - e_{2g}/R_2$$
$$= (e_s - e_{2g})/R_1 - e_{2g}/R_2$$

Noting that $e_{2g} = q_C/C(t)$,

$$dq_C/dt = [-(R_1+R_2)/R_1R_2]q_C/C(t) + e_s/R_1 \quad . . (7)$$

b) Linearizing (7) and noting that $e_s = 0$,

$$d\hat{q}_C/dt = [-(R_1+R_2)/R_1R_2\bar{C}]\hat{q}_C +$$
$$[(R_1+R_2)\bar{q}_C/R_1R_2\bar{C}^2]\hat{C}(t) \quad . . (8)$$

c) To obtain d. e. for e_{2g}, we need to linearize (1),

$$\hat{q}_C = \bar{C}\hat{e}_{2g} + \bar{e}_{2g}\hat{C}(t) \quad . . (9)$$

and the derivative with respect to time,

$$d\hat{q}_C/dt = \bar{C}d\hat{e}_{2g}/dt + \bar{e}_{2g}d\hat{C}(t)/dt \quad . . (10)$$

Substituting (9) and (10) in (8),

$$\bar{C}d\hat{e}_{2g}/dt + \bar{e}_{2g}d\hat{C}(t)/dt = [-(R_1+R_2)/R_1R_2\bar{C}](\bar{C}\hat{e}_{2g} + \bar{e}_{2g}\hat{C}(t)) + [(R_1+R_2)\bar{q}_C/R_1R_2\bar{C}^2]\hat{C}(t) \quad . . (11)$$

Since $q_C \equiv Ce_{2g}$,

$$d\hat{e}_{2g}/dt + [(R_1+R_2)/R_1R_2\bar{C}]\hat{e}_{2g} = (-\bar{e}_{2g}/\bar{C})d\hat{C}/dt \quad . . (12)$$

Problem 7.14.

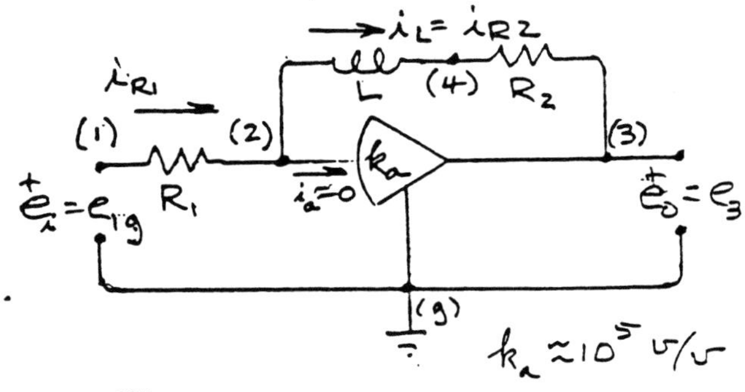

a) For R, $i_{R1} = e_{12}/R_1$ . . (1)

For L, $e_{24} = Ldi_L/dt$ . . (2)

For R_2, $i_{R2} = i_L = e_{43}/R_2$ . . (3)

For the OpAmp, $e_{3g} = k_a e_{1g}$ . . (4)

K's current law at node (2), ($i_a \approx 0$)

$$i_{R1} = i_L \quad . . (5)$$

K's voltage law for outer loop,

$$e_{1g} = e_{12} + e_{24} + e_{43} + e_{3g} \quad . . (6)$$

Starting with (2) and (6),

$$di_Ldt = (1/L)(e_{1g} - e_{12} - e_{43} - e_{3g}) \quad . . (7)$$

Then using (5), (1), and (4),

$$i_L = e_{12}/R_1 = (1/R_1)(e_{1g}-e_{2g}) = e_{1g}/R_1 + e_{3g}/k_aR_1 \quad . . (8)$$

Differentiating with respect to time,

$$di_L/dt = (1/R_1)de_{1g}/dt + (1/k_aR_1)de_{3g}/dt \quad . . (9)$$

Then substituting (9) for di_L/dt in (7), using $e_{12} = e_{1g} - e_{3g}/k_aR_1$, and (3),

$$(1/R_1)de_{1g}/dt + (1/k_aR_1)de_{3g}/dt = (1/L)(\,e_{1g} - e_{1g} + e_{3g}/k_aR_1 - R_2i_L - e_{3g}) \quad .\ .\ (10)$$

Substituting (8) for i_L in (10),

$$(1/R_1)de_{1g} + (1/k_aR_1)de_{3g}/dt = (1/L)[e_{3g}/k_aR_1 - e_{3g} - R_2(e_{1g}/R_1 + e_{3g}/k_aR_1)] \quad .\ .\ (11)$$

Eliminating the very small terms with k_a in their denominator,

$$de_{1g}/dt \approx (-R_1/L)[e_{3g} + (R_2/R_1)e_{1g}]$$

Rearranging this approximation with the output e_{3g} on the l-h side,

$$e_{3g} \approx (-L/R_1)de_{1g}/dt + (-R_2/R_1)e_{1g} \quad .\ .\ (12)$$

This circuit is therefore one way to approximate the "proportional-plus-derivative" action,

$$e_o = k_pe_i + k_dde_i/dt$$

where

$$k_p = -L/R_1 = 1.5/1200 = .00125$$

$$k_d = -R_2/R_1 = 2000/1200 = 1.667$$

The need for this type of action will be discussed later for use in automatic control systems.

CHAPTER 8

PROBLEM 8.1

a) The flowrate of heat is the same in both parts of the system (no heat losses through side walls),

$$(1) \qquad Q_h = \frac{1}{R_1}(T_1 - T_c) = \frac{1}{R_2}(T_c - T_2)$$

where R_1 and R_2 are the thermal resistances of the two parts, and T_c is the temperature at the interface of the two materials. Using equation 8.17, the values of R_1 and R_2 are found to be

$$(2) \qquad R_1 = \frac{L_1}{k_1 A} = 0.8 \ ^\circ C/W$$

$$R_2 = \frac{L_2}{k_2 A} = 2.0 \ ^\circ C/W$$

From equation (1)

$$(3) \qquad T_c = \frac{R_2}{R_1+R_2}\left(T_1 + \frac{R_1}{R_2} T_2\right)$$

Substituting numerical values for R_1, R_2, T_1, and T_2, gives

$$T_c = 148.6 \ ^\circ C$$

b) The temperature distribution T(x) is linear within each part of the system. Knowing the values of T_1, T_c, and T_2, the temperature distribution can be sketched as shown below.

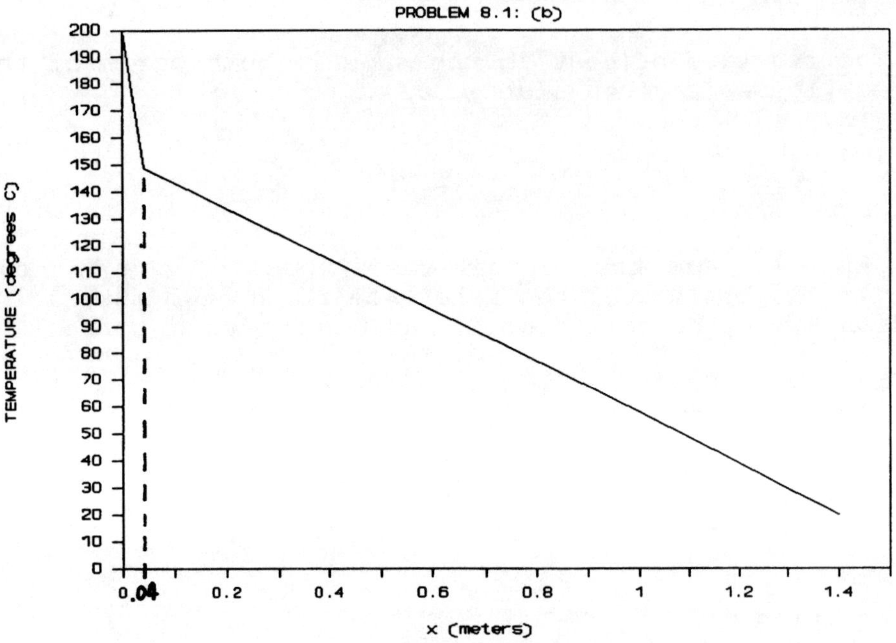

c) The equivalent thermal resistance is defined as

$$R_{eq} = \frac{T_1 - T_2}{Q_h} \tag{4}$$

Hence

$$Q_h = \frac{1}{R_{eq}} (T_1 - T_2) \tag{5}$$

From equations (1) and (3)

$$Q_h = \frac{1}{R_1} [T_1 - \frac{R_2}{R_1+R_2} (T_1 + \frac{R_1}{R_2} T_2)] \tag{6}$$

From equations (5) and (6)

$$\frac{1}{R_1+R_2} T_1 - \frac{1}{R_1+R_2} T_2 = \frac{1}{R_{eq}} (T_1 - T_2)$$

and hence

$$R_{eq} = R_1 + R_2$$

PROBLEM 8.2

a) It is implied in the problem statement that the heat flow in one-dimensional in the horizontal direction only. The heat flowrates in the two materials are

$$(1) \qquad Q_1 = \frac{k_1A_1}{L} (T_1 - T_2)$$

$$(2) \qquad Q_2 = \frac{k_2A_2}{L} (T_1 - T_2)$$

The total heat flowrate is

$$(3) \qquad Q = Q_1 + Q_2$$

and it can be expressed as

$$(4) \qquad Q = \frac{1}{R_{eq}} (T_1 - T_2)$$

From equations (3) and (4) we have

$$(5) \qquad \frac{1}{R_{eq}} (T_1 - T_2) = \frac{1}{R_1} (T_1 - T_2) + \frac{1}{R_2} (T_1 -T_2)$$

Hence

$$(6) \qquad \frac{1}{R_{eq}} = \frac{1}{R_1} + \frac{1}{R_2}$$

or

$$(7) \qquad R_{eq} = \frac{R_1R_2}{R_1+R_2}$$

b) The steady-state temperature distribution will be the same in both parts of the system since there will be no temperature gradient in the vertical direction. Also, the temperature distribution will be linear because both k_1 and k_2 are constant.

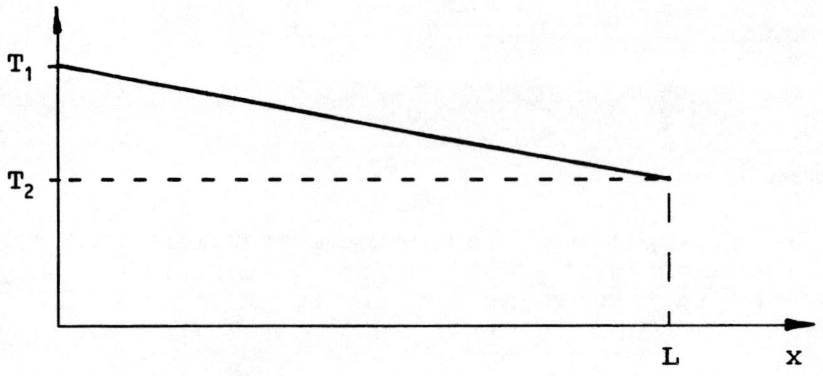

PROBLEM 8.3

From equation 8.3, the rate of heat transfer in the radial direction is

$$(1) \qquad Q_k = - k\,A(r)\,\frac{dT}{dr}$$

The area A(r) is

$$(2) \qquad A(r) = 2\pi r L$$

Hence

$$(3) \qquad Q_k = - k\,2\pi r L\,\frac{dT}{dr}$$

Separating variables

$$(4) \qquad Q_k\,\frac{dr}{r} = - k\,2\pi L\,dT$$

Integrating both sides of equation (4) gives

$$Q_k \int_{D_i/2}^{D_o/2} \frac{dr}{r} = - k\,2\pi L \int_{T_i}^{T_o} dT$$

(5) $Q_k[\ln(D_o/2) - \ln(D_i/2)] = - k\, 2\pi L\, (T_o - T_i)$

Hence, the conductive thermal resistance of the cylinder is

(6) $$R_{hk} = \frac{T_i - T_o}{Q_k} = \frac{\ln(D_o/D_i)}{2\pi kL}$$

PROBLEM 8.4

The lumped model can be used if

(1) $$Bi = \frac{R_{hk}}{R_{hc}} < 0.1$$

The conductive thermal resistance is, from the solution to Problem 8.3,

(2) $$R_{hk} = \frac{\ln(D_o/D_i)}{2\pi kL}$$

The convective thermal resistance is

(3) $$R_{hc} = \frac{1}{h_c A} = \frac{1}{2.24 v_a \pi D_o L}$$

Hence the Biot number

(4) $$Bi = \frac{\ln(D_o/D_i)\, 2.24 v_a D_o}{2k}$$

The condition (1) can be expressed as

(5) $$v_a < \frac{0.1(2k)}{\ln(D_o/D_i)\, 2.24 D_o}$$

Substituting numerical values for the system parameters gives

$$v_a < 3.48 \text{ m/sec}$$

PROBLEM 8.5

a) The energy balance equation for the hot junction is

(1) $$m_t c_t \frac{dT_t}{dt} = h_c A(T_L - T_t)$$

where

$$m_t = \rho_t (4/3)\pi r_t^3$$

and

$$A = 4\pi r_t^2$$

From equation (1), the state variable equation takes the form

(2) $$\dot{T}_t = (-1/R_{hc}C_h)T_t + (1/R_{hc}C_h)T_L$$

Subtituting $T_t = e_{21}/a$ gives

(3) $$\dot{e}_{21} = (-1/R_{hc}C_h)e_{21} + (a/R_{hc}C_h)T_L$$

b) Let the step change of $T_L(t)$ be

(4) $$T_L(t) = \Delta T_L U_s(t)$$

The steady-state value of the system response,

$$(e_{21})_{ss} = a\Delta T_L$$

Hence, the sketch of the step response is

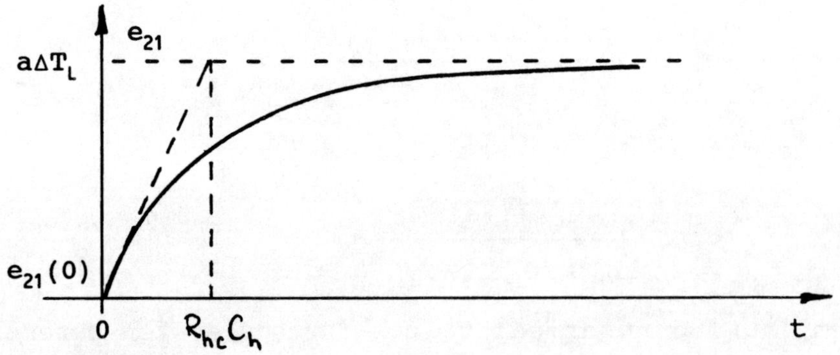

c) It takes three time constant periods for the output of a first order model to reach 95% of its steady-state value. The time constant is

$$\tau = R_{hc}C_h = 1.39 \text{ sec}$$

Hence, the time required

$$t_{95\%} = 4.16 \text{ sec}$$

PROBLEM 8.6

The energy balance equations for the three main system components are

(1) $$m_1c_1 \frac{dT_1}{dt} = h_{c1}A_1 \ (T_2 - T_1)$$

(2) $$m_2c_2 \frac{dT_2}{dt} = Q_i(t) - h_{c1}A_1 \ (T_2 - T_1) - h_{c2}A_2 \ (T_2 - T_3)$$

(3) $$m_3c_3 \frac{dT_3}{dt} = h_{c2}A_2 \ (T_2 - T_3) - h_{c3}A_3 \ (T_3 - T_a)$$

where c_1, c_2, and c_3 are specific heats of the packing, air inside the furnace, and the walls, respectively. The packing surface area is A_1, the inside wall surface area is A_2, and A_3 is the surface area of the outside walls.

Introduce lumped thermal resistances

$$R_1 = \frac{1}{h_{c1}A_1} \qquad R_2 = \frac{1}{h_{c2}A_2} \qquad R_3 = \frac{1}{h_{c3}A_3}$$

and the lumped thermal capacitances

$$C_{h1} = m_1c_1 \qquad C_{h2} = m_2c_2 \qquad C_{h3} = m_3c_3$$

Using T_1, T_2, and T_3 as the state variables and Q_i and T_a as the input variables, the state variable equations in matrix form are

$$\begin{bmatrix} \dot{T}_1 \\ \dot{T}_2 \\ \dot{T}_3 \end{bmatrix} = \begin{bmatrix} \dfrac{-1}{R_1C_{h1}} & \dfrac{1}{R_1C_{h1}} & 0 \\ \dfrac{1}{R_1C_{h2}} & \dfrac{-1}{C_{h2}}\left[\dfrac{1}{R_1} + \dfrac{1}{R_2}\right] & \dfrac{1}{R_2C_{h2}} \\ 0 & \dfrac{1}{R_2C_{h3}} & \dfrac{-1}{C_{h3}}\left[\dfrac{1}{R_2} + \dfrac{1}{R_3}\right] \end{bmatrix} \begin{bmatrix} T_1 \\ T_2 \\ T_3 \end{bmatrix} + \begin{bmatrix} 0 & 0 \\ \dfrac{1}{C_{h2}} & 0 \\ 0 & \dfrac{1}{R_3C_{h3}} \end{bmatrix} \begin{bmatrix} Q_i \\ T_a \end{bmatrix}$$

PROBLEM 8.7

a) The energy balance equations for the two layers of ceramic material are

$$(1)\quad C_{h1}\frac{dT_1}{dt} = \sigma F_E F_A A_1 (T_r^4 - T_1^4) + h_c(A_1 + A_s)(T_a - T_1) - \frac{1}{R_{12}}(T_1 - T_2)$$

$$(2)\quad C_{h2}\frac{dT_2}{dt} = \frac{1}{R_{12}}(T_1 - T_2) + h_c A_s (T_a - T_2)$$

Introduce the convective thermal resistances R_{c1} abd R_{c2} defined as

$$(3)\qquad R_{c1} = \frac{1}{h_c(A_1 + A_s)} \qquad\qquad R_{c2} = \frac{1}{h_c A_s}$$

The nonlinear state variable equations take the form

$$(4)\quad \dot{T}_1 = \frac{1}{C_{h1}}\left[\frac{1}{R_{c1}} + \frac{1}{R_{12}}\right]T_1 - \frac{\sigma F_E F_A A_1}{C_{h1}}T_1^4 + \frac{1}{R_{12}C_{h1}}T_2 + \frac{1}{R_{c1}C_{h1}}T_a$$

$$+ \frac{\sigma F_E F_A A_1}{C_{h1}}T_r^4$$

$$(5)\quad \dot{T}_2 = \frac{1}{R_{12}C_{h2}} T_1 - \frac{1}{C_{h2}} \left[\frac{1}{R_{12}} + \frac{1}{R_{c2}} \right] T_2 + \frac{1}{R_{c2}C_{h2}} T_a$$

b) The nonlinear terms in equation (4) can be linearized using Taylor's method

$$(6)\qquad T_1^4 \approx \bar{T}_1^4 + \hat{T}_1(4\bar{T}_1^3)$$

$$(7)\qquad T_r^4 \approx \bar{T}_r^4 + \hat{T}_r(4\bar{T}_1^3)$$

Substituting the approximating expressions (6) and (7) into equations (4) and (5) and cancelling constant terms yields

$$(8)\quad \dot{\hat{T}}_1 = \frac{-1}{C_{h1}} \left[\frac{1}{R_{c1}} + \frac{1}{R_{12}} + \sigma F_E F_A A_1 4\bar{T}_1^3 \right] \hat{T}_1 + \frac{1}{R_{12}C_{h1}} \hat{T}_2 + \frac{1}{R_{c1}C_{h1}} \hat{T}_a$$

$$+ \frac{\sigma F_E F_A A_1 4\bar{T}_r^3}{C_{h1}} \hat{T}_r$$

$$(9)\quad \dot{\hat{T}}_2 = \frac{1}{R_{12}C_{h2}} \hat{T}_1 - \frac{1}{C_{h2}} \left[\frac{1}{R_{12}} + \frac{1}{R_{c2}} \right] \hat{T}_2 + \frac{1}{R_{c2}C_{h2}} \hat{T}_a$$

Equations (8) and (9) constitute the linearized model of the system.

PROBLEM 8.8

Assuming that no heat losses occur in the system (storage tank and pipes perfectly insulated), the energy balance is

$$(1)\qquad m_w c_w \frac{dT_s}{dt} = Q_{col}(t)$$

Employing the Hottel-Whillier-Bliss model for the solar collector, equation (1) takes the following form

$$(2) \qquad \dot{T}_s = -(A_cF_RU_L/m_wc_w)T_s + (A_cF_R/m_wc_w)S(t) + (A_cF_RU_L/m_wc_w)T_a(t)$$

Substituting numerical values for the system parameters yield

$$(3) \qquad \dot{T}_s = -11.2\text{x}10^{-6}\ T_s + 2.8\text{x}10^{-6}\ S(t) + 11.2\text{x}10^{-6}\ T_a(t)$$

PROBLEM 8.9

The storage tank consisting of three layers can be presented schematically as shown below

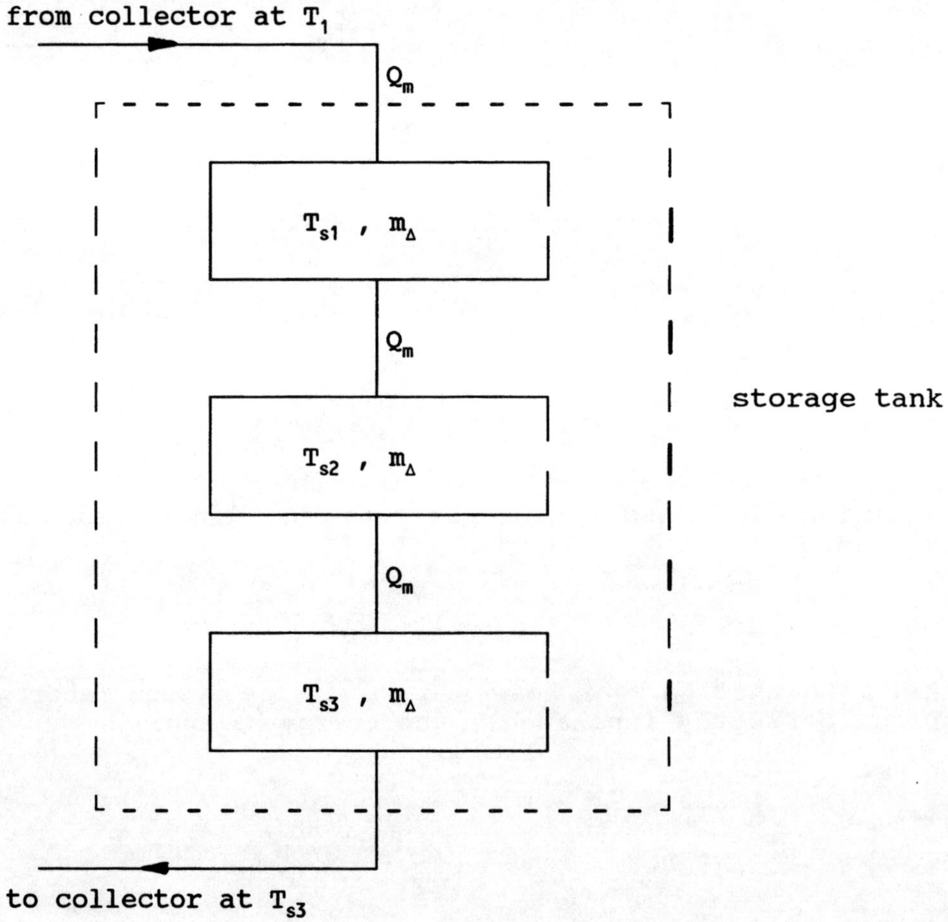

The heat balance equations for the three layers are

(1) $$m_\Delta c_w \frac{dT_{s1}}{dt} = Q_m c_w (T_1 - T_{s1}) - Q_m c_w (T_{s1} - T_{s1})$$

(2) $$m_\Delta c_w \frac{dT_{s2}}{dt} = Q_m c_w (T_{s1} - T_{s2}) - Q_m c_w (T_{s2} - T_{s3})$$

(3) $$m_\Delta c_w \frac{dT_{s3}}{dt} = Q_m c_w (T_{s2} - T_{s3})$$

The heat balance equation for the collector is

(4) $$Q_m c_w (T_1 - T_{s3}) = A_c F_R S(t) - A_c F_R U_L T_{ss} + A_c F_R U_L T_a(t)$$

Hence

(5) $$T_1 = \left[1 - \frac{A_c F_R U_L}{Q_m c_w} \right] T_{s3} + \frac{A_c F_R}{Q_m c_w} S(t) + \frac{A_c F_R U_L}{Q_m c_w} T_a(t)$$

Substituting this result for T_1 in equation (1) yields

(6) $$m_\Delta \frac{dT_{s1}}{dt} = -2Q_m T_{s1} + Q_m T_{s2} + \left[Q_m - \frac{A_c F_R U_L}{c_w} \right] T_{s3} + \frac{A_c F_R}{c_w} S(t) + \frac{A_c F_R U_L}{c_w} T_a(t)$$

From equations (6), (2), and (3) the following state model is obtained in matrix form

$$\begin{bmatrix} \dot{T}_{s1} \\ \dot{T}_{s2} \\ \dot{T}_{s3} \end{bmatrix} = \begin{bmatrix} -2Q_m/m_\Delta & Q_m/m_\Delta & (Q_m c_w - A_c F_R U_L)/m_\Delta c_w \\ Q_m/m_\Delta & -2Q_m/m_\Delta & Q_m/m_\Delta \\ 0 & Q_m/m_\Delta & -Q_m/m_\Delta \end{bmatrix} \begin{bmatrix} T_{s1} \\ T_{s2} \\ T_{s3} \end{bmatrix}$$

$$+ \begin{bmatrix} A_c F_R/m_\Delta c_w & A_c F_R U_L/m_\Delta c_w \\ 0 & 0 \\ 0 & 0 \end{bmatrix} \begin{bmatrix} S(t) \\ T_a(t) \end{bmatrix}$$

CHAPTER 9

PROBLEM 9.1

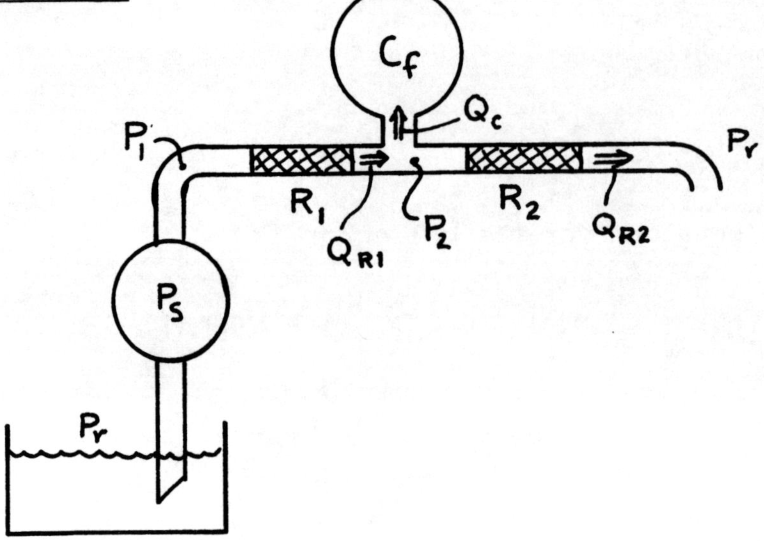

a) For R_1,

(1) $Q_{R1} = P_{12}/R_1$

For C_f,

(2) $Q_c = C_f \dfrac{dP_{2r}}{dt}$

For R_2,

(3) $Q_{R2} = \dfrac{P_{2r}}{P_2}$

Compatability,

(4) $P_S = P_{12} + P_{2r}$

Continuity at (2),

(5) $Q_{R1} = Q_c + Q_{R2}$

Starting with (2), then (5), (1), and (2)

$$C_f \frac{dP_{2r}}{dt} = Q_c = Q_{R1} - Q_{R2} = \frac{P_{12}}{R_1} - \frac{P_{2r}}{R_2}$$

Using (4) and rearranging,

$$C_f \frac{dP_{2r}}{dt} + (1/R_1 + 1/R_2)P_{2r} = P_s/R_1$$

or

$$\left[\frac{C_f R_1 R_2}{R_1+R_2}\right]\frac{dP_{2r}}{dt} + P_{2r} = \left[\frac{R_2}{R_1+R_2}\right]P_s$$

b)

$$\tau = \frac{C_f R_1 R_2}{R_1+R_2}$$

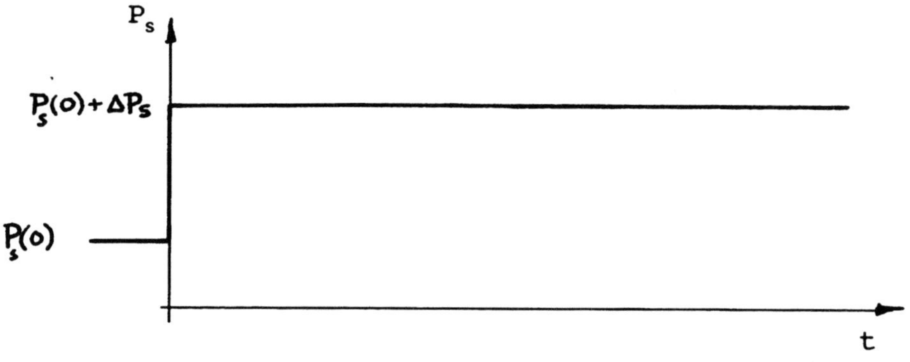

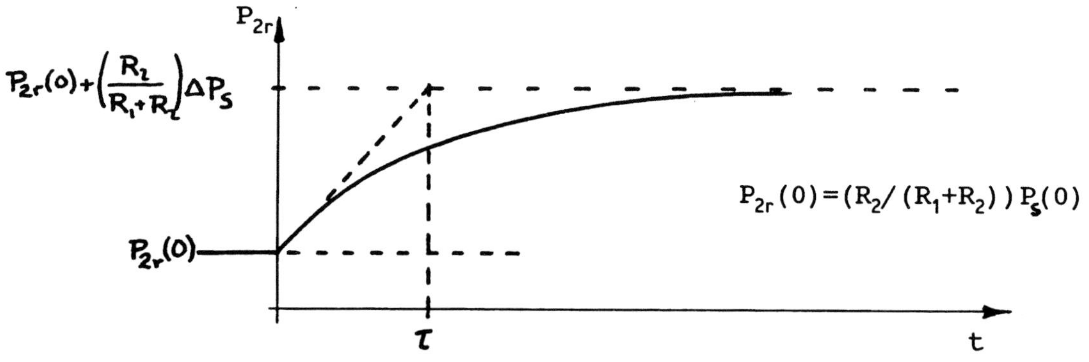

PROBLEM 9.2

a) For R_1,

(1) $P_{12} = R_1 Q_1$

For I,

(2) $P_{23} = I \frac{dQ_1}{dt}$

For C_f,

(3) $Q_c = C_f \frac{dP_{3r}}{dt}$

For R_2,

(4) $P_{3r} = R_2 Q_2$

Compatability,

(5) $P_s = P_{12} + P_{23} + P_{3r}$

Continuity,

(6) $Q_1 = Q_c + Q_2$

Starting with (2), then (5), and (1)

$$I \frac{dQ_1}{dt} = P_{23} = P_s - P_{12} = P_s - R_1 Q_1 - P_{3r}$$

$$= -R_1 Q_1 - P_{3r} + P_s$$

Rearranging,

(7) $\frac{dQ_1}{dt} = (-R_1/I)Q_1 + (-1/I)P_{3r} + (1/I)P_s$

Then using (3), then (6), and (4)

$$C_f \frac{dP_{3r}}{dt} = Q_c = Q_1 - Q_2 = Q_1 + (-1/R_2)P_{3r}$$

Rearranging,

$$(8)\qquad \frac{dP_{3r}}{dt} = (1/C_f)Q_1 + (-1/R_2C_f)P_{3r}$$

Combining (7) and (8) to eliminate Q_1,

$$C_f\frac{d^2P_{3r}}{dt^2} + \left[\frac{1}{R^2} + \frac{R_1C_f}{I}\right]\frac{dP_{3r}}{dt} + \left[\frac{R_1}{R_2I} + \frac{1}{I}\right]P_{3r} = (1/I)P_s$$

$$\begin{matrix}\uparrow & \qquad\qquad & \uparrow & \qquad\qquad & \uparrow\\ a_2 & & a_1 & & a_0\end{matrix}$$

b)

$$\omega_n = (a_0/a_2)^{.5} = [(R_1+R_2)/R_2C_fI]^{.5}$$

$$\zeta = \frac{a_1}{2(a_2a_0)^{.5}} = \frac{I + R_1R_2C_f}{2[R_2IC_f(R_1+R_2)]^{.5}} = .3 \text{ (given)}$$

Therefore the response is under damped.

$$\omega_d = \omega_n(1 - \zeta^2)^{.5} = .954\omega_n$$

The period of the ocsillation is,

$$T_d = \frac{2\pi}{\omega_d} = \frac{6.28}{.954\omega_n} = 6.58/\omega_n$$

The per-cycle decay ratio is,

$$DR = e^{-\zeta\omega_nT_d} = e^{-\zeta\omega_n2\pi/\omega_d} = e^{-2\pi\zeta/(1-\zeta^2)^{.5}}$$

$$= e^{-(6.28)(.3)/(.954)} = e^{-1.97} = .138$$

To sketch the response, we first need to know $P_{3r}(0+)$ and $\dot{P}_{3r}(0+)$

i) Because there is no infinite source of flowrate to change C_f at t=0,

$$P_{3r}(0+) = P_{3r}(0-) = [R_2/(R_1+R_2)]P_s(0-)$$

and

$$Q_2(0+) = Q_2(0-) = P_{3r}(0-)/R_2 = [1/(R_1+R_2)]P_s(0-)$$

ii) Because there is no infinite source of pressure to suddenly change the flow in I at t=0,

$$Q_1(0+) = Q_1(0-)$$

And since $Q_c(0+)=Q_1(0+)-Q_2(0+)=Q_1(0-)-Q_2(0-)$

$$Q_c(0+) = Q_c(0-) = 0$$

Therefore

$$\dot{P}_{3r}(0+) = (1/C_f)Q_c(0+) = 0$$

The solution for $\hat{P}_{3r}=P_{3r}-P_{3r}(0)$ is of the form

$$\hat{P}_{3r}(t)=(\hat{P}_{3r})_p+(\hat{P}_{3r})_h=[R_2/(R_1+R_2)]\Delta P_s + Ae^{-\zeta\omega_n t}\cos(\omega_d t+\phi)$$

To find A and ϕ, we need to use $\hat{P}_{3r}(0+)$ and $\dot{\hat{P}}_{3r}(0+)$ to develop two equations in A and ϕ:

iii) From the first initial condition, $\hat{P}_{3r}(0+)=0$, the solution at t=0+ is:

$$0 = [R_2/(R_1+R_2)]\Delta P_s + Ae^0\cos(\phi)$$

or

(a) $$A\cos(\phi) = [-R_2/(R_1+R_2)]\Delta P_2$$

iv) From the second initial condition, $\dot{\hat{P}}_{3r}(0+)=0$, the derivative of the solution at t=0+ is:

(b) $$0 = 0 + A[e^0(-\omega_d)\sin(\phi) + (-\zeta\omega_n)e^0\cos(\phi)]$$

or

$$A\cos(\phi)[-\omega_d\tan(\phi) - \zeta\omega_n] = 0$$

$$\tan(\phi) = -\zeta\omega_n/[\omega_n(1-\zeta^2)^{.5}] = -\zeta/(1-\zeta^2)^{.5}$$

$$\cos(\phi) = (1-\zeta^2)^{.5} = .954$$

$$\phi = 17.4^\circ \text{ or } .3 \text{ rad}$$

Now from equation (a) above

$$A = (1/\cos(\phi))[-R_2/(R_1+R_2)]\Delta P_s = (-1.048)[-R_2/(R_1+R_2)]\Delta P_s$$

With this information the response is readily sketched,

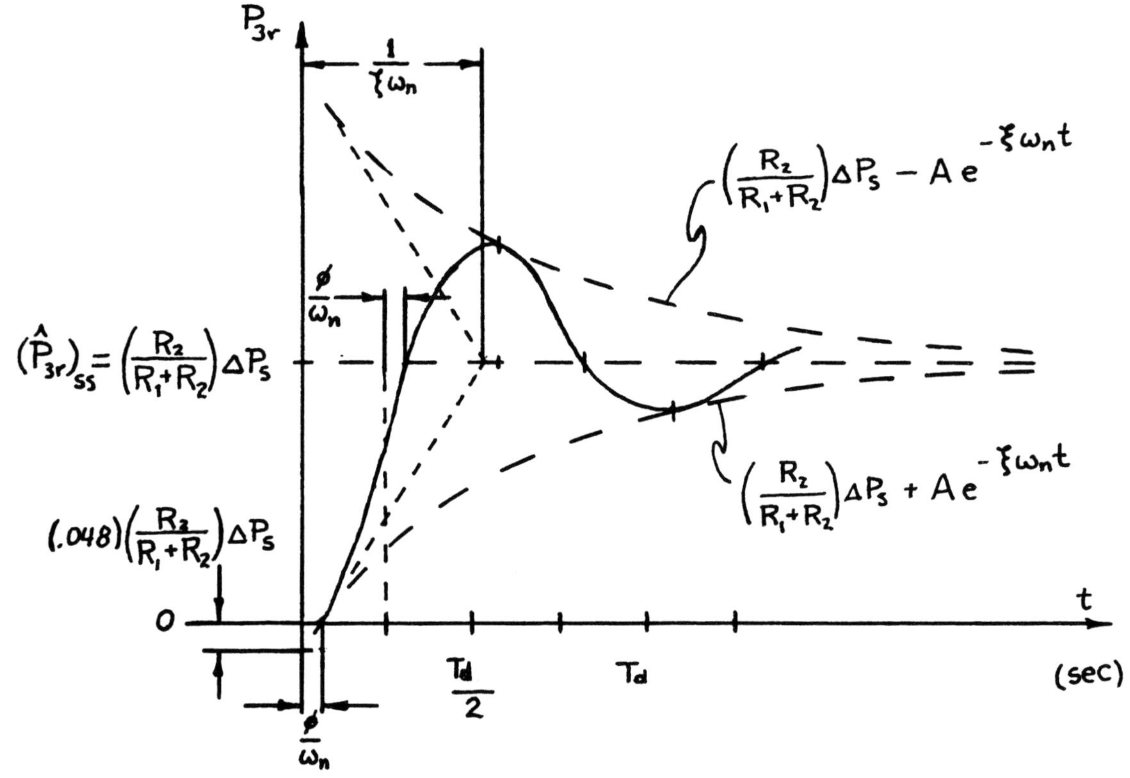

PROBLEM 9.3

a)

$$R_f = \frac{128\mu L}{\pi d^4} = \frac{(128)(1.03x10^{-2}N\text{-}sec/m)(50m)}{(3.14)(.02m)^4}$$

$$= 1.312x10^8 \ N\text{-}sec/m^5$$

$$= 1.312x10^{-2} \ N\text{-}sec/cm^5$$

For laminar flow

$$I = \frac{2\rho L}{\pi d^2/4} = \frac{2(\gamma/g)L}{\pi d^2/4} = \frac{2(8.74x10^{-3}N/cm^3)(50m)(4)(10^6cm^3/m^3)}{(3.8N/Kg)(3.14)(.02m)^2}$$

$$= 2.84x10^8 \ Kg/m^4 \quad or \quad (N\text{-}sec^2/m^5)$$

$$= 2.84x10^{-2} \ N\text{-}sec^2/cm^5$$

$$C_f = \frac{v_{line}}{\beta} = \frac{L(\pi d^2/4)}{\beta} = \frac{(50m)(3.14)(.02m)^2}{(1.38x10^9N/m^2)(4)}$$

$$= 1.138x10^{-11} \ m^5/N$$

$$= 1.138x10^{-1} \ cm^5/N$$

$$C_t = \frac{A_t}{\gamma} = \frac{\pi d^2/4}{\gamma} = \frac{(3.14)(.25m)^2}{(8.74x10^{-3}N/cm^3)(10^6cm^3/m^3)(4)}$$

$$= 5.61x10^{-7} \ m^5/N$$

$$= 5.61x10^3 \ cm^5/N$$

b)

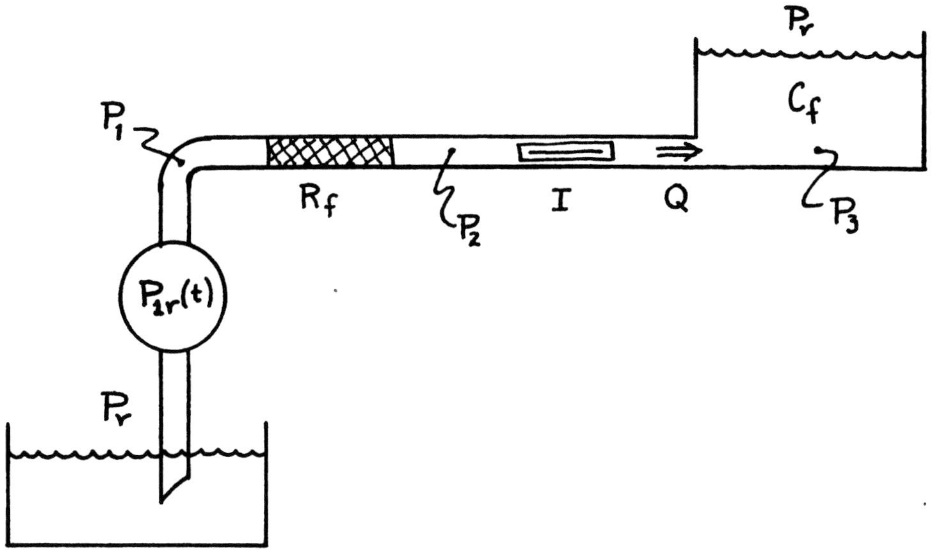

For R_f,

(1) $\quad Q = P_{12}/R_f$

For I,

(2) $\quad P_{23} = I \dfrac{dQ}{dt}$

For C_t,

(3) $\quad Q = C_t \dfrac{dP_{3r}}{dt}$

Compatability,

(4) $\quad P_{1r} = P_{12} + P_{23} + P_{3r}$

Continuity is satisfied by using Q for all elements!

c) Starting with (2), then (4) and (1)

$$I \frac{dQ}{dt} = P_{23} = P_{1r} - P_{12} - P_{3r} = P_{1r} - R_f Q - P_{3r}$$

Rearranging,

$$(5) \qquad \frac{dQ}{dt} = (-R_f/I)Q + (-1/I)P_{3r} + (1/I)P_{1r}$$

Next, using (3)

$$C_t \frac{dP_{3r}}{dt} = Q$$

Substituting for Q from (3) into (5),

$$(6) \qquad C_t \frac{d^2P_{3r}}{dt^2} + \frac{R_f C_t}{I} \frac{dP_{3r}}{dt} + (1/I)P_{3r} = (1/I)P_{1r}$$

$$\uparrow \qquad \uparrow \qquad \uparrow \qquad \uparrow$$

$$a_2 \qquad a_1 \qquad a^0 \qquad b_0$$

d)

$$\omega_n = (a_0/a_2)^{.5} = (1/C_tI)^{.5} = 1/[(5.61)(2.84)(10)]^{.5}$$

$$= 1/12.6 = .079 \text{ rad/sec}$$

$$\zeta = a_1/[2(a_2a_0)^{.5}] = R_f/2 \ (C_t/I)^{.5}$$

$$= (1.312x10^{-2}/2)(5.61x10^3/2.84x10^{-2})^{.5}$$

$$= 6.56x10^{-3}(19.75x10^5)$$

$$= (6.56)(4.44)x10^{-1} = 2.916$$

e)

$$\frac{C_t}{C_f} = 4.93x10^4$$

Therefore

$$C_t <<< C_f$$

so that C_f is negligible.

PROBLEM 9.4

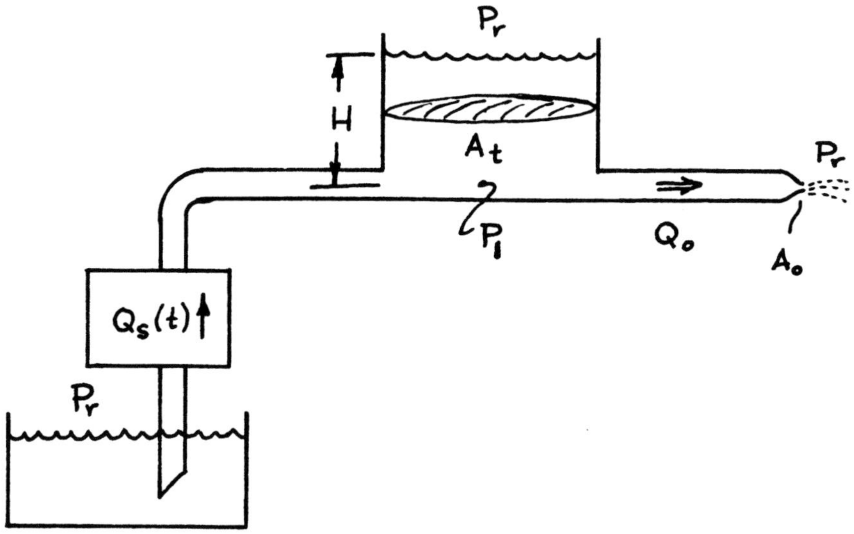

a) For the reservoir,

(1) $$A_t \frac{dH}{dt} = Q_s - Q_o$$

For the orifice

(2) $$Q_o = A_o C_d (2P_{1r}/\rho)$$

Definition relating P_{1r} to H,

(3) $$P_{1r} = \gamma H$$

Combining (2) and (3)

(4) $$Q_o = A_o C_d (2gH)^{.5}$$

$$\hat{Q}_o = A_o C_d (2g)^{.5} [\hat{H}/2(\bar{H})^{.5}]$$

b) Combining (1) and (4),

(5) $$A_t \frac{dH}{dt} = -A_o C_d (2g)^{.5} (H)^{.5} + Q_s$$

Linearizing and rearranging,

$$A_t \frac{d\hat{H}}{dt} + A_o C_d (2g)^{.5}[\hat{H}/2(\bar{H})^{.5}] = \hat{Q}_s$$

or

$$A_t \frac{d\hat{H}}{dt} + [A_o C_d (g/2\bar{H})^{.5}]\hat{H} = \hat{Q}_s$$

Rearranging again

$$\left[\frac{A_t}{A_o C_d}(2H/g)^{.5}\right]\frac{d\hat{H}}{dt} + \hat{H} = \hat{Q}_s\left[\frac{(2\bar{H}/g)^{.5}}{A_o C_d}\right]$$

$$\uparrow \qquad\qquad\qquad\qquad \uparrow$$

$$\tau \qquad\qquad\qquad\qquad b_o$$

c)

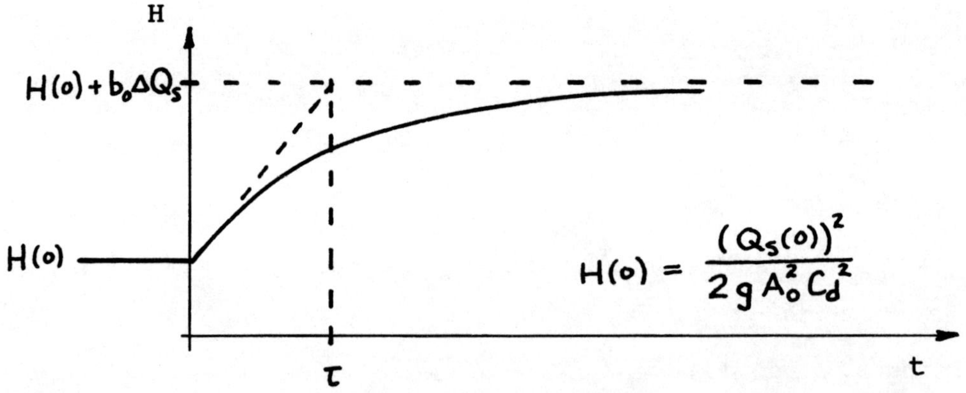

PROBLEM 9.5

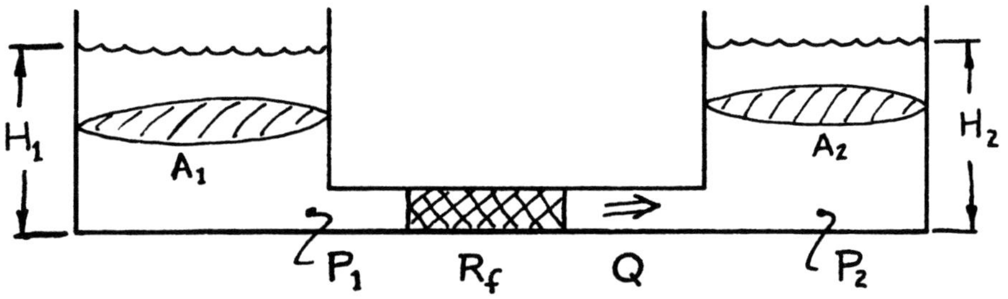

a) At $t = 0-$

(1) $P_{1r}(0-) = \gamma H_1(0-)$

(2) $P_{2r}(0-) = \gamma H_2(0-)$

At $t = 0+$

(3) $P_{1r}(0+) = P_{1r}(0-) = \gamma H_1(0-)$

(4) $P_{2r}(0+) = P_{2r}(0-) = \gamma H_2(0-)$

For tank(1),

(5) $$A_1 \frac{dH_1}{dt} = -Q$$

For tank(2),

(6) $$A_2 \frac{dH_2}{dt} = Q$$

For R_f,

(7) $Q = P_{12}/R_f = \gamma(H_1-H_2)/R_f$

Compatability,

(8) $P_{1r} = P_{12} + P_{2r}$

Definitions relating P to H

(9) $P_{1r} \equiv \gamma H_1$; $P_{2r} = \gamma H_2$

Starting with (8), then (9), then (7) and (6)

$$P_{1r} = \gamma H_1 = R_f Q + \gamma H_2 = R_f A_2 \frac{dH_2}{dt} + \gamma H_2$$

or

(10) $$H_1 = \frac{R_f A_2}{\gamma} \frac{dH_2}{dt} + H_2$$

From (5) and (6)

(11) $$A_1 \frac{dH_1}{dt} = -A_2 \frac{dH_2}{dt}$$

Integrating with respect to time to get at initial conditions,

$$A_1 H_1 \Big|_{0+}^{t} = -A_2 H_2 \Big|_{0+}^{t}$$

or

$$A_1 H_1(t) - A_1 H_1(0+) = -A_2 H_2(t) + A_2 H_2(0+)$$

$$H_1(t) = (-A_2/A_1) H_2(t) + H_1(0+) + (A_2/A_1) H_2(0+)$$

Combining (10) and (12)

$$\left[\frac{R_f A_2}{\gamma}\right] \frac{dH_2}{dt} + H_2(t) = (-A_2/A_1) H_2(t) + H_1(0+) + (A_2/A_1) H_2(0+)$$

$$\left[\frac{R_f A_2}{\gamma}\right] \frac{dH_2}{dt} + [(A_1 + A_2)/A_1] H_2(t) = H_1(0+) + (A_2/A_1) H_2(0+)$$

Rearranging

$$\left[\frac{R_f A_1 A_2}{\gamma(A_1+A_2)}\right]\frac{dH_2}{dt}+H_2(t)=[A_1/(A_1+A_2)]H_1(0+)+[A_2/(A_1+A_2)]H_2(0+)$$

$\uparrow$

τ

Note that at $T\rightarrow\infty$, when $dH_2/dt\rightarrow 0$,

$$H_2(\infty) = H_1(\infty) = [A_1/(A_1+A_2)]H_1(0+) + [A_2/(A_1+A_2)]H_2(0+)$$

PROBLEM 9.6

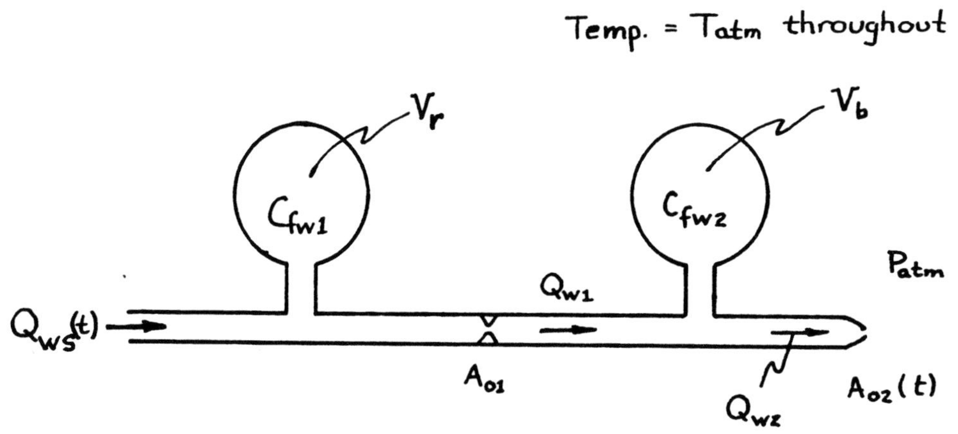

a) At the normal operating point

(1) $\bar{Q}_{w2} = 0.05$ N/sec

(2) $\bar{P}_2 = 5 \times 10^5$ N/m^2

(3) $\dfrac{P_{atm}}{\bar{P}_2} = \dfrac{1}{5}$

Therefore, the flow thru A_{02} is choked so that

(4) $\bar{Q}_{w2} = C_{d2}A_{02}\dfrac{C_2\,\bar{P}_2}{[\,T_{atm}\,]^{.5}}$

where $T_{atm} = 293° K$ (room temperature).

(5) $$A_{o2} = (1/C_{d2}) \frac{\bar{Q}_{w2} [T_{atm}]^{.5} C_2}{\bar{P}_2} = (1/C_{d2}) \frac{(.05)[293]^{.5}(.532)}{5 \times 10^5}$$

$$= 4.94 \times 10^{-6} \text{ m} = .049 \text{ cm}^2$$

b) The set of describing equations are:

For the reservoir,

(6) $$Q_{ws} - Q_{w1} = C_{fw1} \frac{dP_1}{dt}$$

where

(7) $$C_{fw1} = \frac{V_r}{R\ T_{atm}}$$ ("slow" changes)

For A_{01},

(8) $$Q_{w1} = \frac{C_{d1}A_{01}C_2}{[T_{atm}]^{.5}} \cdot 2 [P_2(P_1 - P_2)]^{.5}$$

For the ballast tank,

(9) $$Q_{w1} - Q_{w2} = C_{fw2} \frac{dP_2}{dt}$$

where

(10) $$C_{fw2} = \frac{g\ V_b}{R\ T_{atm}}$$

For A_{02},

(11) $$Q_{w2} = C_{d2}A_{02} \frac{C_2\ P_2}{[T_{atm}]^{.5}}$$

c) Linearizing,

$$\frac{d\hat{P}_1}{dt} = \frac{1}{C_{fw1}} \left(\hat{Q}_{ws}(t) - \hat{Q}_{w1} \right) \tag{12}$$

with

$$\hat{Q}_{w1} = k_1\hat{P}_1 + k_2\hat{P}_2 \tag{13}$$

$$k_1 = \frac{\partial Q_{w1}}{\partial P_1} = \frac{C_{d1}A_{o1}C_2\overline{P}_2}{[\ T_{atm}\ \overline{P}_2(\overline{P}_1 - \overline{P}_2)\ ]^{.5}}$$

$$k_2 = \frac{\partial Q_{w1}}{\partial P_2} = \frac{-C_{d1}A_{o1}C_2(2\overline{P}_2 - \overline{P}_1)}{[\ T_{atm}\ \overline{P}_2(\overline{P}_1 - \overline{P}_2)\ ]^{.5}}$$

yielding the state variable equation for $\hat{P}_1$:

$$\frac{d\hat{P}_1}{dt} = \underbrace{(-k_1/C_{fw1})}_{a_{11}}\hat{P}_1 + \underbrace{(-k_2/C_{fw1})}_{a_{12}}\hat{P}_2 + \underbrace{(1/C_{fw1})}_{b_{11}}\hat{Q}_{ws}(t) \tag{14}$$

then

$$\frac{d\hat{P}_2}{dt} = \frac{1}{C_{fw2}} \left(\hat{Q}_{w1} - \hat{Q}_{w2} \right) \tag{15}$$

with

$$\hat{Q}_{w2} = k_3\hat{P}_2 + k_4\hat{A}_{02} \tag{16}$$

and

$$k_3 = \frac{dQ_{w2}}{dP_2} = \frac{C_{d2}\overline{A}_{02}}{[\ T_{atm}\ ]^{.5}}$$

$$k_4 = \frac{C_{d2}\overline{P}_2}{[\ T_{atm}\ ]^{.5}}$$

which yields the state variable equation for $\hat{P}_2$

(17) $$\frac{d\hat{P}_2}{dt} = (k_1/C_{fw2})\hat{P}_1 + \{(k_2 - k_3)/C_{fw}\}\hat{P}_2$$

$$\begin{matrix} \updownarrow & & \updownarrow \\ a_{21} & & a_{22} \end{matrix}$$

Combining to eliminate $\hat{P}_1$

(18) $$\frac{d^2\hat{P}_2}{dt^2} + (-a_{11} - a_{22})\frac{d\hat{P}_2}{dt} + (a_{11}a_{22} - a_{12}a_{21})\hat{P}_2 = b_{11}a_{21}\hat{Q}_{ws}$$

where

$$a_{11} + a_{22} = (R\ T_{atm}/g)[\ (k_2 - k_3)/V_b - k_1/V_r\ ]$$

$$a_{11}a_{22} = (R\ T_{atm}/g)[\ (k_2 - k_3)/V_b\ ](-k_1/V_r)$$

$$a_{12}a_{21} = (\ -k_2\ R\ T_{atm}/gV_r\ )(\ k_1\ R\ T_{atm}/gV_b\ )$$

$$= (\ R\ T_{atm}/g\ )^2(\ k_1\ R\ T_{atm}/gV_b\ )$$

$$a_{11}a_{22} - a_{12}a_{21} = (\ R\ T_{atm}/g\ )^3(\ -k_1k_3/V_rV_b\ )$$

$$b_{11} = R\ T_{atm}/gV_r$$

$$b_{11}a_{21} = (\ R\ T_{atm}/gV_r\ )(\ k_1\ R\ T_{atm}/gV_b\ )$$

$$= (\ R\ T_{atm}/g\ )^2(\ k_1/V_rV_b\ )$$

recalling that

$$k_1 = \frac{\partial Q_{w1}}{\partial P_1} = \frac{C_{d1}A_{o1}C_2\bar{P}_2}{[\ T_{atm}\ \bar{P}_2(\bar{P}_1 - \bar{P}_2)\ ]^{.5}}$$

$$k_2 = \frac{\partial Q_{w1}}{\partial P_2} = \frac{-C_{d1}A_{o1}C_2(2\bar{P}_2 - \bar{P}_1)}{[\ T_{atm}\ \bar{P}_2(\bar{P}_1 - \bar{P}_2)\ ]^{.5}}$$

$$k_3 = \frac{dQ_{w2}}{dP_2} = \frac{C_{d2}\overline{A}_{02}C_2}{[\ T_{atm}\ ]^{.5}}$$

$$k_4 = \frac{C_{d2}\overline{P}_2C_2}{[\ T_{atm}\ ]^{.5}}$$

CHAPTER 10

PROBLEM 10.1

a) Complete free-body diagram:

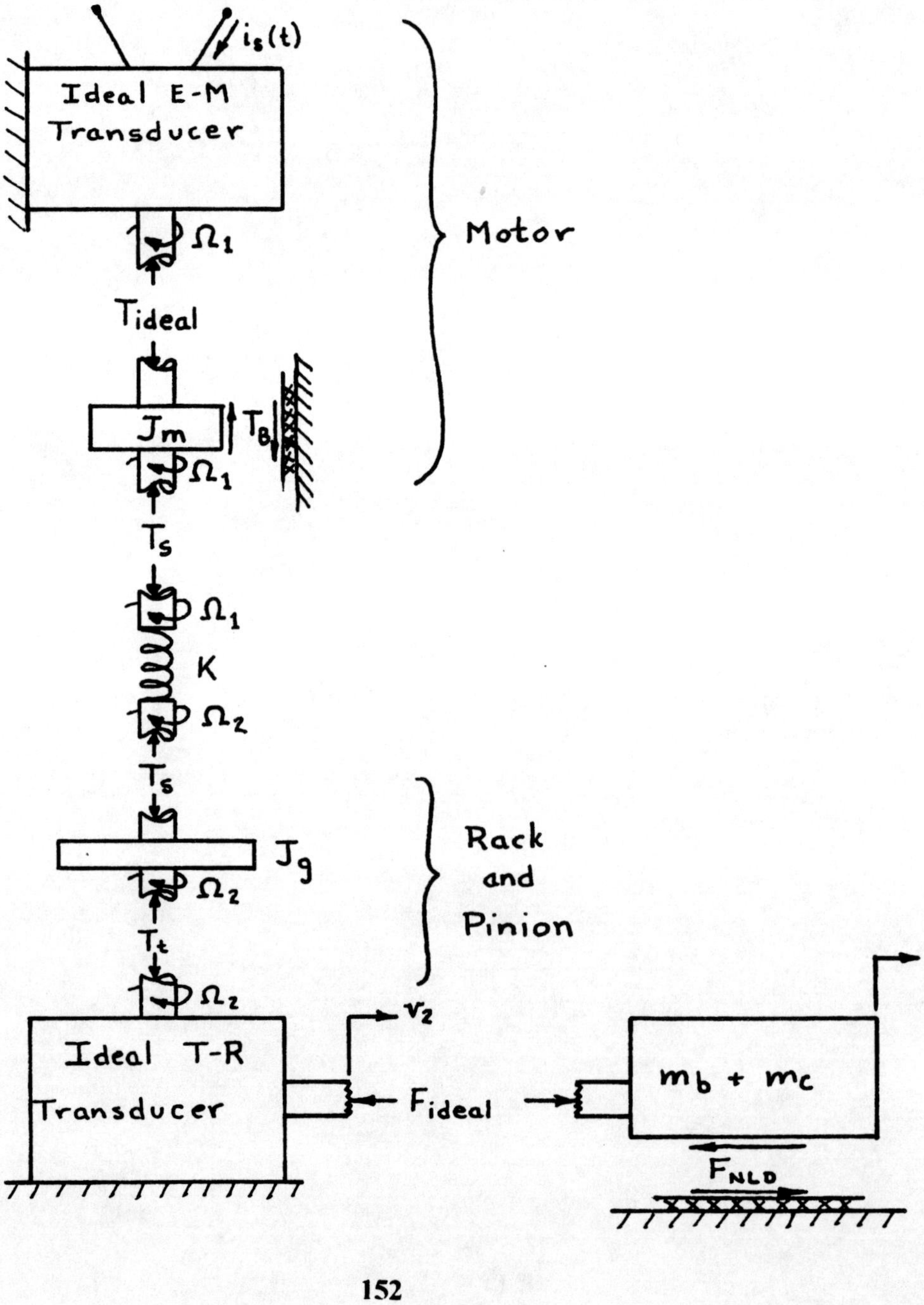

b) For ideal E-M transducer,

(1) $T_i = \alpha i_s(t)$

For J_m,

(2) $$J_m \frac{d\Omega_{1g}}{dt} = T_i - T_o - T_s$$

For B_m,

(3) $T_B = B_m \Omega_{1g}$

For K,

(4) $$\frac{dT_s}{dt} = K(\Omega_{1g} - \Omega_{2g})$$

For J_g,

(5) $$J_g \frac{d\Omega_{2g}}{dt} = T_s - T_t$$

For ideal T-R transducer,

(6) $\Omega_{2g} = (1/r)v_{2g} = n \cdot v_{2g}$

(7) $T_t = r \cdot F_{ideal} = (1/n) F_i$

For $m_b + m_c$,

(8) $$(m_b + m_c) \frac{dv_{2g}}{dt} = F_i - F_{NLD}$$

For NLD,

(9) $F_{NLD} = \text{sign}(v_{2g}) \cdot F_o + b \cdot v_{2g} = f_{NL}(v_{2g})$

Note: From equation (6) it is seen that Ω_{2g} and v_{2g} are different versions of the same state variables, the gear inertia J_g and the mass $(m_b + m_c)$ may be combined into a single A-type element

$$m_{tot} = ((J_g/r^2) + m_b + m_c)$$

as follows: Using (5) and (6) and dividing thru by r:

$$\text{(5mod)} \quad \frac{J_g}{r^2} \cdot \frac{dv_{2g}}{dt} = (T_s/r) - F_i$$

and adding (8)

$$\text{(10)} \quad \left[\frac{J_g}{r^2} + m_b + m_c\right]\frac{dv_{2g}}{dt} = (T_s/r) - F_{NLD}$$

c) Replacing Ω_{2g} with v_{2g}/r in equation (4), we now have the system described be equations (1), (2), (3), (4), (9), and (10) involving six unknowns: T_i, Ω_{1g}, T_B, T_s, v_{2g}, and F_{NLD}.

Using (2), then (1), and (3) yields the first state-variable equation,

$$\text{(11)} \quad \frac{d\Omega_{1g}}{dt} = (-B_m/J_m)\Omega_{1g} + (-1/J_m)T_s + (0)v_{2g} + (\alpha/J_m)i_s$$

Then using modified (4) yields the second state-variable equation,

$$\text{(12)} \quad \frac{dT_s}{dt} = (K)\Omega_{1g} + (0)T_s + (-K/r)v_{2g}$$

And combining (10) with (9) yields the third state-variable,

$$\text{(13)} \quad \frac{dv_{2g}}{dt} = (0)\Omega_{1g} + [1/(r \cdot m_{tot})]T_s + (-1/m_{tot})f_{NL}(v_{2g})$$

The problem has now been reduced to working with three equations and three unknowns.

d) The normal operating point values of Ω_{1g}, T_s, and v_{2g} are found from employing equations (11), (12), and (13) with all time derivatives set equal to zero.

$$\text{(14)} \quad (B_m)\overline{\Omega}_{1g} + (1)\overline{T}_s = (\alpha)\overline{i}_s$$

$$\text{(15)} \quad (K)\overline{\Omega}_{1g} = (K/r)\overline{v}_{2g} \quad ; \quad \therefore \quad \overline{\Omega}_{1g} = (1/r)\overline{v}_{2g}$$

$$\text{(16)} \quad \overline{T}_s = r \cdot f_{NL}(\overline{v}_{1g}) = r[\text{sign}(\overline{v}_{2g}) \cdot F_o + b \cdot \overline{v}_{2g}]$$

Combining (14), (15), and (16) to eliminate $\bar{\Omega}_{1g}$ and $\bar{T}_s$,

$$(B_m/r)\bar{v}_{2g} + r[\text{sign}(\bar{v}_{2g})\cdot F_o + b\cdot\bar{v}_{2g}] = \alpha\cdot\bar{i}_s$$

Solving for $\bar{v}_{2g}$

$$(17) \qquad \bar{v}_{2g} = \frac{\alpha\cdot\bar{i}_s - r\cdot\text{sign}(\bar{v}_{2g})\cdot F_o}{(B_m/r + r\cdot b)} = 1.42 \text{ m/sec}$$

Then

$$(18) \qquad \bar{\Omega}_{1g} = (1/r)\bar{v}_{2g} = 14.28 \text{ rad/sec}$$

and

$$(19) \qquad \bar{T}_s = \alpha\cdot\bar{i}_s - B_m\bar{\Omega}_{1g} = 4.572 \text{ N-m}$$

e) Linearization, valid only when $\bar{v}_{2g}$ is near zero, yields

$$(20) \qquad \frac{d\hat{\Omega}_{1g}}{dt} = \underset{\substack{\uparrow \\ a_{11}}}{(-B_m/J_m)}\hat{\Omega}_{1g} + \underset{\substack{\uparrow \\ a_{12}}}{(-1/J_m)}\hat{T}_s + \underset{\substack{\uparrow \\ a_{13}}}{(0)}\hat{v}_{2g} + \underset{\substack{\uparrow \\ b_{11}}}{(\alpha/J_m)}\hat{i}_s$$

$$(21) \qquad \frac{d\hat{T}_s}{dt} = \underset{\substack{\uparrow \\ a_{21}}}{(K)}\hat{\Omega}_{1g} + \underset{\substack{\uparrow \\ a_{22}}}{(0)}\hat{T}_s + \underset{\substack{\uparrow \\ a_{23}}}{(-K/r)}\hat{v}_{2g}$$

$$(22) \qquad \frac{d\hat{v}_{1g}}{dt} = \underset{\substack{\uparrow \\ a_{31}}}{(0)}\hat{\Omega}_{1g} + \underset{\substack{\uparrow \\ a_{32}}}{(1/m_{tot})}\hat{T}_s + \underset{\substack{\uparrow \\ a_{33}}}{(-b/m_{tot})}\hat{v}_{2g}$$

Solving (21) for $\hat{\Omega}_{1g}$,

$$(23) \qquad \hat{\Omega}_{1g} = (1/a_{21})\frac{d\hat{T}_s}{dt} + (-a_{23}/a_{21})\hat{v}_{2g}$$

Substituting for Ω_{1g} in (20),

$$(24) \qquad (1/a_{21})\frac{d^2\hat{T}_s}{dt^2} + (-a_{23}/a_{21})\frac{d\hat{v}_{2g}}{dt} = (a_{11}/a_{21})\frac{d\hat{T}_s}{dt}$$

$$+ (-a_{11}a_{23}/a_{21})\hat{v}_{2g} + a_{12}\hat{T}_s + b_{11}\hat{i}_s$$

Substituting for $\hat{T}_s$ in (24)

$$\left[(1/a_{21})\frac{d^2}{dt^2} - (a_{11}/a_{21})\frac{d}{dt}\right]\left[(1/a_{32})\frac{d}{dt} + (-a_{33}/a_{32})\right]\hat{v}_{2g}$$

$$-(a_{23}/a_{21})\frac{d\hat{v}_{2g}}{dt} + (a_{11}a_{23}/a_{21})\hat{v}_{2g}$$

$$-(a_{12})\left[(1/a_{32})\frac{d}{dt} + (-a_{33}/a_{32})\right]\hat{v}_{2g} = b_{11}\hat{i}_s$$

After rearranging

$$\underset{\substack{\uparrow \\ a_3}}{(1)}\frac{d^3\hat{v}_{2g}}{dt^3} + \underset{\substack{\uparrow \\ a_2}}{(-a_{11}-a_{33})}\frac{d^2\hat{v}_{2g}}{dt^2} + \underset{\substack{\uparrow \\ a_1}}{(a_{33}a_{11}-a_{23}a_{32}-a_{12}a_{21})}\frac{d\hat{v}_{2g}}{dt}$$

$$+ \underset{\substack{\uparrow \\ a_0}}{(a_{11}a_{23}a_{32}+a_{12}a_{21}a_{33})}\hat{v}_{2g} = \underset{\substack{\uparrow \\ b_0}}{a_{21}a_{32}b_{11}}\hat{i}_s$$

or

$$(a_3D^3 + a_2D^2 + a_1D + a_0)\hat{v}_{2g} = b_0\hat{i}_s$$

where $a_3 = 1$

$$a_2 = (-a_{11}-a_{33}) = (B_m/J_m + b/m_{tot}) = (.03/.0075 + 11/62.25)$$

$$= 4 + .1767 = \underline{4.1767}$$

$$a_1 = (a_{33}a_4 - a_{23}a_{32} - a_{12}a_{21})$$

$$= [(b/m_{tot})(B_m/J_m) + (K/r^2m_{tot}) + (K/J_m)]$$

$$= (.177)(4.0) + (85000/6.225) + (8500/.0075)$$

$$= .707 + 13{,}654 + 1{,}133{,}333$$

$$= \underline{1{,}146{,}987}$$

$$a_0 = (a_{11}a_{23}a_{32} + a_{12}a_{21}a_{33}) = [(B_mK/J_mr^2m_{tot}) + (Kb/J_mm_{tot})]$$

$$= [(4)(85000)/6.225] + [(8500)(11)/(.0075)(6.225)]$$

$$= 54{,}619 + 200{,}268$$

$$= \underline{254{,}876}$$

f) Thus the characteristic equation is

$$D^3 + 4.1767D^2 + 1{,}147{,}000D + 255{,}000 = 0$$

At least one root must be real, and it is readily found iteratively as follows:

Step 1: Form a characteristic equation from the two largest adjacent terms (in this case $a_1D+a_0=0$) and solve for D:

$$D = -a_0/a_1$$

this is a first estimate for r_1.

Step 2: Rearranging the 3rd order characteristic equation as follows:

$$D(a_3D^2 + a_1) + a_2D^2 + a_0 = 0$$

$$D = -(a_2r_1^2+a_0)/(a_3D^2+a_1)$$

$$= -(a_2r_1^2+a_0)/(a_3r_1^2+a_1) = r_1 \quad \{\text{this is a better estimate for } r_1\}$$

$$D = -(a_2r_1^2+a_0)/(a_3r_1^2+a_1) = r_1 \quad \{\text{repeat until it converges}\}$$

For this problem:

Step 1: $r_1 = -a_0/a_1 = -254{,}876/1{,}146{,}987 = -.2223$

$r_1^2 = .049$

Step 2: $r_1 = -(a_2(.049)+a_0)/(a_3(0.49)+a_1)$

$= [(4.177)(.049)+254{,}876]/[.049+1{,}147{,}000]$

$= \underline{.2223}$

We should be so lucky! (Sometimes it takes several iterations)

Now the other roots come from long division:

$$\begin{array}{r|l}
 & a_3D^2 + (a_2+r_1a_3)D + (a_1+r_1a_2+r_1^2a_3) \\ \hline
(D-r_1) & a_3D^3 + a_2D^2 + a_1D + a_0 \\
 & a_3D^3 - r_1a_3D^2 \\ \hline
 & (a_2+r_1a_3)D^2 + a_1D \\
 & (a_2+r_1a_3)D^2 - r_1(a_2+r_1a_3)D \\ \hline
 & (a_1+r_1a_2+r_1^2a_3)D + a_0 \\
 & (a_1+r_1a_2+r_1^2a_3)D - r_1a_1 - r_1^2a_2 - r_1^3a_3 \\ \hline
 & a_0 + r_1a_1 + r_1^2a_2 + r_1^3a_3 = 0
\end{array}$$

{By definition because r_1 is a known root!}

The quotient just obtained contains the other two roots.

$$a_3D^2 + (a_2+r_1a_3)D + (a_1+r_1a_2+r_1^2a_3) = 0$$

$$r_2, r_3 = \frac{-(a_2+r_1a_3) \pm [(a_2+r_1a_3)^2 - 4a_3(a_1+r_1a_2+r_1^2a_3)]^{.5}}{2a_3}$$

Their natural frequency

$$\omega_n = [(a_1+r_1a_2+r_1^2a_3)/a_3]^{.5}$$

$$= [\{1.146\text{x}10^6 + (.2223)(4.176) + (.049)(1)\}/1]^{.5}$$

$$= \underline{1070 \text{ rad/sec}}$$

And their damping ratio

$$\zeta = (a_2+r_1a_3)/\{2[a_3(a_1+r_1a_2+r_1^2a_3)]^{.5}\}$$

$$= (4.176 + .2223)/\{2[1(1.146\text{x}10^6 + .928 + .049)]^{.5}\}$$

$$= \underline{.0021}$$

g) The nonlinear friction function can be considered as the sum of two functions:

The nonlinear coulomb part:

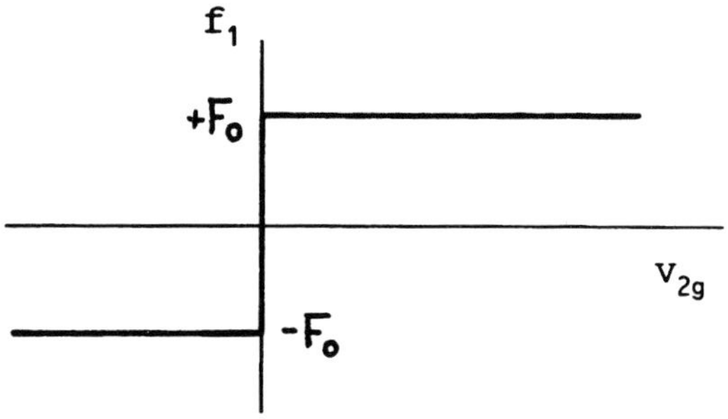

The linear part:

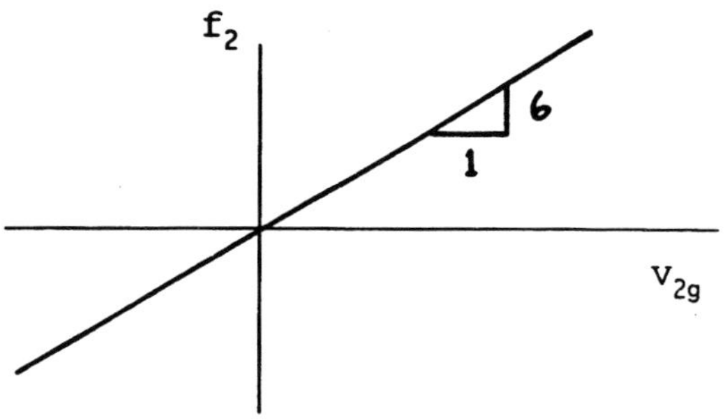

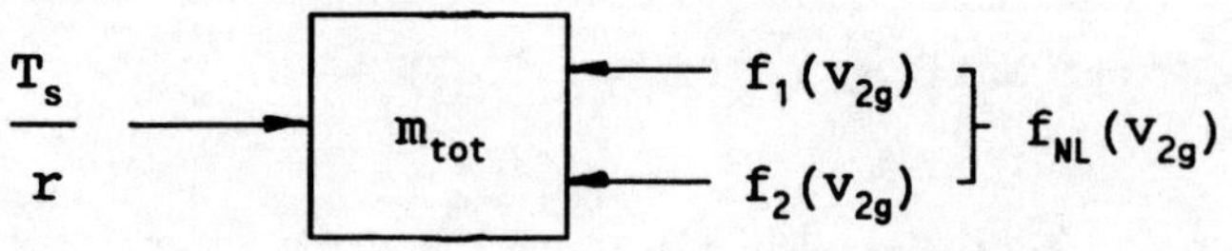

Then there are three cases to consider for the coulomb friction part:

i) mass in motion, $|v_{2g}| > 0$

$$f_1 = F \, \text{sign}(v_{2g})$$

ii) mass standing still,

$$|F_{sum}| = |T_s/r - f_2/v_{2g}| \le F_0$$

and

$$-|v_{2gmin}| < v_{2g} < |v_{2gmin}|$$

approximating

$$v_{2g} \approx 0$$

$$f_1 = F_{sum}$$

iii) mass on the verge of moving

$$|F_{sum}| \ge F_0$$

$$v_{2g} \approx 0$$

$$f_1 = F_0 \, \text{sign}(F_{sum})$$

In the program:

$QDOT(1) \leftrightarrow \dot{\Omega}_g$; $Q(1) \leftrightarrow \Omega_{2g}$

$QDOT(2) \leftrightarrow \dot{T}_s$; $Q(2) \leftrightarrow T_s$

$QDOT(3) \leftrightarrow \dot{v}_{2g}$; $Q(3) \leftrightarrow v_{2g}$

$U(1) \leftrightarrow i_s$

$A(1,1) = (-B_m/J_m)$; $A(1,2) = (-1/J_m)$; $A(1,3) = 0$

$A(2,1) = (K)$; $A(2,2) = 0$; $A(2,3) = (-K/r)$

$A(3,1) = 0$; $A(3,2) = (1/r)$; $A(3,3) = (-1/m_{tot})$

$B(1,1) = (\alpha/J_m)$

$C(1,1) = (-b)$; $C(2,2) = ((v_{2g})_{min})$; $C(3,3) = (F_0)$

Fortran Statements:

```
QDOT(1)=A(1,1)*Q(1)+A(1,2)*Q(2)+A(1,3)*Q(3)+B(1,1)*U(1)
QDOT(2)=A(2,1)*Q(1)+A(2,2)*Q(2)+A(2,3)*Q(3)
FSUM=A(3,1)*Q(1)+A(3,2)*Q(2)+C(1,1)*Q(3)
F1=DSIGN(C(3,3),Q(3))
V2MIN=(.001)*C(2,2)
IF(DABS(Q(3)).LE.V2MIN) F1=FSUM
IF(DABS(F1).GE.C(3,3)) F1=DSIGN(C(3,3),FSUM)
QDOT(3)=A(3,3)*(FSUM+F1)
```

PROBLEM 10.2

a) Free-body and electric circuit diagram

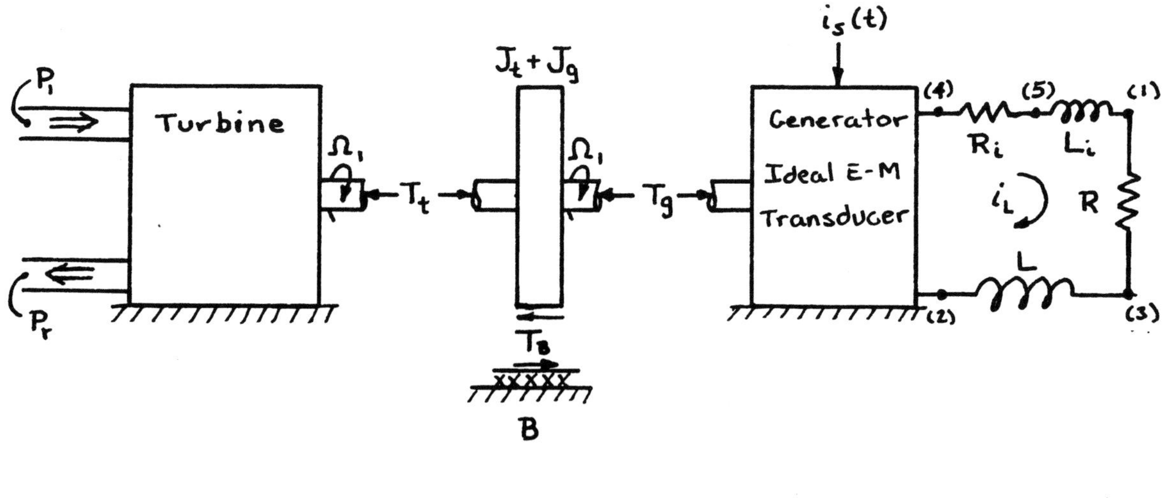

b) For the inertialess trubine,

(1) $$T_t = f_{NL}[(\bar{\Omega}_{1g} + \hat{\Omega}_{1g}),\ (\bar{P}_{1r} + \cancelto{0}{\hat{P}_{1r}}),\ \Omega_0,\ P_0]$$

For the lumped inertia, $J=J_t+J_g$

(2) $$J \frac{d\Omega_{1g}}{dt} = T_t - T_B - T_g$$

For the generator damper, B

(3) $$T_B = B\Omega_{1g}$$

For the ideal generator,

(4) $$T_g = (1/C_r i_s(t))i_L$$

(5) $$\Omega_{1g} = C_r i_s(t) e_{42}$$

For R_i,

(6) $$e_{45} = R_i i_L$$

For L_i,

(7) $$e_{51} = L_i \frac{di_L}{dt}$$

For R,

(8) $$e_{13} = Ri_L$$

For L,

(9) $$e_{32} = L \frac{di_L}{dt}$$

Compatability,

(10) $$e_{42} = e_{45} + e_{51} + e_{13} + e_{32}$$

c) Starting with (2), then (1), (4), and (3),

$$J \frac{d\Omega_{1g}}{dt} = f_{NL}[(\bar{\Omega}_{1g}+\hat{\Omega}_{1g}), \bar{P}_{1r}, \Omega_0, P_0] + (-1/C_r i_s(t))\, i_L - B\Omega_{1g}$$

or

$$(11) \quad \frac{d\Omega_{1g}}{dt} = (1/J) f_{NL}[(\bar{\Omega}_{1g}+\hat{\Omega}_{1g}), \bar{P}_{1r}, \Omega_0, P_0] + (-B/J)(\bar{\Omega}_{1g}+\hat{\Omega}_{1g})$$

$$+ (-1/C_r J)(i_L/i_s(t))$$

which is state variable equation I.

For the electric circuit, lumping the R's and L's,

$$R_{tot} = R_i + R \quad ; \quad L_{tot} = L_i + L$$

$$L_{tot} \frac{di_L}{dt} = e_{51} + e_{32} = e_{42} - e_{45} - e_{13} = \frac{\Omega_{1g}}{C_r i_s(t)} - R_{tot} i_L$$

or

$$(12) \quad \frac{di_L}{dt} = (1/L_{tot} C_r)(\Omega_{1g}/i_s(t)) + (-R_{tot}/L_{tot})\, i_L$$

which is state variable equation II.

d) The terms to be linearized are:

$$\frac{f_{NL}(\Omega_{1g})}{J}, \quad \left(\frac{-1}{C_r J}\right)\frac{i_L}{i_s(t)}, \text{ and } \left(\frac{1}{L_{tot} C_r}\right)\frac{\Omega_{1g}}{i_a(t)}$$

After differentiation they are

$$\frac{1}{J} \left.\frac{\partial f_{NL}(\Omega_{1g})}{\partial \Omega_{1g}}\right|_{\bar{\Omega}_{1g}} \hat{\Omega}_{1g} = \frac{1}{J} \cdot \frac{T_0}{3\Omega_o}(1-\bar{\Omega}_{1g}/\Omega_0)\hat{\Omega}_{1g} = (-B_{inc}/J)\hat{\Omega}_{1g}$$

where $B_{inc} = T_0/3\Omega_0^2(\bar{\Omega}_{1g} - \Omega_0)$

$$(-1/C_rJ)\left[\frac{\partial}{\partial i_L}\left(\frac{i_L}{i_s(t)}\right)\Bigg|_{\bar{\Omega}_{1g},\bar{i}_s}\hat{i}_L + \frac{\partial}{\partial i_s}\left(\frac{i_L}{i_s(t)}\right)\Bigg|_{\bar{i}_L,\bar{i}_s}\hat{i}_s\right]$$

$$= (-1/C_rJ)\left[\left(\frac{i_L}{\bar{i}_s}\right)\hat{i}_L + \left(\frac{-\bar{i}_L}{\bar{i}_s^{\,2}}\right)\hat{i}_s\right]$$

$$= \left[\frac{-1}{C_rJ\bar{i}_s}\right]\hat{i}_L + \left[\frac{\bar{i}_L}{C_rJ\bar{i}_s^{\,2}}\right]\hat{i}_s$$

$$(-1/C_rL_{tot})\left[\frac{\partial}{\partial \Omega_{1g}}\left(\frac{\Omega_{1g}}{i_s(t)}\right)\Bigg|_{\bar{\Omega}_{1g},\bar{i}_s}\hat{\Omega}_{1g} + \frac{\partial}{\partial i_s}\left(\frac{\Omega_{1g}}{i_s(t)}\right)\Bigg|_{\bar{\Omega}_{1g},\bar{i}_s}\hat{i}_s\right]$$

$$= (-1/C_rL_{tot})\left[\left(\frac{i_L}{\bar{i}_s}\right)\hat{\Omega}_{1g} + \left(\frac{-\bar{\Omega}_{1g}}{\bar{i}_s^{\,2}}\right)\hat{i}_s\right]$$

$$= \left[\frac{1}{C_rL_{tot}\bar{i}_s}\right]\hat{\Omega}_{1g} + \left[\frac{-\bar{\Omega}_{1g}}{C_rL_{tot}\bar{i}_s^{\,2}}\right]\hat{i}_s$$

Thus the linearized state variable equations are

(13) $$\frac{d\hat{\Omega}_{1g}}{dt} = a_{11}\hat{\Omega}_{1g} + a_{12}\hat{i}_L + b_{11}\hat{i}_s$$

where $a_{11} = -(B_{inc}+B)/J$

$a_{12} = -(1/C_rJ\bar{i}_s)$

$$b_{11} = (i_L/C_r J\bar{i}_s^{\,2})$$

and

(14) $$\frac{d\hat{i}_L}{dt} = a_{21}\hat{\Omega}_{1g} + a_{22}\hat{i}_L + b_{21}\hat{i}_s$$

where $a_{21} = (1/L_{tot}C_r\bar{i}_s)$

$$a_{22} = -(R_{tot}/L_{tot})$$

$$b_{21} = -(\bar{\Omega}_{1g}/L_{tot}C_r\bar{i}_s^{\,2})$$

The output equation is

$$\hat{e}_{12} = R\hat{i}_L$$

e) Combine (13) and (14) to eliminate $\hat{\Omega}_{1g}$. First, rearrange (14).

$$\hat{\Omega}_{1g} = (1/a_{21})\left[\frac{d}{dt} - a_{22}\right]\hat{i}_L + \left[\frac{-b_{21}}{a_{21}}\right]\hat{i}_s$$

Substituting for $\hat{\Omega}_{1g}$ in (13)

$$\left[\frac{d}{dt} - a_{22}\right]\left[(1/a_{21})\left[\frac{d}{dt} - a_{22}\right]\hat{i}_L + \left[\frac{-b_{21}}{a_{21}}\right]\hat{i}_s\right] = a_{12}\hat{i}_L + b_{11}\hat{i}_s$$

Combining terms

$$\left[\frac{1}{a_{21}}\left[\frac{d^2}{dt^2} + (-a_{11}-a_{22})\frac{d}{dt} + a_{11}a_{22}\right] - a_{12}\right]\hat{i}_L$$

$$= \left[b_{11} + \frac{b_{21}}{a_{21}}\left[\frac{d}{dt} - a_{11}\right]\right]\hat{i}_s$$

Rearranging

$$(15)\qquad \frac{d^2\hat{i}_L}{dt^2} + (-a_{11}-a_{22})\frac{d\hat{i}_L}{dt} + (a_{11}a_{22}-a_{12}a_{21})\hat{i}_L$$

$$= b_{21}\frac{d\hat{i}_s}{dt} + (-a_{11}b_{21}+b_{11}a_{21})\hat{i}_s$$

And then for the output equation, $\hat{e}_{12}=R\hat{i}_L$, use $\hat{i}_L=\hat{e}_{12}/R$, so that

$$(16)\qquad \frac{d^2\hat{e}_{12}}{dt^2} + (-a_{11}-a_{22})\frac{de_{12}}{dt} + (a_{11}a_{22}-a_{12}a_{21})\hat{e}_{12}$$

$$= Rb_{21}\frac{d\hat{i}_s}{dt} + R(b_{11}a_{21}-b_{21}a_{11})\hat{i}_s$$

PROBLEM 10.3

a) Fluid circuit and free-body diagram:

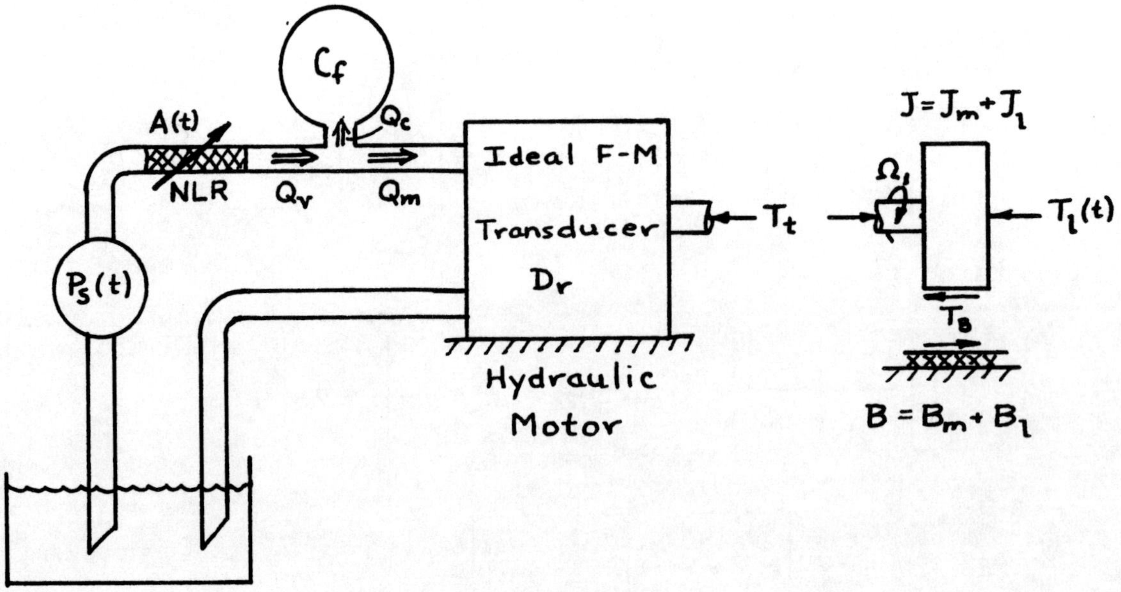

b) For NLR,

(1) $$Q_v = C_d(1/\rho)^{.5}A(t)[P_{12}/(|P_{12}|)^{.5}]$$

For C_f,

(2) $$C_f\frac{dP_{2r}}{dt} = Q_v - Q_m$$

For F-M transducers,

(3) $$Q_m = D_r\Omega_{1g}$$

(4) $$T_t = D_rP_{2r}$$

For $J=J_m+J_l$,

(5) $$J\frac{d\Omega_{1g}}{dt} = T_t - T_B - T_l$$

For $B=B_m+B_l$

(6) $$T_B = B\Omega_{1g}$$

Compatability for fluid loop,

(7) $$P_s = P_{1r} = P_{12} + P_{2r}$$

c) Starting with (2), then (1), and (3) and (7)

(8) $$\frac{dP_{2r}}{dt} = \frac{C_d}{} \left[\frac{2}{\rho}\right]^{.5} \cdot A(t) \cdot \left[\frac{P_s - P_{2r}}{[|P_s-P_{2r}|]^{.5}}\right] + \frac{-D_r}{C_f}\Omega_{1g}$$

Then using (5), (4), and (6)

(9) $$\frac{d\Omega_{1g}}{dt} = \frac{D_r}{J}P_{2r} + \frac{-B}{J}\Omega_{1g} + \frac{-1}{J}T_l(t)$$

Linearizing (1)

(10) $$\hat{Q}_v = C_d\left[\frac{1}{2\rho|\bar{P}_{12}|}\right]^{.5} \cdot \bar{A} \cdot \hat{P}_{12} + C_d\left[\frac{2}{\rho|\bar{P}_{12}|}\right]^{.5} \cdot \bar{P}_{12} \cdot \hat{A}(t)$$

Using (8) with (10)

$$\frac{d\hat{P}_{2r}}{dt} = \frac{-C_d}{C_f}\bar{A}\left[\frac{1}{2\rho|\bar{P}_{12}|}\right]^{.5}(\hat{P}_{2r}-\overset{0}{\not{\hat{P}}_s}(t)) + \frac{-D_r}{C_f}\hat{\Omega}_{1g} \tag{11}$$

$$+\frac{C_d}{C_f}\left[\frac{2}{\rho|\bar{P}_{12}|}\right]^{.5}\bar{P}_{12}\cdot\hat{A}(t)$$

(Note: $\bar{P}_{12} = \bar{P}_s - \bar{P}_{2r}$)

or

$$\frac{d\hat{P}_{2r}}{dt} = a_{11}\hat{P}_{2r} + a_{12}\hat{\Omega}_{1g} + b_{11}\hat{A}(t) \tag{12}$$

where $a_{11} = \frac{-C_d\bar{A}}{C_f}\left[\frac{1}{2\rho|\bar{P}_{12}|}\right]^{.5}$

$a_{12} = -D_r/C_f$

$b_{11} = \frac{C_d}{C_f}\left[\frac{2}{\rho|\bar{P}_{12}|}\right]^{.5}\bar{P}_{12}$

Linearizing (9)

$$\frac{d\hat{\Omega}_{1g}}{dt} = a_{21}\hat{P}_{2r} + a_{22}\hat{\Omega}_{1g} + b_{22}\hat{T}_l(t) \tag{13}$$

where $a_{11} = D_r/J$

$a_{22} = -B/J$

$b_{22} = 1/J$

Solving (13) for $\hat{P}_{2r}$,

$$(14) \qquad \hat{P}_{2r} = \frac{1}{a_{21}}\left[(\frac{d}{dt} - a_{22})\hat{\Omega}_{1g} - b_{22}\hat{T}_l(t) \right]$$

Substituting in (12) for $\hat{P}_{2r}$ from (14),

$$(\frac{d}{dt} - a_{11})\frac{1}{a_{21}}\left[(\frac{d}{dt} - a_{22})\hat{\Omega}_{1g} - b_{22}\hat{T}_l(t) \right] = a_{12}\hat{\Omega}_{1g} + b_{11}\hat{A}(t)$$

Combinig terms,

$$(\frac{d^2}{dt^2} + (-a_{11}-a_{22})\frac{d}{dt} + (a_{11}a_{22}-a_{21}a_{21}))\hat{\Omega}_{1g}$$

$$= b_{22}(\frac{d}{dt} - a_{11})T_l(t) + a_{21}b_{11}\hat{A}(t)$$

PROBLEM 10.4

a) Find the system differential equation relating P_{1r} to $\Psi(t)$ and $R_l(t)$.

For the variable displacement hydraulic pump,

$$(1) \qquad Q_P = C_1 \Psi(t) \Omega_{1g} - (1/R_{fP}) P_{1r}$$

For the air-charged accumulator,

$$(2) \qquad Q_P - Q_{Rl} = (V_{air}/kP_1)(dP_{1r}/dt) \qquad \text{("fast" changes)}$$

For the load resistor,

$$(3) \qquad Q_{Rl} = (1/R_l(t)) P_{1r}$$

Combining to eliminate Q's

$$(4) \qquad \frac{dP_{1r}}{dt} = (\ kP_1/V_{air}\ )[\ (1/R_{fp}) + (1/R_l(t))\ ]P_{1r}$$

$$= (\ k\ P_1\ C_1\ \Omega_{1g}/V_{air}\ )\ \Psi(t)$$

b) Find the normal operating point values, $\overline{\Psi}$ and $\overline{Q}_p$

$$(5) \qquad \overline{\Psi} = (\ 1/C_1\Omega_{1g}\ )[\ (1/R_{fp}) + (1/\overline{R}_l)\ ]\overline{P}_{1r}$$

$$= (1240)/[\ (4.4)(180)(1200)(40)\ ]$$

$$= .0326 \text{ Rad.}$$

$$(6) \qquad \overline{Q}_p = C_1\ \overline{\Psi}\ \Omega_{1g} - P_{1r}/R_{fP}$$

$$= \overline{P}_{1r}/R_l$$

$$= 1000/40$$

$$= 25 \text{ in}^3/\text{sec}$$

c) Linearizing the system differential equation:

$$(7) \qquad \frac{d\hat{P}_{1r}}{dt} + \frac{kP_1}{V_{air}}\left[(1/R_{fP})+(1/\overline{R}^l)\right]\hat{P}_{1r} = \frac{kP_1}{V_{air}}\left[C_1\Omega_{1g}\hat{\Psi}(t)-(\overline{P}_{1r}/\overline{R}_l^{\,2})\hat{R}_l(t)\right]$$

with the system time constant

$$(8) \qquad \tau = \frac{V_{air}R_{fP}\overline{R}_l}{kP_1(R_{fP} + \overline{R}_l)}$$

where

$$V_{air} = m_{air}R\ T_{atm}/P_1$$

Using the given data

$$\tau = [\ (300)(1200)(40)\ ]/[\ (1.4)(1015)(1240)\ ]$$

$$= 8.17 \text{ sec.}$$

d)

$$(9)\qquad \left[\frac{\Delta P_r}{\Delta \hat{R}_l}\right]_{ss} = \frac{-\overline{P}_{1r}(R_{fP}\overline{R}_l)}{\overline{R}_l^{\,2}(R_{fP} + \overline{R}_l)} = \frac{-3000}{124} = -24.19 \quad in^3/sec$$

$$(10)\qquad \left[\frac{\Delta P_r}{\Delta \hat{\Psi}}\right]_{ss} = \frac{C_1\Omega_{1g}R_{fP}\overline{R}_l}{R_{fP} + \overline{R}_l} = \frac{(4.4)(180)(1200)(40)}{1240}$$

$$= 5110 \text{ psi/rad}$$

PROBLEM 10.5

a)

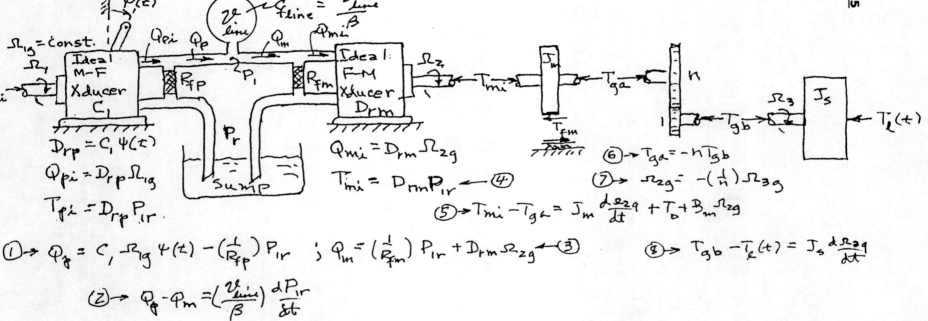

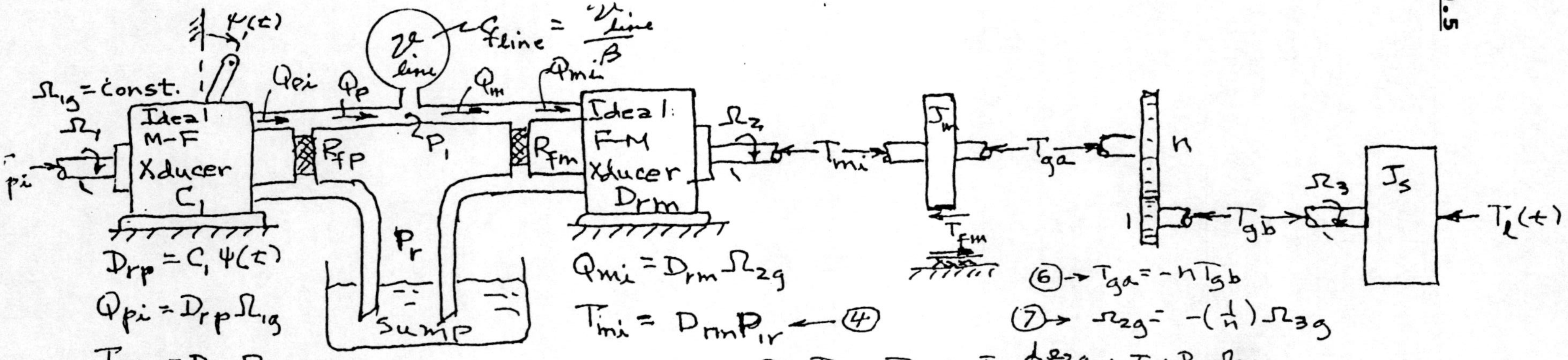

$D_{rp} = C_1 \psi(t)$

$Q_{pi} = D_{rp}\Omega_{1g}$

$T_{pi} = D_{rp}P_{1r}$

$Q_{mi} = D_{rm}\Omega_{2g}$

$T_{mi} = D_{rm}P_{1r}$ ← (4)

(6) → $T_{ga} = -nT_{gb}$

(7) → $\Omega_{2g} = -\left(\frac{1}{n}\right)\Omega_{3g}$

(5) → $T_{mi} - T_{ga} = J_m \frac{d\Omega_{2g}}{dt} + T_o + B_m\Omega_{2g}$

(1) → $Q_p = C_1\Omega_{1g}\psi(t) - \left(\frac{1}{R_{fp}}\right)P_{1r}$; $Q_m = \left(\frac{1}{R_{fm}}\right)P_{1r} + D_{rm}\Omega_{2g}$ ← (3)

(8) → $T_{gb} - T_l(t) = J_s \frac{d\Omega_{3g}}{dt}$

(2) → $Q_p - Q_m = \left(\frac{\mathcal{V}_{line}}{\beta}\right)\frac{dP_{1r}}{dt}$

b) Normal operating point values:

(i) $\bar{T}_{mi} = T_o + B_m(-\bar{\Omega}_{3g}/n) + \bar{T}_{ga} = D_{rm}\bar{P}_{1r}$

or

$$D_{rm} = [\ T_o - B_m(\bar{\Omega}_{3g}/n) - n\bar{T}_l\ ]/\bar{P}_{1r}$$

$$= [\ 30 + (.65)(260/3) + 4500\ ]/1000$$

$$= 4.59$$

(ii) $\bar{Q}_m = D_{rm}(-\bar{\Omega}_{3g}/n) + (1/R_{fm})\bar{P}_{1r}$

(iii) $\bar{Q}_p = \Omega_{1g}C_1\bar{\Psi} - (1/R_{fp})\bar{P}_{1r} = \bar{Q}_m$

$$\bar{D}_{rp} = C_1\bar{\Psi} = [\ \bar{Q}_m + (1/R_{fp})\bar{P}_{1r}\ ]/\Omega_{1g}$$

c) The necessary and sufficient set of describing equations (1) through (8) contain the eight unknowns: Q_p, P_{1r}, Q_m, Ω_{2g}, T_{mi}, T_{ga}, T_{gb}, Ω_{3g}. The state variable equations for P_{1r} comes from equations (1), (2), and (3).

$$\frac{dP_{1r}}{dt} = (\beta/V_{line})\ \{\ C_1\Omega_{1g}\Psi(t) - [(R_{fp}+R_{fm})/R_{fp}R_{fm}]P_{1r} - D_{rm}\Omega_{2g}\ \}$$

or

$$\frac{dP_{1r}}{dt} = \underbrace{\frac{-\beta}{V_{line}}\ \frac{R_{fp}+R_{fm}}{R_{fp}R_{fm}}}_{a_{11}} P_{1r} + \underbrace{\frac{-\beta D_{rm}}{V_{line}}}_{a_{12}}\Omega_{2g} + \underbrace{\frac{\beta C_1\Omega_{1g}}{V_{line}}}_{b_{11}}\Psi(t) \tag{9}$$

The state variable equation for Ω_{2g} comes from equations (4) through (8). First combine (6), (7), and (8) with (5).

$$T_{mi} = -nT_{gb} + J_m(d\Omega_{2g}/dt) + T_o + B_m\Omega_{2g}$$

$$T_{mi} = -n[\ T_l(t) + J_s(-n)\frac{d\Omega_{2g}}{dt}\ ] + J_m\frac{d\Omega_{2g}}{dt} + T_o + B_m\Omega_{2g} \tag{10}$$

Then combine equation (4) with equation (10) and rearrange

$$D_{rm}P_{1r} = (n^2J_s+J_m)\frac{d\Omega_{2g}}{dt} + B_m\Omega_{2g} + T_o - nT_l(t)$$

let $(n^2J_s + J_m) = J_{tot}$, and put in state variable format

$$(11) \qquad \frac{d\Omega_{2g}}{dt} = \frac{D_{rm}}{J_{tot}} P_{1r} + \frac{-B_m}{J_{tot}} \Omega_{2g} + (-1/J_{tot})T_o + (n/J_{tot})T_l(t)$$

$$\qquad\qquad \updownarrow \qquad\qquad \updownarrow \qquad\qquad\qquad\qquad \updownarrow$$

$$\qquad\qquad a_{21} \qquad\qquad a_{22} \qquad\qquad\qquad\qquad b_{22}$$

Output:

$$\Omega_{3g} = -n\Omega_{2g}$$

d) For small perturbations:

State variable equation (A):

$$(A) \qquad \frac{d\hat{P}_{1r}}{dt} = a_{11}\hat{P}_{1r} + a_{12}\hat{\Omega}_{2g} + b_{11}\hat{\Psi}(t)$$

State variable equation (B):

$$(B) \qquad \frac{d\hat{\Omega}_{2g}}{dt} = a_{21}\hat{P}_{1r} + a_{22}\hat{\Omega}_{2g} + b_{22}\hat{T}_l(t)$$

Output equation:

$$\hat{\Omega}_{3g} = -n\hat{\Omega}_{2g}$$

where

$$a_{11} = -\beta(R_{fm}+R_{fp})/(V_{line}R_{fm}R_{fp})$$

$$= -2x10^5(520 + 480)/[(10)(540)(480)]$$

$$= -77.16 \text{ sec}^{-1}$$

$$a_{12} = -\beta D_{rm}/V_{line} = (-4.59)(2x10^5)/10$$

$$= -9.18x10^4 \text{ psi/rad}$$

$$a_{21} = D_{rm}/(n^2J_s + J_m) = 4.59/[(9)(6) + .11]$$

$$= .0848 \quad \text{in}^2\text{rad/lb sec}^2$$

$$a_{22} = -B_m/(n^2 J_s + J_m) = -.65/54.11$$

$$= -.012 \text{ sec}^{-1}$$

$$b_{11} = C_1 \Omega_{1g} \beta / V_{line} = (190)(2\text{x}10^5) C_1/10$$

$$= 3.8 \ C_1 \text{ lb/in}^2 \text{rad sec}$$

$$b_{22} = n/J_{tot} = 3/54.11$$

$$= .055 \text{ rad}^2/\text{in lb sec}$$

Combining (A) and (B) to eliminate $\hat{P}_{1r}$ yields

$$\frac{d^2\Omega_{2g}}{dt^2} - (a_{11}+a_{22})\frac{d\Omega_{2g}}{dt} + (a_{11}a_{22}-a_{12}a_{21})\Omega_{2g}$$

$$= b_{22}\frac{d\hat{T}_l(t)}{dt} + a_{11}b_{22}\hat{T}_l(t) + b_{11}a_{21}\hat{\Psi}(t)$$

and

$$\xi = \frac{-(a_{11} + a_{22})}{2[\ a_{11}a_{22} - a_{12}a_{21}\ ]^{.5}}$$

$$= \frac{77.16 + .012}{2[\ (77.16)(.012) + (91800)(.0848)\ ]^{.5}}$$

$$= .437$$

$$\omega_n = [\ a_{11}a_{22} - a_{12}a_{21}\ ]^{.5}$$

$$= 88.24 \text{ rad/sec} = 14.05 \text{ Hertz}$$

$$I_{line} = \rho L/A = (.032/380)(40)/[\ (3.14)(.5)^2/4\ ]$$

$$= .0169 \text{ lb sec}^2/\text{in}^5$$

$$D_{rm}^{\ 2} I_{line} = .356 \text{ in lb sec}^2/\text{rad}$$

$$J_m = .11 \text{ in lb sec}^2/\text{rad}$$

$$n^2 J_s = 54 \text{ in lb sec}^2/\text{rad}$$

if J_s were removed from the system, I_{line} would not be negligible.

PROBLEM 10.6

a)

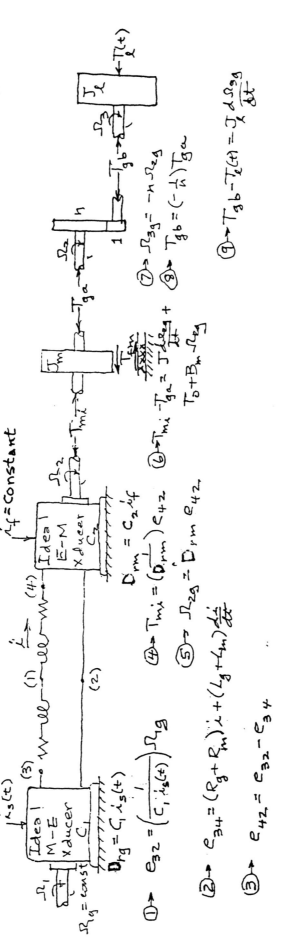

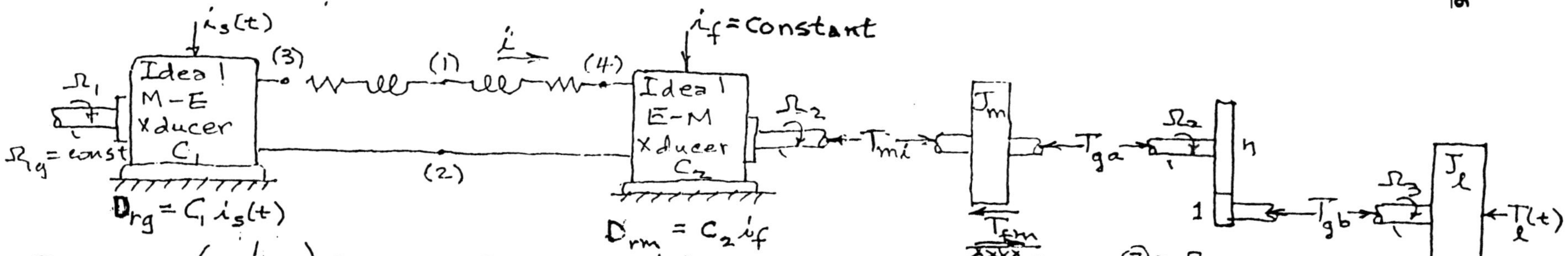

$D_{rg} = C_1 i_s(t)$

$D_{rm} = C_2 i_f$

① → $e_{32} = \left(\frac{1}{C_1 i_s(t)}\right)\Omega_{1g}$

② → $e_{34} = (R_g + R_m)i + (L_g + L_m)\frac{di}{dt}$

③ → $e_{42} = e_{32} - e_{34}$

④ → $T_{mi} = \left(\frac{1}{D_{rm}}\right)e_{42}$

⑤ → $\Omega_{2g} = D_{rm}\, e_{42}$

⑥ → $T_{mi} - T_{ga} = J\frac{d\Omega_{eg}}{dt} + T_0 + B_m \Omega_{eg}$

⑦ → $\Omega_{3g} = -n\,\Omega_{eg}$

⑧ → $T_{gb} = \left(-\frac{1}{n}\right)T_{ga}$

⑨ → $T_{gb} - T_\ell(t) = J_\ell \frac{d\Omega_{3g}}{dt}$

b) Find $\overline{D}_{rm} = f(\overline{i}, \overline{T}_l, \overline{\Omega}_{3g})$

$$\overline{D}_{rm} = \overline{i}/\overline{T}_{mi} = \overline{i}/(\ \overline{T}_{ga} + T_o + B_m\overline{\Omega}_{2g}\ )$$

$$= \overline{i}/(\ -n\overline{T}_l + T_o + B_m(-1/n)\overline{\Omega}_{3g}\ )$$

$$= 30/(4500 + 10 + (.4)260/3)$$

$$= .0066$$

Find $\overline{e}_{12} = f(\overline{\Omega}_{3g}, \overline{i}, D_{rm})$

$$\overline{e}_{12} = R_m\overline{i} + \overline{e}_{42} = R_m\overline{i} + \overline{\Omega}_{2g}/D_{rm}$$

$$= R_m\overline{i} - \overline{\Omega}_{3g}/nD_{rm}$$

Find $\overline{D}_{rg} = C_1\overline{i}_s = f(\overline{e}_{12}, \overline{i}, \overline{\Omega}_{1g})$

$$\overline{D}_{rg} = \overline{\Omega}_{1g}/\overline{e}_{32} = \Omega_{1g}/(\ \overline{e}_{12} + R_g\overline{i})$$

c) Equations (1) through (9) above describe the system on term of the nine unknowns, e_{32}, T_{mi}, Ω_{2g}, e_{42}, e_{34}, T_{mi}, T_{ga}, T_{gb}, and Ω_{3g}. Combining equations (1), (2), (3), and (5)

$$e_{42} = \Omega_{2g}/\alpha_{rm} = \Omega_{1g}/C_1 i_s(t) - (R_g+R_m)i - (L_g+L_m)(di/dt)$$

Rearranging, yields the state variable equation for i.

$$\text{(A)} \qquad \frac{di}{dt} = \frac{-(R_g+R_m)}{L_g+L_m} i + \frac{-1}{D_{rm}(l_g+L_m)} \Omega_{2g} + \frac{1}{C_1(L_g+L_m)} \frac{\Omega_{1g}}{i_s(t)}$$

Combining (4), (6), (7), (8), and (9)

$$T_{mi} - T_{ga} = i/\alpha_{rm} + nT_{gb} = I_m \frac{d\Omega_{2g}}{dt} + T_o + B\Omega_{2g}$$

$$i/D_{rm} + n\left[\ -nJ_l\frac{d\Omega_{2g}}{dt} + T_l(t)\ \right] = J_m\frac{d\Omega_{2g}}{dt} + T_o + B\Omega_{2g}$$

Rearranging yields the state variable equation for Ω_{2g}

(B) $$\frac{d\Omega_{2g}}{dt} = \frac{1}{D_{rm}(J_m+n^2J_l)} i + \frac{-B}{J_m+n^2J_l} \Omega_{2g} + \frac{-1}{J_m+n^2J_l} (T_o - nT_l(t))$$

The output equation is

(C) $$\Omega_{3g} = -n\Omega_{2g}$$

d) Linearizing equations (A), (B), and (C):

$$\frac{di}{dt} = a_{11}\hat{i} + a_{12}\hat{\Omega}_{2g} + b_{11}\hat{i}_s(t)$$

$$\frac{d\hat{\Omega}_{2g}}{dt} = \hat{a}_{21}i + a_{22}\hat{\Omega}_{2g} + b_{22}\hat{T}_l(t)$$

$$\hat{\Omega}_{3g} = -n\hat{\Omega}_{2g}$$

where

$$a_{11} = -(R_g+R_m)/(L_g+L_m) = -1.0/10$$
$$= -.1$$

$$a_{12} = -1/[\ D_{rm}(L_g+L_m)\ ] = -1.0/(.0066)(10)$$
$$= -15.15$$

$$a_{21} = 1/[\ D_{rm}(J_m + n^2J_l)\ ] = 1/(.0066)(30+54)$$
$$= 1.804$$

$$b_{11} = -\Omega_{1g}/[\ C_1(L_g+L_m)\bar{i}_s^{\,2} = -190/C_1(10)(\bar{i}_s)^2$$
$$= -19/C_1(\bar{i}_s)^2$$

$$b_{22} = n/(J_m+n^2J_l) = -3/84$$
$$= .0357$$

$$\xi = -(a_{11}+a_{22})/(2\ [a_{11}a_{22}-a_{12}a_{21}]^{.5})$$
$$= (.1+.0048)/(2\ [(.1)(.00476)+(15.15)(1.804)]^{.5})$$
$$= .1$$

$$\omega_n = [a_{11}a_{22} - a_{12}a_{21}]^{.5} = [\ 27.33\ ]^{.5}$$

$$= 5.22 \text{ rad/sec} = .831 \text{ Hertz}$$

PROBLEM 10.7

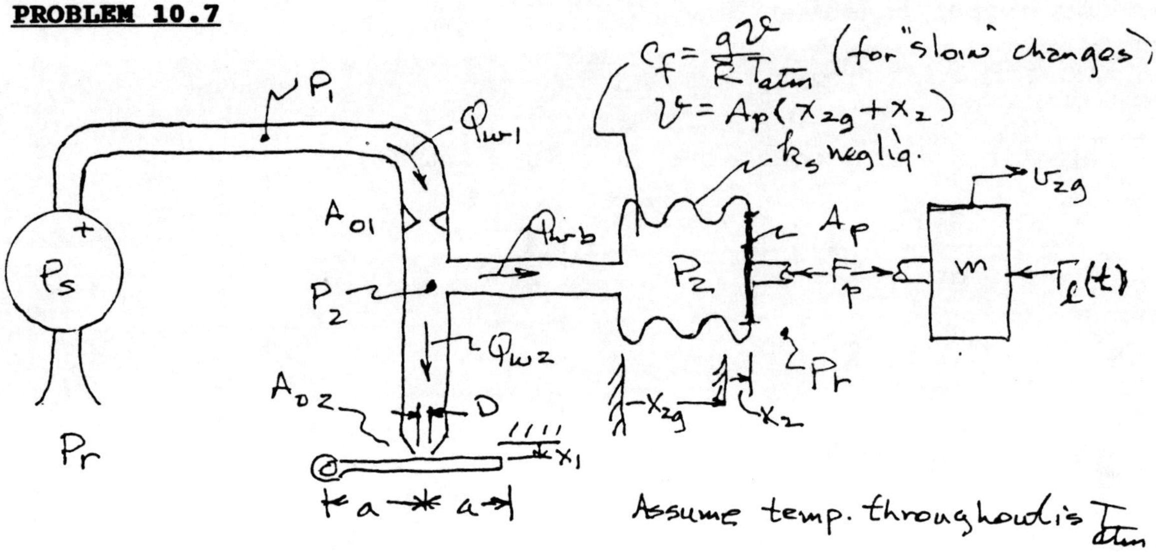

(1) $Q_{w1} = C_{d1}A_{01}C_2P_1/[T_{atm}]^{.5}$

(2) $Q_{w2} = (\ C_{d2}\pi Dx_1(t)2C_2/2[T_{atm}]^{.5}\ )\ [P_r(P_2 - P_r)]^{.5}$

(3) $Q_{wb} = Q_{w1} - Q_{w2}$

(4) $Q_{wb} = \underbrace{(gV/RT_{atm})\ (dP_2/dt)}_{\text{due to pressure changes}} + \underbrace{\gamma A_p v_{2g}}_{\text{due to volume changes}}$

(5) $F_p = A_p(P_2 - P_r)$

(6) $m\dfrac{dv_{2g}}{dt} = F_p - F_l(t)$

Combining equations (1) through (6)

$$\frac{gV}{RT_{atm}}\frac{dP_2}{dt} = \frac{C_{d1}A_{01}C_2P_1}{[\ T_{atm}\ ]^{.5}} - \frac{C_{d2}\pi Dx_1(t)C_2}{[\ T_{atm}\ ]^{.5}}[P_r(P_2-P_r)]^{.5}$$

$$- \gamma A_p v_{2g}$$

Rearranging yields the state variable equation for P_2.

$$\frac{d\hat{P}_2}{dt} = \frac{-C_{d2}\pi D x_1(t) C_2 R[T_{atm}P_r]^{.5}}{gV}[P_2 - P_r]^{.5}$$

$$+ \frac{-\gamma A_p R T_{atm}}{gV} v_{2g} + \frac{C_{d1}A_{01}C_2R[T_{atm}]^{.5}}{gV} P_1$$

Linearizing:

$$\text{(A)} \qquad \frac{d\hat{P}_2}{dt} = a_{11}\hat{P}_2 + a_{12}\hat{v}_{2g} + b_{11}\hat{x}_1(t) + \cancelto{0}{b_{12}\hat{P}_1}$$

where

$$a_{11} = \frac{-C_{d2}\pi D\bar{x}_1 C_2 R[T_{atm}P_r]^{.5}}{2gV\ [\bar{P}_2 - P_r]^{.5}} \quad 1/\text{sec}$$

$$a_{12} = \frac{-\gamma A_p R T_{atm}}{gV} \quad \text{lb/in}^3$$

$$b_{11} = \frac{-C_{d2}\pi D C_2 R[T_{atm}P_r(\bar{P}_2 - P_r)]^{.5}}{gV} \quad \text{lb/in}^3\ \text{sec}$$

$$b_{21} = \frac{C_{d1}A_{01}C_2R[T_{atm}]^{.5}}{gV} \quad 1/\text{sec}$$

Combining (5) and (6),

$$\frac{dv_{2g}}{dt} = (1/m)[\ A_p(P_2 - P_r) - F_l(t)\ ]$$

$$= (A_p/m)P_2 + (0)v_{2g} + (-A_p/m)P_r + (-1/m)F_2(t)$$

Linearizing for small perturbations,

$$\text{(B)} \qquad \frac{d\hat{v}_{2g}}{dt} = a_{21}\hat{P}_2 + a_{22}\hat{v}_{2g} + \cancelto{0}{b_{21}\hat{P}_r} + b_{22}\hat{F}_l(t)$$

where

$$a_{21} = A_p/m \quad \text{in}^3/\text{lb sec}$$

$a_{22} = 0$

$b_{21} = -A_p/m \quad in^3/lb\ sec$

$b_{22} = -1/m \quad in/lb\ sec$

Combining (A) and (B) to eliminate $\hat{P}_2$,

$$\frac{d^2\hat{v}_{2g}}{dt_2} - a_{11}\frac{d\hat{v}_{2g}}{dt} - a_{12}a_{21}\hat{v}_{2g} = b_{11}a_{21}\hat{x}_1$$

$$\left[\frac{\Delta\hat{v}_{2g}}{\Delta\hat{x}_1}\right|_{ss} = \frac{-b_{11}}{a_{12}} = \frac{-C_{d2}\pi DC_2R[T_{atm}P_r(\bar{P}_2-P_r)]^{.5}}{\gamma A_p\ R\ T_{atm}}$$

or

$$\left[\frac{\Delta\hat{v}_{2g}}{\Delta\hat{x}_1}\right|_{ss} = \frac{C_{d2}\pi DC_2[P_r(\bar{P}_2-P_r)]^{.5}}{\gamma A_p\ [T_{atm}]^{.5}}$$

For the damping ratio

$$\xi = \frac{-a_{11}}{2[-a_{21}a_{21}]^{.5}} = \frac{\dfrac{-C_{d2}\pi D\bar{x}_1C_2R[T_{atm}P_r]^{.5}}{2gV[P_2-\bar{P}_r]^{.5}}}{2\left[\dfrac{\gamma A_pR\ T_{atm}}{gV}(A_p/m)\right]^{.5}}$$

$$= \frac{C_{d2}\pi D\bar{x}_1C_2R[RP_r]^{.5}}{A_p[\ (\gamma gV/m)(\bar{P}_2-P_r)\ ]^{.5}}$$

Ask instructor for parameter values to continue with numerical parameters.

PROBLEM 10.8

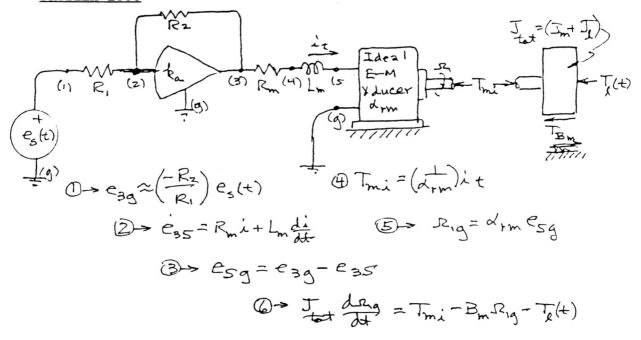

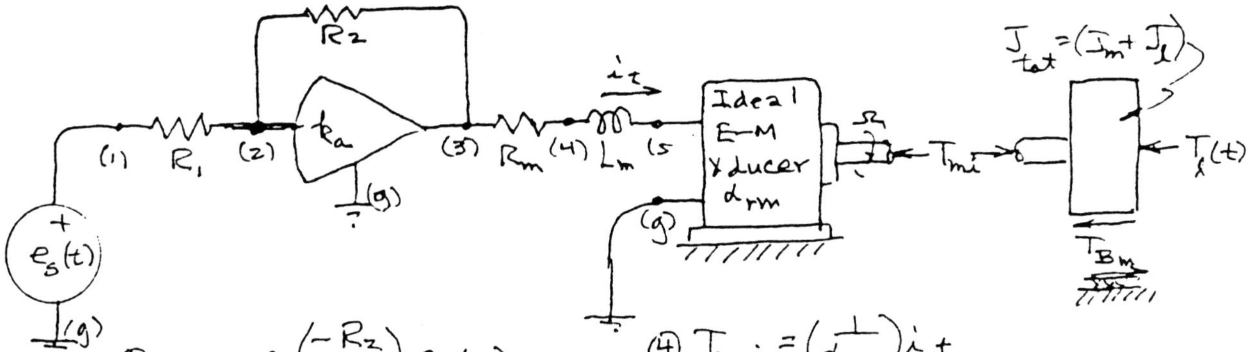

① → $e_{3g} \approx \left(\frac{-R_2}{R_1}\right) e_s(t)$

④ $T_{mi} = \left(\frac{1}{\alpha_{rm}}\right) i_t$

② → $e_{35} = R_m i + L_m \frac{di}{dt}$

⑤ → $\Omega_{1g} = \alpha_{rm} e_{5g}$

③ → $e_{5g} = e_{3g} - e_{35}$

⑥ → $J_{tot} \frac{d\Omega_{1g}}{dt} = T_{mi} - B_m \Omega_{1g} - T_l(t)$

Combining equations (1), (2), (3), and (5) yields,

$$L_m \frac{di_t}{dt} = -R_m i_t + (-R_2/R_1)\, e_s(t) + (-1/\alpha_{rm})\, \Omega_{1g}$$

Rearranging to form the state variable equation for i_f,

$$\text{(A)} \qquad \frac{di_t}{dt} = \underbrace{(-R_m/L_m)}_{a_{11}} i_t + \underbrace{(-1/\alpha_{rm} L_m)}_{a_{12}} \Omega_{1g} + \underbrace{(-R_2/R_1 L_m)}_{b_{11}} e_s(t)$$

Combining (4) and (2) yields

$$J_{tot} \frac{d\Omega_{1g}}{dt} = (1/\alpha_{rm})\, i_t - B_m \Omega_{1g} - T_l(t)$$

or

$$\text{(B)} \qquad \frac{d\Omega_{1g}}{dt} = \underbrace{(1/\alpha_{rm} J_{tot})}_{a_{21}} i_t - \underbrace{(B_m/J_{tot})}_{a_{22}} \Omega_{1g} - \underbrace{(1/J_{tot})}_{b_{22}} T_l(t)$$

Combining (A) and (B) to eliminate i_t and $T_l(t)$

$$\frac{d^2\Omega_{1g}}{dt^2} - (a_{11}+a_{22})\frac{d\Omega_{1g}}{dt} + (a_{11}a_{22}-a_{12}a_{21})\Omega_{1g} = b_{11}a_{21}e_s(t)$$

$$\left[\frac{\Delta\Omega_{1g}}{\Delta e_s}\right]_{ss} = \frac{b_{11}a_{21}}{a_{11}a_{22}-a_{12}a_{21}} = \frac{\dfrac{-R_2}{R_1L_m\alpha_{rm}J_{tot}}}{\dfrac{-R_m}{L_m}\dfrac{-B_m}{J_{tot}} + \dfrac{1}{L_m\alpha_{rm}^2J_{tot}}}$$

$$= \frac{-R_2\alpha_{rm}}{R_1(R_m\alpha_{rm}^2B_m + 1)}$$

$$\xi = \frac{-(a_{11}+a_{22})}{2[a_{11}a_{22}-a_{12}a_{21}]^{.5}}$$

$$= \frac{(R_m/L_m) + (B_m/J_{tot})}{2[\ (R_mB_m/L_mJ_{tot}) + (1/\alpha_{rm}^2L_mJ_{tot})\ ]^{.5}}$$

$$= \frac{R_mJ_{tot} + B_mL_m}{2\ [\ L_mJ_{tot}(R_mB_m + 1/\alpha_{rm}^2)\ ]^{.5}}$$

CHAPTER 11

PROBLEM 11.1

$$\frac{\dfrac{\overline{\Omega}_{1g}K}{\overline{\Omega}_{2g}J_e}}{s^2 + \dfrac{K}{2C_c\Omega_{2g}}s + \dfrac{\overline{\Omega}_{1g}K}{\overline{\Omega}_{2g}J_e} + \dfrac{K}{J_p}}$$

$T_e \longrightarrow \qquad \longrightarrow T_K$

$$\frac{\dfrac{K}{J_p}}{s^2 + \dfrac{K}{2C_c\Omega_{2g}}s + \dfrac{\overline{\Omega}_{1g}K}{\overline{\Omega}_{2g}J_e} + \dfrac{K}{J_p}}$$

$T_w \longrightarrow \qquad \longrightarrow T_K$

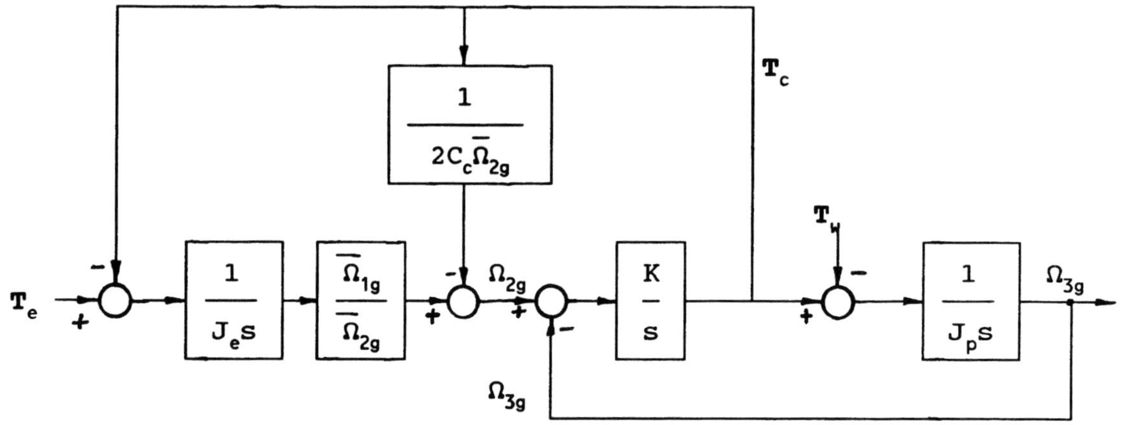

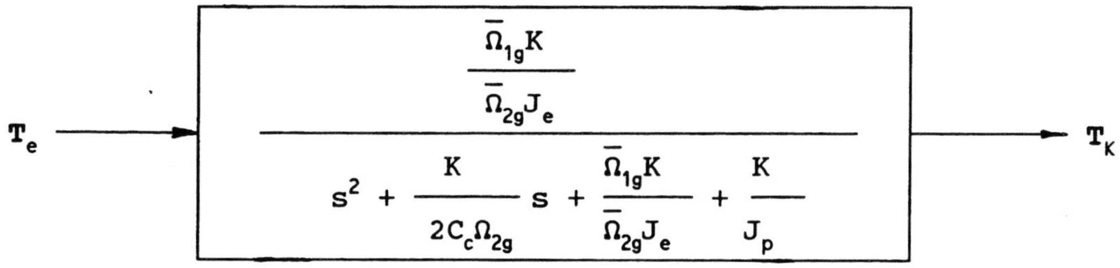

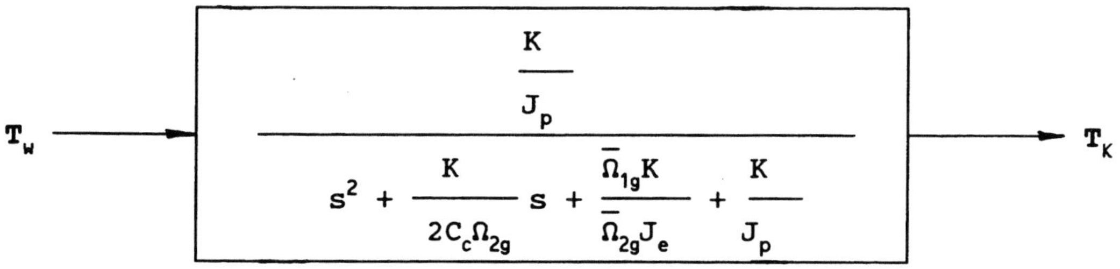

PROBLEM 11.2

a)

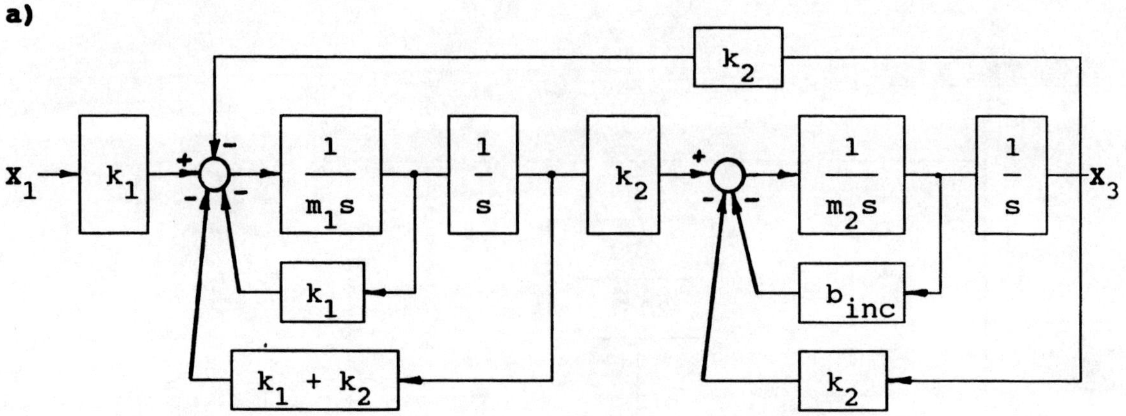

b)

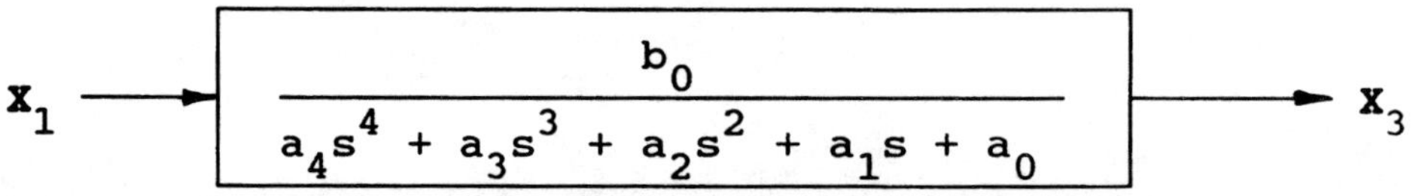

$$\frac{b_0}{a_4 s^4 + a_3 s^3 + a_2 s^2 + a_1 s + a_0}$$

$X_1 \longrightarrow$ | | $\longrightarrow X_3$

c)

$$\frac{b_2 s^2 + b_1 s + b_0}{a_4 s^4 + a_3 s^3 + a_2 s^2 + a_1 s + a_0}$$

$X_1 \longrightarrow$ | | $\longrightarrow X_2$

where

$$a_4 = m_1 m_2 \qquad\qquad b_2 = k_1 m_2$$

$$a_3 = m_1 b_{inc} + m_2 b_1 \qquad\qquad b_1 = k_1 b_{inc}$$

$$a_2 = m_1 k_2 + m_2 (k_1 + k_2) \qquad\qquad b_0 = a_0 = k_1 k_2$$

$$a_1 = b_1 k_2 + b_{inc}(k_1 + k_2)$$

$$a_0 = k_1 k_2$$

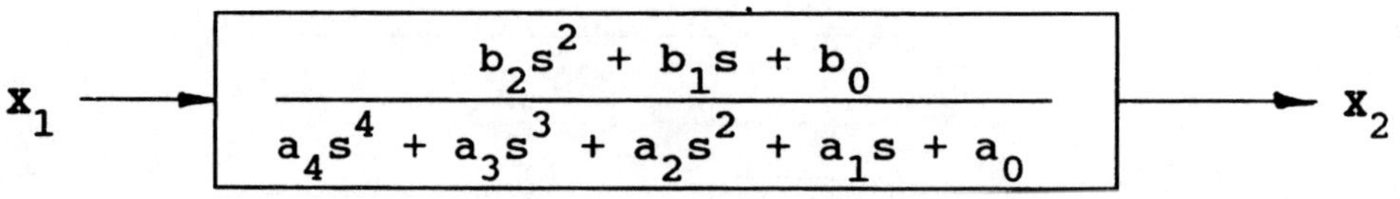

PROBLEM 11.3

a) The state-ariable equations and output equation are

$$\frac{di_L}{dt} = (-R_2/L)\ i_L + (1/L)\ e_{2g}$$

and

$$\frac{de_{2g}}{dt} = (-1/C)\ i_L + (-1/R_1C)\ e_{2g} + (1/R_1C)\ e_s$$

with

$$e_0 = e_{2g}$$

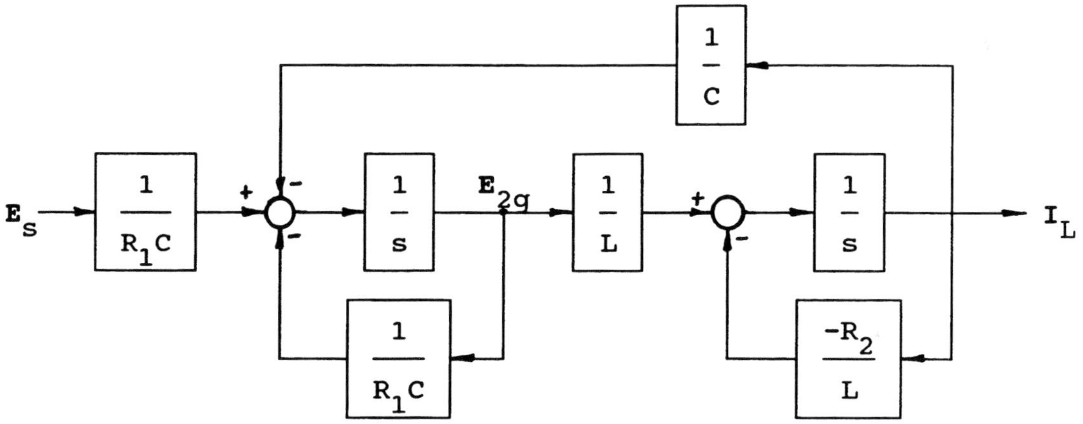

b) For the overall transfer function relating $\mathbf{E}_0$ to $\mathbf{E}_s$ combine the two state-variable equations and the output equation to eliminate i_L and e_{2g}.

$$LC\frac{d^2e_0}{dt} + \left(\frac{L}{R} + R_2C\right)\frac{de_0}{dt} + \left(\frac{R_2}{R_1} + 1\right)e_0 = \frac{L}{R}\frac{de_s}{dt} + \left(\frac{R_2}{R_1}\right)e_s$$

$$\text{E}_s \longrightarrow \boxed{\dfrac{\dfrac{L}{R}s + \dfrac{R_2}{R_1}}{LCs^2 + \left(\dfrac{L}{R} + R_2 C\right)s + \left(\dfrac{R_2 + R_1}{R_1}\right)}} \longrightarrow \text{E}_0$$

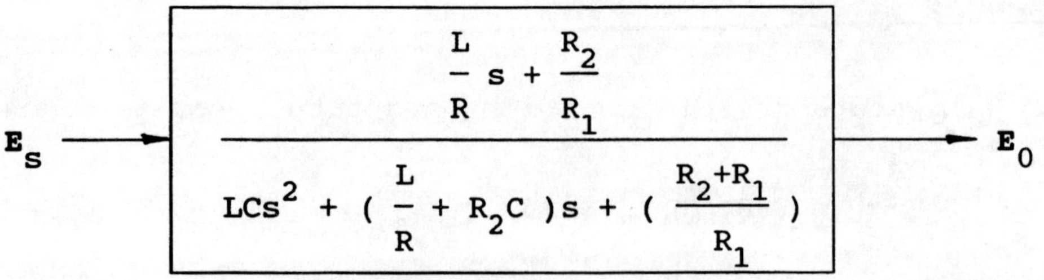

PROBLEM 11.4

a) Using

$$R_{inc} = \frac{de_{2g}}{di_L}$$

the solution for this problem is the same as for Problem 11.3 with R_2 replaced by R_{inc}.

PROBLEM 11.5

a) The detailed functional block diagram developed in Problem 11.1 solution is modified by adding a negative feedback path through a block labeled

$$2C_2\overline{\Omega}_{3g}$$

from Ω_{3g} to the summer having input T_c:

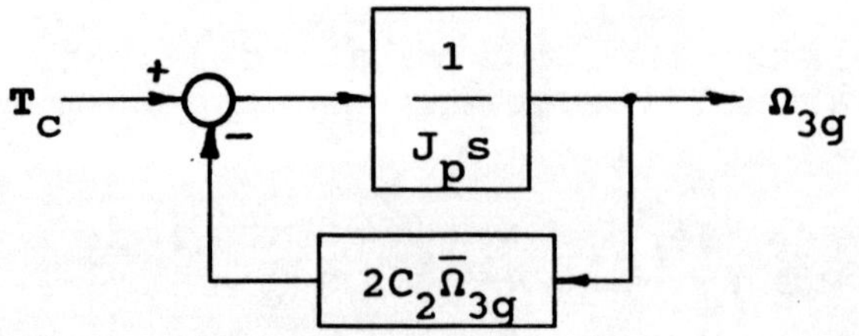

When the system equations are modified and transformed into the s-domain state variable equations:

$$s\Omega_{1g} = (0)\Omega_{1g} + (-1/J_e)T_c + (0)\Omega_{3g} + (1/J_e)T_e$$

$$\updownarrow \quad \updownarrow \quad \updownarrow \quad \updownarrow$$

$$a_{11} \quad a_{12} \quad a_{13} \quad b_{11}$$

$$sT_c = (K\bar{\Omega}_{1g}/\bar{\Omega}_{2g})\Omega_{1g} + (-K/2\bar{C}_c\Omega_{2g})T_c + (0)\Omega_{3g}$$

$$\updownarrow \quad \updownarrow \quad \updownarrow$$

$$a_{21} \quad a_{22} \quad a_{23}$$

$$s\Omega_{3g} = (0)\Omega_{1g} + (1/J_p)T_c + (-2C_2\bar{\Omega}_{3g}/J_p)\Omega_{3g}$$

$$\updownarrow \quad \updownarrow \quad \updownarrow$$

$$a_{31} \quad a_{32} \quad a_{33}$$

Cramer's rule may now be used to eliminate T_c and Ω_{1g}. Collecting terms for the three state-variables:

$$(s-a_{11})\Omega_{1g} - a_{12}T_c - a_{13}\Omega_{3g} = b_{11}T_e$$

$$-a_{21}\Omega_{1g} + (s-a_{22})T_c - a_{23}\Omega_{3g} = 0$$

$$-a_{31}\Omega_{1g} - a_{32}T_c + (s-a_{33})\Omega_{3g} = 0$$

$$\Omega_{3g} = \frac{\begin{vmatrix} (s-0) & -a_{12} & b_{11}T_c \\ -a_{21} & (s-a_{22}) & 0 \\ 0 & -a_{32} & (s-a_{33}) \end{vmatrix}}{\begin{vmatrix} s & -a_{12} & 0 \\ -a_{21} & (s-a_{22}) & 0 \\ 0 & -a_{32} & (s-a_{33}) \end{vmatrix}}$$

$$= \frac{b_{11}a_{21}a_{32}T_c}{s(s-a_{22})(s-a_{33})-a_{21}a_{12}(s-a_{33})}$$

$$(s^3+(-a_{22}-a_{33})s^2+a_{22}a_{33}s-a_{21}a_{12}s+a_{21}a_{12}a_{33})\Omega_{3g} = b_{11}a_{21}a_{32}T_e$$

Substituting for the a's

$$s^3+((k/2C_c\bar{\Omega}_{2g})+(2C_c\bar{\Omega}_{3g}/J_p)s^2+((k/2C_c\bar{\Omega}_{2g})(C_2\bar{\Omega}_{3g}/J_p)+(k\bar{\Omega}_{1g}/J_e\bar{\Omega}_{2g})s$$

$$+ (k/J_e)(\bar{\Omega}_{1g}/\bar{\Omega}_{2g})(2C_2\bar{\Omega}_{2g}/J_p)$$

PROBLEM 11.6

Emloying the s-domain versions of the state-variable equations for the electric motor driven inertia and damper system:

$$sT_t = (-R/L)I_t + (-1/\alpha_r L)\Omega_{1g} + (1/L)E_s$$

$$s\Omega_{1g} = (1/\alpha_r J_{tot})I_t + (-B_{tot}/J_{tot})\Omega_{1g}$$

facilitates preparation of the detailed transfer function block diagram:

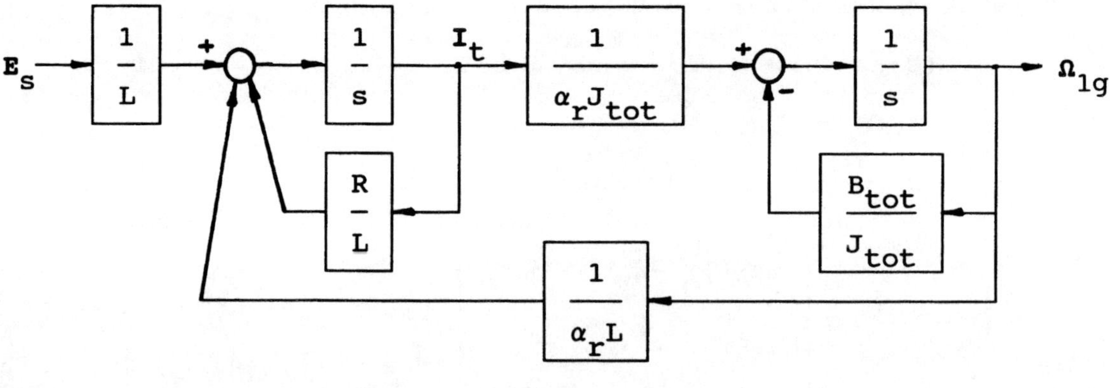

Then closing the inner loops:

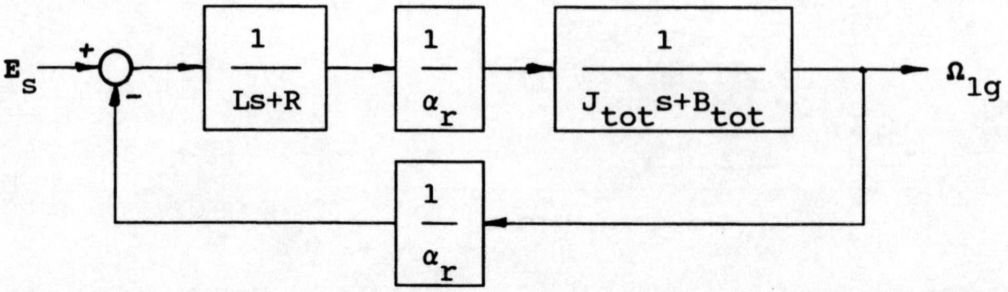

So that

$$\frac{\Omega_{1g}}{E_s} = \frac{\dfrac{1}{\alpha_r(Ls+R)(J_{tot}s+B_{tot})}}{1 + \dfrac{1}{\alpha_r^2(Ls+R)(J_{tot}s+B_{tot})}}$$

yielding:

$$E_s \longrightarrow \boxed{\frac{\alpha_r}{\alpha_r^2 LJ_{tot}s^2 + \alpha_r^2(LB_{tot} + J_{tot}R)s + \alpha_r^2 RB_{tot} + 1}} \longrightarrow \Omega_{1g}$$

PROBLEM 11.7

a)

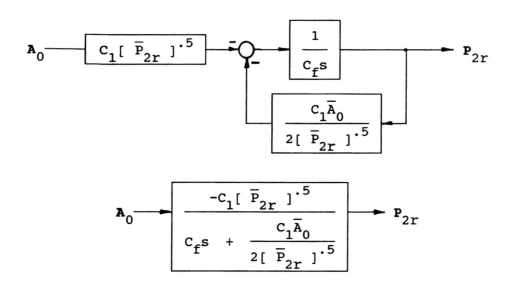

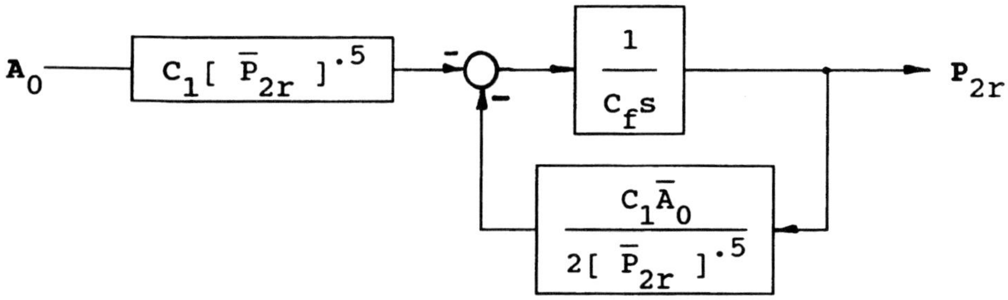

$$A_0 \longrightarrow \boxed{\frac{-C_1[\,\bar{P}_{2r}\,]^{.5}}{C_f s + \dfrac{C_1\bar{A}_0}{2[\,\bar{P}_{2r}\,]^{.5}}}} \longrightarrow P_{2r}$$

PROBLEM 11.8

a) The s-transformed and rearranged state-variable equations are

$$(s-a_{11})\mathbf{X}_1 - a_{12}\mathbf{X}_2 + (0)\mathbf{X}_3 = b_{11}\mathbf{U}_1$$

$$-a_{21}\mathbf{X}_1 + (s-0)\mathbf{X}_2 - a_{23}\mathbf{X}_3 = 0$$

$$a_{31}\mathbf{X}_1 - a_{32}\mathbf{X}_2 - (s-a_{33})X_3 = 0$$

and the detailed functional block diagram is

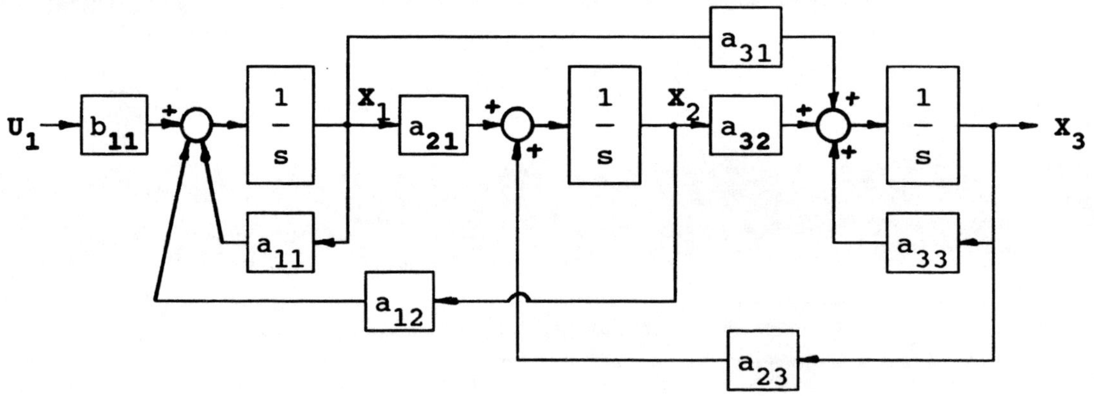

b) Using Cramer's determinants

$$\mathbf{X}_3 = \frac{\begin{vmatrix} (s-a_{11}) & -a_{12} & b_{11}\mathbf{U} \\ -a_{21} & s & 0 \\ -a_{31} & -a_{32} & 0 \end{vmatrix}}{\begin{vmatrix} (s-a_{11}) & -a_{12} & 0 \\ -a_{21} & s & -a_{23} \\ -a_{31} & -a_{32} & (s-a_{33}) \end{vmatrix}}$$

$$\frac{X_3}{U_1} = \frac{a_{31}b_{11}s + a_{21}a_{32}b_{11}}{s^3 - (a_{11}+a_{33})s^2 + (a_{11}a_{33}-a_{32}a_{23}-a_{21}a_{12})s - a_{12}a_{23}a_{31}}$$

$$+a_{32}a_{23}a_{11}+a_{21}a_{12}a_{33}$$

Let

$$a_2 = -(a_{11}+a_{33})$$

$$a_1 = a_{11}a_{33}-a_{32}a_{23}-a_{21}a_{12}$$

$$a_0 = -a_{12}a_{23}a_{31}+a_{32}a_{23}a_{11}+a_{21}a_{12}a_{33}$$

$$U_1 \longrightarrow \boxed{\frac{a_{31}b_{11}s + a_{21}a_{32}b_{11}}{s^3 + a_2s^2 + a_1s + a_0}} \longrightarrow X_3$$

c)

For $y = c_{21}x_2 + c_{13}x_3$

$$U_1 \longrightarrow \boxed{\frac{b_1s + b_0}{s^3 + a_2s^2 + a_1s + a_0}} \longrightarrow Y$$

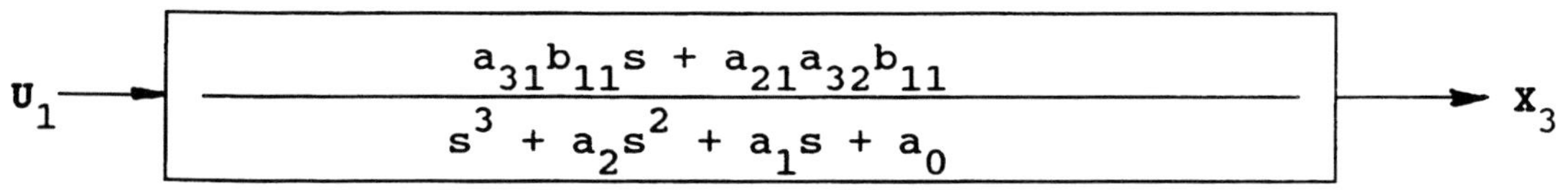

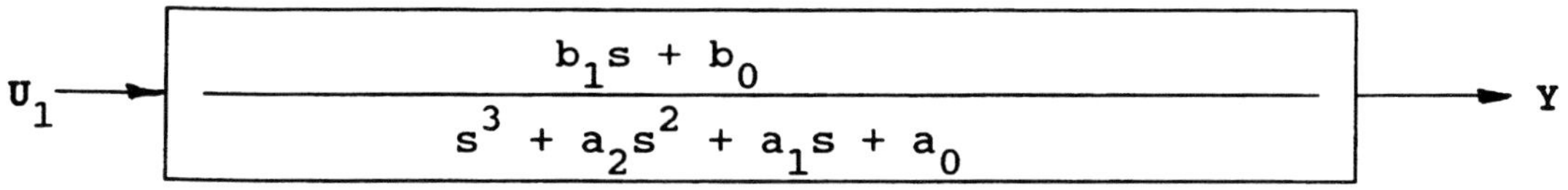

where

$$b_1 = c_{12}a_{31}a_{23} - c_{12}a_{21}a_{33} + c_{13}a_{21}a_{32}$$

$$b_0 = c_{12}a_{21} + c_{13}a_{31}$$

CHAPTER 12

PROBLEM 12.1

a) $$\mathbf{T}(j\omega) = \mathbf{T}(s)\Big|_{s=j\omega} = \frac{k}{j\omega} = -j\,\frac{k}{\omega}$$

Magnitude: $$|\mathbf{T}(j\omega)| = \frac{k}{\omega} \quad ; \quad \log|\mathbf{T}(j\omega)| = \log(k) - \log(\omega)$$

Phase: $$\phi_T = \tan^{-1}\left[\frac{-k/\omega}{0}\right] = -\frac{\pi}{2}$$

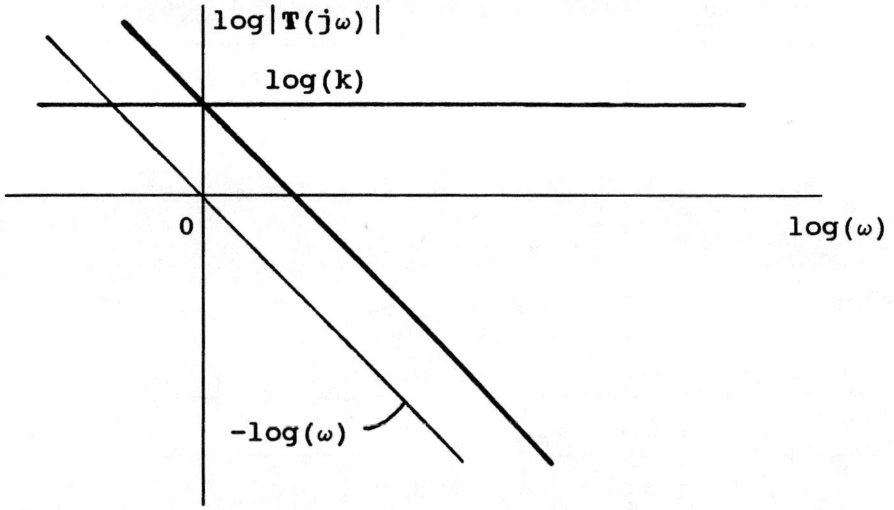

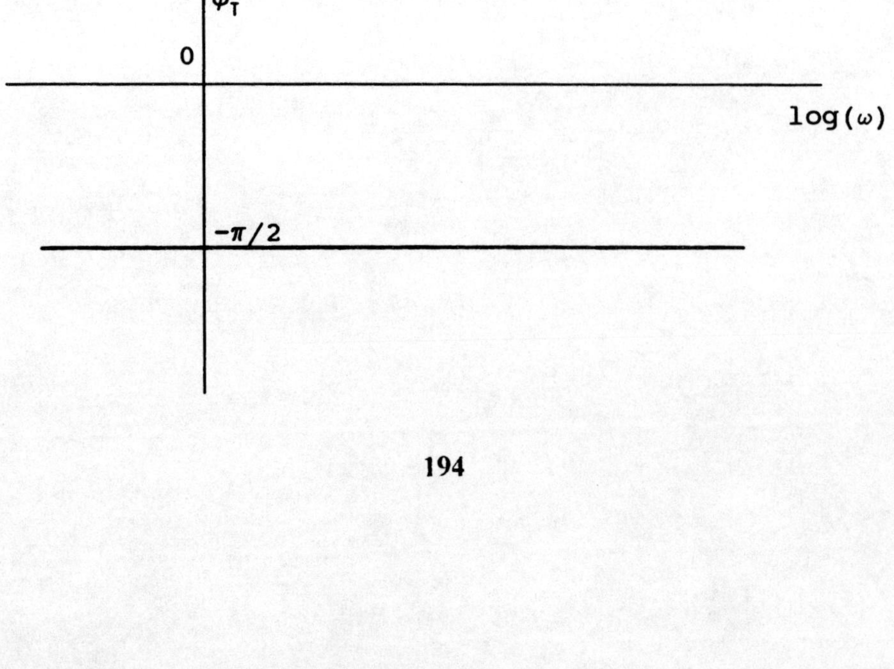

b) $$\mathbf{T}(j\omega) = \left.\frac{k}{s(\tau s+1)}\right|_{s=j\omega} = \frac{k}{j\omega(j\omega\tau+1)}$$

<u>Magnitude</u>: $\log|\mathbf{T}(j\omega)| = \log(k) - \log|j\omega| - \log|j\omega\tau+1|$

<u>Phase</u> : $\phi_T = 0 - \tan^{-1}(\omega/0) - \tan^{-1}(\omega\tau) = -\frac{\pi}{2} - \tan^{-1}(\omega\tau)$

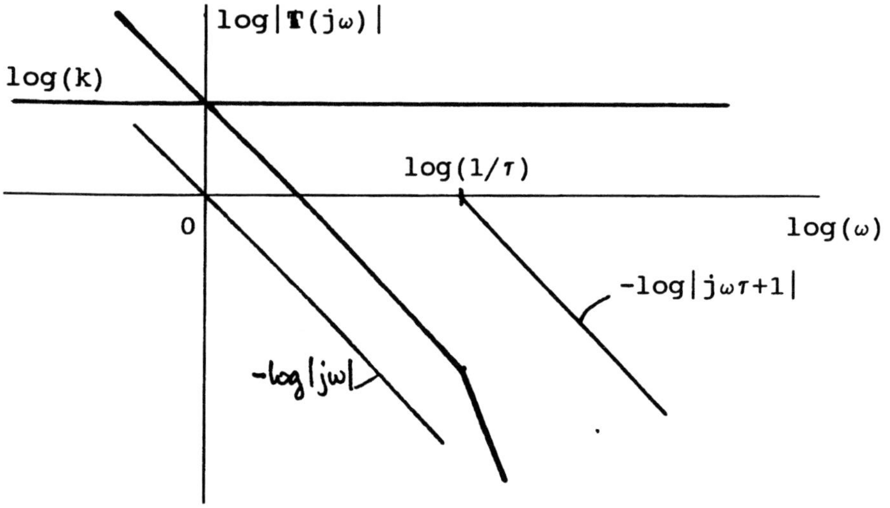

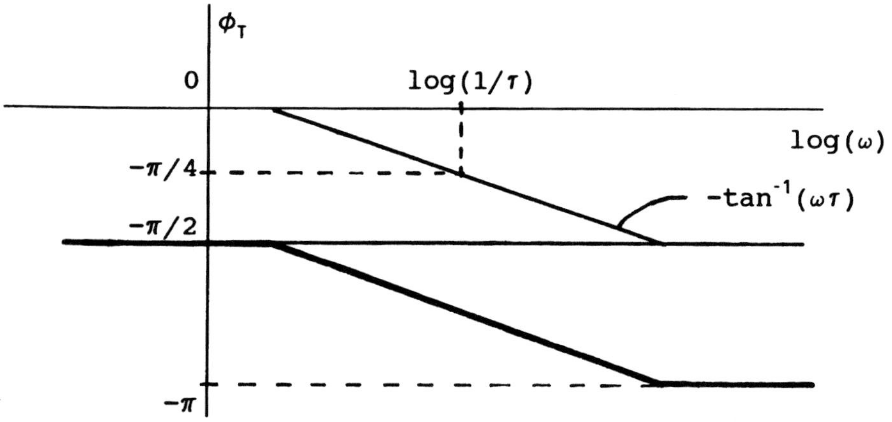

c) $\mathbf{T}(j\omega) = \dfrac{j\omega k}{1+j\omega\tau}$

<u>Magnitude</u>: $\log|\mathbf{T}(j\omega)| = \log(\omega k) - \log|1+j\omega\tau|$

$$= \log(k) + \log(\omega) - \log|1+j\omega\tau|$$

<u>Phase</u>: $\phi_T = \tan^{-1}(\omega k/0) - \tan^{-1}(\omega\tau) = \dfrac{\pi}{2} - \tan^{-1}(\omega\tau)$

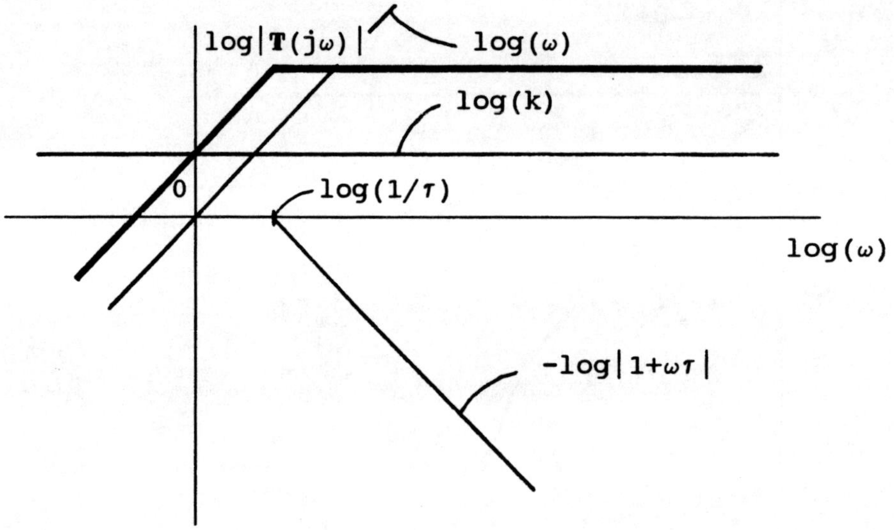

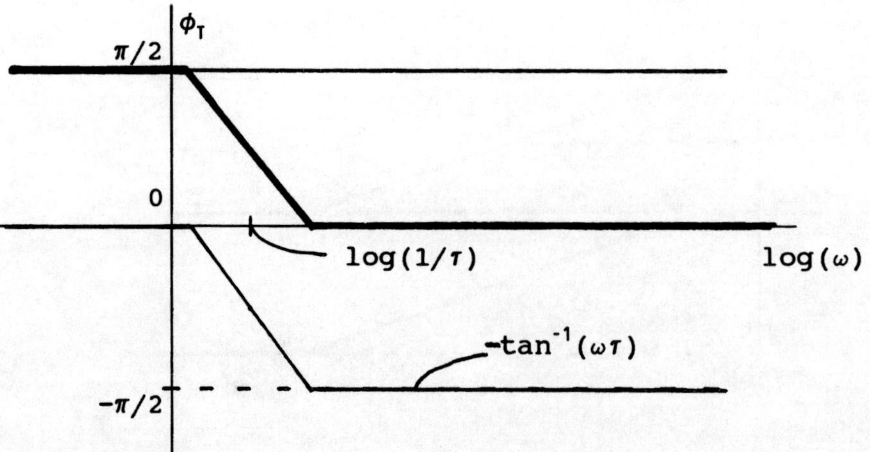

d) $\mathbf{T}(j\omega) = \dfrac{k}{(j\omega\tau+1)^2}$

Magnitude: $\log|\mathbf{T}(j\omega)| = \log(k) - 2\log|1+j\omega\tau|$

Phase: $\phi_T = 0 - 2\tan^{-1}(\omega\tau)$

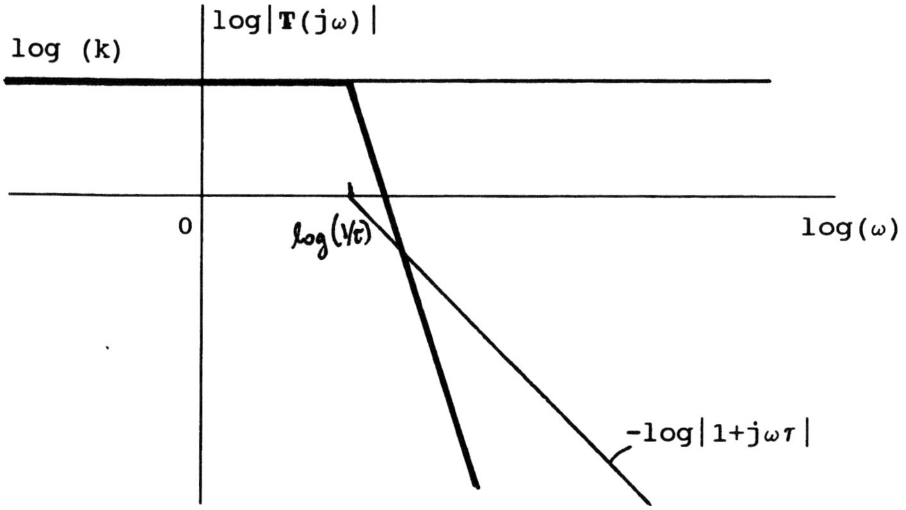

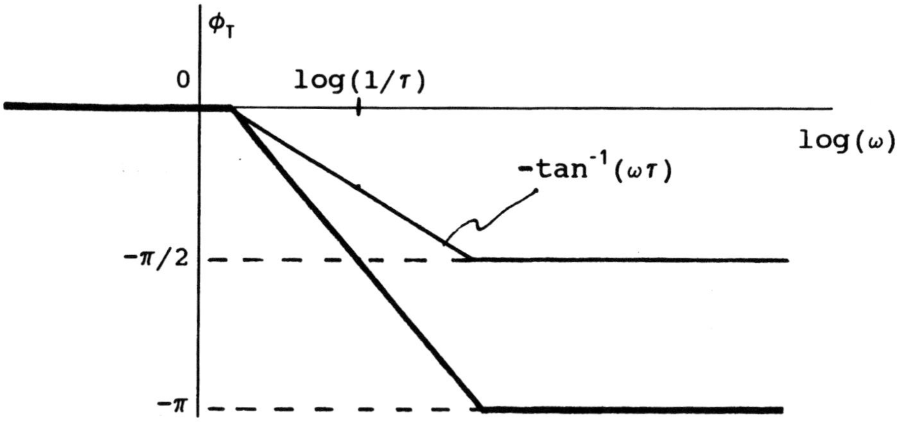

e) $\mathbf{T}(j\omega) = \dfrac{k(j\omega\tau_1+1)}{j\omega(j\omega\tau_2+1)}$

<u>Magnitude</u>: $\log|\mathbf{T}(j\omega)| = \log(k) + \log|j\omega\tau_1+1| - \log|\omega|$

$\qquad - \log|j\omega\tau_1+1|$

<u>Phase</u>: $\phi_T = 0 + \tan^{-1}(\omega\tau_1) - \pi/2 - \tan^{-1}(\omega\tau_2)$

For plotting assume $\tau_1 > \tau_2$

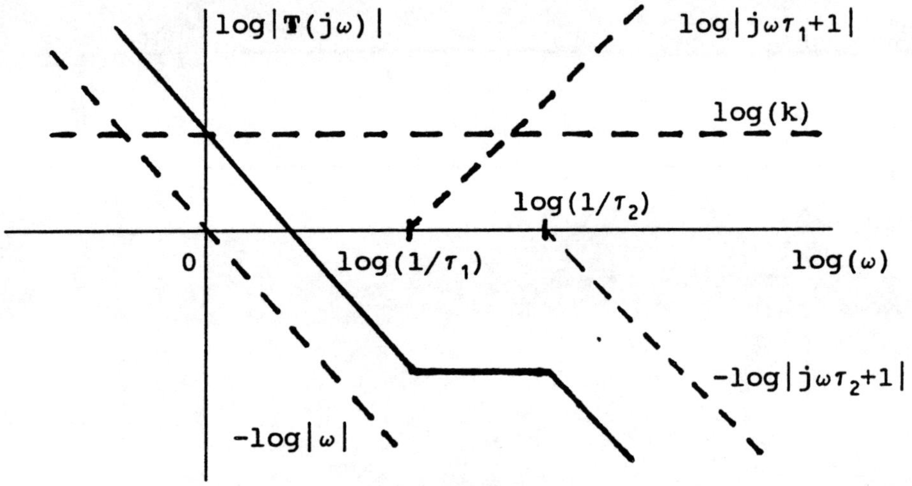

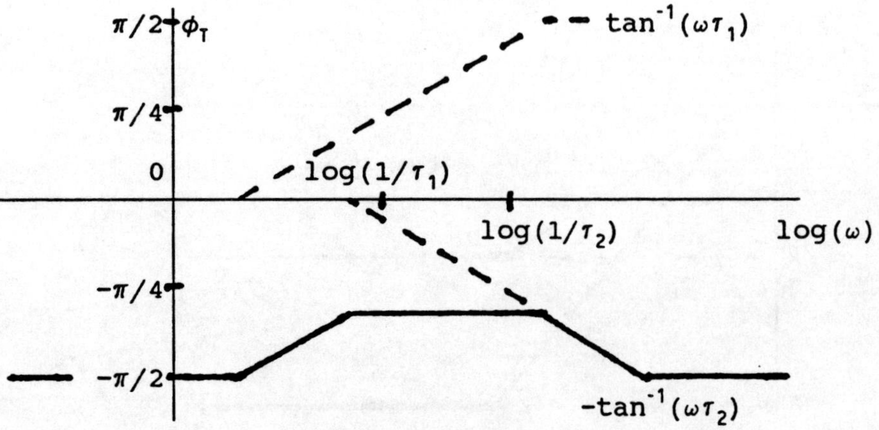

f) $$\mathbf{T}(j\omega) = \frac{10j\omega(0.1j\omega+1)}{(j\omega+1)^2}$$

Magnitude: $\log|\mathbf{T}(j\omega)| = \log(10)+\log(\omega)+\log|0.1j\omega+1|-2\log|j\omega+1|$

Phase: $\phi_T = \frac{\pi}{2} + \tan^{-1}(0.1\omega) - 2\tan^{-1}(\omega)$

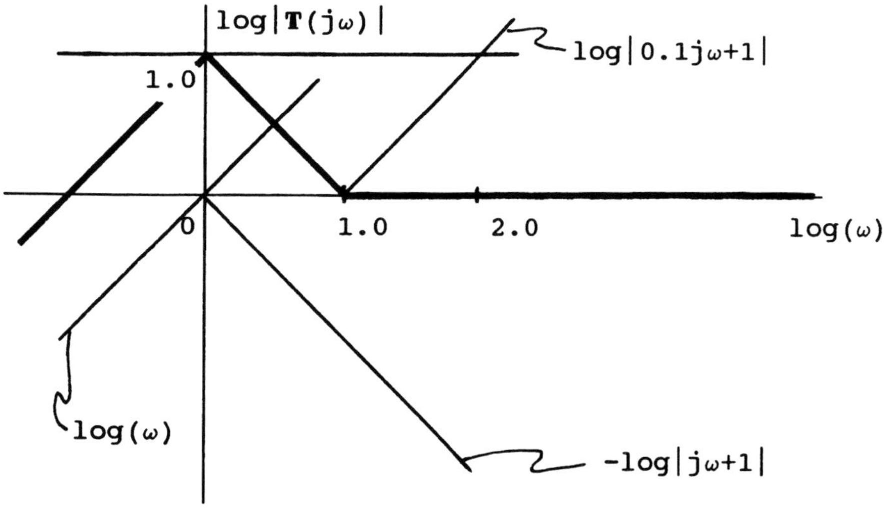

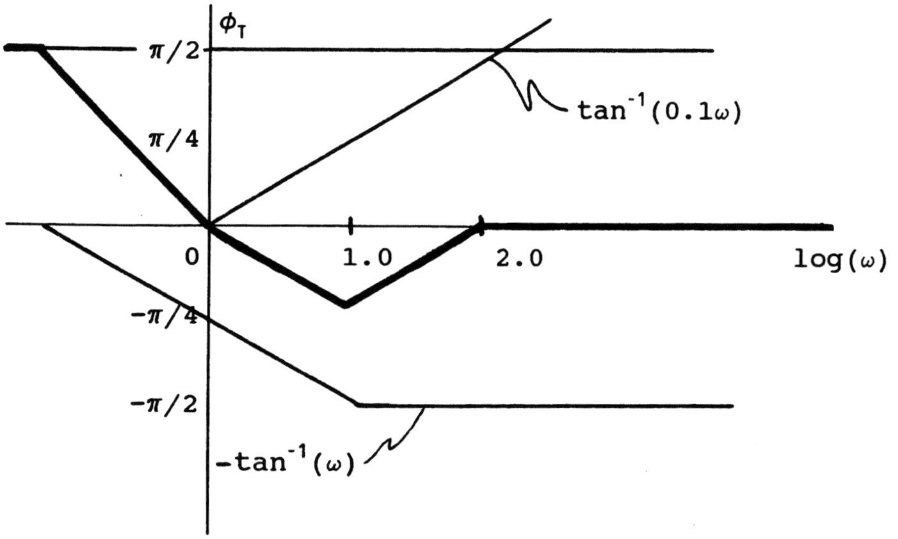

PROBLEM 12.2

a) $\mathbf{T}(j\omega) = \dfrac{k}{j\omega} = -j\,\dfrac{k}{\omega}$

Real part: $Re[\mathbf{T}(j\omega)] = 0.0$

Imaginary part: $Im[\mathbf{T}(j\omega)] = -\dfrac{k}{\omega}$

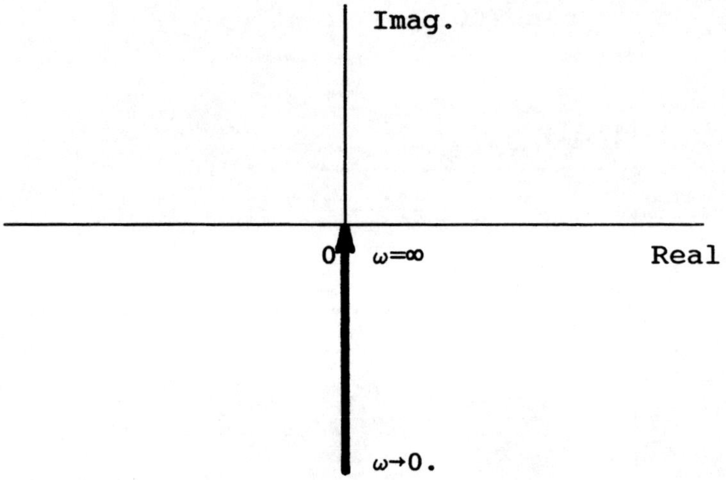

b) $\mathbf{T}(j\omega) = \dfrac{k}{-\tau\omega^2+j\omega} = \dfrac{-k\tau-j(k/\omega)}{\tau^2\omega^2+1}$

Real part: $Re[\mathbf{T}(j\omega)] = \dfrac{-k\tau}{\tau^2\omega^2+1}$

Imaginary part: $Im[\mathbf{T}(j\omega)] = \dfrac{-(k/\omega)}{\tau^2\omega^2+1} = (1/\tau\omega)\ Re[\mathbf{T}(j\omega)]$

As $\omega \to 0.0$: $Re[\mathbf{T}(j\omega)] \to -k\tau$

$Im[\mathbf{T}(j\omega)] \to -\infty$

As $\omega \to \infty$: $Re[\mathbf{T}(j\omega)] \to 0.0(-)$

$Im[\mathbf{T}(j\omega)] \to 0.0(-)$

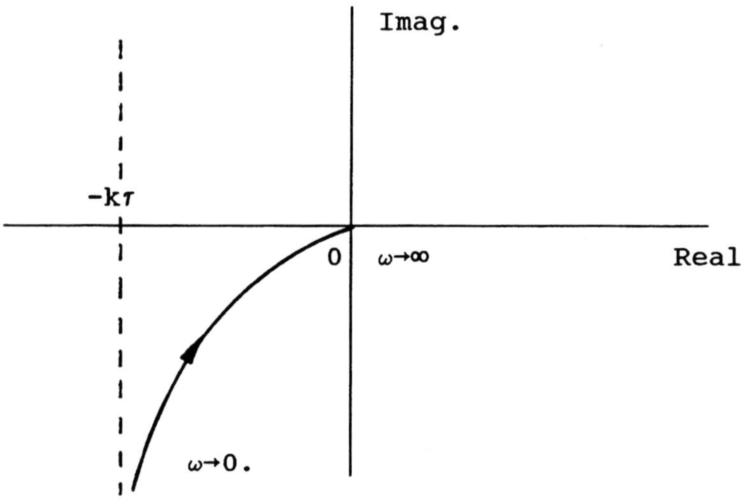

c) $$\mathbf{T}(j\omega) = \frac{\omega_n^2}{\omega_n^2-\omega^2+j2\xi\omega_n\omega}$$

<u>Real part</u>: $$\mathrm{Re}[\mathbf{T}(j\omega)] = \frac{\omega^2(\omega_n^2-\omega^2)}{(\omega_n^2-\omega^2)^2+(2\xi\omega_n\omega)^2}$$

<u>Imaginary part</u>: $$\mathrm{Im}[\mathbf{T}(j\omega)] = \frac{-\omega_n^3 2\xi\omega}{(\omega_n^2-\omega^2)^2+(2\xi\omega_n\omega)^2}$$

$$= \frac{-\omega_n 2\xi\omega}{\omega_n^2-\omega^2}\ \mathrm{Re}[\mathbf{T}(j\omega)]$$

As $\omega \to \omega_n$: $\mathrm{Re}[\mathbf{T}(j\omega)] \to 0.0$

$$\mathrm{Im}[\mathbf{T}(j\omega)] \to \frac{-1}{2\xi\omega_n^2}$$

As $\omega \to 0.$: $\mathrm{Re}[\mathbf{T}(j\omega)] \to 1.0$

$\mathrm{Im}[\mathbf{T}(j\omega)] \to 0.0(-)$ if $\xi > 0.$
$\to 0.0(+)$ if $\xi < 0.$

As $\omega \to \infty$: $\mathrm{Re}[\mathbf{T}(j\omega)] \to 0.0$

$\mathrm{Im}[\mathbf{T}(j\omega)] \to 0.0(-)$ if $\xi > 0.$
$\to 0.0(+)$ if $\xi < 0.$

For $\xi > 0$

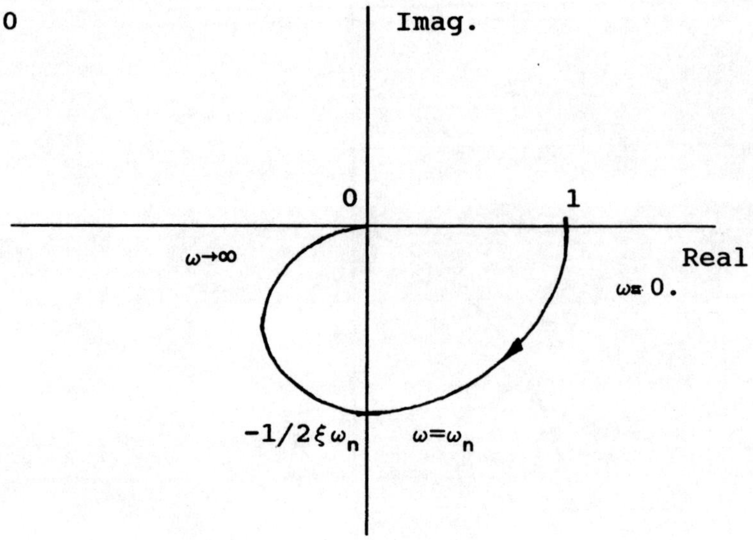

For $\xi < 0$.

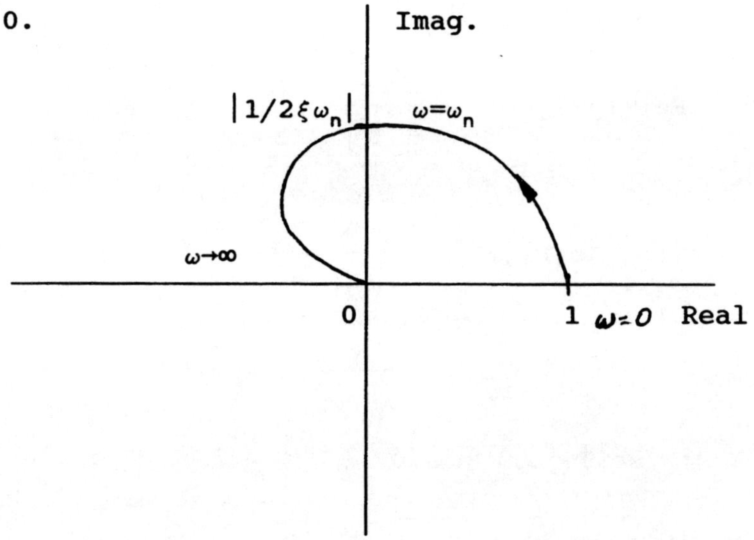

d) $\mathbf{T}(j\omega) = k\, e^{-j\omega\tau_o} = k\cos(\omega\tau_o) - j\, k\sin(\omega\tau_o)$

<u>Real part</u>: $\mathrm{Re}[\mathbf{T}(j\omega)] = k\cos(\omega\tau_o)$

<u>Imaginary part</u>: $\mathrm{Im}[\mathbf{T}(j\omega)] = k\sin(\omega\tau_o)$

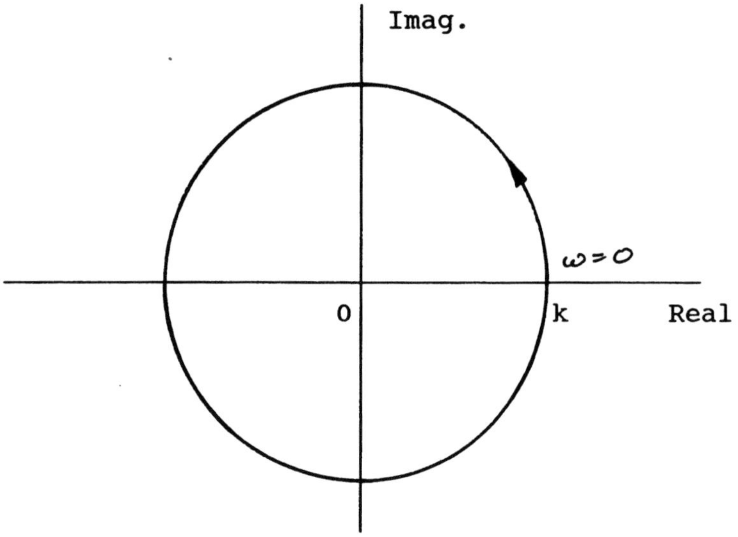

e) $$\mathbf{T}(j\omega) = \frac{1+j\omega}{10-\omega^2+j7\omega}$$

<u>Real part</u>: $$\mathrm{Re}[\mathbf{T}(j\omega)] = \frac{10+6\omega^2}{(10-\omega^2)^2+(7\omega)^2}$$

<u>Imaginary part</u>: $$\mathrm{Im}[\mathbf{T}(j\omega)] = \frac{3\omega-\omega^3}{(10-\omega^2)^2+(7\omega)^2}$$

ω	$\mathrm{Re}[\mathbf{T}(j\omega)]$	$\mathrm{Im}[\mathbf{T}(j\omega)]$
.01	.1	.0003
.05	.1	.0015
1.00	.123	.0154
5.00	.110	-.0759
10.00	.0469	-.0746
100.00	.0006	-.000007

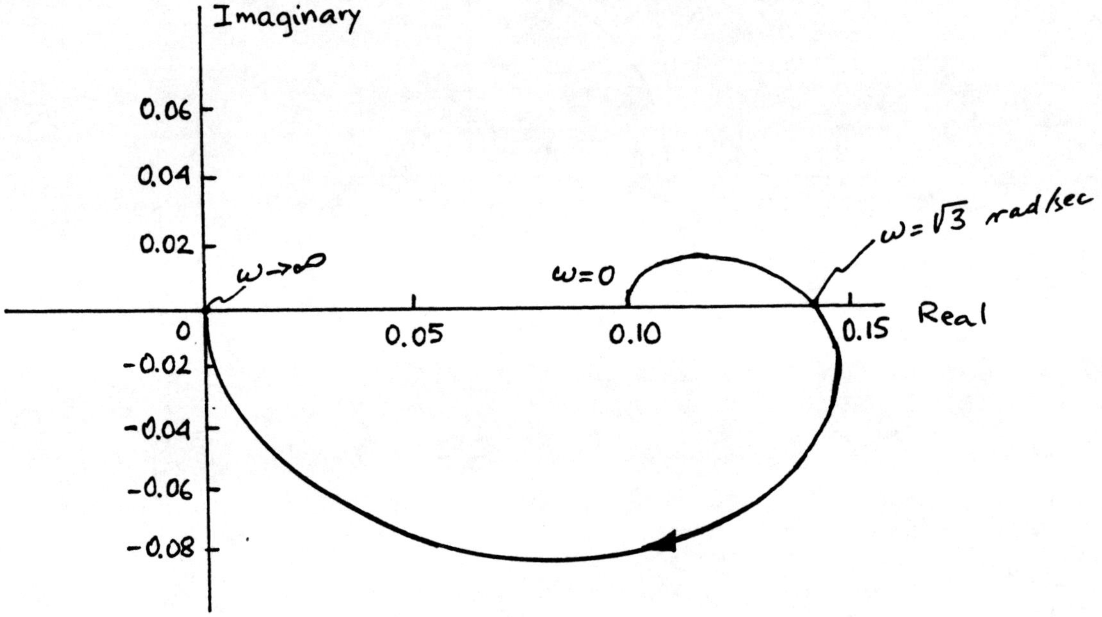
Imaginary
0.06
0.04
0.02
0
-0.02
-0.04
-0.06
-0.08
ω→∞
ω=0
ω=√3 rad/sec
0.05
0.10
0.15
Real

f) $$\mathbf{T}(j\omega) = \frac{100}{-15\omega^2+j(50\omega-\omega^3)}$$

Real part: $$\mathrm{Re}[\mathbf{T}(j\omega)] = \frac{-1500\omega^2}{(15\omega^2)^2+(50\omega-\omega^3)^2}$$

Imaginary part: $$\mathrm{Im}[\mathbf{T}(j\omega)] = \frac{-5000\omega+100\omega^3}{(15\omega^2)^2+(50\omega-\omega^3)^2}$$

ω	Re[**T**(jω)]	Im[**T**(jω)]
.01	-.6000	-200.00
.10	-.5997	-19.99
1.00	-.5712	-1.87
5.00	-.2400	-.08
7.07	-.1333	.00
10.00	-.0600	.02
100.00	-.000015	.0001

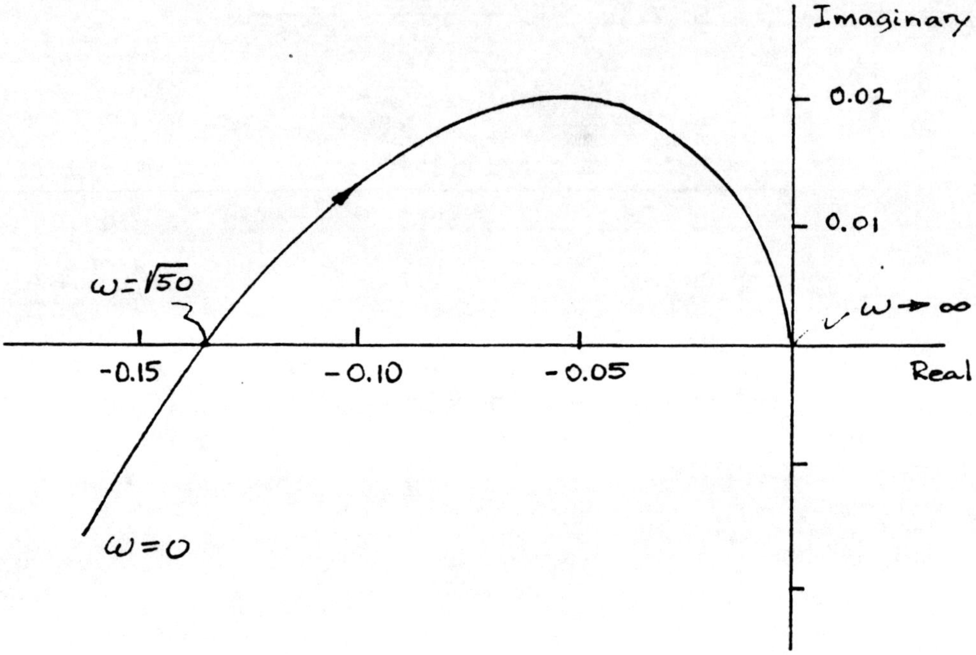
Imaginary
0.02
0.01
ω=√50
ω→∞
-0.15
-0.10
-0.05
Real
ω=0

PROBLEM 12.3

a) Notice that when $\omega = \omega_\phi$, the phase angle $\phi_T = -180°$.

Drawing a horizontal line $\phi_T = -180°$ on the phase angle Bode diagram and reading the value of ω for the point of intersection with the phase angle curve gives

$$\omega_\phi \approx 12 \text{ rad/sec}$$

For $\omega = \omega_g$, from the polar plot we have

$$|\mathbf{T}(j\omega)|\Big|_{\omega_g} = 1 \quad \text{or} \quad \log|\mathbf{T}(j\omega)|\Big|_{\omega_g} = 0$$

From the magnitude Bode diagram, the value of ω_g is found at the intersection of the horizontal zero line and the magnitude curve

$$\omega_g \approx 30 \text{ rad/sec}$$

b) The static gain k can be found as

$$k = |\mathbf{T}(j\omega)|\Big|_{\omega=0}$$

From the magnitude Bode diagram,

$$k = 5 \text{ dB} \quad \text{or} \quad k = 1.778$$

PROBLEM 12.4

For the sinusoidal input, $x(t) = U\sin(\omega_f t)$, the output of this linear system will also be sinusoidal, $y(t) = Y\sin(\omega_f t+\phi_T)$, where

(1) $$Y = U\cdot|\mathbf{T}(j\omega)|\Big|_{\omega=\omega_f}$$

(2) $$\phi_T = \angle\mathbf{T}(j\omega)\Big|_{\omega=\omega_f}$$

$\mathbf{T}(j\omega)$ is the system sinusoidal transfer function, which has to be found. The system input-output equation transformed into the domain of the complex variable s becomes

(3) $$\mathbf{Y}(s)(a_2s^2+a_1s+a_0) = \mathbf{U}(s)(b_2s^2+b_1s+b_0)$$

Hence

$$(4)\qquad \mathbf{T}(s) = \frac{\mathbf{Y}(s)}{\mathbf{U}(s)} = \frac{b_2s^2+b_1s+b_0}{a_2s^2+a_1s+a_0}$$

The sinusoidal transfer function

$$(5)\qquad \mathbf{T}(j\omega) = \mathbf{T}(s)\Big|_{s=j\omega} = \frac{b_0-b_2\omega^2+j\omega b_1}{a_0-a_2\omega^2+j\omega a_1}$$

Now, the amplitude of the output signal is

$$(6)\qquad Y = U|T(j\omega)|\Big|_{\omega=\omega_f} = U\frac{[\ (b_0-b_2\omega_f^2)^2 + \omega_f^2b_1^2\ ]^{.5}}{[\ (a_0-a_2\omega_f^2)^2 + \omega_f^2a_1^2\ ]^{.5}}$$

Substituting $\omega_f = (a_0/a_2)^{.5}$ into equation (6) yields

$$(7)\qquad Y = U\frac{[\ (b_0 - a_0b_2/a_2)^2 + a_0b_1^2/a_2\ ]^{.5}}{[\ a_1^2a_0/a_2\ ]^{.5}}$$

$$= \frac{U}{a_1}\left[\frac{a_2(b_0 - a_0b_2/a_2)^2 + a_0b_1^2}{a_0}\right]^{.5}$$

From equation (5) the phase angle is

$$(8)\qquad \phi_T = \tan^{-1}\left[\frac{\omega b_1}{b_0-b_2\omega^2}\right] - \tan^{-1}\left[\frac{\omega a_1}{a_0-a_2\omega^2}\right]$$

Substituting $\omega = \omega_f = (a_0/a_2)^{.5}$ gives

$$(9)\qquad \phi_T = \tan^{-1}\left[\frac{b_1(a_0a_2)^{.5}}{a_2b_0 - a_0b_2}\right] - \frac{\pi}{2}$$

The output signal is

$$(10)\qquad y(t) = Y\sin[\ (a_0/a_2)^{.5}t + \phi_T\ ]$$

where Y and ϕ_T are given by equations (7) and (9) respectively.

PROBLEM 12.5

a) The transfer function **T**(s) will be found by reducing the block diagram shown in Figure P12.2.

First reduce the two feedback loops involving a_{11} and a_{12}

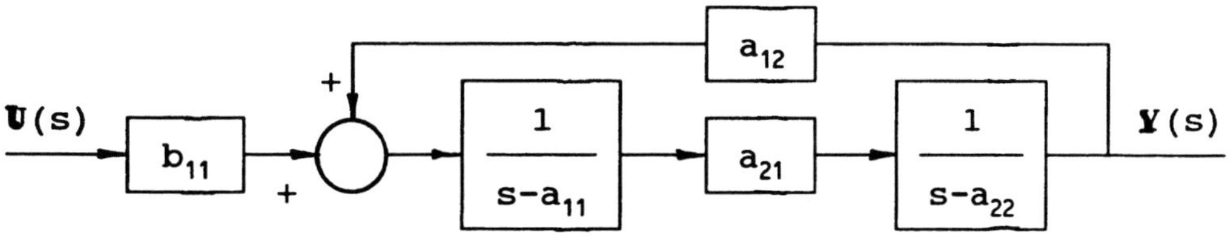

Now combining the three blocks in series $\dfrac{1}{s-a_{11}}$, a_{21}, and $\dfrac{1}{s-a_{22}}$, gives

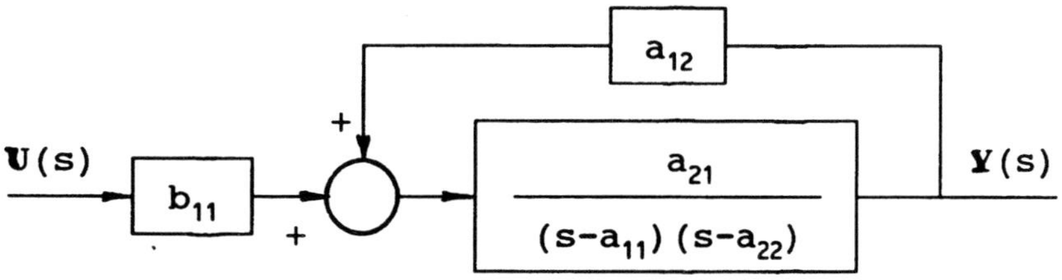

The single-block transfer function can now be obtained

$$(1)\quad \mathbf{T}(s) = \frac{\mathbf{Y}(s)}{\mathbf{U}(s)} = b_{11}\frac{\dfrac{a_{21}}{(s-a_{11})(s-a_{22})}}{1 - \dfrac{a_{21}a_{12}}{(s-a_{11})(s-a_{22})}} = \frac{b_{11}a_{21}}{(s-a_{11})(s-a_{22})a_{12}a_{21}}$$

Substituting numerical values for the system parameters yields

$$(2)\qquad \mathbf{T}(s) = \frac{70}{s^2+0.1s+8.}$$

b) From the given expression for the input signal, it can be deduced that the input amplitude is 0.001 and the frequency of the input signal is ω = 1.5 rad/sec. Since the system model is linear, the output signal will also be sinusoidal,

$$y(t) = Y\sin(1.5t + \phi_T).$$

To find Y and ϕ_T, the sinusoidal transfer function must be obtained.

$$(3) \qquad \mathbf{T}(j\omega) = \mathbf{T}(s)\Big|_{s=j\omega} = \frac{70}{-\omega^2+0.1j\omega+8}$$

Substituting ω = 1.5 rad/sec

$$(4) \qquad \mathbf{T}(j\omega)\Big|_{\omega=1.5} = \frac{70}{5.75 + 0.15j}$$

Hence, the amplitude of the output signal is

$$(5) \qquad Y = 0.001\ |\mathbf{T}(j\omega)|\Big|_{\omega=1.5} = 0.01217$$

and the phase angle

$$(6) \qquad \phi_T = \tan^{-1}(0/70) - \tan^{-1}(0.15/5.75) = -0.026 \text{ rad}$$

The mathematical expression for the output signal is

$$(7) \qquad y(t) = 0.01217 \sin(\ 1.5t - 0.026\ )$$

PROBLEM 12.6

a) The elemental equation for the tank as a fluid capacitance is

$$(1) \qquad C_f \frac{dp}{dt} = Q_i - Q_L$$

The output flow rate is

$$(2) \qquad Q_L = 1/R_L\ (p-p_a)$$

where p_a is the atmospheric pressure. To introduce liquid height as the state variable substitute

(3) $p = \rho g h + p_a$ and $\dfrac{dp}{dt} = \rho g \dfrac{dh}{dt}$

Using the expression for fluid capacitance of an open reservoir shown in Figure 9.2, $C_f = A/\rho g$, equation (4) can be written as follows

$$\frac{dh}{dt} = -\frac{\rho g}{AR_L} h + \frac{1}{A} Q_i \tag{5}$$

which constitutes the system state variable equation.

b) At steady-state equation (5) takes the form

$$0 = -\frac{\rho g}{R_L} \bar{h} + \bar{Q}_i \tag{6}$$

Hence

$$\bar{h} = \frac{R_L}{\rho g} \bar{Q}_i = 2.0 \text{ m}$$

c) The input flowrate consists of a constant and an incremental component, $Q_i = \bar{Q}_i + \hat{Q}_i$, given by

$$Q_i = 0.5 + 0.1 \sin(0.4t) \tag{7}$$

Since the system is assumed to be linear, the liquid height will also have a constant and an incremental component, $h = \bar{h} + \hat{h}$. The constant component was found in part (b), $\bar{h} = 2.0$ m. The incremental component is

$$\hat{h}(t) = H \sin(0.4t + \phi_T) \tag{8}$$

where H is the amplitude and ϕ_T is the phase angle of sinusoidal oscillations of the liquid height. It is required here that $H \le 0.2$ m. However, since

$$H = |Q_i| \, |\mathbf{T}(j\omega)| \tag{9}$$

the condition for amplitude H can be written as

$$|Q_i| \, |\mathbf{T}(j\omega)| \le 0.2 \tag{10}$$

From equation (7), $|Q_i| = 0.1$, and thus inequality (10) reduces to

(11) $$|\mathbf{T}(j\omega)| \leq 2$$

The above condition must be satified for $\omega = 0.4$ rad/sec.

(12) $$|\mathbf{T}(j\omega)|\Big|_{\omega=0.4} \leq 2$$

Thus, to solve the problem, the magnitude of the system sinusoidal transfer has to be found. From equation (5)

(13) $$s\mathbf{H}(s) = -\frac{\rho g}{AR_L}\mathbf{H}(s) + \frac{1}{A}\mathbf{Q}_i(s)$$

Hence

(14) $$\mathbf{T}(s) = \frac{\mathbf{H}(s)}{\mathbf{Q}_i(s)} = \frac{R_L}{AR_L+1}$$

The sinusoidal transfer function

(15) $$\mathbf{T}(j\omega)\Big|_{\omega=0.4} = \frac{R_L}{j\omega AR_L+1} = \frac{39.24}{j15.7A + 9.81}$$

The condition (12) becomes

(16) $$\frac{39.24}{[\ 15.7^2A^2 + 9.81^2\ ]^{.5}} \leq 2$$

Solving for A yeilds

(17) $$A \geq 1.08\ m^2$$

d) The time delay between any two corresponding points of two sinusoidal signals of the same frequency can be found from the expression for the phase shift between the two signals

(18) $$\phi = \omega t_d$$

In this case ϕ is the phase angle of the sinusoidal transfer function, ϕ_T, and $\omega = 0.5$ rad/sec. From equation (15) the phase angle can be calculated

(19) $$\phi_T = 0 - \tan^{-1}(15.7A/9.81)$$

Substituting $A = 1.0\ m^2$,

(20) $\phi_T = 1.0$ rad

Now, from equation (18), the time delay is

(21) $t_d = \phi_T/\omega = 1.0/0.4 = 2.5$ sec

e) From equations (2) and (3), the incremental output flowrate is

(22) $\hat{Q}_L = (1/R_L)\rho g\hat{h} = (\rho g/R_L)\ H \sin(0.4t + \phi_T)\ m^3/sec$

For $A = 1.0\ m^2$, $\phi_T = 1.0$ rad (equation 20), and thus the only unknown in equation (22) is H. From equation (9) and (16)

$$H = |Q_i||\mathbf{T}(j\omega)| = 0.1 \frac{39.24}{[\ a5.7^2 + 9.81^2\ ]^{.5}} = 0.212\ m$$

Hence, the expression for $\hat{Q}_L$

$$\hat{Q}_L = (0.25)(0.212)\sin(0.4t + 1.0)$$

(23) $\hat{Q}_L = 0.053 \sin(0.4t+1)\ m^3/sec$

PROBLEM 12.7

a) The closed-loop transfer function of the feedback system shown in Figure P12.4 is

(1) $$\mathbf{T}_{CL}(s) = \frac{\mathbf{T}_C(s)\mathbf{T}_P(s)}{1 + \mathbf{T}_C(s)\mathbf{T}_P(s)}$$

Substituting the expressions for $\mathbf{T}_C(s)$ and $\mathbf{T}_P(s)$ gives

(2) $$\mathbf{T}_{CL}(s) = \frac{10s+10}{10s^2+17s+11}$$

b) The output signal of this linear system for

$$u(t) = 0.2 \sin(3t)$$

will be

(3) $$y(t) = Y \sin(3t+\phi_T)$$

where the amplitude

(4) $$Y = 0.2|\mathbf{T}_{CL}(j\omega)|\Big|_{\omega=3 \text{ rad/sec}}$$

and the phase angle

(5) $$\phi_T = \angle\mathbf{T}_{CL}(j\omega)\Big|_{\omega=3 \text{ rad/sec}}$$

From equation (2), the sinusoidal transfer function is

(6) $$\mathbf{T}_{CL}(j\omega) = \frac{j\omega 10+10}{-10\omega^2+j\omega 17+11}$$

and for $\omega = 3$ rad/sec

(7) $$\mathbf{T}_{CL}(j\omega)\Big|_{\omega=3 \text{ rad/sec}} = \frac{10+j30}{-79+j51}$$

Hence, the magnitude

(8) $$|\mathbf{T}_{CL}(j\omega)|\Big|_{\omega=3 \text{ rad/sec}} = \frac{[\ 10^2+30^2\ ]^{.5}}{[\ 79^2+51^2\ ]^{.5}} = 0.335$$

and the amplitude of the output

(9) $$Y = (0.2)(0.335) = 0.067$$

The phase angle ϕ_T is

(10) $$\phi_T = \phi_N - \phi_D$$

where ϕ_N and ϕ_D are phase angles of the numerator and denominator of $\mathbf{T}(j\omega)$, respectively. The two angles are shown in the following figure.

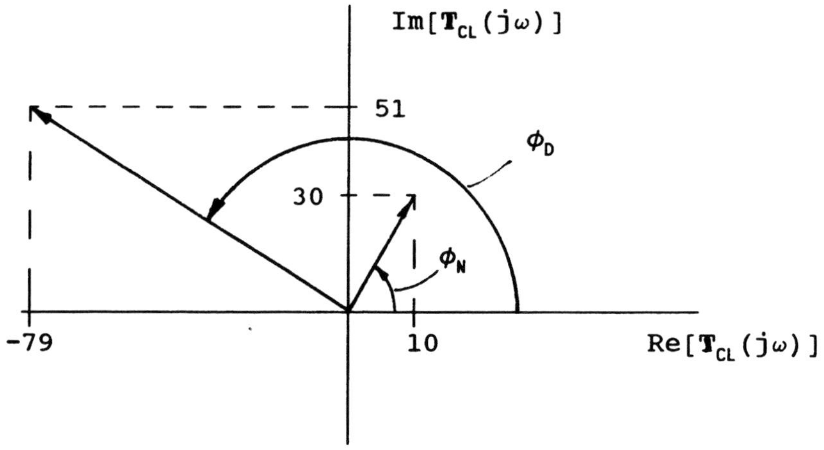

$$\phi_N = \tan^{-1}(30/10) = 71.56°$$

$$\phi_D = 180° - \tan^{-1}(51/79) = 180° - 32.85° = 147.15°$$

Hence

$$\phi_T = 71.56° - 147.15° = -75.59°$$

PROBLEM 12.8

The input to the system is the temperature of the air, $T_a(t)$, varying in a sinusoidal fashion, as sketched below.

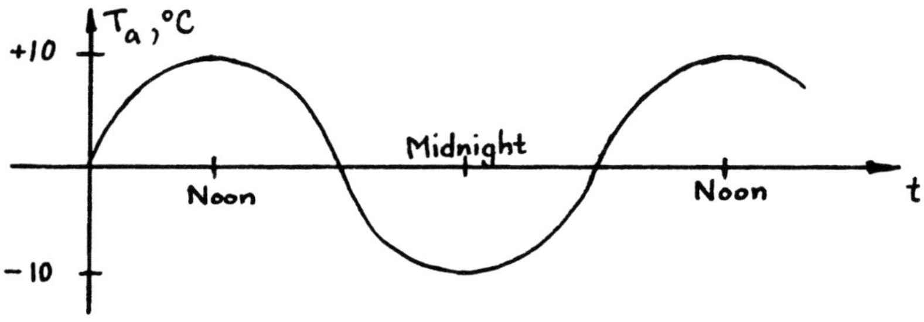

The amplitude of this signal is 10° C, and the frequency is

(1) $$\omega = \frac{2\pi}{(24)(3600)} = 72.7 \times 10^{-6} \text{ rad/sec}$$

The system transfer function can be found from the input-output equation

$$(2) \qquad T(s) = \frac{T_w(s)}{T_a(s)} = \frac{3}{0.58j+3}$$

For the frequency obtained in equation (1), the sinusoidal transfer function is

$$(3) \qquad T(j\omega)\Big|_{\omega=72.7\times10^{-6}} = \frac{3}{0.58j+3}$$

The amplitude of oscillations of T_w can now be calculated

$$(4) \qquad |T_w(j\omega)| = 10\ |T(j\omega)| = 10\ \frac{3}{[\ 0.58^2+3^2\ ]^{.5}} = 9.8°\ C$$

The phase angle is, from equation (3),

$$(5) \qquad \phi_T = 0 - \tan^{-1}(0.58/3.0) = -0.19 \text{ rad}$$

Hence, the time delay between T_a and T_w, t_d, can be calculated from the equation

$$(6) \qquad t_d = \phi_T/\omega = -(0.19/72.7)\times10^6 = -2613.5 \text{ sec} = -43.6 \text{ min.}$$

The maximum of T_a will occur at 12:44 PM and the minimum will occur 44 minutes after midnight.

CHAPTER 13

PROBLEM 13.1

The system characteristic equation is

(1) $10s^4+10s^3+20s^2+s+1 = 0.0$

The necessary conditions for stability are satisfied since all coeficients on the left hand side of equation (1) are positive.

To check if the sufficient conditions for stability are satisfied, evaluate the sign of the Hurwitz determinants.

$$D_1 = |10| > 0$$

$$D_2 = \begin{vmatrix} 10 & 10 \\ 1 & 20 \end{vmatrix} = 200 - 10 = 190 > 0$$

$$D_3 = \begin{vmatrix} 10 & 10 & 0 \\ 1 & 20 & 10 \\ 0 & 1 & 1 \end{vmatrix} = 200 + 0 + 0 - 0 - 100 - 10 = 90 > 0$$

Thus both the necessary and sufficient conditions are satisfied. The system is stable.

PROBLEM 13.2

a) The open-loop transfer function is

(1) $$\mathbf{T}_{OL}(s) = \mathbf{G}(s)\mathbf{H}(s) = \frac{10(2s+1)}{3s^3+2s^2+s+1}$$

The set of necessary conditions is satisfied because all coefficients in the characteristic equation of the open-loop system

(2) $3s^3+2s^2+s+1 = 0$

are positive. To check if the set of sufficient conditions for stability is satisfied, consider the Hurwitz determinants

(3) $D_1 = |2| = 2 > 0$

(4) $$D_2 = \begin{vmatrix} 2 & 3 \\ 1 & 1 \end{vmatrix} = 2 - 3 = -1 < 0$$

The sufficient conditions are not satisfied, $D_2 < 0$, and thus the open-loop system is unstable.

b) The transfer function of the closed-loop system is

(5) $$T_{CL}(s) = \frac{G(s)}{1+G(s)H(s)} = \frac{2s+1}{3s^3+2s^2+21s+11}$$

The system characteristic equation is

(6) $$3s^3+2s^2+21s+11 = 0$$

The necessary conditions for stability are satisfied since all coefficients on the left hand side of equation (6) are positive.

The Hurwitz determinants are

$$D_1 = |2| = 2 > 0$$

$$D_2 = \begin{vmatrix} 2 & 3 \\ 11 & 21 \end{vmatrix} = 42 - 33 = 9 > 0$$

The set of sufficient conditions is satisfied and thus the closed-loop system is stable.

PROBLEM 13.3

The system open-loop transfer function is

(1) $$T_{OL}(s) = T_C(s)T_P(s) = \frac{5ks+1.25k}{100s^3+20s^2+s}$$

The system characteristic equation is

(2) $$100s^3+20s^2+s = 0$$

The necessary conditions are satisfied and the Hurwitz determinants are

$$D_1 = |20| = 20 > 0$$

$$D_2 = \begin{vmatrix} 20 & 0 \\ 100 & 1 \end{vmatrix} = 20 - 0 = 20 > 0$$

The sufficient conditions are also satisfied. Therfore, the system is stable. The open-loop system stability is independent of k.

The system closed-loop transfer function is

$$(3) \qquad T_{CL}(s) = \frac{T_C(s)T_P(s)}{1+T_C(s)T_P(s)} = \frac{5ks+1.25k}{100s^3+20s^2+(5k+1)s+1.25k}$$

Hence the system characteristic equation is

$$(4) \qquad 100s^3+20s^2+(5k+1)s+1.25k = 0$$

The necessary conditions for stability wiil be satisfied if

$$(5) \qquad 5k+1 > 0 \qquad \text{and} \qquad 1.25k > 0$$

or, if

$$(6) \qquad k > -1/5 \qquad \text{and} \qquad k > 0$$

Both conditions are satisfied for $k > 0$.

The Hurwitz determinants are

$$D_1 = |20| = 20 > 0$$

$$(7) \qquad D_2 = \begin{vmatrix} 20 & 100 \\ 1.25k & 5k+1 \end{vmatrix} = 100k + 20 - 125k = 20 - 25k$$

Thus, the sufficient condition for stability is

$$(8) \qquad 20 - 25k > 0$$

which gives

$$(9) \qquad k < 0.8$$

Combining (6) and (9), the necessary and sufficient conditions for stability of this system are that the controller gain is positive and less than 0.8, i.e.

$$0.0 < k < 0.8$$

PROBLEM 13.4

The closed-loop system transfer function is

(1) $$T_{CL}(s) = \frac{2k}{\tau^2 s^3 + 2\tau s^2 + s + 2k}$$

The characteristic equation is

(2) $$\tau^2 s^3 + 2\tau s^2 + s + 2k = 0$$

The necessary conditions for stability are

(3) $$\tau > 0 \qquad \text{and} \qquad k > 0$$

The set os sufficient conditions involves Hurwitz determinants D_1 and D_2

(4) $$D_1 = |2\tau| = 2\tau > 0$$ if the necessary conditions are met

(5) $$D_2 = \begin{vmatrix} 2\tau & \tau^2 \\ 2k & 1 \end{vmatrix} = 2\tau - 2k\tau^2$$

For stability D_2 must be greater than zero

$$2\tau - 2k\tau^2 > 0$$

$$2\tau(1-k\tau) > 0$$

Hence

(6) $$k < 1/\tau$$

Equations (3) and (6) constitute the set of necessary and sufficient conditions for stability of the closed-loop system.

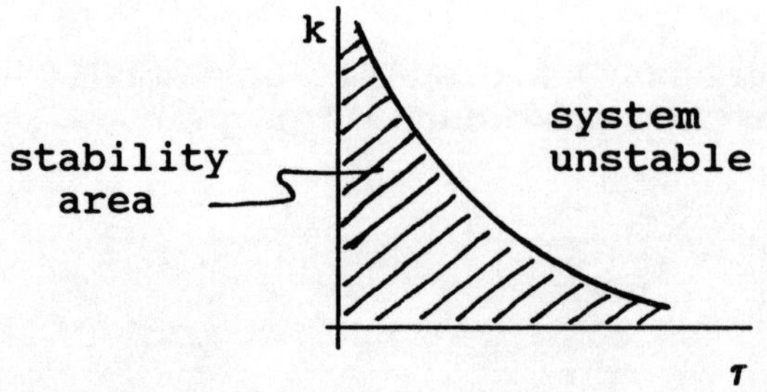

PROBLEM 13.5

a) Identify the coefficients in the system characteristic equation

(1) $a_0 = 42$ $a_1 = 41$ $a_2 = 12$ $a_3 = 1$

Set up the Routh array

s^3	1	41	
s^2	12	42	
s^1	37.5		$b_1 = (a_2a_1-a_3a_0)/a_2=37.5$; $b_2=0$
s^0	42		$c_1 = (b_1a_0-a_2b_2)/b_1=42$

All elements in the first column of the Routh array are positive, and thus the system is stable. Also, all roots of the characteristic equation are located in the left hand side of the complex plane.

b) Identify the **a** coefficients in the characteristic equation

$a_0 = 10$ $a_1 = 44$ $a_2 = 80$ $a_3 = 400$

The Routh array is

s^3	400	44	
s^2	80	10	
s_1	-6		$b_1 = (a_2a_1-a_3a_0)/a_2 = -6$
s^0	10		$c_1 = (b_1a_0-a_2b_2)/b_1 = 10$

The system is unstable and there are two roots in the right hand side of the complex plane since there are two sign changes in the first column of the Routh array.

c) The system is unstable because the necessary conditions for stability are not met. To find the number of roots of the characteristic equation with positive real parts, form the Routh array.

s^4	1	-14	-20	$a_4=1$; $a_2=-14$; $a_0=-20$
s^3	1	26		$a_3=1$; $a_1=26$
s^2	-40	-20		$b_1=-40$; $b_2=-20$
s^1	25.5			$c_1=25.5$
s^0	-20			$d_1=-20$

There are three sign changes in the first column of the Routh array (from +1 to -40, from -40 to +25.5, and from +25.5 to -20), therefore the number of roots of the characteristic equation located in the right hand side of the complex plane is three.

PROBLEM 13.6

The transfer function of the open-loop system is

(1) $$\mathbf{T}_{OL}(s) = \frac{k}{s(0.2s+1)(0.08s+1)} = \frac{k}{0.016s^3+0.28s^2+s}$$

The sinusoidal transfer function, $\mathbf{T}_{OL}(j\omega)$, is

(2) $$\mathbf{T}_{OL}(j\omega) = \mathbf{T}_{OL}(s)\Big|_{s=j\omega} = \frac{k}{-j0.016\omega^3-0.28\omega^2+j\omega}$$

The real and imaginary parts of $\mathbf{T}_{OL}(j\omega)$ can be found by multiplying numerator and denominator of the above expression by $[-0.28\omega^2-j\omega(1-0.016\omega^2)]$

(3) $$\text{Re}[\mathbf{T}_{OL}(j\omega)] = \frac{-0.28k\omega^2}{(0.28\omega^2)^2+\omega^2(1-0.016\omega^2)^2}$$

(4) $$\text{Im}[\mathbf{T}_{OL}(j\omega)] = \frac{k\omega(1-0.016\omega^2)}{(0.28\omega^2)^2+\omega^2(1-0.016\omega^2)^2}$$

The frequency at which the polar plot will cross the real axis can found by solving the equation

(5) $$\text{Im}[\mathbf{T}_{OL}(j\omega)] = 0$$

which yields

(6) $$\omega_\phi = 7.9 \text{ rad/sec}$$

On the basis of equations (3) through (7), and also calculating the limit of the phase angle for frequency approaching infinity from equation (12.41),

(7) $\lim \phi_T(\omega) = (0-3)(\pi/2) = -3\pi/2$

the polar plot can be sketched as shown below

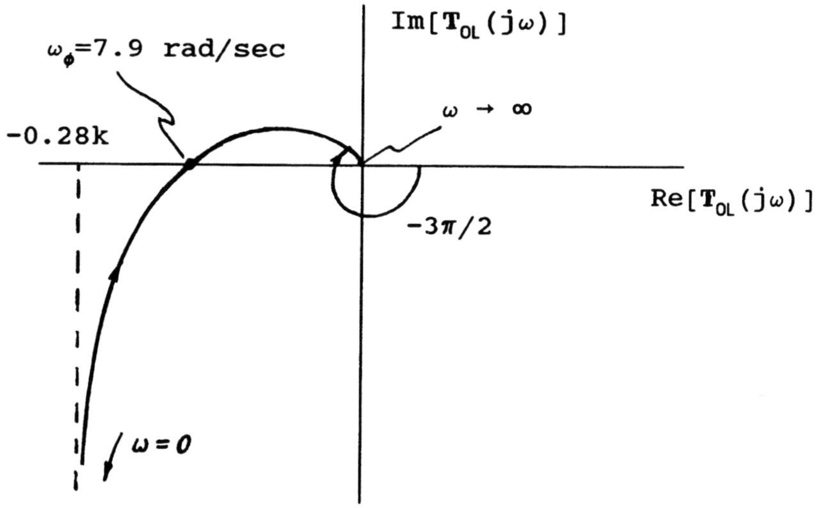

The Nyquist stability condition is

(8) $\left| \mathrm{Re}[\mathbf{T}_{OL}(j\omega)] \Big|_{\omega_\phi} \right| \leq 1$

which yields (after substituting ω=7.9 into equation (3))

(9) $k \leq 17.5$

PROBLEM 13.7

The system stability can be determined using Hurwitz, Routh or Nyquist criterion. Since the stability margins will have to be found in part (b), the Nyquist criterion is the most suitable for solving the entire problem.

a) First find the system open-loop transfer function

(1) $$\mathbf{T}_{OL}(s) = \frac{k_c k_p k_f}{\tau_i s(\tau_c s+1)(\tau_p s+1)}$$

Substituting numerical values for the system parameters gives

(2) $$\mathbf{T}_{OL}(s) = \frac{13.8}{0.49s^3+5.25s^2+3.5s}$$

Hence the sinusoidal transfer function is

(3) $$\mathbf{T}_{OL}(j\omega) = \frac{13.8}{-5.25\omega^2+j\omega(3.5-0.49\omega^2)}$$

The real. and imaginary parts of $\mathbf{T}_{OL}(j\omega)$ have to be found

(4) $$\mathbf{T}_{OL}(j\omega) = \frac{13.8[-5.25\omega^2-j\omega(3.5-0.49\omega^2)]}{(-5.25\omega^2)^2+\omega^2(3.5-0.49\omega^2)^2}$$

Hence

(5) $$\mathrm{Re}[\mathbf{T}_{OL}(j\omega)] = \frac{-72.45\omega^2}{27.5625\omega^4+\omega^2(3.5-0.49\omega^2)^2}$$

(6) $$\mathrm{Im}[\mathbf{T}_{OL}(j\omega)] = \frac{-13.8\omega(3.5-0.49\omega^2)}{27.5625\omega^4+\omega^2(3.5-0.49\omega^2)^2}$$

The polar plot will cross the real axis for $\omega = \omega_\phi$, which satisfies the following equation

(7) $$\mathrm{Im}[\mathbf{T}_{OL}(j\omega)]\Big|_{\omega_\phi} = 0$$

The non-zero solution of this equation is

(8) $\omega_\phi = 2.67$ rad/sec

Substituting (8) into (9) and checking the Nyquist stability condition

(9) $|\mathrm{Re}[\mathbf{T}_{OL}(j\omega)|_{\omega_\phi}]| < 1$

we obtain

(10) $|\mathrm{Re}[\mathbf{T}_{OL}(j\omega)|_{\omega_\phi}]| = 72.45/(27.5625\omega_\phi^2) = 0.368 < 1$

The closed-loop system is stable.

b) The stability gain margin is

(11) $$k_g = \frac{1}{|\mathrm{Re}[\mathbf{T}_{OL}(j\omega_\phi)]|} = 2.717 \text{ or } k_g = 8.68 \text{ dB}$$

To determine the stability phase margin, first the frequency ω_g, for which the magnitude of the $\mathbf{T}_{OL}(j\omega)$ is unity, has to found. The magnitude of the open-loop transfer function given by equation (3) is

(12) $$|\mathbf{T}_{OL}(j\omega)| = \frac{13.8}{[\ 27.5625\omega^4+\omega^2(3.5-0.49\omega^2)^2\ ]^{.5}}$$

The frequency ω_g will be found by solving

(13) $|\mathbf{T}_{OL}(j\omega)|_{\omega_\phi}| = 1$

Substituting (12) into (13) leads to the following equation

(14) $0.24\omega_g^6+24.1325\omega_g^4+12.25\omega_g^2-190.44 = 0$

The only real, positive root of this equation is

(15) $\omega_g = 1.59$ rad/sec

The values of real and imaginary parts of $\mathbf{T}_{OL}(j\omega)$ for $\omega = \omega_g$ are

(16) $\mathrm{Re}[\mathbf{T}_{OL}(j\omega)|_{\omega_g}] = -0.970$

(17) $\text{Im}[\mathbf{T}_{OL}(j\omega)\Big|_{\omega_g}] = -0.262$

Since both parts are negative, the phase angle is

(18) $$\angle\mathbf{T}_{OL}(j\omega)\Big|_{\omega_g} = -180 + \tan^{-1}\left[\frac{\text{Im}[\mathbf{T}_{OL}(j\omega_g)]}{\text{Re}[\mathbf{T}_{OL}(j\omega_g)]}\right] = -164.88°$$

Hence, the stability phase margin is

$$\gamma = 180 + \angle\mathbf{T}_{OL}(j\omega_g) = 15.12°$$

PROBLEM 13.8

a) The transfer function of the open-loop system is

(1) $$\mathbf{T}_{OL}(s) = \frac{0.1k_T}{s(1+0.1s)(1+0.2s)} = \frac{k_T}{0.2s^3+3s^2+10s}$$

The corresponding sinusoidal transfer function is

(2) $$\mathbf{T}_{OL}(j\omega) = \frac{k_T}{-j0.2\omega^3-3\omega^2+j10\omega}$$

Multiplying numerator and denominator by the complex conjugate to the expression in the denominator gives

(3) $$\mathbf{T}_{OL}(j\omega) = \frac{k_T[-3\omega^2-j\omega(10-0.2\omega^2)]}{9\omega^4+\omega^2(10-0.2\omega^2)^2}$$

Hence, the real and imaginary parts are

(4) $$\text{Re}[\mathbf{T}_{OL}(j\omega)] = -\frac{3k_T}{9\omega^2+(10-0.2\omega^2)^2}$$

(5) $$\text{Im}[\mathbf{T}_{OL}(j\omega)] = -\frac{k_T\omega(10-0.2\omega^2)}{9\omega^4+\omega^2(10-0.2\omega^2)^2}$$

The frequency for which the phase angle is equal to -180° can be found from the equation

(6) $$\text{Im}[\mathbf{T}_{OL}(j\omega)] = 0$$

Substituting (5) into (6) and solving for ω yields

(7) $\omega_\phi = 7.07$ rad/sec

The value of the real part at this frequency is calculated using equation (4)

(8) $$\mathrm{Re}[\mathbf{T}_{OL}(j\omega)]\Big|_{\omega_\phi} = k_T/150$$

For $k_T = 150$, the real part is equal to -1 and thus the system is marginally stable.

b) For the gain margin of 1.2 the following condition must be satisfied

(9) $$k_g = \frac{1}{|\mathrm{Re}[\mathbf{T}_{OL}(j\omega_\phi)]|} = 1.2$$

Combining (8) and (9) gives the tachometer gain necessary for the gain margin of 1.2

(10) $150/k_T = 1.2$

and hence

(11) $k_T = 125$

c) First find the frequency ω_g, for which the magnitude of the open-loop transfer function is unity and the phase angle is -180°+45° = -135°. Using the phase condition yields

(12) $$\frac{\mathrm{Im}[\mathbf{T}_{OL}(j\omega_g)]}{\mathrm{Re}[\mathbf{T}_{OL}(j\omega_g)]} = \tan(-135°) = 1$$

Substituting the expressions for the real and imaginary parts of $\mathbf{T}_{OL}(j\omega)$ gives the quadratic equation

(13) $0.2\omega_g^2 + 3\omega_g - 10 = 0$

and hence

(14) $\omega_g = 2.8$ rad/sec

Now, the magnitude condition is

(15) $$\frac{k_T}{[\ 9\omega_g^4+\omega_g^2(10-0.2\omega_g^2)^2\ ]^{.5}} = 1$$

Substituting ω_g = 2.8 rad/sec and solving for k_T, we find

(16) $k_T = 33.3$

CHAPTER 14

PROBLEM 14.1

The error transfer function is

$$(1) \qquad \mathbf{T}_E(s) = \frac{1}{1 + \mathbf{T}_{OL}(s)} = \frac{(s+5)(s+2)^2}{(s+5)(s+2)^2 + k}$$

For a unit step input, the steady-state error is

$$(2) \qquad e_{ss} = \lim_{s\to 0} s\,\mathbf{U}(s)\mathbf{T}_E(s) = \lim_{s\to 0} s\,\frac{1}{s}\,\frac{(s+5)(s+2)^2}{(s+5)(s+2)^2 + k} = \frac{20}{20 + k}$$

The steady-state performance requirement can be expressed as

$$(3) \qquad \frac{20}{20 + k} < 0.1$$

Hence

$$(4) \qquad k > 180.$$

To evaluate system stability consider the characteristic equation of the closed-loop system

$$(5) \qquad 1 + \mathbf{T}_{OL}(s) = 0$$

Substituting the expression for $\mathbf{T}_{OL}(s)$ gives

$$1 + \frac{k}{(s+5)(s+2)^2} = 0$$

and hence

$$(6) \qquad s^3 + 9s^2 + 24s + 20 + k = 0$$

Employing the Hurwitz stability criterion yields the following conditions

$$(7) \qquad D_1 = 9 > 0$$

(8) $D_2 = \begin{vmatrix} 9 & 1 \\ 20+k & 24 \end{vmatrix} = 9(24)-20-k > 0$

Solving (8) gives the stability condition for k

(9) $k < 196.$

Combining (4) and (9), the range of k for which the system meets the specified steady-state performance and stability requirements is

(10) $180. < k < 196.$

PROBLEM 14.2

a) The closed-loop transfer function is

(1) $$T_{CL}(s) = \frac{\Omega_o(s)}{\Omega_d(s)} = \frac{\dfrac{110}{s^2+150s+110} \cdot \dfrac{K}{0.1s+1} \cdot \dfrac{10}{20s+1}}{1 + \dfrac{110}{s^2+150s+110} \cdot \dfrac{K}{0.1s+1} \cdot \dfrac{10}{20s+1}}$$

$$= \frac{1100\ K}{(s^2+150s+110)(0.1s+1)(20s+1) + 1100\ K}$$

$$= \frac{1100\ K}{2s^4 + 320.1s^3 + 3236s^2 + 2361s + 110 + 1100\ K}$$

Hence the input-output equation is

(2) $$2\ddddot{\Omega}_o + 320.1\dddot{\Omega}_o + 3236\ddot{\Omega}_o + 2361\dot{\Omega}_o + (110+1100K)\Omega_o = 1100\ K\ \Omega_d$$

b) The steady-state error must be

(3) $e_{ss} < 0.01\ \Delta\Omega_d$

where

(4) $$e_{ss} = \left. \frac{1}{1 + T_{OL}(s)} \right|_{s=0}$$

The open-loop transfer function for $s=0$, $\mathbf{T}_{OL}(0)$, is

(5) $$\mathbf{T}_{OL}(0) = \frac{1100\ K}{110} = 10\ K$$

Hence

(6) $$e_{ss} = \frac{1}{1 + 10\ K}$$

Assuming a unit step input, $\Delta\Omega_d=1$, we have

(7) $$\frac{1}{1 + 10\ K} < 0.01$$

or

(8) $$K > 9.9$$

PROBLEM 14.3

a) The system closed-loop transfer function is

(1) $$\mathbf{T}_{CL}(s) = \frac{\dfrac{\alpha}{(Ls+R)(Js+B)}}{1 + \dfrac{\alpha(\alpha+k_T)}{(Ls+R)(Js+B)}} = \frac{\alpha}{(Ls+R)(Js+B) + \alpha(\alpha+k_T)}$$

The system characteristic equation is

(2) $$L{\cdot}Js^2 + (L{\cdot}B+R{\cdot}J)s + R{\cdot}B + \alpha^2 + \alpha k_T = 0$$

Substituting numerical values for the known system parameters

(3) $$0.4s^2 + 49.5s + 4804. + 68.k_T = 0$$

Hence, the damping ratio is

(4) $$\zeta = \frac{49.5}{2[\ 0.4(4804.+68.k_T)\ ]^{.5}}$$

which will be greater than 0.5 if

(5) $$k_T < 19.436 \text{ V sec/rad}$$

The disturbance sensitivity is defined as

$$(6) \qquad S_{DC} = \frac{\mathbf{E}_V(0)}{1 + \mathbf{T}_{OL}(0)}$$

Substituting expressions for $\mathbf{E}_V$ and $\mathbf{T}_{OL}$ from the system block diagram gives

$$(7) \qquad S_{DC} = \left. \frac{1/B}{1 + \dfrac{\alpha(\alpha + k_T)}{(Ls+R)(Js+B)}} \right|_{s=0} = \frac{R}{R \cdot B + \alpha^2 + \alpha k_T}$$

The condition $S_{DC} < 2.0 \times 10^{-3}$ will be met if

$$(8) \qquad \frac{R}{R \cdot B + \alpha^2 + \alpha k_T} < 0.002$$

Solving for k_T yields

$$(9) \qquad k_T > 17.6 \text{ V sec/rad}$$

The damping ratio and disturbance sensitivity conditions will both be satisfied for the range of k_T

$$(10) \qquad 17.6 < k_T < 19.436$$

b) The steady-state error is

$$(11) \qquad e_{ss} = \frac{1}{1 + \mathbf{T}_{OL}(0)} = \frac{1}{1 + \dfrac{\alpha(\alpha + k_T)}{R \cdot B}}$$

Selecting $k_T = 18$ V sec/rad gives

$$(12) \qquad e_{ss} = 0.029 \text{ rad/sec}$$

PROBLEM 14.4

a) We will use the Nyquist stability criterion in this part, therefore the open-loop transfer function has to be found first

$$(1) \qquad \mathbf{T}_{OL}(s) = \frac{50\ k_p}{(10s+1)(20s+1)(2s+1)}$$

The sinusoidal open-loop transfer function is obtained by substituting $s = j\omega$ in equation (1)

$$(2) \qquad \mathbf{T}_{OL}(j\omega) = \frac{50\ k_p}{-400j\omega^3 - 260\omega^2 + 32j\omega + 1}$$

The real and imaginary parts of $\mathbf{T}_{OL}(j\omega)$ are found to be

$$(3) \qquad Re[\mathbf{T}_{OL}(j\omega)] = \frac{50\ k_p\ (1-260\omega^2)}{(1-20\omega^2)^2 + \omega^2(32-400\omega^2)^2}$$

$$(4) \qquad Im[\mathbf{T}_{OL}(j\omega)] = \frac{50\ k_p\ \omega(32-400\omega^2)}{(1-20\omega^2)^2 + \omega^2(32-400\omega^2)^2}$$

The polar plot of $\mathbf{T}_{OL}(j\omega)$ is sketched below.

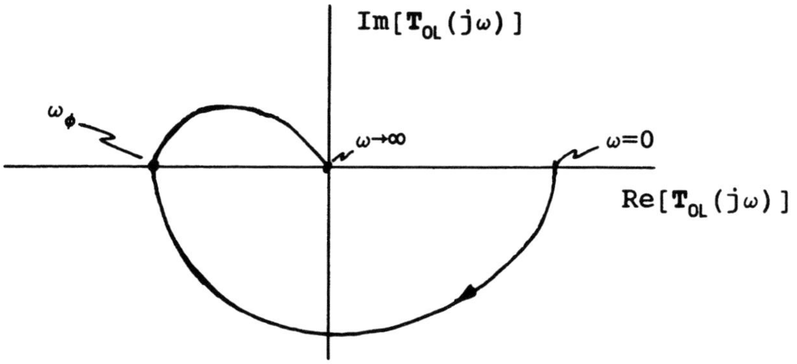

The value of frequency ω_ϕ for which the phase angle is equal to -180° is found from the equation

$$(5) \qquad Im[\mathbf{T}_{OL}(j\omega)] = 0$$

which yields

(6) $\omega_\phi = 0.28$ rad/sec

For the required gain margin, $k_g = 1.2$, the following must be satisfied

$$(7) \qquad \frac{1}{|Re[\mathbf{T}_{OL}(j\omega)]|} = 1.2$$

Using equations (3) and (6), the above condition becomes

$$(8) \qquad \left[\frac{50\ k_p}{|\ 1 - 260(0.28)^2\ |}\right]^{-1} = 1.2$$

Hence

(9) $k_p = 0.33$

b) The system error transfer function is

$$(10) \qquad \mathbf{T}_E(s) = \frac{1}{1+\mathbf{T}_{OL}(s)} = \frac{400s^3 + 260s^2 + 32s + 1}{400s^3 + 260s^2 + 32s + 1 + 50k_p}$$

The steady error for the step input of magnitude 10°C is

$$(11) \qquad e_{ss} = \lim_{s \to 0} s \frac{10}{s} \frac{400s^3 + 260s^2 + 32s + 1}{400s^3 + 260s^2 + 32s + 1 + 50k_p} = \frac{10}{1 + 50k_p}$$

For $k_p = 0.33$, the steady-state error is

(12) $e_{ss} = 0.57$°C

PROBLEM 14.5

The error transfer function is

$$(1) \qquad \mathbf{T}_E(s) = \frac{1}{1 + \mathbf{T}_{OL}(s)} = \frac{s^2(\tau s+1)}{s^2(\tau s+1) + 1 + k}$$

The steady-state error is

$$(2) \qquad e_{ss} = \lim_{s\to 0} s\,\mathbf{U}(s)\mathbf{T}_E(s) = \lim_{s\to 0} s \frac{2}{s^3} \frac{s^2(\tau s+1)}{s^2(\tau s+1) + 1 + k} = \frac{2}{1 + k}$$

The acceleration error coefficient for this system is

$$(3) \qquad K_a = \lim_{s\to 0} s^2\mathbf{T}_{OL}(s) = k$$

Hence, the steady-state error

$$(4) \qquad e_{ss} = \frac{2}{1 + K_a}$$

PROBLEM 14.6

First, consider the system with the P controller, $\mathbf{T}_c(s) = 9$. The closed-loop transfer function in this case is

$$(1) \qquad \mathbf{T}_{CL}(s) = \frac{\mathbf{T}_c(s)\mathbf{T}_p(s)}{1 + \mathbf{T}_c(s)\mathbf{T}_p(s)} = \frac{9}{10s + 10}$$

The system is of first order with the characteristic equation

$$(2) \qquad 10s + 10 = 0$$

The time constant is 1.0 second, and there will be no overshoot in the system response.

To find the steady-state error, first obtain the error transfer function

$$(3) \qquad \mathbf{T}_E(s) = \frac{1}{1 + \mathbf{T}_{OL}(s)} = \frac{10s + 1}{10s + 10}$$

Hence the steady-state error for a unit step input is

$$(4) \qquad e_{ss} = \lim_{s\to 0} \mathbf{T}_E(s) = 0.1$$

Now, consider the system with the PI controller. The closed-loop transfer function now becomes

$$(5) \qquad \mathbf{T}_{CL}(s) = \frac{9s + 5}{10s^2 + 10s + 5}$$

which gives the system characteristic equation

(6) $$10s^2 + 10s + 5 = 0$$

The damping ratio is

(7) $$\zeta = \frac{10}{2(10 \cdot 5)^{.5}} = 0.707$$

and the corresponding maximum overshoot is

(8) $$M_p\% = 4.3\%$$

The error transfer function will be found using the open-loop transfer function

(9) $$T_{OL}(s) = 9(1 + 1/1.8s)\frac{1}{10s + 1} = \frac{9s + 5}{s(10s + 1)}$$

Now the error transfer function is

(10) $$T_E(s) = \frac{s(10s + 1)}{s(10s + 1) + 9s + 5}$$

The steady-state control error for a unit step input is

(11) $$e_{ss} = \lim_{s \to 0} T_E(s) = 0$$

The results for the two controllers are summarized in the following table.

	CONTROLLER	
	P	PI
$M_p\%$	0.0	4.3
e_{ss}	0.1	0.0

PROBLEM 14.7

First, the system with the P controller will be considered. The system closed-loop transfer function is

$$(1) \qquad \mathbf{T}_{CL}(s) = \frac{k\,k_p}{\tau_1\tau_2 s^2 + (\tau_1 + \tau_2)s + 1 + k\,k_p}$$

The characteristic equation is

$$(2) \qquad \tau_1\tau_2 s^2 + (\tau_1 + \tau_2)s + 1 + k\,k_p = 0$$

The damping ratio for the system with the P controller is thus

$$(3) \qquad \zeta_P = \frac{\tau_1 + \tau_2}{2(\tau_1\tau_2(1 + k\,k_p))^{.5}}$$

To evaluate steady-state performance, first find the open-loop transfer function

$$(4) \qquad \mathbf{T}_{OL}(s) = \frac{k\,k_p}{(\tau_1 s + 1)(\tau_2 s + 1)}$$

Now, the error transfer function is

$$(5) \qquad \mathbf{T}_E(s) = \frac{(\tau_1 s + 1)(\tau_2 s + 1)}{(\tau_1 s + 1)(\tau_2 s + 1) + k\,k_p}$$

Hence the steady-state error for a unit step input with the P controller is

$$(6) \qquad (e_{ss})_P = \lim_{s\to 0} \mathbf{T}_E(s) = \frac{1}{1 + k\,k_p}$$

Now, the system with the PD controller will be evaluated. The closed-loop transfer function is

$$(7) \qquad \mathbf{T}_{CL}(s) = \frac{k\,k_p(1 + T_d s)}{(\tau_1 s + 1)(\tau_2 s + 1) + k\,k_p(1 + T_d s)}$$

Hence the system characteristic equation

$$(8) \qquad (\tau_1 s + 1)(\tau_2 s + 1) + k\,k_p(1 + T_d s) = 0$$

or

$$(9) \qquad \tau_1\tau_2 s^2 + (\tau_1 + \tau_2 + k\,k_p T_d)s + 1 + k\,k_p = 0$$

The damping ratio can be found from equation (9)

$$(10) \qquad \zeta_{PD} = \frac{\tau_1 + \tau_2 + k\,k_p T_d}{2(\tau_1\tau_2(1 + k\,k_p))^{.5}}$$

Comparing with the damping ratio for the system with the P controller, notice that

$$(11) \qquad \frac{\zeta_{PD}}{\zeta_P} = \frac{\tau_1 + \tau_2 + k\,k_p T_d}{\tau_1 + \tau_2} = 1 + \frac{k\,k_p T_d}{\tau_1 + \tau_2}$$

The above ratio is always greater than unity for positive values of k, k_p, and T_d. Therefore, the PD controller provides more damping than the P controller.

The open-loop transfer function with the PD controller is

$$(12) \qquad \mathbf{T}_{OL}(s) = \frac{k\,k_p(1 + T_d s)}{(\tau_1 s + 1)(\tau_2 s + 1)}$$

and the error transfer function is

$$(13) \qquad \mathbf{T}_E(s) = \frac{(\tau_1 s + 1)(\tau_2 s + 1)}{(\tau_1 s + 1)(\tau_2 s + 1) + k\,k_p(1 + T_d s)}$$

Hence the steady-state error for a unit step input is given by

$$(14) \qquad (e_{ss})_{PD} = \lim_{s \to 0} \mathbf{T}_E(s) = \frac{1}{1 + k\,k_p}$$

which is the same as the steady-state error with the P controller, given by equation (6).

PROBLEM 14.8

The system is of type 1 and thus the first requirement of the steady-state error after a step input equal to zero is satisfied for all nonzero values of k_p.

Now, consider the steady-state load sensitivity requirement. The system open-loop transfer function is

$$(1) \qquad T_{OL}(s) = \frac{k_p k_m k_a}{Js^2 + Bs}$$

The load torque is acting on the system through $G_v(s)$

$$(2) \qquad G_v(s) = \frac{1}{Js^2 + Bs}$$

Hence, the steady-state load sensitivity is

$$(3) \qquad S_{DC} = \lim_{s \to 0} \frac{G_v(s)}{1 + T_{OL}(s)} = \frac{1}{k_p k_m k_a}$$

which must be less than 0.1 rad/N-m

$$(4) \qquad \frac{1}{k_p k_m k_a} < 0.1$$

Thus the gain of the controller must be

$$(5) \qquad k_p > \frac{1}{0.1 k_m k_a} \qquad \text{or} \qquad k_p > 5 \ \text{volt/volt}$$

The system characteristic equation is

$$(6) \qquad Js^2 + Bs + k_p k_m k_a = 0$$

The damping ratio

$$(7) \qquad \zeta = \frac{1}{2\ [\ J k_p k_m k_a\ ]^{.5}} = 0.1$$

and the natural frequency

$$(8) \qquad \omega_n = [\ (k_p k_m k_a)/J\ ]^{.5} = 1.63 \ \text{rad/sec}$$

PROBLEM 14.9

The open-loop transfer function of the modified system is

$$(1) \qquad T_{OL}(s) = \frac{k_p k_m k_a}{s(Js + B + k_m k_v)}$$

The system closed-loop transfer function is

$$(2) \qquad T_{CL}(s) = \frac{k_p k_m}{Js^2 + (B + k_m k_v)s + k_p k_m k_a}$$

This second order system is stable if $J > 0$, $(B + k_m k_v) > 0$, and $k_p k_m k_a > 0$. The requirement that the damping ratio be greater than 0.5 can be expressed methematically as

$$(3) \qquad \zeta = \frac{B + k_m k_v}{2\,[\,J k_p k_m k_a\,]^{.5}} = \frac{1.25 + k_v}{12.25} \geq 0.5$$

which gives the condition for k_v

$$(4) \qquad k_v \geq 4.88 \text{ volt-sec/rad}$$

The modified system is still of type 1 and thus the steady-state error requirement from Problem 14.8 is satisfied. The steady-state load sensitivity is

$$(5) \qquad S_{DC} = \lim_{s \to 0} \frac{1}{Js^2 + (B + k_m k_v)s + k_p k_m k_a} = \frac{1}{k_p k_m k_a}$$

which is the same as for the original system considered in Problem 14.8.

Since both the original and the modified systems produce oscillatory step responses, their speed of response can be evaluated by the peak times, $t_p = \pi/\omega_d$. For the original system

$$(6) \qquad t_p = \frac{\pi}{\omega_n\,[\,1 - \zeta^2\,]^{.5}} = \frac{\pi}{1.63\,[\,1 - 0.1^2\,]^{.5}} = 1.94 \text{ sec}$$

For the modified system, which has the same natural frequency but larger damping ratio, the peak time is

$$t_p = \frac{\pi}{1.63\,[\,1 - 0.5^2\,]^{.5}} = 2.23 \text{ sec}$$

Thus the feedback velocity dcreases the system speed of response.

CHAPTER 15

PROBLEM 15.1

A recursive formula for $y(k)$ is

$$y(k) = 1.2y(k-1) - 0.6y(k-2) + u(k-1) + u(k-2)$$

a) For a unit step input, the recursive formula gives the following results:

$$y(0) = 0$$

$$y(1) = 1.2y(0) + u(0) = 1.0$$

$$y(2) = 1.2y(1) - 0.6y(0) + u(1) + u(0) = 1.2 + 1 + 1 = 3.2$$

.
.
.

The values of $y(k)$ for $k = 0, 1, \ldots, 25$ are tabulated below.

k	y(k)
0	0.000
1	1.000
2	3.200
3	5.240
4	6.368
5	6.498
6	5.976
7	5.273
8	4.742
9	4.526
10	4.587
11	4.788
12	4.994
13	5.120

k	y(k)
14	5.147
15	5.105
16	5.038
17	4.982
18	4.956
19	4.958
20	4.976
21	4.996
22	5.010
23	5.014
24	5.011
25	5.005

b) For a unit impulse function, using the recursive formula for y(k) yields the following results:

k	y(k)	k	y(k)
0	0.000	14	0.028
1	1.000	15	-0.042
2	2.200	16	-0.067
3	2.040	17	-0.056
4	1.128	18	-0.026
5	0.130	19	0.002
6	-0.521	20	0.018
7	-0.703	21	0.021
8	-0.531	22	0.014
9	-0.215	23	0.004
10	0.060	24	-0.003
11	0.202	25	-0.006
12	0.206		
13	0.126		

PROBLEM 15.2

The input-output equation for the system in Example 5.1 is

(1) $$m\dot{v}_{1g} + bv_{1g} = F(t)$$

Substituting numerical values for m and b

(2) $$5\dot{v}_{1g} + 2v_{1g} = F(t)$$

The system transfer function is

(3) $$\mathbf{T}(s) = \frac{\mathbf{V}_{1g}(s)}{\mathbf{F}(s)} = \frac{1}{5s + 2} = \frac{0.5}{2.5s + 1}$$

Substituting $s=j\omega$ gives the sinusoidal transfer function

(4) $$\mathbf{T}(j\omega) = \frac{0.5}{2.5j\omega + 1}$$

The bandwidth of the system is determined by the break frequency

(5) $$\omega_b = \frac{2\pi}{2.5} = 2.5 \text{ rad/sec}$$

Shannon's Theorem requires $\omega_s > 2\omega_b$ or $\omega_s > 5$ rad/sec.

Selecting $\omega_s = 10\omega_b$ gives $\omega_b = 25$ rad/sec, where 10 is an arbitrarily selected factor, usually taken between 6 and 50.

PROBLEM 15.3

The frequency of oscillations of the sstem step response is

$$\omega_d = \omega_n[1 - \zeta^2]^{.5} = 0.63 \text{ rad/sec}$$

According to Shannon

$$\omega_s > 1.26 \text{ rad/sec}$$

Select $\omega_s = 10\omega_d = 6.3$ rad/sec, which gives a sampling period $T_s = 1$ sec.

PROBLEM 15.4

According to Shannon, the sampling frequency must be

(1) $\omega_s > 2(200)$ rad/sec

or

(2) $\omega_s > 400$ rad/sec

Select $\omega_s = 500$ rad/sec.

The radial frequency of the electric noise is

(3) $\omega_{noise} = 2\pi(60) = 377$ rad/sec

which will produce an aliasing signal with a frequency of

(4) $\omega_a = \omega_s - \omega_{noise} = 500 - 377 = 123$ rad/sec

The aliasing frequency is below the frequency of the signal that is to be measured and thus a guard filter is necessary. Select the break frequency of the guard filter ω_f half way between the measuring signal frequency and the noise frequency

(5) $$\omega_f = \frac{200 + 377}{2} = 280.5 \text{ rad/sec}$$

which gives the filter time constant

(6) $$\tau_f = \frac{2\pi}{\omega_f} = 0.0244 \text{ sec}$$

Hence, the filter transfer function is

(7) $$\mathbf{T}_f(s) = \frac{1}{0.0224s + 1}$$

PROBLEM 15.5

a) Using linearity of the z-transform

(1) $$\mathbf{F}(z) = \mathbf{Z}\{\ a(1 - e^{-bkT})\ \} = \mathbf{Z}\{a\} - \mathbf{Z}\{\ ae^{-bkT}\ \}$$

Now, find the two z-transforms.

(2) $$\mathbf{Z}\{a\} = \frac{az}{z - 1}$$

(3) $$\mathbf{Z}\{\ ae^{-bkT}\ \} = \frac{az}{z - e^{-bT}}$$

Hence

(4) $$\mathbf{F}(z) = \frac{az}{z - 1} - \frac{az}{z - e^{-bT}} = \frac{a(1 - e^{-bT})z}{(z - 1)(z - e^{-bT})}$$

b)

(5) $$\mathbf{F}(z) = \mathbf{Z}\{\ (1 - akT)e^{-bkT}\ \} = \mathbf{Z}\{\ e^{-bkT}\ \} - \mathbf{Z}\{\ akTe^{-bkT}\ \}$$

The z-transform of the exponential function is

(6) $$\mathbf{Z}\{\ e^{-bkT}\ \} = \frac{z}{z - e^{-bT}}$$

To find the second term in $\mathbf{F}(z)$, first note the following property of the z-transform known as the complex translation theorem

(7) $$\mathbf{Z}\{x(k)e^{-bk}\} = \sum_{k=0}^{\infty} x(k)e^{-bk}z^{-k} = \sum_{k=0}^{\infty} x(k)(e^{b}z)^{-k} = \mathbf{X}(e^{b}z)$$

Before applying this theorem to the second term of **F**(z), first find

(8) $$\mathbf{Z}\{\ akT\ \} = \frac{aTz}{(z - 1)^2}$$

Now

(9) $$\mathbf{Z}\{akTe^{-bkT}\} = \frac{aTe^{bT}z}{(e^{bt}z - 1)^2} = \frac{aTe^{-bT}z}{(z - e^{-bT})^2}$$

The complete z-transform is

(10) $$\mathbf{F}(z) = \frac{1}{z - e^{-bT}} - \frac{aTe^{-bT}z}{(z - e^{-bT})^2} = \frac{z(z-e^{-bT}) - aTe^{-bT}z}{(z - e^{-bT})^2}$$

c) First, in tables of z-transforms, find

(11) $$\mathbf{Z}\{\ \sin(\omega kT)\ \} = \frac{z\ \sin(\omega T)}{z^2 - 2z\ \cos(\omega T) + 1}$$

Applying the complex translation theorem from part **b)**

(12) $$\mathbf{F}(z) = \mathbf{Z}\{\ e^{-bkT}\sin(\omega kT)\ \} = \frac{ze^{-bT}\ \sin(\omega T)}{z^2 + 2ze^{-bT}\ \cos(\omega T) + e^{-bT}}$$

d) Denoting

(13) $$f(k) = \cos(\omega kT)$$

and

(14) $$f(k-2) = \cos(\ \omega(k-2)T\ )$$

The z-transform of $f(k-2)$ is

(15) $$\mathbf{Z}\{\ f(k-2)\ \} = z^{-2}\mathbf{F}(z)$$

where

(16) $$\mathbf{F}(z) = \mathbf{Z}\{\ f(k)\ \} = \mathbf{Z}\{\ \cos(\omega kT)\ \} = \frac{z(z - \cos(\omega T))}{z^2 - 2z\ \cos(\omega T) + 1}$$

Hence,

$$(17) \qquad \mathbf{Z}\{\cos(\omega(k-2)T)\} = z^{-2}\frac{z(z - \cos(\omega T))}{z^2-2z\cos(\omega T)+1} = \frac{z - \cos(\omega T)}{z^3-2z^2\cos(\omega T)+z}$$

PROBLEM 15.6

a) The sequence x(k) is plotted below.

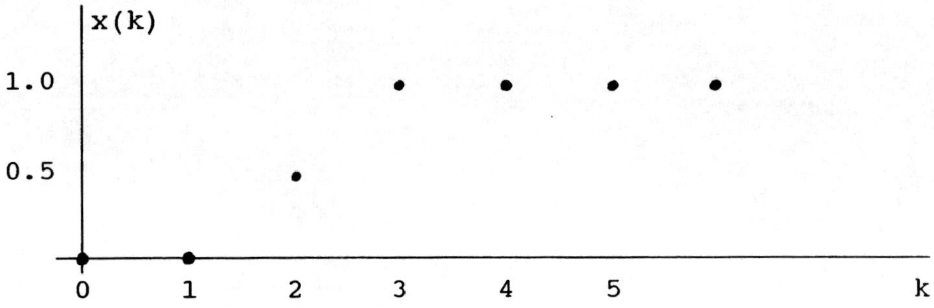

The mathematical expression is

$$(1) \qquad f(kT) = 0.5 [(k-1)T - (k-3)T]$$

where T = 1 sec in this case. The z-transform can be written as

$$(2) \qquad \mathbf{F}(z) = 0.5 [\mathbf{F}_1(z) + \mathbf{F}_2(z)]$$

where

$$(3) \qquad \mathbf{F}_1(z) = \mathbf{Z}\{ (k-1)T \}\Big|_{T=1} = z^{-1}\mathbf{Z}\{ kT \}\Big|_{T=1} = \frac{1}{(z - 1)^2}$$

and

$$(4) \qquad \mathbf{F}_2(z) = \mathbf{Z}\{ (k-3)T \}\Big|_{T=1} = z^{-3}\mathbf{Z}\{ kT \}\Big|_{T=1} = \frac{1}{z^2(z -1)^2}$$

Hence,

$$(5) \qquad \mathbf{F}(z) = \frac{1}{(z - 1)^2} - \frac{1}{z^2(z - 1)^2} = \frac{z^2 - 1}{z^2(z - 1)^2} = \frac{z + 1}{z^2(z - 1)}$$

b) Using the property of linearity, the z-transform of the sequence x(k) can be expressed as

(6) $$\mathbf{F}(z) = \mathbf{F}_1(z) + \mathbf{F}_2(z)$$

where

(7) $$\mathbf{F}_1(z) = \mathbf{Z}\{ e^{0.5k} \} = \frac{z}{z - e^{0.5}} = \frac{z}{z - 1.65}$$

and

(8) $$\mathbf{F}_2(z) = \mathbf{Z}\{ U_s(k-2) \} = z^{-2}\mathbf{Z}\{ U_s(k) \} = \frac{1}{z^2 - z}$$

Hence,

(9) $$\mathbf{F}(z) = \frac{z}{z - 1.65} + \frac{1}{z^2 - z} = \frac{1}{z^2 - 2.65z + 1.65}$$

PROBLEM 15.7

The z-transform of the system unit step response is

(1) $$\mathbf{Y}(z) = \frac{z(z + 1)}{(z^2 - 1.1z + 0.28)(z - 1)}$$

Factoring the denominator leads to

(2) $$\mathbf{Y}(z) = \frac{z(z + 1)}{(z - 0.4)(z - 0.7)(z - 1)}$$

Since $\mathbf{Y}(z)$ has a zero at the origin, it will be convenient to find an inverse z-transform of $\mathbf{Y}(z)/z$ first.

(3) $$\frac{\mathbf{Y}(z)}{z} = \frac{z + 1}{(z - 0.4)(z - 0.7)(z - 1)} = \frac{C_1}{z-0.4} + \frac{C_2}{z-0.7} + \frac{C_3}{z-1}$$

The constants C_1, C_2, and C_3 are

(4) $$C_1 = \left. \frac{\mathbf{Y}(z)\ (z - 0.4)}{z} \right|_{z=0.4} = 7.78$$

$$(5) \qquad C_2 = \left. \frac{Y(z)\ (z - 0.7)}{z} \right|_{z=0.7} = -18.89$$

$$(6) \qquad C_3 = \left. \frac{Y(z)\ (z - 1)}{z} \right|_{z=1} = 11.11$$

Hence,

$$(7) \qquad \frac{Y(z)}{z} = \frac{7.78}{z - 0.4} - \frac{18.89}{z - 0.7} + \frac{11.11}{z - 1}$$

Multiplying both sides by z gives

$$(8) \qquad Y(z) = \frac{7.78z}{z - 0.4} - \frac{18.89z}{z - 0.7} + \frac{11.11z}{z - 1}$$

The inverse z-transforms for the three terms on the right hand side can be found in the table of z-transforms in Appendix 2.

$$(9) \qquad y(k) = 7.78\ (0.4)^k - 18.89\ (0.7)^k + 11.11$$

From this equation, the steady-state value of $y(k)$ is

$$(10) \qquad y_{ss} = \lim_{k\to\infty} y(k) = 11.11$$

To verify this result, apply the final value theorem to $Y(z)$.

$$(11) \qquad y_{ss} = \lim_{z\to 1} (z-1)Y(z) = \left. \frac{z(z + 1)}{(z - 0.4)(z - 0.7)} \right|_{z=1} = 11.11$$

which verifies the steady-state value of the solution for $y(k)$.

PROBLEM 15.8

From the table of values of $w(kT)$ it can be seen that the sequence can be described mathematically by

$$(1) \qquad w(kT) = 0.5^k$$

Hence the system transfer function is

$$(2) \qquad T(z) = Z\{\ w(kT)\ \} = \frac{z}{z - 0.5}$$

For a unit step input the z-transform of the output is

(3) $$\mathbf{Y}(z) = \frac{z}{z - 1} \cdot \frac{z}{z - 0.5}$$

And hence the unit step response in the time domain

(4) $$y(k) = \mathbf{Z}^{-1}\{ \mathbf{Y}(z) \}$$

To find the inverse transform of $\mathbf{Y}(z)$, proceed as in the previous problems

(5) $$\frac{\mathbf{Y}(z)}{z} = \frac{z}{(z - 1)(z - 0.5)} = \frac{C_1}{z - 1} + \frac{C_2}{z - 0.5}$$

The constants C_1 and C_2 are

(6) $$C_1 = \left. \frac{\mathbf{Y}(z)\ (z - 1)}{z} \right|_{z=1} = 2$$

(7) $$C_2 = \left. \frac{\mathbf{Y}(z)\ (z - 0.5)}{z} \right|_{z=0.5} = -1$$

Hence,

(8) $$\mathbf{Y}(z) = \frac{2z}{z - 1} - \frac{z}{z - 0.5}$$

Taking the inverse z-transform gives

(9) $$y(k) = 2 - 0.5^k$$

PROBLEM 15.9

The weighting sequence is an inverse z-transform of $\mathbf{T}(z)$. In order to find $\mathbf{Z}^{-1}\{ \mathbf{T}(z) \}$, first apply method of partial fraction expansion to $\mathbf{T}(z)/z$.

(1) $$\frac{\mathbf{T}(z)}{z} = \frac{z + 1}{(z^2 - 0.988z + 0.49)(z - 0.6)}$$

$$= \frac{C_1 z + C_2}{z^2 - 0.988z + 0.49} + \frac{C_3}{z - 0.6}$$

The constant C_3 is

$$(2) \qquad C_3 = \left. \frac{\mathbf{T}(z)\ (z - 0.6)}{z} \right|_{z=0.6} = 6.22$$

Now, to find C_1 and C_2 bring $\mathbf{T}(z)/z$ to a common denominator.

$$(3) \qquad \frac{C_1 z + C_2}{z^2 - 0.988z + 0.49} + \frac{6.22}{z - 0.6}$$

$$= \frac{(C_1+6.22)z^2+(C_2-0.6C_1-6.145)z+(3.05-0.6C_2)}{(z^2-0.988z+0.49)(z-0.6)}$$

Equating coefficients of terms involving the same powers of z in the numerator of the above expression and the numerator of the original form of $\mathbf{T}(z)/z$ gives

$$(4) \qquad C_1 = -6.22$$

$$(5) \qquad C_2 = 3.413$$

Thus the partial fraction expansion of $\mathbf{T}(z)/z$ is

$$(6) \qquad \frac{\mathbf{T}(z)}{z} = \frac{-6.22z + 3.413}{z^2 - 0.988z + 0.49} + \frac{6.22}{z - 0.6}$$

or

$$(7) \qquad \frac{\mathbf{T}(z)}{z} = \mathbf{F}_1(z) + \mathbf{F}_2(z)$$

where

$$(8) \qquad \mathbf{F}_1(z) = \frac{-6.22z + 3.413}{z^2 - 0.988z + 0.49}$$

$$(9) \qquad \mathbf{F}_2(z) = \frac{6.22}{z - 0.6}$$

First find the inverse z-transform of $\mathbf{F}_1(z)$. The following formulas will be employed.

$$(10) \qquad \mathbf{Z}\{\ e^{-akT}\cos(\omega t)\ \} = \frac{z^2 - e^{-aT}z\ \cos(\omega T)}{z^2 - 2e^{-aT}z\ \cos(\omega T) + e^{-2aT}}$$

$$(11) \qquad \mathbf{Z}\{\ e^{-akT}\sin(\omega t)\ \} = \frac{e^{-aT}z\ \sin(\omega T)}{z^2 - 2e^{-aT}z\ \cos(\omega T) + e^{-2aT}}$$

Comparing the denominator of $\mathbf{F}_1(z)$ with the denominator in the above expression allows us to find e^{-aT} and ωT

$$(12) \qquad e^{-2aT} = 0.49 \quad \rightarrow \quad e^{-aT} = 0.7$$

and

$$(13) \qquad 2e^{-aT}\ \cos(\omega T) = 0.988 \quad \rightarrow \quad \omega T = 0.79 \text{ rad}$$

Now rearrange $\mathbf{F}(z)$ to match the z-transform of $e^{-akT}\ \cos(\omega t)$ and $e^{-akT}\ \sin(\omega t)$

$$(14) \qquad \mathbf{F}_1(z) = -6.22 \frac{z - 0.49 - 0.06}{z^2 - 0.988z + 0.49}$$

$$= -6.22\left[\frac{z - 0.49}{z^2-0.988z+0.49} - \frac{1}{8.17}\frac{8.17(0.06)}{z^2-0.988z+0.49}\right]$$

$$= -6.22\left[\frac{z - 0.49}{z^2-0.988z+0.49} - 0.76\frac{0.49}{z^2-0.988z+0.49}\right]$$

Hence

$$(15) \qquad \mathbf{T}(z) = -6.22\frac{z^2 - 0.49z}{z^2-0.988z+0.49} - 0.76\frac{0.49z}{z^2-0.988z+0.49} + \frac{6.22}{z-0.6}$$

Taking the invers transform yields

$$(16) \qquad w(k) = e^{-0.357k}(-6.22\cos(0.79k)+0.76\sin(0.79k))+6.22(.6)^k$$

PROBLEM 15.10

The z-transform of the input-output equation is

(1) $$\mathbf{Y}(z)\,(z^2 - 0.7z + 0.1) = z\mathbf{U}(z)$$

Hence the pulse transfer function $\mathbf{T}(z)$ is

(2) $$\mathbf{T}(z) = \frac{\mathbf{Y}(z)}{\mathbf{U}(z)} = \frac{z}{z^2 - 0.7z + 0.1}$$

The weighting sequence is the inverse z-transform of $\mathbf{T}(z)$. Applying the method of partial fraction expansion gives

(3) $$\frac{\mathbf{T}(z)}{z} = \frac{1}{(z - 0.5)(z - 0.2)} = \frac{C_1}{z - 0.5} + \frac{C_2}{z - 0.2}$$

where the constants C_1 and C_2 are found as follows

(4) $$C_1 = \left.\frac{\mathbf{T}(z)\,(z - 0.5)}{z}\right|_{z=0.5} = 3.33$$

(5) $$C_2 = \left.\frac{\mathbf{T}(z)\,(z - 0.2)}{z}\right|_{z=0.2} = -3.33$$

which gives

(6) $$\mathbf{T}(z) = \frac{3.33z}{z - 0.5} - \frac{3.33z}{z - 0.2}$$

Taking the inverse z-transform yields

(7) $$w(k) = 3.33(0.5)^k - 3.33(0.2)^k$$

PROBLEM 15.11

a) The z-transform of the Kronecker delta is $\mathbf{U}(z) = 1$. Therefore the output sequence in this case is

(1) $$y(k) = \mathbf{Z}^{-1}\{\ \mathbf{T}(z)\ \}$$

Applying partial fraction expansion to $\mathbf{T}(z)/z$ gives

(2) $$\frac{\mathbf{T}(z)}{z} = \frac{1}{(z - 1)(z - 0.125)} = \frac{C_1}{z - 1} + \frac{C_2}{z - 0.125}$$

The constants C_1 and C_2 are

(3) $$C_1 = \left. \frac{T(z)\ (z - 1)}{z} \right|_{z=1} = 1.143$$

(4) $$C_2 = \left. \frac{T(z)\ (z - 0.125)}{z} \right|_{z=0.125} = -1.143$$

Hence,

(5) $$T(z) = \frac{1.143z}{z - 1} - \frac{1.143z}{z - 0.125}$$

Taking the inverse z-transform gives the output sequence

(6) $$y(k) = 1.143(1 - 0.125^k)$$

b) The system transfer function can be rewritten as

(7) $$T(z) = \frac{Y(z)}{U(z)} = \frac{z^{-1}}{1 - 1.125z^{-1} + 0.125z^{-2}}$$

Hence the input-output equation is

(8) $$y(k) - 1.125y(k-1) + 0.125y(k-2) = u(k-1)$$

The recursive formula for the output sequence is

(9) $$y(k) = 1.125y(k-1) - 0.125y(k-2) + u(k-1)$$

Assuming $y(k) = 0$ for $k < 0$, the values of $y(k)$ for $k = 0, 1, 2, \ldots$ can be calculated as follows:

$$y(0) = 0$$

$$y(1) = 1.125y(0) - 0.125y(-1) + u(0) = 1.0$$

$$y(2) = 1.125y(1) - 0.125y(0) + u(1) = 1.625$$

$$y(3) = 3.703$$

$$y(4) = 3.9603$$

$$\vdots$$

To find the steady-state value of y_k, use the final value theorem

(10) $\quad y_{ss} = \lim_{k \to \infty} y(k) = \lim_{z \to 1} (z - 1)\mathbf{Y}(z)$

where

(11) $\quad \mathbf{Y}(z) = \mathbf{T}(z)\mathbf{U}(z)$

The z-transform of the input sequence can be obtained using the definition of the z-transform

(12) $$\mathbf{U}(z) = 1 + 0.5z^{-1} + 2z^{-2} = \frac{z^2 + 0.5z + 2}{z^2}$$

Also notice that

(13) $$\mathbf{T}(z) = \frac{z}{(z - 1)(z - 0.125)}$$

Now the steady-state solution y_{ss} is

(14) $$y_{ss} = \lim (z - 1) \frac{z}{(z - 1)(z - 0.125)} \frac{z^2 + 0.5z + 2}{z^2} = 4.0$$

which agrees with the recursive solution.

CHAPTER 16

PROBLEM 16.1

The two conditions that have to be transformed from the s domain to the z domain are

(1) $\zeta > 0.7$ and $\omega_d < 3.93$ rad/sec

The curve in the z plane representing loci of $\zeta = 0.707$ is described by Equation (16.22)

(2) $d = e^{-0.54}$

This curve is shown in Figure 16.4. The area corresponding to $\zeta > 0.707$ is enclosed between this curve and the real axis.

The second condition for T = 2 sec. gives

(3) $$\frac{\omega_d}{\omega_s} = \frac{3.93}{31.4} = 0.125$$

The shaded area in the figure below is where both conditions are satisfied.

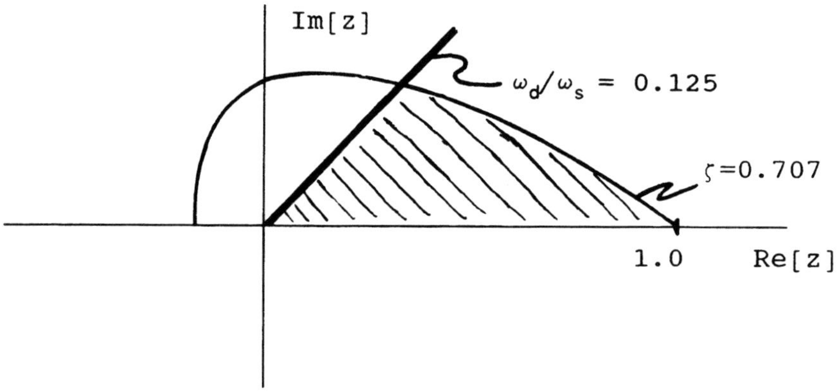

PROBLEM 16.2

In general, a pole in the s plane, $p = a + jb$, is transformed into the z plane by the mapping given by Equation (16.15)

(1) $$z = e^{(a + jb)T} = e^{aT}e^{jbT}$$

which is a circle of radius e^{aT} having its center at the origin of the z plane.

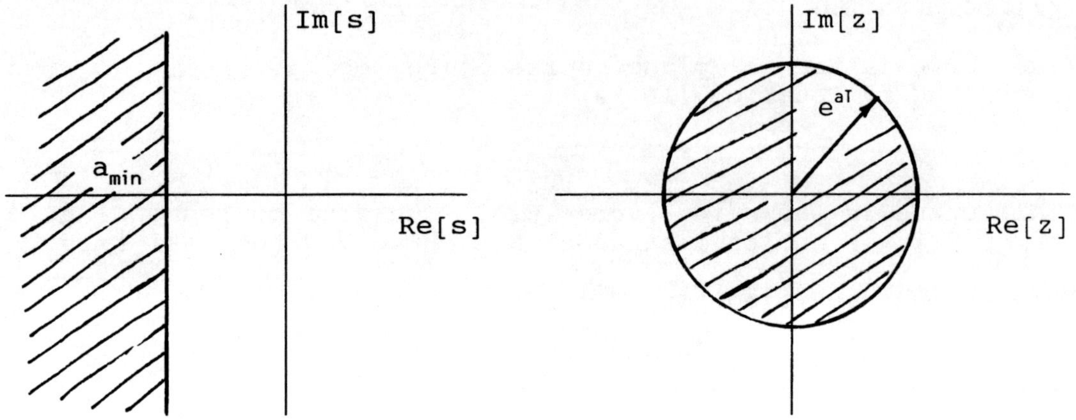

PROBLEM 16.3

The z-transform of Equation (16.53) is

(1) $$\mathbf{U}(z)(1-z^{-1}) = K_p\mathbf{E}(z)(1-z^{-1})+K_I\mathbf{E}(z)z^{-1}+K_D\mathbf{E}(z)(1-2z^{-1}+z^{-2})$$

Hence the pulse transfer function

(2) $$\mathbf{T}(z) = \frac{\mathbf{U}(z)}{\mathbf{E}(z)} = K_p + K_I \frac{z^{-1}}{1 - z^{-1}} + K_D (1 - z^{-1})$$

Arranging into a ratio of polynomials

(3) $$\mathbf{T}(z) = \frac{(K_p+K_D)z^2 + (K_I-K_p-2K_D)z + K_D}{z^2 - z}$$

PROBLEM 16.4

a) The controller pulse transfer function is

$$(1) \qquad \mathbf{T}_c(z) = K_p \frac{z - 0.9512}{z - 1}$$

The pulse transfer function of the process with zero order hold is

$$(2) \qquad \mathbf{T}_p(z) = (1 - z^{-1})\ \mathbf{Z}\{\ 0.25/[(s + 1)s]\ \}$$

$$= (1 - z^{-1}) \frac{0.25(1 - e^{-0.1})z^{-1}}{(1 - z^{-1})(1 - e^{-0.1}z^{-1})} = \frac{0.0238}{z - 0.905}$$

The system open-loop pulse transfer function is

$$(3) \qquad \mathbf{T}_{OL}(z) = \mathbf{T}_c(z)\mathbf{T}_p(z) = \frac{0.0238\ K_p\ (z - 0.9512)}{(z - 1)(z - 0.905)}$$

Hence the closed-loop pulse transfer function

$$(4) \qquad \mathbf{T}_{CL}(z) = \frac{0.0238\ K_p\ (z - 0.9512)}{(z - 1)(z - 0.905) + 0.0238\ K_p\ (z - 0.9512)}$$

The system characteristic equation is

$$(5) \qquad z^2 + (0.0238K_p - 1.905)z + (0.905 - 0.02264K_p) = 0$$

Employing the bilinear transformation defined by Equation (16.24) gives

$$(6) \qquad (0.19 + 0.0453K_p)w + (3.81 - 0.04644K_p) = 0$$

To assume stability the root of this equation must be negative

$$(7) \qquad w = \frac{0.04644K_p - 3.81}{0.0453K_p + 0.19} < 0$$

which gives

$$(8) \qquad -4.19 < K_p < 82.04$$

or

$$(9) \qquad K_{pmax} = 82.04$$

b) Using Equation (16.38) the steady-state error for a ramp input is

(10) $$e_{ss} = \lim_{z\to 1} \frac{T}{(1 - z^{-1})\, \mathbf{T}_{OL}(z)}$$

For $K_p = 82.04$, the steady-state error is

(11) $$e_{ss} = 0.1$$

PROBLEM 16.5

The system characteristic equation is

(1) $$z^3 + (0.025K_p - 1.6)z^2 + (0.06K_p + 0.73)z + 0.008K_p - 0.1 = 0$$

Applying the bilinear transformation $z = (1+w)/(w-1)$ yields the cubic equation

(2) $$(0.027K_p + 3.43)w^3 + (-0.06K_p + 3.57)w^2 + (-0.059K_p + 0.97)w + (0.093K_p + 0.03) = 0$$

To satisfy the necessary conditions for stability all coefficients in the above equation must be positive, which yields the following conditions in terms of K_p.

$$K_p > -127.04$$

$$K_p < 58.52$$

$$K_p < 16.44$$

$$K_p > -0.32$$

The range of K_p for which all necessary conditions are satidfied is thus

(3) $$-0.32 < K_p < 16.44$$

To determine sufficient conditions use the Hurwitz determinant

(4) $$\begin{vmatrix} -0.061K_p + 3.57 & 0.027K_p + 3.43 \\ 0.093K_p + 0.03 & -0.059K_p + 0.97 \end{vmatrix} > 0$$

which gives a quadratic inequality

(5) $$0.0011K_p^2 - 0.589K_p + 3.36 > 0$$

Solving for K_p, we find the sufficient conditions

(6) $K_p < 5.91$ or $K_p > 527.7$

Combining the necessary and sufficient sets of stability conditions gives

(7) $-0.32 < K_p < 5.91$

PROBLEM 16.6

a) A closed-loop transfer function of the continuous control system is

(1) $$T_{CL} = \frac{k_p(1+T_d s)}{s^2 + (2+k_p T_d)s + k_p}$$

To meet the required transient response specifications, the natural frequency of the closed-loop system must be

(2) $$\omega_n = \frac{\omega_d}{\sqrt{1-\zeta^2}} = \frac{2\pi}{5\sqrt{1-0.7^2}} = 1.7 \text{ rad/sec}$$

The system characteristic equation is

(3) $$s^2 + (2+k_p T_d)s + k_p = 0$$

From (3) and (4)

(4) $$k_p = \omega_n^2 = 3.1$$

To achieve desired damping in the system, we must have

$$2 + k_p T_d = 2\zeta\,\omega_n = 2.464$$

Hence

$$T_d = 0.15 \text{ sec}$$

Thus, the transfer function of the continuous PD controller is

$$T_c(s) = 3.1(1+0.15s)$$

b) Using equations (16.49) and (16.51), the digital proportional and derivative gains are

$$K_p = k_p = 3.1$$

$$K_d = \frac{k_p T_d}{T} = 23.25$$

It should be noted that the sampling time T was selected small enough to make the dynamic effects of the zero-order hold negligible. The position control law is

(6) $$u(k) = 3.1\ e(k) + 23.25\ [e(k)-e(k-1)]$$

or, at time (k-1)T,

(7) $$u(k-1) = 3.1\ e(k-1) + 23.25\ [e(k-1) - e(k-2)]$$

Subtracting (7) from (6) gives the velocity algorithm

(8) $$\Delta u(k) = 26.35\ e(k) - 49.6\ e(k-1) + 23.25\ e(k-2)$$

c) The pulse transfer function of the controller is

(9) $$T_c(z) = 26.35 - 23.25z^{-1}$$

The pulse transfer function of the process preceded by a zero-order hold is

(10) $$T_p(s) = (1-z^{-1})\ \mathcal{Z}\left\{\frac{1}{s^2(s+2)}\right\} = \frac{0.07z+0.062}{4(z-1)(s-0.67)}$$

Hence, the pulse transfer function of the closed-loop system is

$$T_{CL}(z) = \frac{T_c(z)T_p(z)}{1+T_c(z)T_p(z)} = \frac{1.845z^{-1}+0.0062z^{-2}-1.4415z^{-3}}{4-4.8355z^{-1}+2.6822z^{-2}-1.4415z^{-3}}$$

d) From (11), the input-output equation is

$$4y(k) - 4.8355y(k-1) + 2.6822y(k-2) - 1.4415y(k-3) = 1.8445\ r(k-1) + 0.0062\ r(k-2) - 1.4415\ r(k-3)$$

PART II SPECIAL PROBLEMS.

Introduction

The end-of-chapter problems in the text, limited in scope and mostly susceptible of analytical treatment, have been provided for the student to assimilate a working knowledge of each new chapter as new material is encountered. In addition to providing home problem solutions in PART I of this Instructors Manual, the authors have collected a number of special in-depth problems which serve to give the serious student a chance to integrate the knowledge and experience gained from progressing through successive chapters in the book.

In most cases these problems require a period of several days (assuming a normal full-time load of other courses) to execute, and they usually involve a certain amount of programming to carry out a digital computer simulation. Classical solution of linearized models is expected in addition to linear and nonlinear model simulation in order to provide a means of validating computer results and to provide insights that help in "debugging" computer programs which inevitably acquire "glitches" that are sometimes difficult to find. Either access to a mainframe computer or a moderately-priced personal computer are suitable for these digital simulations. (See Appendix III for a program of the type suitable for simulation on a PC.)

Solutions are not provided for these special problems, and they are offered mainly to suggest possibilities to the instructor whose own experience may be used to enrich a given problem through incorporation of his own ideas, or ideas picked up from technical papers appearing in the literature.

Special Problem A

The nonlinear electric circuit shown below is to be subjected to an input voltage $e_i(t)$ which consists of a constant normal operating point value $\bar{e}_i = 5.0$ volts, and an incremental portion Δe_i which suddenly starts at t=0. Thus:

$$e_i(t) = \begin{cases} 0 \text{ for } t<0 \\ \Delta e_i \text{ for } t>0 \end{cases}$$

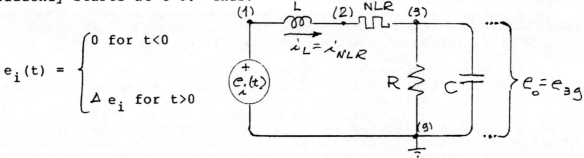

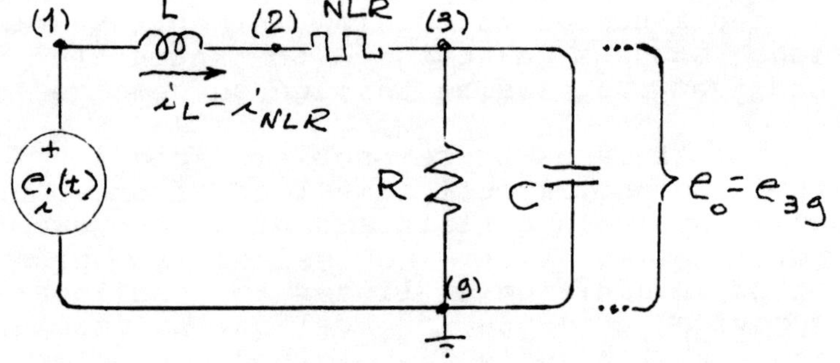

The nonlinear resistor NLR is a square-law device described by:

$$e_{23} = K_1 |i_{NLR}| i_{NLR}$$

a) For the values of R, K_1, C, and L assigned by your instructor find the normal operating point values of the output voltage $\bar{e}_o = \bar{e}_{3g}$, the voltage drop $\bar{e}_{23}$, and the current $\bar{i}_L$. Also develop an expression for the incremental resistance R_{inc} of the nonlinear resistor NLR and compute its value for this normal operating point.

R = ; K_1 = ; C = ; L =

b) Develop the nonlinear state variable equations for this system using e_{1g} as the state variable q_1 and i_L as the state variable q_2 and develop the output equation for the output e_o as the output variable y_1.

c) Develop the linearized state-variable equations using $\hat{e}_{3g}$ and $\hat{i}_L$ as the state variables q_1 and q_2 respectively, and develop the output equation for the output $e_o = \bar{e}_{3g} + \hat{e}_{3g}$ as the output variable y_1.

d) Draw the simulation block diagram for the linearized system, derive the overall linear input-output sytem differential equation relating $\hat{e}_o$ to $\hat{e}_i$, and develop expressions for the damping ratio ζ and the undamped natural frequency ω_n (or time constants τ_1 and τ_2) in terms of R, K_1, C, and L.

e) Calculate the values for ζ and ω_n (or τ_1 and τ_2) using the parameter values given for part a), and obtain the analytical expression for the response of $\hat{e}_o$ to a 0.5 v step change in $\hat{e}_i$ at t=0.

f) Use the program given in Appendix 3 to simulate first the linearized response and then the nonlinear response of this system on a personal

computer.
Alternatively prepare a program (preferably in FORTRAN) to carry out the digital simulations of this system on a main-frame computer that you have access to, employing a proprietary differential equation-solving subroutine available from the main-frame library.

Compare the results of the two digital simulations with each other and with the analytical solution for the linearized model of this system developed in part e).

Special Problem B

The drive system shown below is being designed to drive the spindle and chuck of a variable speed lathe.

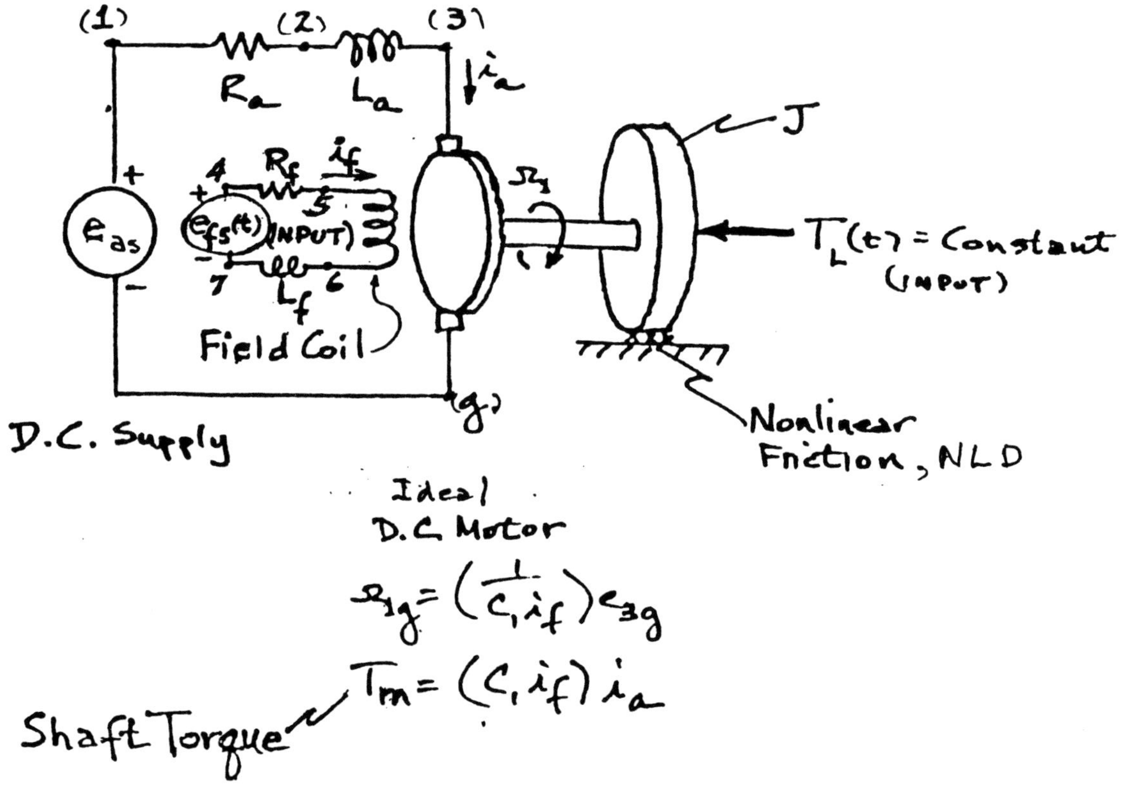

To gain an understanding of the dynamic response characteristics of this spindle drive system you are asked to simulate the response of this system to changes in the field circuit input voltage source e_{fs}, using a digital computer. This simulation may be carried out on a personal computer or on a main-frame digital computer.

The electric drive-motor has been modeled as an ideal electromechanical transducer together with resistors and inductors in the armature and field circuits. The motor inertia is to be lumped with the spindle and chuck inertia, and the motor friction is lumped with the friction of the spindle bearings. The nonlinear damping characteristic of this friction is modeled as shown graphically and analytically below.

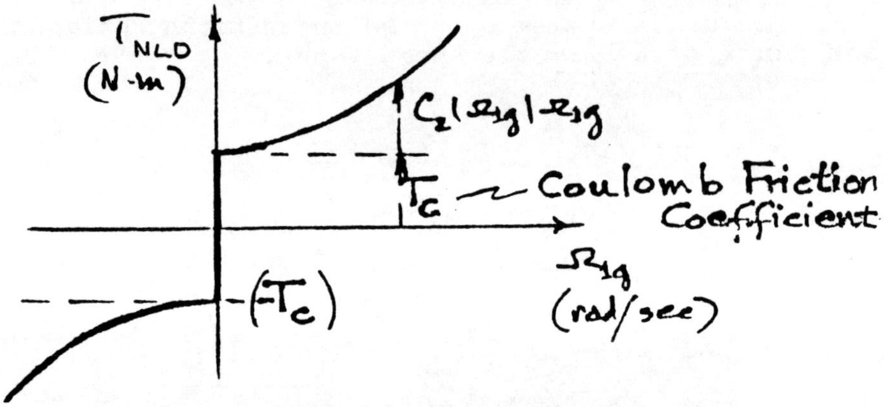

In words, the action of the motor is as follows:

The direct result of increasing $e_{fs}(t)$ is to increase i_f which in turn has a two-fold effect: a) it tends to increase the voltage at the armature terminals of the transducer (sometimes called the back-emf of the armature) for a given motor speed Ω_{1g}; and b) it tends to increase the motor torque T_m for a given armature current i_a. The armature current i_a concurrently changes due to changes in e_{3g}.

a) Draw a complete free-body diagram of the mechanical part of the system showing the motor torque T_m, the nonlinear friction torque T_{NLD}, and the load torque T_L, and write the necessary and sufficient set of describing equations for this system.

b) Formulate the set of nonlinear state-variable equations employing i_f, i_a, and Ω_{1g} as the state variables q_1. q_2, and q_3 respectively.

c) Determine the operating-point values of i_f, i_a, Ω_{1g}, and T_m, employing pertinent items from the following list of physical parameters for this system:

e_{as} = 120 v.	R_a = .48 ohm (1 ohm=1 v/a)
$\bar{e}_{fs}$ = 100 v.	L_a = 3.0 h (1 h=1 v-sec/a)
R_f = 100 ohms	J = 3.75 n-m-sec/rad^2

T_L = 23.0 N-m T_c = 2.66 N-m

C_1 = 1.15 v-sec/a-rad C_2 = 3.5×10^{-4} N-m-sec^2/rad^2

L_f = 50 h

d) Combine the linearized state variable equations to obtain the input-output system differential equation relating Ω_{1q} to e_{fs} for the linearized model of the system. Find the roots of the system characteristic equation and calculate the values of the field circuit time constant, τ_f, and the damping ratio, ζ, and the undamped natural frequency, ω_n, of the linearized model.

e) Use the program given in Appendix 3 to simulate first the linearized response and then the nonlinear response of this system to a small step input on a personal computer. Alternatively prepare a program (preferably in FORTRAN) to cary out the digital simulations of this system on a main-frame computer that you may have access to, employing a proprietary differential equation solving routine from the main-frame library. Compare the results of the two digital simulations with each other, and qualitatively evaluate their reasonableness in light of your knowledge of τ_f, ζ, and ω_n.

S.P.C. on next page

Special Problem C

A hydrostatic variable-speed transmission employing a variable displacement hydraulic pump has been modeled as shown below. As the displacement of the pump is varied by the pump stroke control lever, the variation of the resulting flowrate to the hydraulic motor causes the output speed of the load to change.

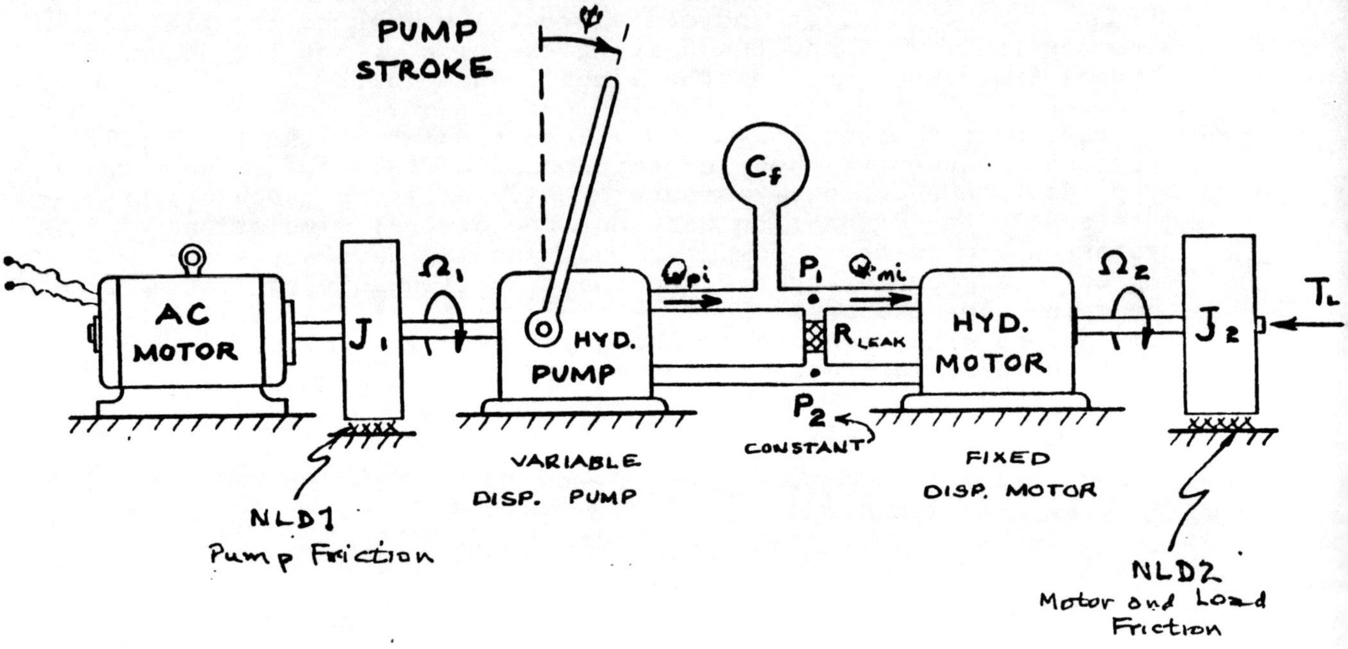

IDEAL PUMP EQNS:

$$T_{pi} = D_p P_{12}$$

$$\Omega_{1g} = \frac{1}{D_p} Q_{pi}$$

where $D_p = \dfrac{\phi}{\phi_{MAX}} D_{p\,MAX}$

IDEAL HYD. MOTOR EQNS:

$$T_{mi} = D_m P_{12}$$

$$\Omega_{2g} = \frac{1}{D_m} Q_{mi}$$

ψ is in rad
Ω is in rad/sec
N is in rev/min

The rotational inertias of the electric motor and the hydraulic pump have been lumped together in J_1 and the inertias of the hydraulic motor and the load have been lumped together in J_2. The steady-state torque-speed characteristic of the electric motor and the steady torque-speed characteristics of the nonlinear hydraulic pump friction (NLD1) and the nonlinear lumped hydraulic motor-load friction (NLD2) are shown below.

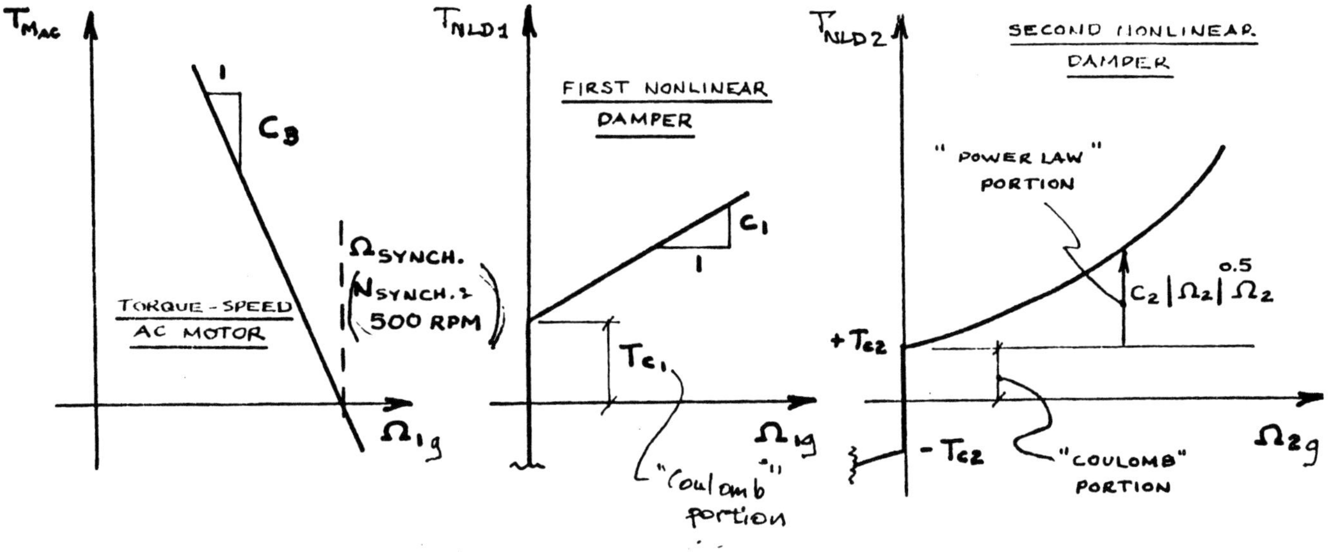

This problem will involve the digital simulation of the response of this system to a sinusoidally varying perturbation of the pump stroke $\hat{\psi} = A_m \psi_{max} \sin\omega t$ about its normal operating value .

a) Draw a complete free-body diagram of the mechanical parts of the system showing each element and the torques T_{mac}, T_{pi}, T_{mi}, T_{NLD}, and T_L, and then write the necessary and sufficient set of describing equations for this system.

b) Formulate the set of state variables for this system using Ω_{1g}, P_{12}, and Ω_{2g} as the state variables q_1, q_2, and q_3 respectively.

c) Working back into the system from the load end, use the following normal operating values and parameters to determine the normal operating values of P_{12}, Q_{mi}, T_{mi}, and Q_{pi}.

$\bar{\Omega}_{2g}$ = 45.0 rad/sec	C_2 = 0.30 N-m/(rad/sec)$^{1.5}$
$\bar{T}_L$ = 300.0 N-m	T_{c2} = 40.0 N-m
D_m = 93.2x10^{-5} m^3/rad	J_2 = 0.6 N-m-sec^2/rad
R_{leak} = 8x10^9 N-sec/m^5	

d) Continue back into the system to find the operating value of the normalized pump stroke $(\bar{\psi}/\psi_{max})$, $\bar{T}_{pi}$, $\bar{\Omega}_{1g}$, and $\bar{T}_{em}$ using the normal operating values found in c) together with the system parameters which also include the following:

$D_{pmax} = 2.18x10^{-4} m^3/rad$ $\qquad$ $C_f = 1.2x10^{-11} m^5/N$

$N_{synch} = 500$ rev/min $\qquad$ $C_3 = 240.0$ N-m-sec/rad

$C_1 = 0.6$ N-m-sec/rad $\qquad$ $J_1 = 0.6$ N-m-sec^2/rad

$T_{cl} = 50.0$ N-m

e) Use the program in Appendix 3 with a PC (or your own program on a a main-frame computer) to simulate the response of this system, using $y_1 = \Omega_{2g}$ and $y_2 = (\Omega_{2g} - \bar{\Omega}_{2g})$, when the input is $u = (\psi - \bar{\psi})/\psi_{max} = A_m \sin \omega t$ suddenly started at t=0.
Given: $\omega/2\pi = f = 5.0$ hertz, and $A_m = .02$, then .60

Suggested $T_{step} = .005$ sec.

f) Develop the linearized state variable equations for this system and prepare the system transfer function relating $\Omega_{2g}(s)$ to $\psi(s)$ for small perturbations of all variables. (Assume that the signs of Ω_{1g} and Ω_{2g} do not change). Use this model to verify your nonlinear simulations obtained in e). In particular compare the amplitude and phase of Ω_{2g} obtained from this linear model with the amplitude and phase of the plot of y_2 vs. time obtained from the simulations with the two values of A_m used above.

Special Problem D

This project involves the use of closed-loop control for the turbine-generator system introduced in Problem 10.2. The object of using this control system is to maintain a system output voltage e_{12} which is as nearly constant as possible at all times, with zero deviation from its desired value under steady operating conditions. The most significant disturbances to the system are variations in the pressure P_1 supplied to the turbine, and variations of the load resistance R.

I. As a prelude to carrying out this project it is first necessary to execute the parts a) through e) of problem 10.2, modified to include $P_{1r}(t)$ and $R(t)$ as system inputs, in addition to the generator field current $i_s(t)$. Thus the nonlinear and the linearized state-variable equations will need to include appropriate terms for $P_{1r}(t)$, $R(t)$, and $i_s(t)$; and $\hat{P}_{1r}(t)$, $\hat{R}(t)$, and $\hat{i}_s(t)$ respectively. And the system differential equation called for in part e) will need to include terms for $\hat{P}_{1r}(t)$, $\hat{R}(t)$, and $\hat{i}_s(t)$.

II. The controller for this system is to be designed to manipulate the field current $i_s(t)$ in such a way as to control the output voltage

e_{12} as shown below.

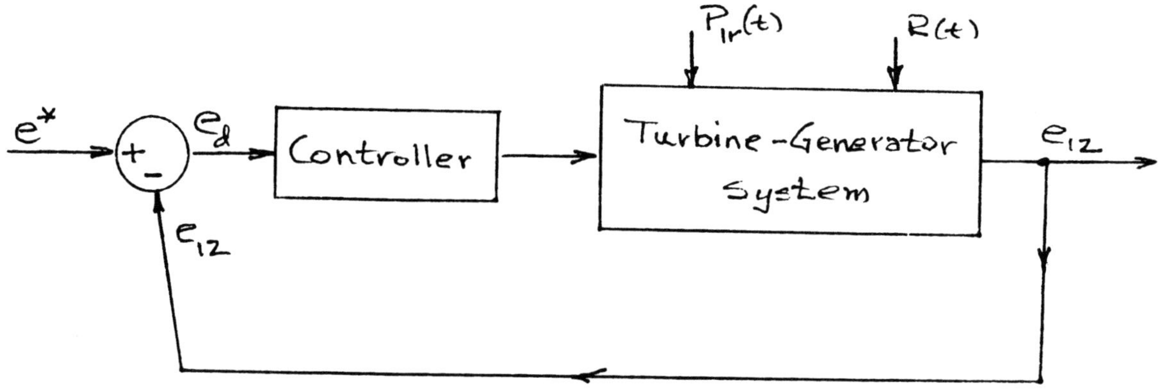

Since a zero steady-state error is required, the controller will need to include an integral control term. The object here is to employ linear control theory, reinforced by linear and nonlinear dynamic simulation to determine suitable values for the gain factors k_p and T_i of a P-I controller that will achieve the fastest possible reduction of the voltage deviation e_d following a small (5%) step perturbation of either $P_{1r}(t)$ or $R(t)$. The system must have a gain margin of at least 1.5, and a phase margin of at least 30°. Employ the following set of system parameters:

$P_0 = 30$ lb/in.^{2} $\qquad R_i = .008$ ohm

$\Omega_0 = -5.0$ rad/sec

$\bar{e}_{12} = 110$ v $\qquad L_i = .1$ h

$\bar{i}_L = 680.$ a $\qquad L = .5$ h

$\bar{\Omega}_{1g} = 100$ rad/sec (approx. 900 rpm)

$\bar{P}_{12} = 25$ lb/in.^{2}

$\bar{i}_s = 1.2$ a

a) Find the normal operating value of R and then the value of the generator field constant C_r required to meet the normal operating voltage, the normal operating shaft speed, and the normal operating field current given above. Noting that 1.0 HP = 6600 in-lb/sec = 746 watts, find the normal operating power delivered by this generator, and the value of the transducer coefficient $K_c \bar{\alpha}_r$ relating the normal operating torque $\bar{T}_{g_{ideal}}$ to the normal operating current $\bar{i}_L$, where $K_c = 6600/746$ in.-lb/watt-sec.

b) Find the normal operating turbine torque $\bar{T}_t = \bar{T}_{g_{ideal}} + B_g \bar{\Omega}_{1g}$, and then the torque parameter T_0 needed for the hydraulic turbine.

Given: $B_g = 330$ lb-sec/in.

$J_t = 500$ lb-in-sec^2

$J_g = 1500$ lb-in-sec^2

c) Carry out the numerical computations needed for analytical solution and then digital simulations for the closed loop system response. Your digital simulations should include finding the response of the system to large (50%) changes in the load resistance R(t).